ROUTLEDGE LIBRARY EDITIONS: MACROECONOMICS

Volume 5

MACROECONOMIC ANALYSIS

MACROECONOMIC ANALYSIS

Essays in Macroeconomics and Econometrics

Edited by
D. CURRIE, R. NOBAY AND D. PEEL

Routledge
Taylor & Francis Group
LONDON AND NEW YORK

First published in 1981 by Croom Helm

This edition first published in 2016
by Routledge
2 Park Square, Milton Park, Abingdon, Oxon OX14 4RN

and by Routledge
711 Third Avenue, New York, NY 10017

Routledge is an imprint of the Taylor & Francis Group, an informa business

British Library Cataloguing in Publication Data
A catalogue record for this book is available from the British Library

ISBN: 978-1-138-93746-8 (Set)
ISBN: 978-1-315-67362-2 (Set) (ebk)
ISBN: 978-1-138-94096-3 (Volume 5) (hbk)
ISBN: 978-1-138-94097-0 (Volume 5) (pbk)
ISBN: 978-1-315-67394-3 (Volume 5) (ebk)

MACROECONOMIC ANALYSIS:

ESSAYS IN MACROECONOMICS AND ECONOMETRICS

Edited by
D. Currie, R. Nobay and D. Peel

CROOM HELM LONDON

Croom Helm Ltd, 2-10 St John's Road, London SW11

British Library Cataloguing in Publication Data

Macroeconomic analysis.
1. Macroeconomics
I. Currie, D. II. Nobay, R.
III. Peel, D.
339 HB171

ISBN 0-7099-0311-1

Printed and bound in Great Britain

Contents

LIST OF CONTRIBUTORS

G. Akerlof	University of California, Berkley
J.E. Alt	University of Washington
R.W. Blundell	University of Manchester
M. Brech	N.E.D.O.
T.S. Breusch	University of Southampton
S. Brittan	Financial Times
W.H. Buiter	University of Bristol
M. Chatterji	University of Essex
V. Chick	University College, London
K.A. Chrystal	University of Essex
M.S. Feldstein	Harvard University
L. Godfrey	University of York
S. Holly	London Business School
A. Ingham	University of Southampton
D.W. Jorgenson	Harvard University
N.Kaldor	Kings College Cambridge
L.J. Lau	Stanford University
J. Matatko	University of Exeter
D.G. Mayes	N.I.E.S.R.
P.Minford	University of Liverpool
D.R. Osborn	University of Manchester
W.B. Reddaway	University of Cambridge
K. Schott	University College, London
P. Simmons	University of York
J.E. Spencer	New University of Ulster
T. Stoker	Stanford University
M.T. Sumner	University of Salford
M. Wickens	University of Southampton
A. Zellner	University of Chicago

EDITORS' INTRODUCTION

The proceedings of the 1979 and 1980 annual conferences of the Association of University Teachers of Economics, have been brought together here, and in a companion volume of essays in contemporary economic analysis. These annual meetings provide an important, and indeed the only well-established annual forum for professional economists in the United Kingdom. The activities of the Association date back to the 1920s, and include amongst its past participants and officers such economic luminaries as John Maynard Keynes and Sir William Beueridge. That the association meetings now represent a thoroughly professional conference venue is in no small measure due to the efforts and endeavours of Frank Paish and the late Harry G. Johnson. In partial tribute, the two keynote lectures of the meetings are named after them.

An A.U.T.E. conference is not drawn upon narrowly defined subjects, and previous conference volumes have not, therefore reflected any specific themes. The simultaneous publication of the 1979 and 1980 papers has offered the editors the opportunity to bring together papers in the general areas of micro-economics and development, (vol 1), and macro-economics and econometrics, (vol 2).

The programme committee endeavours to invite contributions for the main keynote lectures from distinguished scholars actively pursuing research in areas which seem important and promising. This volume includes the Frank W. Paish lectures for 1979 and 1980, which were delivered by Martin Feldstein and Dale Jorgenson, both of Harvard University and the inaugural Association lecture by Arnold Z ellner of the University of Chicago.

The theme of Feldstein's Frank Paish lecture is the effect of social security on private saving. In all countries which attempt to make a general provision for state pensions, the acturial value of such pension rights is a substantial fraction of conventionally measured private wealth; in some, the pension rights are on a sufficiently generous scale to reduce drastically the drop in real income normally expected at retirement. There are thus "common sense" grounds for expecting the existence of general social security schemes to depress private saving substantially, although a number of theories - notably approaches based on optimal intergenerational transfers - have disputed the legitimacy of this inference. Feldstein reviews some reasons for regarding these objections as unconvincing and presents an assortment of empirical evidence to suggest that social security does indeed reduce private saving substantially, even when effects on the timing of the retirement decision are taken into account.

In a lecture which brings together economic theory, measurement and policy analysis, Jorgenson presents an analysis of aggregate consumer behaviour. One important feature of the analysis is the application of recent theoretical developments on exact aggregation, which makes it possible to dispense with the notion of a representative consumer. An illustration of the policy relevance of the approach, is the analysis of the deregulation of U.S. domestic petroleum prices in 1979. An example of the host of interesting implications is that the benefits of decontrol are proportionately greater for higher income consumers. The profession will look forward with some excitement to further extensions of work in this area by Jorgenson and associates.

Arnold Zellner, in a stimulating first Association lecture addresses the somewhat neglected issue of the philosophy and objectives of econometrics. Drawing upon the interrelationship between scientific objectives and methodoly and statistical inference, he emphasises the need for quantitative economists to fruitfully consider the merits of sophisticated simplicity and Bayesian inference within the general framework of economic inquiry.

The other essays in this volume deal with a variety of topics in macroeconomic and econometric analysis. As may be expected of the conference sessions which are for presentation, the papers elicited a considerable amount of discussion from the floor. We are grateful to the participants, formal discussants and referees for their helpful and critical comments. Particular thanks are due to Naomi Canter, Nora Parsley, Simon Blackman and Nora Kelly for efficient secretarial and editorial help.

The Editors.

THE FRANK PAISH AND ASSOCIATION LECTURES

THE EFFECT OF SOCIAL SECURITY ON SAVING

Martin S. Feldstein.

PHILOSOPHY AND OBJECTIVES OF ECONOMETRICS

Arnold Zellner.

AGGREGATE CONSUMER BEHAVIOUR AND INDIVIDUAL WELFARE

Dale W. Jorgenson, Lawrence J. Lau and Thomas Stoker.

1. THE EFFECT OF SOCIAL SECURITY ON SAVING

Martin S. Feldstein[1]

I am pleased and honored to have been asked to deliver the 1979 Frank Paish Lecture. Professor Paish's studies over many years have added to our understanding of the economic system in general and the British economy in particular. The process of saving and capital formation on which I will speak today was one of the many important subjects to which Professor Paish contributed.

The saving rate of an economy is one of the most important parameters governing its long-run performance. A higher saving rate means greater capital intensity, higher productivity and a better standard of living. An economy that increases its savings rate experiences more rapid technical progress and a faster rate of growth over many years until a new equilibrium is established.

Saving rates differ very substantially among industrial nations. For the 15 year period from 1960 through 1974, gross saving accounted for an average of 25 percent of gross domestic product among the 21 O.E.C.D. countries for which data are available. But this gross saving rate ranged from a high of 37.2 percent in Japan to lows of 18.4 percent and 18.6 percent for the U.K. and the U.S. The pattern of high and low saving rate countries has remained quite stable over this period. The correlation between the average saving rate in a country in the 1960-64 period and the 1965-69 period is 0.97. For 1965-69 and 1970-74, the correlation is 0.93 (Feldstein and Horioka, 1979).

Why do saving rates differ so much among countries? How do the government policies pursued in each country affect that country's saving rate? As a profession, we are still disturbingly far from having complete answers to these very important questions. My remarks today will focus on one aspect of this subject that, after several years of research, I believe is extremely important: the impact of social security on private savings.

Social security programs have become extremely important in most of the industrial countries of the world. Social security benefits have come to be relied upon as the major source of finance of post-retirement consumption in the United States and in many other countries. The traditional life cycle theory of saving implies that existing social security programs are likely to depress substantially the aggregate private rate of saving. Moreover, since the social security programs are largely unfunded - i.e. they do not accumulate assets to meet future benefit obligations in the way that a private pension would - the reduction in the private saving rate translates into a corresponding reduction in the national saving rate. But as with so many other subjects, a wider and more general analytic framework reveals a theoretical indeterminacy; we cannot know on the basis of *a priori* consideration alone whether social security increases or decreases the private saving rate. I will discuss the nature of this theoretical indeterminacy in the first part of my lecture.

There is fortunately a growing body of empirical research on this subject. While there are of course ambiguities and problems in the interpretation of these econometric studies, I believe that on balance the evidence strongly supports the implication of the traditional life cycle saving theory that the provision of a large social security pension does substantially reduce real private saving. The second half of my lecture will provide a review of this evidence.

Social Security in the Theory of Saving

The life cycle model is the central idea in the modern theory of saving because it provides the crucial link between the microeconomics of rational household behavior and the macroeconomics of the rate of saving. The fundamental insight of this theory, that aggregate saving is positive in a growing economy because the younger workers who save are more numerous and have higher earnings than the older retirees who dissave, was presented by Sir Roy Harrod in the second lecture of his famous book, *Towards a Dynamic Economics* (1948). Harrod's description of the household's optimizing behavior, which he noted was an extension of Irving Fisher's (1930) analysis, is remarkably modern and "neoclassical" for someone who is rightly regarded as one of the great developers of Keynesian economic theory. It was then Franco Modigliani and his collaborators (e.g. 1954, 1957, 1963 and 1966) who developed Harrod's insight and metaphor of "hump saving" into a quantitative theory and began the process of empirical verification that has made the life cycle model a central feature of our economic understanding.

Implications of the Life Cycle Model

The traditional Harrod-Modigliani life cycle model implies that the introduction of an actuarially fair social security pension program unambiguously reduces private saving. More specifically, in this life-cycle framework, a government policy alters the time pattern of consumption only if it changes the household's lifetime budget constraint. Since an actuarially fair social security program leaves the budget constraint unchanged, there is also no change in each year's consumption. The social security tax that is paid in each year therefore reduces private saving by an equal amount. For an actuarially fair social security program, this is equivalent to reducing the personal wealth accumulated before retirement by the actuarial present value of future benefits (see Feldstein 1974, 1977).

In the United States, the substantial size of the social security program implies that the magnitude of this reduction in private saving is <u>potentially</u> very great. It is useful to review briefly the size of this potential life cycle effect before going on to discuss the possible offsetting effects suggested by a more general theoretical framework.

Consider the question first from the point of view of an average American worker. A married worker who has had the median level of earnings all his life now retires with social security benefits for himself and his wife equal to 65 percent of his peak before-tax earnings. Since these social security benefits are untaxed, they replace approximately 80 percent of his maximum after-tax earnings. Moreover, the benefits are now permanently inflation-indexed so that they maintain their real value regardless of what happens to the price level. With such a high replacement rate, there is little if any reason for such a worker to want to save or to have a private pension.

The replacement rate is higher for workers with less than the median earnings and somewhat lower for workers with earnings above the median. Social security provides a significant replacement rate except for the relatively small number of employees who earn substantially more than the current maximum yearly earnings of nearly $23,000. The replacement rate is also lower for families in which there is a second earner whose contribution to total family income is relatively large. It is these groups alone that still have some incentive for private saving.

For most American families, social security is the most important form of household "wealth". More precisely, the actuarial present value of the social security benefits to which they will be entitled at age 65 exceeds the value of all their other assets combined. A recent study at the National Bureau of Economic Research concluded that the aggregate value of this social security wealth exceeded $3.5 trillion in 1978.[2] To put this $3.5 trillion of social security pseudo-wealth into perspective, it is useful to note that the most inclusive traditional measure of the total net worth of the private sector is less than $6 trillion. If the current social security wealth had been saved and accumulated as real wealth instead, the stock of real capital would be more than 50 percent larger than it is today.

The potential importance of the social security program is also clear if we look at the volume of social security tax collections. Since social security taxes are widely regarded as a form of compulsory saving, it is interesting to compare the annual social security taxes with the annual volume of private saving. In 1978, social security tax payments by employees and employers exceeded $100 billion. By comparison, total private saving (including corporate retained earnings and net pension contributions as well as individual saving) was also approximately $100 billion. Thus if the social security tax payments would have been saved instead, the private saving rate would have been double its actual level.

Departures from Maximizing Behavior

These figures leave no doubt about the very large potential impact of social security on the process of capital accumulation if the traditional life cycle theory is an appropriate model of individual saving behavior. It has, however, been common in many popular discussions of social security policy to reject this picture of rational life cycle saving and its conclusion that social security depresses private saving (e.g. Meyers, 1965; Pechman *et al.*, 1968; and Schulz, 1974). Individuals are instead viewed as myopic nonplanners who save in a haphazard way or not at all; it is this failure to provide systematically for consumption in retirement that is the primary justification for social security. As a result of such myopia, the introduction of social security or an increase in its scale would have no offsetting effect on private saving.

It is also sometimes argued that much of existing wealth does not reflect life-cycle accumulation but is held in order to make future bequests. According to one form of this view, individuals receive bequests and then act as stewards of that wealth until they pass it on to their own heirs; holding and increasing wealth is a matter of morality and honor, not of utility maximizing economic behavior. Wealth that is held or accumulated in this way will not be affected by social security.

There are undoubtedly some individuals whose saving behavior is largely haphazard and irrational. There are others who regard the spending of inherited wealth as morally wrong and who guide their own accumulation by a principle of stewardship rather than the life-cycle use of funds. I doubt that either form of behavior is as common as is sometimes claimed. In any case, such behavior among part of the population would reduce the effect of social security on savings but not eliminate it.

Some writers have even suggested that the provision of social security may actually cause some individuals to save more. This argument is based largely on the survey evidence of Katona (1965) and Cagan (1965) indicating that persons covered by private pensions did not save less and may have saved more than those persons not covered by pensions. Cagan explained his surprising results in terms of a "recognition effect", i.e. when an individual is forced to participate in a pension plan, he recognizes for the first time the importance of saving for his old age. Participation in a pension plan has an educational effect; more formally, it changes the individual's utility function as he perceives it *ex ante* during his working years. Katona added to this a second explanation: the "goal gradient" hypothesis of psychological aspiration theory according to which "effort is intensified the closer one is to one's goal" (Katona, 1965, p. 4). In more conventional economic terms, this would imply that individual preferences are themselves a function of the opportunity set or of the initial position, a dramatic departure from the usual assumption of economic analysis.

Extending the Life Cycle Model

A theoretical analysis that implies that social security may not depress personal saving need not rest on an assumption of irrational behavior, recognition effects or changing preferences. In an analysis that I called the "extended life cycle model" (Feldstein, 1974), I showed how individual life cycle saving could actually be increased by the introduction of social security or by an increase of social security benefits. The essential feature of that extended life cycle model is that the pattern of working and retirement is not fixed but that retirement and saving decisions are made jointly. This has the important implication that any exogenous variable can influence saving indirectly by altering retirement.

Social security and private pensions are likely to induce earlier retirement because benefits are generally available only to those who are fully or partially retired. The resulting increase in the expected period of retirement will, as such, increase total saving during preretirement years. The net effect of social security or of a private pension depends on the relative strengths of the "wealth replacement effect" of the traditional life cycle model and the "induced retirement effect" suggested by the extended life cycle model. An important implication of this is the possibility that the effect of social security of a private pension on saving is not monotonic; at first, the induced retirement effect might dominate but then, as the probability of retirement reaches a natural maximum, further increases in retirement benefits depress private saving.

A different extension of the life cycle model, the introduction of intergenerational transfers, has recently been proposed by Robert Barro (1974), Levis Kochin (1974) and Merton Miller and Charles Upton (1974). The extreme version of this theory implies that an actuarially fair social security program will have no effect on private saving. The essence of their argument is that the introduction of social security (or a change in an existing program) causes an offsetting change in private intergenerational transfers. To understand and evaluate this argument, it is useful to distinguish three alternative cases that might exist before the introduction of change in social security: (1) parents plan to and do leave positive bequests to their children; (2) parents plan to and do receive substantial support from their children during retirement; and (3) a corner solution with no significant intended bequests or gifts in either direction.

Consider first the case with planned bequests that was emphasized by Barro and the others who developed the current argument. The parent generation chooses an optimal life cycle plan which, because their children's utility enters their own utility function, includes making a bequest to their children. An increase in social security benefits entails a transfer from children (who will pay the future social security taxes) to the parents. This upsets the parents' initial equilibrium by reducing the effective net value of the bequests that parents make to their children. To counteract this, the parents must increase the size of their cash bequest by enough to offset the extra taxes that their children will pay. The extra saving for this enlarged bequest just offsets the reduced saving that would otherwise result from the larger social security benefits.

The process is actually more complex than this because each future generation also receives benefits that are in turn financed by their own children. But since the real rate of return on real capital exceeds the pseudo-return on social security taxes (Samuelson, 1958), each future generation is worse off under social security. Restoring the initial equilibrium requires the first generation of parents to provide an extra bequest that will in effect endow an annuity for all future generations to compensate them for this difference. Barro has shown that the extra saving to establish this endowment just offsets the reduced saving that would otherwise result from the larger social security benefits of the first generation.

This model of offsetting private bequests requires an unlikely degree of rational planning and foresight. More important, it is wrong to assume that parents who are concerned about the utility of their children will necessarily wish to leave bequests. A parent who believes that, because of generally rising productivity and real incomes, his children will be richer than himself, may well decide that the optimal "bequest" is negative, i.e. a transfer from his children to himself. Since this decision cannot be enforced, the "constrained optimum" for the parent is no bequest. This may remain the parent's chosen position after an increase in social security: the increase in social security could alter the parent's unconstrained optimum but have no effect on actual bequests.

It is clear that, for the vast majority of the population and therefore for most social security recipients, there are no significant bequests to children even in the presence of our current social security system. There is no evidence that the typical retiree wishes to offset social security intergenerational transfers from young to old. To the extent that there is no induced offsetting private transfer, social security reduces saving by substituting for private wealth.

Some supporters of the theory of offsetting bequests have tried to broaden their argument to include such other parent-child transfers as the financing of the child's education, the child's consumption at home, and even the amount of parental attention given to the child. There is of course no evidence that any of these have responded to the increase in social security. Moreover, none of them involves the accumulation of physical capital. Thus even if social security did induce such offsetting transfers from parents to children in the form of education or increased childhood consumption, it would still be true that social security reduced real saving and capital accumulation.

Consider therefore the seemingly more plausible second mechanism by which changing intergenerational transfers could offset the basic effect of social security. In this case, parents make no bequests but, in the absence of social security, rely on their children to finance their retirement consumption. In the extreme form of this argument, our pay-as-you-go system of public social security replaces a private pay-as-you-go system of private intra-family transfers. In this extreme case, social security has no effect on private saving precisely because no such saving would have occurred in the absence of social security. More generally, the effect of social security on saving is reduced to the extent that parents rely on children for part of their support in old age and expect their children to reduce their gifts by any increase in the amount of the social security benefits.

The survey evidence on gifts from children to retired parents shows that this second case is also of very limited importance (e.g. Wintworth and Motley, 1970). At no time in recent decades has more than a small fraction of retirees received gifts from their children; moreover, the average gift was extremely small in comparison to concurrent income levels or to the corresponding ratio of social security benefits to income today. I have recently analyzed the experience of older retirees whose total incomes, including social security benefits but excluding gifts received from children and others, is below the official poverty line (Feldstein and Bernheim, 1979). Even among this very low income group, only a small fraction receive gifts from their children and the value of these gifts is very small.

It is beyond belief that the current working generation would, in the absence of social security, have made gifts totalling nearly $100 billion to retired parents in 1978. Moreover, it seems reasonable to believe that, even without social security, the rise in incomes during the past few decades would have made most workers choose to finance their own retirement consumption rather than be dependent on the much lower level of voluntary support that their children might later provide.

The dominant form of behavior is therefore likely to be the "corner solution" in which there are neither bequests nor the general support of retirees by their children. Parents might like to receive gifts from their generally more affluent children but have no way to coerce such behavior. They therefore save to finance their own retirement consumption and reduce their saving when social security benefits are increased. The economtric evidence summarized below supports the conclusion that this "corner solution" case is more important than either of the two cases in which changes in private intergenerational transfers offset the savings effect of social security.

In addition to induced changes in retirement and in transfers between parents and children, there is a third way in which the character of private behavior may partly offset the depressing effect of social security. To some extent, social security substitutes for private pension plans. In the United States, many of these pension plans are only partly funded; i.e. the expected present value of future pension benefits exceeds the value of the assets owned by the pension funds. To the extent that social security merely substitutes for <u>unfunded</u> private pensions, an increase in social security is only the substitution of an unfunded public program for an unfunded private one. There is, however, an important difference. An unfunded private pension is a net corporate liability and should, if correctly perceived by investors, depress the value of corporate equity by an equal amount. The equity owners of the company should respond to this reduction in their wealth by increasing their saving. More explicitly, the effect of a private pension on total saving will not depend on whether or not it is funded if the stock market is efficient in reflecting the full extent of the unfunded liability and if share owners are rational savers whose consumption level depends only on their real lifetime budget constraint.

Although the study of the effect of pensions on private saving is far from complete, a preliminary analysis of time series data on the relation between private pension accumulation and other forms of saving implies that private pensions have not altered the total volume of private savings in the United States (Feldstein, 1979). Moreover, studies of data for individual firms indicate that each dollar of unfunded vested pension liability reduces the market value of a firm's equity by approximately one dollar (Oldfield, 1977; Feldstein and Seligman, 1979). Taken together, these two analyses suggest that private pensions do reduce the direct saving by individual employees and that this is offset through increased pension funding and the saving by individual shareholders. The combination of pension funding and induced shareholder response makes private pensions fundamentally different from social security and imply that substituting social security for private pensions is likely to depress total saving. Again, however, this is not a fully settled issue and is not one on which *a priori* arguments are fully convincing.

Even if we disregard the role of pensions as well as any induced changes in retirement and in private intergenerational transfers, there are reasons why rational savers might not regard "social security wealth" - i.e. the present actuarial value of future social security benefits - and ordinary private fungible wealth as perfect substitutes. First, the social security program provides an annuity rather than a fixed sum at retirement. Even before price indexing was formally incorporated in 1972, benefits were periodically adjusted for rising prices. Because of this "real annuity" character of social security, risk-averse individuals might reasonably regard a dollar of social security wealth as a substitute for more than a dollar's worth of fungible assets. Alternatively, since "social security wealth" lacks the liquidity of ordinary savings, a dollar of social security wealth might substitute for less than a dollar's worth of fungible assets. Second, social security benefits are not a contractual obligation of the government but are determined by legislation. Pessimists might therefore underestimate the value of social security wealth while optimists overestimate it. Finally, social security is not an actuarially fair program but alters lifetime budget constraints; such changes in real lifetime resources will alter consumption and saving.

The implication of the theoretical issues that I have been discussing is that the question of whether social security increases or decreases capital accumulation cannot be answered from theoretical consideration alone. The basic life cycle model suggests a strong presumption in favor of the conclusion that the unfunded social security program depresses national saving. But the possibility of irrational behavior by some individuals, the induced earlier retirement and changes in private intergenerational transfers, the role of unfunded private pensions, and the special characteristics of social security wealth all imply that the promise of social security benefits may not cause an equivalent reduction in private wealth accumulation. Only by the analysis of data on private saving and wealth can we hope to assess the actual effect of social security.

Econometric Evidence on the Effect of Social Security on Saving

Economists are now beginning to use different bodies of data to estimate the impact of social security on saving. In the remaining part of this lecture, I will summarize some of the major findings of that econometric research. I will focus this necessarily brief summary on the studies dealing with the United States and on my own research. I hardly need say that empirical findings for the United States economy should not be extrapolated to other countries where differences in institutions could result in a quite different response to social security.

The Time Series Evidence

During the late 1930s and the succeeding war years, there was a general expectation among economists that the saving rate would continue to rise as people became more affluent and as retirement at age 65 became increasingly common. That increase in saving did not materialize. Even as incomes rose very substantially in the 1960s and the fraction of men over 65 who were still working dropped to less than half of the rate in the 1920s, the aggregate saving rate did not increase significantly. This was also the period in which social security was introduced and in which it grew rapidly. It is worth noting that early American Keynesians like Seymour Harris (1941) and even Keynes himself[3] predicted that the U.S. social security program precluded the rapid growth of private saving. Time series analysis of aggregate saving behavior permits a test of this view and, more generally, an estimate of the effect of changes in the level and scope of the social security program.

The basic problem in doing such time series analysis is measuring the magnitude of the social security program in a way that corresponds most closely to its potential effect on private saving. Surveys confirm that individuals do not have precise estimates of the likely value of their future social security benefits. Although legislative changes create benefit entitlements immediately, these new benefits are only recognized slowly by the individuals affected. There is no completely satisfactory solution to this problem. In practice, all of the researchers have used "social security wealth", i.e. the present actuarial value of the future benefits to which the working population is entitled.[4] This overly precise measure cannot provide an accurate picture of year to year variations in the public's perception of the extent to which they can rely on social security but, hopefully, it does capture the broad sweep of changes including the original introduction, the major extensions of coverage and the provision of dependents' benefits.

When a social security wealth variable is added to a standard aggregate consumption function that is estimated with annual data for the period 1929 through 1974 (without the 6 war years), its coefficient is 0.024 (with a standard error of 0.009).[5] Adding this variable has relatively little effect on the coefficients of the other variables. Since the aggregate value of social security wealth in 1972 was $1.85 trillion (Feldstein and Pellechio, 1979), a coefficient of 0.024 implies that social security increased consumption (and thereby depressed private saving) by $44.4 billion. In 1972, total private saving (including real corporate retained earnings) were $75.3 billion. A reduction in saving of $44.4 billion is thus equivalent to 59 percent of actual saving in 1972.

With any statistical equation there is always the possibility that an estimated coefficient really reflects the effect of some important variable that has been inadvertently omitted. In the first time series study of this question (Feldstein, 1974), I tested the unemployment rate to assess whether the coefficient of the social security variable was only reflecting changes in unemployment rates between and within the pre-war and post-war periods. Including the unemployment rate had the effect of cutting the coefficient of the social security wealth variable by half (to 0.10) and to less than its standard error while the coefficient of the unemployment variable was slightly greater than its standard error. The problem of collinearity between the two series made it impossible to arrive at any firm conclusion unless the unemployment rate could be excluded on *a priori* grounds. Fortunately, shortly after the publication of my 1974 paper, the U.S. Department of Commerce published revised estimates of national income and its components which embody a number of improvements over the information that was previously available. Analysis with this new and better data eliminated the ambiguity previously introduced by unemployment. The unemployment variable became only a fraction of its standard error and its presence had almost no effect on either the coefficient of social security wealth or its statistical significance (Feldstein, 1979).

In an interesting extension of this analysis, Alicia Munnell (1974) added the retirement rate of men over age 65 as an additional variable. This specification makes the social security wealth coefficient a measure of the pure wealth replacement effect; as expected, Munnell's coefficient of 0.30 is greater than my estimated net effect of 0.24. The impact of induced retirement thus offset an average of one-fifth of the pure wealth replacement effect of the traditional life cycle model.

Robert Barro (1978) recently presented estimates that suggest that the effect of social security wealth is more ambiguous. His analysis modifies the basic specification of the consumption function by adding the government surplus as an additional variable. Barro's rationale for this novel specification is that a government surplus implies a reduction in government debt which, in an economy in which intergenerational transfers link all generations together, is equivalent to an increase in current disposable income. Adding the government surplus variable reduces the coefficient of social security wealth from 0.24 to 0.14 with a standard error of 0.10. The depressing effect of social security appears to be smaller and statistically less significant.

I believe Barro's analysis is misleading. I have already explained why the assumption of an operational intergenerational transfer process is not likely to be a realistic description. More specifically, I believe the government surplus variable does not belong in a properly specified consumption function. Although the variable appears to be statistically significant, I believe that the significance is spurious. The government surplus is not an exogenous variable that directly affects consumption, as the Barro specification assumes, but an endogenous variable whose value changes with cyclical variations in consumption. What we really see in the positive coefficient of the government surplus variable is that an increase in consumer spending tends to expand the economy, raising tax collections and therefore increasing the government surplus. This interpretation is confirmed by dividing the surplus into its two components (government spending and tax receipts); the government expenditure variable is insignificant and the tax receipts variable is significant.

In concluding this summary of the time series evidence, I should note that data for the postwar period alone appear to be incapable of providing useful information on the effect of social security. In all of the studies using postwar data, the standard error of the coefficient of the social security wealth variable is so large that no economically interesting hypothesis can be rejected. This reflects not only the shorter period but also our inability to measure accurately enough the perceived changes in the public's expectation about future social security benefits. This inadequacy of the postwar data makes it important to examine other types of information, including cross-section data on individual households and cross-country studies of international differences in saving rates.

Individual Household Evidence

The best microeconomic data on the wealth of individual American households remains the Survey of Consumer Finances that was conducted in 1963 by the U.S. Census Bureau (Projector and Weiss, 1966). This survey of more than 2000 households greatly oversampled the high income population. On the basis of the information collected in the survey, I estimated the social security wealth of each household in the sample with a male between the ages of 35 and 64.

In the first analysis of this data (Feldstein, 1976), I compared the characteristics of the distribution of ordinary "fungible wealth" with the characteristics of the distribution of "total wealth" (defined as the sum of ordinary fungible wealth and social security wealth). The key conclusion of that comparison is that the distribution of total wealth is much less concentrated than the distribution of ordinary fungible wealth. For example, while the top one percent of wealth holders had 28.4 percent of fungible wealth in 1963, they only had 18.9 percent of total wealth. Since the concentration of ordinary wealth has shown no trend over the past 50 years, this evidence indicates a substantial reduction in the concentration of total wealth over this period.

This reduction in the concentration of total wealth is what would be expected because of the reduced concentration of disposable income over this century as well as the growing importance of estate taxes. This helps to resolve the apparent paradox of a stable concentration of wealth as conventionally measured and suggests that the concentration of fungible wealth has remained stable because of the growth of social security wealth.

Within each age group, the distribution of income among income classes is more similar to the distribution of total wealth than to the distribution of fungible wealth. The life cycle theory of wealth accumulation is thus more consistent with the distribution of total wealth than with the distribution of fungible wealth. This provides further indirect evidence that the prospect of social security benefits induces households to reduce their accumulation of private fungible wealth.

To test this relation between social security wealth and individual wealth accumulation more explicitly, Anthony Pellechio and I used these data to estimate the effect of each household's social security wealth on that household's pre-retirement accumulation of ordinary fungible wealth (Feldstein and Pellechio, 1979a). For this study, we limited out sample to households in which there was an employed man aged 55 to 64; households with very low or very high incomes were also eliminated. The basic parameter estimates indicated that social security substantially reduces the accumulation of household wealth as traditionally defined. More specifically, the point estimates generally indicate that each dollar of social security wealth reduces ordinary net worth by somewhat less than one dollar. The standard errors are too large to reject the implication of the traditional life cycle model that there is dollar-for-dollar replacement, but the estimates are also consistent with a rather wide range of other replacement rates. In general, however, the estimates are not compatible with the hypothesis that social security does not depress private wealth accumulation. This microeconomic evidence therefore supports the conclusion reached on the basis of the time series evidence.

New data on household wealth and on social security are just becoming available at this time. These new data represent substantially larger samples and contain information on potential social security benefits based on administrative records. They will therefore provide important opportunities to refine the existing analysis of household behavior.

International Evidence

I turn finally to the evidence on the relation between international differences in social security and the saving rates in the corresponding countries. As I noted at the beginning of my talk, there are very substantial and relatively stable differences in saving rates. There is also substantial variation in the extent of social security coverage and in the ratio of social security benefits to income. More specifically, in a study of fifteen countries for which data could be compiled, I found that benefits per aged individual averaged 40 percent of *per capita* income during the period from 1954 through 1960 and that the standard deviation of this ratio was 26 percent of *per capita* income (Feldstein, 1977).

To assess the effect of these differences in social security benefits, I used data on this cross-section of countries to estimate a model of the saving and retirement behavior implied by the extended life cycle theory. The savings function in this model builds on earlier studies of international savings differences by Houthakker (1961, 1965) and Modigliani (1970). The basic life cycle model implies that a country's saving depends on the growth rate of aggregate income and the demographic structure of the population. To this specification I added an estimate of the ratio of social security benefits to average *per capita* income and a measure of retirement behavior.

The parameter estimates of this model imply that social security has a powerful effect on both saving and retirement. More specifically, if the retirement rate is held constant, an increase in the social security benefit ratio from one standard deviation below the sample average to one standard deviation above implies a reduction in the net private saving rate by 5.4 percentage points or 43 percent of the sample mean rate of saving. This overstates the net impact of social security on saving because an increase in social security benefits reduces the labor force participation of older men which in turn increases the saving rate. In the reduced form of the model, with the retirement rate no longer held constant, the net effect of social security on saving is some 80 percent of this pure wealth replacement value; i.e. an increase in benefits from one standard deviation below the average to one standard deviation above reduces the saving rate by 4.3 percentage points.

One of the most worrisome things about the data used in the study is the crude measure of the social security benefits that employees expect. The observed ratio of actual benefits per aged individual to average *per capita* income may reflect past practices and previous income levels. A new set of data, produced by the U.S. Social Security Administration in cooperation with officials of foreign governments, provides measures of the actual statutory ratio of benefits to the preretirement earnings of typical employees in twelve countries (Olsen, 1978). I have been studying these data in the context of the extended life cycle model. Although this study is not yet complete, the coefficient estimates appear to confirm the results obtained with the cruder measure of social security benefits. It is quite reassuring that, despite the obvious problems of international comparability, the data appear to be rich enough to yield estimates of the impact of social security that are similar in magnitude to the estimates obtained with time-series data and with individual household observations.

Conclusion

This brings to an end my review of the theoretical and empirical analysis of the relation between social security and private saving. There will undoubtedly be further research on this subject in the future. New data and new conceptual insights will refine and could modify significantly the conclusions that emerge from existing research. Additional studies for other countries can indicate the extent to which they share the experience of the United States.

In my opinion, the existing research indicates that social security does substantially depress private saving and therefore national saving in the United States. Each dollar of social security wealth appears to reduce private wealth accumulation by somewhat less than a dollar but more than 50 cents. These studies have also contributed to our understanding of the basic process of saving and capital formation, showing the explanatory power and appropriateness of the life cycle framework as well as the need to extend the traditional life cycle model to a less restricted form of behavior. The more general lesson about the importance of the unintended but adverse consequences of a well-meaning government policy should also not go unnoticed.

REFERENCES

Ando, A. and F. Modigliani (1963). The 'Life Cycle' Hypothesis of Saving: Aggregate Implications and Tests. *American Economic Review* (March), Vol. 53, 55-84.

Barro, R. (1974). Are Government Bonds Net Wealth? *Journal of Political Economy* (November/December), Vol. 82, No. 6, 1095-117.

Barro, R. (1978). The Impact of Social Security on Private Saving. *The American Enterprise Institute Studies* #199.

Cagan, P. (1965). *The Effect of Pension Plans as Aggregate Savings*. New York.

Feldstein, M. (1974). Social Security, Induced Retirement and Aggregate Capital Accumulation. *Journal of Political Economy* (September/October), Vol. 82, No. 5.

Feldstein, M. (1976). Social Security and the Distribution of Wealth. *Journal of the American Statistical Association* (December), Vol. 71, No. 356, 800-7.

Feldstein, M. (1977). Social Security and Private Savings: International Evidence in an Extended Life-Cycle Model, in *The Economics of Public Services*, an International Economic Association Conference Volume, M. Feldstein and R. Inman (eds.).

Feldstein, M. (1978). Do Private Pensions Increase National Saving? *Journal of Public Economics* (December), Vol. 10, No. 3.

Feldstein, M. (1979). The Effect of Social Security on Private Saving: The Time Series Evidence. National Bureau of Economic Research working paper No. 314.

Feldstein, M. and B. Bernheim (1979). The Empirical Irrelevance of Intergenerational Transfers for the Effects of Social Security and Government Deficits. Forthcoming.

Feldstein, M. and C. Horioka (1979). Domestic Savings and International Capital Flows. National Bureau of Economic Research working paper No. 310.

Feldstein, M. and A. Pellechio (1979). Social Security Wealth and the Impact of Alternative Inflation Adjustments, in Colin Campbell (ed.), *Social Security*. Forthcoming.

Feldstein, M. and A. Pellechio (1979a). Social Security and Household Wealth Accumulation: New Microeconometric Evidence. *Review of Economics and Statistics*. Forthcoming.

Feldstein, M. and S. Seligman (1979). The Effect of Unfunded Pension Liabilities on Share Prices. Forthcoming.

Fisher, I. (1930). *The Theory of Interest*. New York: Macmillan.

Harris, S. (1941). *The Economics of Social Security*. New York: McGraw-Hill.

Harrod, R. (1948). *Towards a Dynamic Economics*. London: Macmillan.

Houthakker, H. (1961). An International Comparison of Personal Saving. *Bulletin of the International Statistical Institute*, #38, 56-59.

Houthakker, H. (1965). On Some Determinants of Saving in Developed and Underdeveloped Countries, in *Problems of Economic Development*, E. Robinson (ed.). London: Macmillan, Chapter 10.

Katona, G. (1965). Private Pensions and Individual Saving,

Survey Research Center, Institute for Social Research, University of Michigan.

Kochin, L. (1974). Are Future Taxes Anticipated by Consumers? *Journal of Money, Credit and Banking* (August), Vol. 6, 385-94.

Meyers, R. (1965). *Social Insurance and Allied Government Programs*. Homewood, Illinois: Richard D. Irwin.

Miller, M. and C. Upton (1974). *Macro-economics: A Neo-classical Introduction*. Homewood, Illinois: Irwin Publishing Company.

Modigliani, F. (1966). The Life Cycle Hypothesis of Saving, the Demand for Wealth and the Supply of Capital. *Social Research* (Summer), Vol. 33, No. 2, 160-217.

Modigliani, F. (1970). The Life Cycle Hypothesis of Saving and Intercountry Differences in the Saving Ratio, in W.A. Eltis *et al.*, (eds.) *Induction, Growth and Trade, Essays in Honor of Sir Roy Harrod*, Oxford.

Modigliani, F. and A. Ando (1957). Tests of the Life Cycle Hypothesis of Savings. *Bulletin of the Oxford University Institute of Statistics* (May), Vol. 19, 99-104.

Modigliani, F. and R. Brumberg (1954). Utility Analysis and the Consumption Function: An Interpretation of Cross-Section Data, in K. Kurihara (ed.) *Post Keynesian Economics*. New Brunswick.

Munnell, A. (1974). *The Effect of Social Security on Personal Saving*. Ballinger Publishing Company.

Oldfield, G. (1977). Financial Aspects of the Private Pension System. *Journal of Money, Credit and Banking* (February), Vol. 9, No. 1, Pt. 1, 48-54.

Olsen, Leif Haans- (1978). Earnings-Replacement Rate of Old-Age Benefits, 1965-75, Selected Countries. *Social Security Bulletin* (January), Vol. 41, No. 1, 3-14, Table 1 - p. 4.

Pechman, J., H. Aaron and M. Taussig (1968). *Social*

Security: Perspectives for Reform. Washington: The Brookings Institution.

Projector, D. and G. Weiss (1966). *Survey of Financial Characteristics of Consumers* (August). Washington: Board of Governors of the Federal Research System.

Samuelson, P. (1958). An Exact Consumption-Loan Model of Interest with or without the Social Contrivance of Money. *Journal of Political Economy* (December), Vol. 66, No. 6, 467-482.

Schulz, J. *et al.* (1974). *Providing Adequate Retirement Income: Pension Reform in the United States and Abroad.* Hanover, N.H.: Published for Brandeis University Press by the University Press of New England.

Wintworth, F. and D. Motley (1970). *Resources After Retirement.* Monograph No. 34, Office of Research and Statistics Research Report, Social Security Administration. Washington D.C.: U.S. Government Printing Office.

FOOTNOTES

1. Professor of Economics, Harvard University and President, National Bureau of Economic Research. This paper draws together conclusions of research done as part of the NBER's program of research on Social Insurance and its special research project on Capital Formation. The views expressed here are my own and should not be attributed to any organization.

2. Martin Feldstein and Anthony Pellechio (1978). The estimate of $3.5 trillion refers to individuals over age 34 only.

3. My colleague Richard Musgrave recalls the occasion when Lord Keynes visited the U.S. Treasury and commented that the new U.S. Social Security program would prevent the excess saving that many economists then feared.

4. The idea of social security wealth is introduced and described in Feldstein (1974).

5. This particular equation, presented in Feldstein (1979b), is the same specification as reported in Feldstein (1974) but with a longer sample period and the new national income account revisions that were published in 1976.

2. PHILOSOPHY AND OBJECTIVES OF ECONOMETRICS

A. Zellner

It is a great pleasure and honor to be invited to present the first Association Lecture. I say that it is a pleasure because this occasion affords me the opportunity to record publicly my appreciation for the outstanding British contributions to economics and statistics by Smith, Ricardo, Marshall, Edgeworth, Keynes, Ramsey and others in economics and by Bayes, Edgeworth, Pearson, Fisher, Jeffreys and others in statistics. On the philosophy of science, I have been most strongly influenced by the writings of Sir Harold Jeffreys of your Cambridge University who was born here in Durham on April 22, 1891 and in honor of whom I have edited a recently published volume, *Bayesian Analysis in Econometrics and Statistics: Essays in Honor of Harold Jeffreys*. Thus, my present lecture and economics and statistics in general have a major "made-in-Britain" component.

The first point that I shall make is that unless we have a good grasp of the philosophy and objectives of econometrics, a term which I use almost synonymously with modern quantitative economics, we really do not know what we are doing in economic research and in teaching economics. The same can be said about philosophy and objectives in any area of knowledge. By thinking seriously about the foundations of econometrics, a topic unfortunately not well treated in textbooks of econometrics, we may possibly obtain a clearer understanding of what it is we are doing and trying to accomplish in econometrics and with these insights become more effective in research and teaching.

On the relation of science and econometrics, I have for long emphasized the Unity of Science Principle which Karl Pearson put forward as follows: The unity of science is a unity of methods employed in analyzing and learning from experience and data. The subject matter discipline may be economics, history, physics, etc. but the methods employed in analyzing and learning from data are basically the same. As Jeffreys expresses the idea, "There must be a uniform standard of validity for all hypotheses, irrespective of the subject. Different laws may hold in different subjects, but they must be tested by the same criteria; otherwise we have no guarantee that our decisions will be those warranted by the data and not merely the result of inadequate analysis or of believing what we want to believe." Thus the Unity of Science Principle sets the *same* standards for work in the natural and social sciences. For example, this range of considerations is particularly relevant for those in economics who cross-correlate variables and assert causation on the basis of such correlations alone or those who carelessly test all hypotheses in the "5% accept-reject syndrome." Also, we must emphasize the importance of a general unified set of methods for use in science and the undesirability of unnecessary jargon and *ad hoc* methods.

Given that we take the Unity of Science Principle seriously, we may next ask what are the main objectives of science. As Karl Pearson, Harold Jeffreys and others state, one of the main objectives of science and, I add, of econometrics is that of learning from our experience and data. Knowledge so obtained may be sought for its own sake, for example to satisfy our curiosity about economic phenomena and/or for practical policy and other decision purposes. One part of our knowledge is merely *description* of what we have observed; the more important part is *generalization* or *induction*, that is that part which "... consists of making inferences from past experience to predict future [or as yet unobserved] experience", as Jeffreys puts it.

Thus there are at least two components to our knowledge, *description* and *generalization* or *induction*. While generalization or induction is usually considered to be more important, description plays a significant role in science, including economics. For example Burns' and Mitchell's monumental NBER study, *Measuring Business Cycles* is mainly descriptive but valuable in providing general features of business cycles about which others can generalize. While some have damned this work as "measurement without theory", the opposite sin of "theory without measurement" seems much more serious. In fact there are too many mathematical economic theories which explain no past data and which are incapable of making predictions about future or as yet unobserved experience. Such economic theories are mathematical "denk-spielen" and not inductive generalizations to which I referred above. Further, I shall later mention another important role for description in connection with reductive inference.

In learning from our experience and data, it is critical that we understand the roles and nature of three kinds of inference, namely deductive inference, inductive inference and reductive inference.

As regards deductive inference, Reichenbach explains that, "Logical proof is called *deduction*; the conclusion is obtained by deducing it from other statements, called the premises of the argument. The argument is so constructed that if the premises are true the conclusions must also be true ... It unwraps, so to speak, the conclusion that was wrapped up in the premises." Clearly, much economic theory is an exercise in deductive inference. However, the inadequacies of deductive inference for scientific work must be noted. First, traditional deductive inference leads just to the extreme attitudes of *proof*, *disproof* or *ignorance* with respect to propositions. There is no provision for a statement like, "A proposition is probably true" in deductive inference or logic. This is a deficiency of deduction for scientific work wherein such statements are very widely employed and found to be useful.

Second, deduction or deductive inference alone provides no guide for choice among logically correct alternative explanations or theories. As is well known, for any given set of data, there are an infinity of models which fit the data exactly. Deduction provides no guide for selection among this infinity of models.

Thus there is a need for a type of inference which is broader than deductive inference and which yields statements less extreme than deductive inference. This type of inference is called inductive inference by Jeffreys. It enables us to associate probabilities with propositions and to manipulate them in a consistent, logical way to take account of new information. Deductive statements of proof and disproof are then viewed as limiting cases of inductive logic wherein probabilities approach one or zero, respectively.

Jeffreys who has made major contributions to the development of inductive logic in his book, *Theory of Probability* states that inductive inference involves "... making inferences from past experience to predict future experience" by use of inductive generalizations or laws. And given actual outcomes, the procedures of inductive inference allow us to revise probabilities associated with inductive generalizations or laws to reflect the information contained in new data.

Note that for Jeffreys induction is not an economical description of past data, as Mach suggested since Mach omitted the all important predictive aspect of induction. Further, predictive inductive inferences have an unavoidable uncertainty associated with them as Hume pointed out years ago. For example, it is impossible *to prove*, deductively or inductively that generalizations or laws, even the Chicago Quantity Theory of Money are absolutely true. Even Newton's laws which were considered "absolutely true" by many physicists in the nineteenth century have been replaced by Einstein's laws. Thus there is an unavoidable uncertainty associated with laws in all areas of science, including economics. Inductive logic provides a quantification of this uncertainty by associating probabilities with laws and providing logically consistent procedures for changing these probabilities as new evidence arises. In this regard, probability is viewed as representing a degree of reasonable belief with the limiting values of zero being complete disbelief or disproof and of one being complete belief or proof.

For Jeffreys, Bayesian statistics is implied by his theory of scientific method. Thus Bayesian statistics is the technology of inductive inference. The operations of Bayesian statistics enable us to make probability statements about parameters' values and future values of variables. Also, optimal point estimates and point predictions can be readily obtained by Bayesian methods. Probabilities and/or odds ratios relating to competing hypotheses or models can be evaluated which reflect initial information and sample information. Thus many inference problems encountered in induction can be solved by Bayesian methods and these solutions are compatible with Jeffreys's theory of scientific method.

To illustrate inductive inference in econometrics, consider Milton Friedman's, *Theory of the Consumption Function*. In his book Friedman set forth a bold inductive generalization which he showed explained variation in much past data, a fact which increased most individuals' degree of reasonable belief in his theory. Further, Friedman proposed a number of additional tests of his model and predicted their outcomes, an example of what we referred to above as inductive inference. A number of these tests have been performed with results compatible with Friedman's predictions. Such results enhance the degree of reasonable belief which we have in Friedman's theory. This is the kind of research in economics and econometrics which illustrates well the nature of inductive inference and is, in my opinion, most productive.

As regards inductive generalizations, there are a few points which deserve to be emphasized. First, a useful "starting-point" for inductive generalization in many instances is the proposition that all variation is considered random or non-systematic unless shown otherwise. A good example of the fruitfulness of such a starting point is given by the random walk hypothesis for stock prices in stock market research. Many researchers have put forward models to forecast stock prices by use of variables such as auto sales, changes in money, etc. only to find that their forecasts are no better than those yielded by a random walk model. In other areas, when a researcher proposes a new effect, the burden is on him to show that data support the new effect. The initial hypothesis is thus, "No effect unless shown otherwise."

A second most important guiding principle in the selection of inductive generalizations is the Wrinch-Jeffreys *Simplicity Postulate*, namely, "The simplest law is chosen because it is the most likely to give correct predictions", and "... simpler laws have the greater prior probabilities. This is what Wrinch and I called the *simplicity postulate*." Jeffreys provides much evidence for the simplicity postulate in his book *Scientific Inference* in which he shows that scientists in many fields generally have found simple models to be most fruitful. Also, it should be noted that in addition to Jeffreys, R.A. Fisher, J.W. Tukey, G.E.P. Box, M. Friedman and many others emphasize the virtues of sophisticated simplicity in choice among models, a point of view that is sometimes supported by an appeal to Occam's Razor or the Principle of Parsimony or the Simplicity Postulate.

The concept of sophisticated simplicity in model-building does not stand in one-to-one correspondence with the number of equations of a model. For example, it is possible to have a horribly complicated single non-linear mixed differential-difference equation. Thus I believe that we must have at least a two-way classification of econometric models, namely small/simple, small/complicated, large/simple and large/complicated. The objectives of an analysis and the nature of the available data will often be important in determining the size of a model, for example whether it need and can be large to capture much detail. In any event, whether models are small or large, I maintain that they should be sophisticatedly simple. Input-output models are examples of large, simple models; however the main problem with them is that they are not *sophisticatedly* simple. Marshallian supply and demand models are examples of relatively simple models which have been of great practical value. On the other hand, there are a number of complicated multi-equation macro-econometric models on the scene which violate the Simplicity Postulate. Some of these involve hundreds of non-linear stochastic difference equations. I ask builders of such models if their models have a unique solution. Generally, they are unable to answer this question. Further, when I ask them why they build such complicated models, some respond that reality is complicated and therefore models have to be complicated. This response involves an *a priori* view of nature and a major non-sequitor. How do we know that reality (whatever that is) is complicated and not simple? I believe that when we say that something is complicated, it is equivalent to saying that we have something which is not understood. In my view understanding involves simplification not complication and thus I am unhappy with these complicated, little understood models which don't forecast very well relative to simpler models and which are unreliable guides to policy. For example, our simulation experiments with a major U.S. macro-econometric model have led me to conclude that at best it is to be considered as a very local, not entirely satisfactory approximation to some underlying model and very unreliable for analyses of major recessions, depressions and inflationary periods. Also, its use as a policy instrument leaves much to be desired. In fact, I believe that this large model, and others like it, should be labelled, *Dangerous, Users Beware*.

Very important in improving old inductive generalizations and creating new ones is the third kind of inference, reductive inference or sometimes referred to as abductive or retroductive inference which dates back to Aristotle. C.S. Pierce states, "Abduction or reduction suggests that something may be. It involves studying facts and devising generalizations to explain them". While many features of reductive inference are not very well understood, Jacques Hadamard's book, *The Psychology of Invention in the Mathematical Field* does provide some useful insights. Hadamard surveyed his fellow mathematicians to learn how they made their major discoveries. Almost invariably the responses which he obtained emphasized surprising and unusual facts that played a key role in the production of major discoveries or break-throughs. That is rather than solving a given problem, it appears that leading mathematicians' recognition of unusual and surprising facts caused them to think about possible explanations. This thinking involved forming many combinations of ideas with both the conscious and unconscious minds playing a role. Usually a good deal of hard preparatory work is required before one generates a scientifically esthetically pleasing combination of ideas which explains the unusual fact and is capable of making additional verifiable predictions. Thus hard work appears to be a necessary, though unfortunately not a sufficient condition for the production of fruitful new combinations of ideas.

Examples of unusual or surprising facts leading to major developments in economics are not hard to find. For example Kuznets' finding of the constancy of the savings-income ratio in time-series data contrasted with its non-constancy in cross-section data caused many including Duesenberry, Modigliani, Brumberg, Ando and Friedman to produce new theories of consumption. The surprising linear relation between the logarithm of output per worker and the logarithm of the wage rate across countries prompted Arrow, Chenery, Minhas and Solow to discover the CES production function. Many other examples of surprising and unusual facts leading to new theories could be provided. In view of the potential importance of unusual and surprising data, it is of course troubling to see how often outlying observations are discarded without thought or averaged with usual observations by means of "robust" techniques. Of course statisticians usually average everything. In fact a definition of a statistician is a person who has his feet in the refrigerator and his head in the oven and says that on average he is comfortable. Then he computes a confidence interval and is uncertain.

Since unusual and surprising facts are considered important in reductive inference, I suggested some years ago that we should give a good deal of thought about how to produce unusual facts in economics and econometrics. I shall mention some procedures and hope that you will add to the list.

1. Study of incorrect predictions and forecasts of models can be quite jarring and induce new thoughts on how to reformulate models to explain them. The incorrect econometric models' forecasts of a post-World War II depression in the U.S. prompted a good deal of such model reformulation.

2. Close study of the equations of current macroeconometric models can yield surprising and startling facts. For example, some models' dividend, investment and consumer durable goods expenditure equations have unbelievably long lags. Studies of micro-panel data by several of my doctoral students have convinced me that these long lags are spurious, the result of aggregation over buyers and nonbuyers and firms that change and those that do not change dividend rates. In each of these areas, new models for the micro-panel data were formulated, fitted and compared with macro-formulations. The results were most illuminating.

3. Looking for regularities such as constancy of labor's share or of saving-income ratios is a good source of unusual and surprising facts requiring explanation.

4. Strenuous simulation experiments with current econometric models can produce unusual facts about models' properties which require explanations. For example, putting a model through a major depression may reveal many unusual features. Or simulating a model over long periods may indicate unusual fluctuations (or lack of them).

5. Pushing theories to extremes generally produces unusual results. For example in terms of Friedman's proportionality hypothesis for permanent consumption and permanent income, some years ago I suggested that as permanent income approaches zero, the consumption-income ratio would rise toward one in order to keep body and soul together. Recent analysis of data for low income Indian consumers bears out this contention. Similarly for consumers with very great wealth, it should be the case that

the consumption-income ratio is lower than for consumers of just average wealth. If Rockefeller's wealth is 2.5 billion dollars, with a 10% annual rate of return his permanent income is $250 million a year. It is doubtful that he consumes nine-tenths of $250 million. Thus it is probably the case that the consumption-income ratio is near one at low income levels, about .9 over the mid-range and below .9 for high incomes. By pushing other theories to their extremes, similar departures may be discovered which require explanations, a process which resembles what is done in physics by studying systems under extreme conditions of high pressures, low temperatures, etc.

6. Observing behavior in unusual historical periods, for example periods of hyperinflation or great depression and in very different cultures can yield a number of unusual and surprising facts.

7. Surveys can be designed to produce unusual rather than usual facts by considering measurement of the behavior of unusual groups.

8. Experimental economics, that is experiments with animals and/or humans has produced a number of very intriguing and unusual facts which have as yet not been explained. There is fertile ground here for much reductive inference activity.

In the way of conclusion, let me stress the following points.

First, deduction, induction and reduction deserve to be studied more thoroughly by econometricians and economists in order to achieve a better understanding of their roles in research.

Second, a much heavier emphasis on sophisticated simplicity in econometrics is needed both with respect to models and methods.

Third, the sophisticatedly simple Bayesian learning model and decision-making techniques have been incorporated in econometric textbooks. Further use of them will lead to better analyses of data and decision problems.

Fourth, much greater emphasis on reductive inference in

teaching econometrics, statistics and economics would be desirable. To a certain extent, recent emphasis on exploratory data analysis techniques in statistics is a step in the right direction and would be worth instituting in econometrics.

Finally, I hope that this lecture has provided you with a number of surprising ideas and facts which will stimulate you to reconsider your thoughts about the philosophy and objectives of econometrics.

SELECTED REFERENCES

Bhalla, S.S., Measurement Errors and the Permanent Income Hypothesis: Evidence From Rural India, *American Economic Review, 69* (June, 1979), 295-307.

Box, G.E.P. and G.C. Tiao, *Bayesian Inference in Statistical Analysis*, Reading, Mass.: Addison-Wesley, 1973.

DeGroot, M.H., *Optimal Statistical Decisions*, New York: McGraw Hill Book Company, 1970.

Fienberg, S.E. and A. Zellner (editors), *Studies in Bayesian Econometrics and Statistics in Honor of Leonard J. Savage*, Amsterdam: North-Holland Publishing Company, 1975.

Friedman, M., *A Theory of the Consumption Function*, Princeton, N.J.: Princeton University Press, 1957.

Hadamard, J., *The Psychology of Invention in the Mathematical Field*, New York: Dover Publications, Inc., 1945.

Hanson, N.R., *Patterns of Discovery*, Cambridge: Cambridge University Press, 1958.

Jeffreys, H., *Theory of Probability* (3rd rev. ed.), London: Oxford University Press, 1967.

Jeffreys, H., *Scientific Inference* (2nd ed.), Cambridge: Cambridge University Press, 1957.

Pearson, K., *The Grammar of Science*, London: Everyman, 1938.

Reichenbach, H., *The Rise of Scientific Philosophy*, Berkeley: University of California Press, 1958.

Zellner, A., *An Introduction to Bayesian Inference in Econometrics*, New York: John Wiley & Sons, Inc., 1971.

Zellner, A., Causality and Econometrics, in K. Brunner and A.H. Meltzer (editors), *Three Aspects of Policy and Policy-making*, Carnegie-Rochester Conference Series, Vol. 10, Amsterdam: North-Holland Publishing Company, 1979.

Zellner, A., Statistical Analysis of Econometric Models (invited paper with discussion), *Journal of the American Statistical Association, 74* (September, 1979), 628-643.

Zellner, A. (editor), *Bayesian Analysis in Econometrics and Statistics: Essays in Honor of Harold Jeffreys*, Amsterdam: North-Holland Publishing Company, 1980.

Zellner, A. and S.C. Peck, Simulation Experiments with a Quarterly Macroeconometric Model of the U.S. Economy, in A.A. Powell and R.A. Williams (ed.), *Econometric Studies of Macro and Monetary Relations*, Amsterdam: North-Holland Publishing Company, 1973.

3. AGGREGATE CONSUMER BEHAVIOUR AND INDIVIDUAL WELFARE

D.W. Jorgenson, L.J. Lau and T.M. Stoker

1. INTRODUCTION[1]

The objective of this paper is to present a new econometric model of aggregate consumer behavior and to implement this model for the United States for the period 1958-1974. The model incorporates aggregate time series data on quantities consumed, prices, the level and distribution of income, and demographic characteristics of the population. It also incorporates individual cross section data on the allocation of consumer expenditures for household with different demographic characteristics.

Our econometric model can be applied to the generation of projections of aggregate consumer demand in the United States. For this purpose projected future prices, the future level and distribution of income, and the future demographic development of the population are required. The model can also be used to make projections for groups of individuals within the United States, classified by income and by demographic characteristics. Finally, it can be employed in assessing the impact of economic policies on the welfare of individuals with common demographic characteristics.

Our model of aggregate consumer behavior unifies two distinct lines of empirical research on consumer behavior. The first line of research, issuing from the seminal contributions of Schultz (1938), Stone (1954b), and Wold (1953), has focused on the role of prices and incomes as determinants of consumer expenditures. The theory of consumer behavior is used to derive a model of the representative consumer. This model is implemented on the basis of aggregate time series data on prices, per capita quantities consumed, and per capita income.

A second line of research, realized most fully in the classic study of family budgets by Prais and Houthakker

(1955), has focused on the role of demographic characteristics and incomes of individual households as determinants of consumer expenditures. The theory of consumer behavior is used to derive a model of the individual consumer. This model is implemented on the basis of cross section data on quantities consumed, income, and demographic characteristics of individual households.

Time series and cross section data have been combined by Stone (1954b) and Wold (1953) in aggregate models of consumer behavior based on a model of the representative consumer. Cross section data are used to estimate the impact of per capita income and time series data are used to estimate the impact of prices within a model of per capita quantities consumed. This pioneering research omits an important link between individual and aggregate consumer behavior arising from the fact that aggregate demand functions can be represented as the sum of individual demand functions.

Aggregate demand functions depend on prices and incomes, as in the theory of individual consumer behavior. However, aggregate demand functions depend on individual incomes rather than aggregate income. Models of aggregate consumer behavior based on aggregate income or per capita income imply restrictions that severely limit the dependence of individual demand functions on individual incomes. In the absence of such restrictions the implications of the theory of consumer behavior for aggregate demand functions are extremely limited.

An immediate consequence of the theory of individual consumer behavior is that the weighted sum of aggregate demand functions with each function multiplied by the price of the corresponding commodity is equal to aggregate income. A second consequence is that aggregate demand functions are homogeneous of degree zero in prices and individual incomes. Diewert (1977) and Sonnenschein (1974) have shown that any system of aggregate demand functions that satisfies these two conditions, but is otherwise arbitrary, can be rationalized as the sum of systems of individual demand functions.

Gorman (1953) has provided a complete characterization of the restrictions on individual demand functions that underly models of aggregate consumer behavior based on per capita quantities consumed and per capita income. Individual demand functions must be linear in income with identical slopes for all individuals. This restriction implies that Engel curves for individual consumers are linear and parallel to each other. Furthermore, if aggregate demands are equal to zero when aggregate income is equal to zero, individuals must have identical homothetic preferences.

Homothetic preferences are inconsistent with well-established empirical regularities in the behavior of individual consumers, such as Engel's Law that the proportion of total expenditure devoted to food is a decreasing function of total expenditure.[2] Identical preferences for individual households are inconsistent with empirical findings that expenditure patterns depend on demographic characteristics of individual households.[3] Even the weaker form of Gorman's results, that quantities consumed are linear functions of income with identical slopes for all individuals, is inconsistent with empirical evidence from budget studies.[4]

Despite the conflict between Gorman's characterization of individual consumer behavior and the empirical evidence from cross section data, this characterization has provided an important stimulus to empirical research based on aggregate time series data. The linear expenditure system, proposed by Klein and Rubin (1947) and implemented by Stone (1954a), has the property that individual demand functions are linear in income. The resulting system of aggregate demand functions has been used widely as the basis for econometric models of aggregate consumer behavior. Generalizations of the linear expenditure system that retain the critical property of linearity of individual demand functions in income have also been employed in empirical research.[5]

Muellbauer (1975,1976a,1976b) has substantially generalized Gorman's characterization of the representative consumer model by permitting per capita quantities demanded to depend on prices and on a function of individual incomes not restricted to be per capita income. In Muellbauer's model of the representative consumer individual preferences are identical but not necessarily homothetic. Furthermore, quantities consumed may be nonlinear functions of income rather than linear functions, as in Gorman's characterization. An important consequence of this nonlinearity is that aggregate demand functions depend on the distribution of income among individuals. Berndt, Darrough, and Diewert (1977) have implemented aggregate models of consumer behavior that conform to Muellbauer's characterization of the representative consumer model, retaining the assumption that preferences are identical among individuals.

Lau (1977b) has developed a theory of exact aggregation that makes it possible to dispense with the notion of a representative consumer entirely. One of the most remarkable implications of Lau's theory of exact aggregation is that systems of demand functions for individuals with common demographic characteristics can be recovered uniquely from the system of aggregate demand functions. This feature makes it possible to exploit all of the implications of the theory of the individual consumer in specifying a model of aggregate consumer behavior. The corresponding feature of the model of a representative consumer accounts for the widespread utilization of this model in previous empirical research.

In this paper we develop an econometric model of aggregate consumer behavior based on the theory of exact aggregation. In this theory the assumption that the impact of individual incomes on aggregate demand can be represented by a single function of individual incomes, such as aggregate income or per capita income, is replaced by the assumption that there may be a number of such functions. These functions may depend not only on individual incomes but also on attributes of individuals, such as demographic characteristics, that give rise to differences in preferences.

To incorporate the implications of the theory of individual consumer behavior into a system of individual demand functions, we characterize each individual by means of an indirect utility function. We assume that the indirect utility function for an individual depends on prices and income and on demographic characteristics of the consuming unit that give rise to differences in preferences. Given an indirect utility function for each individual, we can generate a system of individual demand functions by applying Roy's (1942) Identity. This approach to specifying a system of individual demand functions was first implemented in a path-breaking study by Houthakker (1960).

In order to represent aggregate demand functions as the sum of individual demand functions, we employ the theory of exact aggregation. To incorporate the implications of the theory of the individual consumer into a model of aggregate consumer behavior, we first characterize systems of individual demand functions that conform to the theory of exact aggregation. The theory of exact aggregation requires that individual demand functions are linear in a number of functions of individual income and attributes, such as demographic characteristics, that give rise to differences in preferences. We impose integrability on the individual demand functions by generating them from indirect utility functions.

The theory of exact aggregation enables us to specify the dependence of systems of individual demand functions on incomes and attributes. To incorporate the implications of the theory of the individual consumer we must also specify the dependence of systems of individual demand functions on prices. We assume that the indirect utility function for each individual has the transcendental logarithmic or translog form. We present estimates of the parameters of the resulting model of aggregate consumer behavior in Section 2.

To illustrate the application of our model of aggregate consumer behavior, we analyze the impact of a policy of decontrolling U.S. domestic petroleum prices in 1979. We project expenditure patterns with and without oil price decontrol for the period 1979-1985 in Section 2. We evaluate the impact of alternative policies on individual welfare by means of the variation in total expenditure that each consuming unit requires in order to achieve the level of utility after the policy change at prices prevailing before the policy change. Results for oil price decontrol are presented in Section 3 for consuming units classified by demographic characteristics and income. We conclude with an appraisal of new research possibilities created by our applications of the theory of exact aggregation.

2. *Aggregate Consumer Behavior*

In this section we present individual and aggregate models of consumer behavior based on the theory of exact aggregation. The theory of exact aggregation requires that the individual demand functions must be linear in a number of functions of individual income and of attributes that depend on demographic characteristics. Representing aggregate demand functions as the sum of individual demand functions, we find that the aggregate demand functions depend on the distribution of income among individuals as well as the level of per capita income and prices. The aggregate demand functions also depend on the shares of groups of individuals, classified by demographic characteristics, in total expenditure.

We assume that each consuming unit has an indirect utility function that is homogeneous of degree zero in prices and income, nonincreasing in prices and nondecreasing in income, and quasi-convex in prices. To incorporate differences in indidual preferences we allow the indirect utility function to depend on attributes, such as demographic characteristics, that vary among individuals. In our model of consumer behavior the individual consuming units are households. We assume that household expenditures on commodity groups are allocated so as to maximize a household welfare function. As a consequence, the household behaves in the same way as an individual maximizing a utility function.[6]

We assume, further, that there are m commodity groups, indexed by $j = 1, 2, \ldots m$, and n consuming groups, indexed by $\ell = 1,2 \ldots n$. The quantity of the jth commodity group consumed by the ℓth consuming unit is denoted $x_{j\ell}$. The price of the jth commodity group, denoted p_j, is the same for all consuming units. Total expenditure by the ℓth unit on all m commodity groups is denoted $M_\ell = \Sigma\, p_j\, x_{j\ell}$. The expenditure share of the jth group in the budget of the ℓth unit is $w_{j\ell} = p_j\, x_{j\ell} \,/\, M_\ell$.

To allow for differences in preferences among consuming units, we allow the indirect utility functions for the ℓth unit to depend on a vector of attributes, say A_ℓ; each attribute is represented by a dummy variable equal to unity when the consuming unit has the corresponding characteristic and zero otherwise. In our model of consumer behavior there are several groups of attributes. Each consuming unit is assigned one of the attributes in each of the groups.

To represent our model of consumer behavior we require the following additional notation:

$w_\ell = (w_{1\ell}, w_{2\ell} \ldots w_{m\ell})$ -- vector of expenditure shares for the ℓth consuming unit ($\ell = 1, 2 \ldots n$).

$\ln \frac{p}{M_\ell} = (\ln \frac{p_1}{M_\ell}, \ln \frac{p_2}{M_\ell} \ldots \ln \frac{p_m}{M_\ell})$ -- vector of logarithms of ratios of prices in total expenditure by the ℓth consuming unit ($\ell = 1, 2 \ldots n$). $\ln p = (\ln p_1, \ln p_2 \ldots \ln p_m)$ -- vector of logarithms of prices.

We assume that the ℓth consuming unit allocates its expenditures in accord with the transcendental logarithmic or translog[7] indirect utility function, say V_ℓ, where:

$$\ln V_\ell = F(A_\ell) + \ln \frac{p}{M_\ell}' \alpha_p + \frac{1}{2} \ln \frac{p}{M_\ell}' \beta_{pp} \ln \frac{p}{M_\ell} + \ln \frac{p}{M_\ell}' \beta_{pA} A_\ell, \quad (\ell = 1, 2 \ldots n)$$

In this representation the function F depends on the attribute vector A_ℓ, but is independent of the prices p and total expenditure M_ℓ. The vector α_p and the matrices β_{pp} and β_{pA} are constant parameters that are the same for all consuming units.

The expenditure shares of the ℓth consuming unit can be derived by the logarithmic form of Roy's Identity:[8]

$$w_{j\ell} = \frac{\partial \ln V_\ell}{\partial \ln (p_j/M_\ell)} \Big/ \Sigma \frac{\partial \ln V_\ell}{\partial \ln (p_j/M_\ell)}, \quad (j = 1,2 \ldots m;$$

$\ell = 1, 2 \ldots n)$.

Applying this identity to the translog indirect utility function, we obtain the system of individual expenditure shares:

$$w_\ell = \frac{1}{D_\ell}\left(\alpha_P + \beta_{PP} \ln \frac{P}{M_\ell} + \beta_{PA} A_\ell\right), \qquad (\ell = 1, 2 \ldots n),$$

where the denominators $\{D_\ell\}$ take the form:

$$D_\ell = \iota' \alpha_P + \iota' \beta_{PP} \ln \frac{P}{M_\ell} + \iota' \beta_{PA} A_\ell, (\ell = 1, 2 \ldots n).$$

and ι is a vector of ones.

We first observe that the function F that appears in the translog indirect utility function does not enter into the determination of the individual expenditure shares. This function is not identifiable from observed patterns of individual expenditure allocation. Second, since the individual expenditure shares can be expressed as ratios of functions involving the unknown parameters -- α_P, β_{PP}, β_{PA} -- these shares are homogeneous of degree zero in the parameters. By multiplying a given set of the unknown parameters by a constant we obtain another set of parameters that generates the same system of individual budget shares. Accordingly, we can choose a normalization for the parameters without affecting observed patterns of individual expenditure allocation. We find it convenient to employ the normalization:

$$\iota'\alpha_P = -1.$$

Under this restriction any change in the set of unknown parameters will be reflected in changes in individual expenditure patterns.

The conditions for exact aggregation are that the individual expenditure shares are linear in functions of the attributes $\{A_\ell\}$ and total expenditure $\{M_\ell\}$ for all consuming units.[9] These conditions will be satisfied if and only if the terms involving the attributes and total expenditures do not appear in the denominators of the expressions given above for the individual expenditure shares, so that:

$$\iota' \beta_{PP} \iota = 0$$

$$\iota' \beta_{pA} = 0$$

These restrictions imply that the denominators $\{D_\ell\}$ reduce to:

$$D = -1 + \iota' \beta_{PP} \ln P ,$$

where the subscript ℓ is no longer required, since the denominator is the same for all consuming units. Under these restrictions the individual expenditure shares can be written:

$$w_\ell = \frac{1}{D} (\alpha_P + \beta_{PP} \ln P - \beta_{PP} \iota \cdot \ln M_\ell + \beta_{PA} A_\ell) , \quad (\ell = 1, 2 \dots n).$$

The individual expenditure shares are linear in the logarithms of total expenditures $\{\ln M_\ell\}$ and the attributes $\{A_\ell\}$, as required for exact aggregation.

Aggregate expenditure shares, say w, are obtained by multiplying individual expenditure shares by total expenditure for each consuming unit, adding over all consuming units, and dividing by total expenditures for all units:

$$w = \frac{\Sigma M_\ell w_\ell}{\Sigma M_\ell} .$$

The aggregate expenditure shares can be written

$$w = \frac{1}{D} \left(\alpha_P + \beta_{PP} \ln P - \beta_{PP} \iota \frac{\Sigma M_\ell \ln M_\ell}{\Sigma M_\ell} + \beta_{PA} \frac{\Sigma M_\ell A_\ell}{\Sigma M_\ell}\right).$$

Aggregate expenditure shares depend on prices p. They also depend on the distribution of total expenditures over all consuming units through the statistic $\Sigma M_\ell \ln M_\ell / \Sigma M_\ell$. This single statistic summarizes the impact of changes in the distribution of total expenditures among individual consuming units on aggregate expenditure allocation. Finally, aggregate expenditure shares depend on the distribution of total expenditure among demographic groups through the vector of statistics $\{\Sigma M_\ell A_\ell / \Sigma M_\ell\}$. Since the attributes are represented as dummy variables, equal to one for a consuming unit with that characteristic and zero otherwise, these statistics are equal to the shares of the corresponding demographic groups in total expenditures. We conclude that aggregate expenditure patterns depend on the distribution of total expenditures over all consuming units through the statistic $\Sigma M_\ell \ln M_\ell / \Sigma M_\ell$ and the distribution among demographic groups through the vector of statistics $\{\Sigma M_\ell A_\ell / \Sigma M_\ell\}$.

The parameters $\beta_{PP}\iota$ and β_{PA} can be estimated from cross section data for expenditures on all commodity groups, total expenditure, and demographic characteristics of all consuming units. Time series data on prices are required to estimate the remaining parameters of the model. To implement our model of aggregate consumer behavior we pool time series data for the period 1958-1974 with cross section data for 1972 from the 1972-1973 *Survey of Consumer Expenditures*. We estimate $\Sigma M_k \ln M_k / \Sigma M_k$ and $\{\Sigma M_k A_k / \Sigma M_k\}$ on a time series basis from the *Current Population Reports*.[10] The resulting estimates are presented in Table 1. The first part of Table 1 gives the notation for expenditure shares, prices, total expenditures, and the five sets of demographic characteristics employed in our model. The second part gives parameter estimates and standard errors for all five equations of the model.

We illustrate the application of our model of aggregate consumer behavior by analyzing the impact of a policy of decontrolling the prices of oil products in 1979. We measure the impact on patterns of consumer expenditures over a seven year period for individual consuming units with

Table 1 : Notation

Expenditure shares:

WEN	Energy
WAG	Agricultural products
WTNT	Trade and transportation
WCAP	Capital services
WSERV	Consumer services

Prices:

p_{EN}	Energy
p_{AG}	Agricultural products
p_{TNT}	Trade and transportation
p_{CAP}	Capital services
p_{SERV}	Consumer services

Total expenditures:

M

Family size:

F2	2 persons
F3	3 persons
F4	4 persons
F5	5 persons
F6	6 persons
F7	7 or more persons

Age of head:

A30	25-34 years
A40	35-44 years
A50	45-54 years
A60	55-64 years
A70	65 years and over

Region of residence:

RNC	North Central
RS	South
RW	West

Race:

BLK	Nonwhite

Type of residence:

RUR	Rural

TABLE 1

FINAL POOLED ESTIMATION RESULTS

	WEN		WAG		WTNT		WCAP		WSERV	
	Coefficient	S.E.	Coefficient	S.E.	Coefficient	S.E.	Coefficient	S.E.	Coefficient	S.E.
Constant	-.17945	.00601	-.7199	.0126	-.4453	.0110	1.0914	.0273	-.7467	.0255
$\ell n\ p_{EN}$	-.03125	.0125	-.09940	.0254	.06733	.0191	-.04842	.0207	.09416	.0243
$\ell n\ p_{AG}$	-.09940	.0254	.1029	.110	-.02619	.0906	.1834	.0514	-.2238	.0900
$\ell n\ p_{TNT}$	.06733	.0191	-.02619	.0906	-.08615	.123	.006093	.0362	.007744	.0357
$\ell n\ p_{CAP}$	-.04842	.0207	.1834	.0514	.006093	.0362	.1207	.0480	-.1106	.0540
$\ell n\ p_{SERV}$	.09416	.0243	-.2238	.0900	.007744	.0357	-.1106	.0540	.1931	.105
ℓn M	.01758	.000660	.06304	.00137	.03117	.00123	-.1512	.00308	.03942	.00286
F2	-.01554	.000974	-.03470	.00203	-.01595	.00182	.006120	.00456	.06008	.00424
F3	-.01905	.00114	-.05271	.00239	-.02679	.00214	.01662	.00537	.08192	.00500
F4	-.02207	.00125	-.06800	.00260	-.03379	.00234	.02374	.00585	.1001	.00545
F5	-.02214	.00143	-.08318	.00299	-.03725	.00268	.02648	.00671	.1161	.00625
F6	-.02527	.00173	-.08975	.00361	-.04337	.00324	.03812	.00811	.1202	.00755
F7	-.02371	.00182	-.1151	.00380	-.05590	.00341	.06605	.00853	.1287	.00794
A30	-.001611	.00134	-.02210	.00281	-.01319	.00252	.03640	.00632	.0005067	.00588
A40	-.003721	.00144	-.04026	.00302	-.01648	.00270	.04143	.00678	.01904	.00631
A50	-.005706	.00138	-.04776	.00288	-.01933	.00258	.04648	.00646	.02632	.00602
A60	-.008298	.00137	-.04695	.00287	-.01751	.00257	.03183	.00645	.04093	.00600
A70	-.007458	.00133	-.03445	.00279	-.003353	.00250	-.002690	.00627	.04795	.00584
RNC	-.008689	.000910	.01795	.00189	.009602	.00170	-.04191	.00426	.02305	.00397
RS	-.007450	.000908	.01222	.00189	-.0001429	.00169	-.02916	.00425	.02453	.00396
RW	.004270	.000978	.01385	.00204	.009010	.00183	-.01796	.00458	-.009167	.00426
BLK	.003649	.00116	-.01128	.00242	-.004184	.00217	.02132	.00543	-.009507	.00506
RUR	-.01767	.000904	.007565	.00188	-.00008160	.00169	-.04599	.00423	.05618	.00394

$$D = -1 \underset{(.000660)}{-.01758} \ell n\, p_{EN} - \underset{(.00137)}{.06304} \ell n\, p_{AG} - \underset{(.00123)}{.03117} \ell n\, p_{TNT} + \underset{(.00308)}{.1512} \ell n\, p_{CAP} - \underset{(.00286)}{.03942} \ell n\, p_{SERV}$$

different demographic characteristics and different income levels. For this purpose we employ projections of prices for the five commodity groups included in our model with and without oil price decontrol for the period 1979-1985. We also employ projections of income, say I, and total expenditure M for households with 1979 incomes of \$17,000 and \$8,000. The projections are given in Table 2 for the Base Case and the Case with Decontrol.

Changes in economic policy result in changes in expenditure patterns. To illustrate the application of our model to projection of expenditure patterns for groups of individuals classified by income and by demographic characteristics. Table 3 provides typical expenditure patterns for households with four members, age of head of household in the range from 35-44 years, Urban residence, and White race. Results are given for households with 1979 incomes of \$17,000 and \$8,000. Expenditure on energy, the first commodity group, increase with an increase in prices for households with 1979 incomes of \$8,000; expenditures decrease for households with 1979 incomes of \$17,000. These changes in expenditure patterns reflect the offsetting influence of positive income effects and negative price effects on the demand for energy.

3 Individual Welfare

To evaluate the impact of alternative economic policies on individual welfare we employ the equivalent variation in total expenditure required for each consuming unit to achieve the level of utility after the policy change at prices prevailing before the policy change. If the equivalent variation is negative, the total expenditure of the consuming unit must be increased in order to compensate for the policy change. If the equivalent variation is positive, the total expenditure of the consuming unit must be decreased to compensate for the change. Differences in equivalent variations among consuming units reflect the fact that preferences and economic circumstances differ among units.

Under the exact aggregation condition the indirect utility function for each consuming unit takes the form:

$$\ln V_\ell = \ln P' \left(\alpha_p + \frac{1}{2} \beta_{PP} \ln P + \beta_{PA} A_\ell\right) - \ln M_\ell D(P) .$$

TABLE 2. PRICE, INCOME, AND EXPENDITURE PROJECTIONS

PRICES (1972 = 1,000)

YEAR	BASE CASE 1	2	3	4	5	CASE WITH DECONTROL 1	2	3	4	5
1979	2.1170	1.6193	1.6553	1.6000	1.6989	2.1276	1.6193	1.6553	1.6000	1.6989
1980	2.3048	1.7246	1.7878	1.7246	1.8404	2.3537	1.7229	1.7878	1.7246	1.8423
1981	2.4818	1.8313	1.9309	1.8552	1.9957	2.5883	1.8368	1.9348	1.8571	1.9997
1982	2.6698	1.9367	2.0709	1.9858	2.1511	2.8039	1.9484	2.0751	1.9897	2.1598
1983	2.8691	2.0442	2.2034	2.1170	2.3117	3.0072	2.0565	2.2144	2.1276	2.3233
1984	3.0771	2.1555	2.3420	2.2547	2.4818	3.2123	2.1684	2.3561	2.2660	2.4943
1985	3.2772	2.2728	2.4818	2.3941	2.6538	3.4281	2.2864	2.4968	2.4061	2.6671

INCOME AND EXPENDITURES

YEAR	BASE CASE I (1979 = $17,000)	M (1979 = $17,000)	I (1979 = $8,000)	M (1979 = $8,000)	CASE WITH DECONTROL I (1979 = $17,000)	M (1979 = $17,000)	I (1979 = $8,000)	M (1979 = $8,000)
1979	17000.00	15740.98	8000.00	7407.52	17000.00	15740.98	8000.00	7407.52
1980	18720.93	17334.46	8809.85	8157.39	18750.20	17368.97	8827.39	8173.63
1981	20651.22	19121.79	9718.22	8998.49	20766.33	19228.38	9772.39	9048.65
1982	22354.96	20699.35	10519.98	9740.87	22527.57	20859.18	10601.21	9816.08
1983	24520.38	22704.40	11539.00	10684.42	24705.32	22875.64	11626.03	10765.01
1984	26970.78	24973.32	12692.13	11752.15	27180.49	25167.50	12790.82	11843.53
1985	29450.61	27269.50	13859.11	12832.70	29710.52	27510.16	13981.42	12945.96

Source Edward Novicky, Scientific Time Sharing Corporation based on the DRI Quarterly Model of the United States.

TABLE 3
TYPICAL EXPENDITURE PATTERNS
1979 Income $17,000

	BASE					WITH DECONTROL				
	1	2	3	4	5	1	2	3	4	5
1979	663.54	4276.99	2900.03	4036.11	3864.31	665.91	4284.36	2894.54	4039.53	3856.64
1980	698.92	4746.70	3168.48	4557.24	4163.12	707.40	4793.99	3147.71	4592.50	4127.37
1981	719.60	5271.13	3479.21	5163.37	4488.48	746.55	5368.69	3442.63	5233.37	4437.14
1982	737.56	5762.08	3749.30	5692.12	4758.29	774.93	5890.04	3706.69	5783.77	4703.75
1983	767.21	6361.59	4070.18	6412.11	5093.32	803.42	6493.30	4032.23	6505.97	5040.72
1984	795.53	7034.42	4429.19	7251.54	5462.65	830.20	7172.03	4397.04	7354.18	5414.04
1985	825.00	7703.51	4797.05	8094.21	5849.73	864.67	7865.40	4761.92	8222.69	5795.49

1979 Income $8,000

	BASE					WITH DECONTROL				
	1	2	3	4	5	1	2	3	4	5
1979	409.57	2361.54	1537.23	1062.52	2036.66	410.68	2364.98	1534.63	1064.20	2033.03
1980	436.10	2618.02	1681.08	1222.76	2199.44	440.27	2640.91	1671.62	1237.83	2183.01
1981	456.93	2904.58	1846.98	1412.58	2377.42	470.17	2952.47	1830.74	1440.78	2354.49
1982	475.19	3170.76	1991.45	1577.11	2526.36	493.61	3233.98	1972.89	1613.02	2502.58
1983	501.58	3497.48	2164.50	1808.95	2711.91	519.57	3562.85	2148.33	1844.98	2689.28
1984	528.99	3864.59	2358.42	2082.87	2917.29	546.39	3933.23	2345.21	2121.85	2896.85
1985	557.10	4230.52	2556.78	2356.92	3131.38	577.13	4311.56	2542.65	2405.72	3108.90

Given the indirect function for each unit, we can solve explicitly for the expenditure function:

$$\ln M_\ell = \frac{1}{D} \left[\ln P' \left(\alpha_P + \frac{1}{2} \beta_{PP} \ln P + \beta_{PA} A_\ell\right) - \ln V_\ell\right]$$

The expenditure function gives the minimum expenditure required for the consuming unit to achieve the utility level V_ℓ, given prices P.

To analyze the impact of the change in economic policy on the ℓth household, we first evaluate the indirect utility function after the change in policy has taken place. Suppose that prices are P^1 and expenditure for the ℓth household is M_ℓ^1. Now, suppose that the prices prevailing before the change in policy are P^0. We define the equivalent variation in total expenditure for the ℓth household, say E_ℓ, as the additional expenditure required to achieve the same level of utility after the change in policy, say V_ℓ^0, at the old prices P^0:

$$E_\ell = M_\ell^1 - M_\ell(P^0, V_\ell^1, A_\ell) .$$

The equivalent depends on the attributes A_ℓ of the ℓth consuming unit, the final expenditure and prices, which enter through the indirect utility function of the ℓth consuming unit V_ℓ^1 (P^1, A_ℓ, M_ℓ^1), on the prices P^1 prevailing before the policy change, and on expenditure M_ℓ^1 after the policy change.

Alternative economic policies result in differences in the prices facing the individual consuming units. They also result in differences in total expenditures for the individual units. To evaluate the impact of alternative policies on individual welfare, we must compare the equivalent variation in total expenditure required to achieve the level of utility resulting from each policy with the change in total expenditure that actually takes place. For this purpose we define the net equivalent variation in total expenditure for the ℓth household, say N_ℓ, as the difference between the equivalent and the change in total expenditure:

$$N_\ell = E_\ell - (M_\ell^1 - M_\ell^0) = M_\ell\ (P^0,\ V_\ell^1,\ A_\ell) - M_\ell^0\ .$$

If the net equivalent variation is negative, the welfare of the consuming unit is increased by the policy change; if the net equivalent variation is positive, the welfare of the consuming unit is decreased.

To evaluate the impact of oil price decontrol on consumer welfare we first evaluate the equivalent variation in total expenditure for each consuming unit at prices P^0 without decontrol and total expenditure M_ℓ^1 and utility level V_ℓ^1 with decontrol. In Table 4 we give the equivalent variation for households with $17,000 of income in 1979, having four members and age of head of household in the range from 35-44 years. Similarly, in Table 5 we give the equivalent variation for households with $8,000 in income in 1979 with the same demographic characteristics. Results are given for consuming units in each of four regions of the United States, for Urban versus Rural residents, and four White versus Nonwhite racial groups.

A comparison of equivalent variations among groups reveals that the additional expenditure required to achieve the same level of utility without oil price decontrol is proportionately greater for consumer groups with lower incomes. Second, at a given level of income these additional expenditures are greater for Rural than for Urban households. Again, at a given level of income Whites must be compensated by larger amounts than Nonwhites. Finally, households in the Northeast and North Central regions must be compensated more than households in the South and West. Since prices have increased for all households, the equivalent variations are positive for all groups we have examined.

Our second step in evaluating the impact of oil price decontrol on consumer welfare is to evaluate net variations for each consuming unit at prices P^0 and total expenditures M^0 without decontrol and utility level V_ℓ^1 with decontrol.

TABLE 4

EQUIVALENT VARIATIONS

1979 Income $17,000

	NORTHEAST				NORTH CENTRAL			
	URBAN		RURAL		URBAN		RURAL	
YEAR	WHITE	NONWHITE	WHITE	NONWHITE	WHITE	NONWHITE	WHITE	NONWHITE
1979	3.32	3.04	4.70	4.41	4.00	3.71	5.37	5.09
1980	14.34	13.00	19.86	18.51	17.37	16.03	22.89	21.55
1981	68.05	65.88	80.48	78.32	73.53	71.37	85.96	83.80
1982	110.16	107.98	124.24	122.06	116.07	113.90	130.15	127.98
1983	153.32	150.12	169.88	166.68	161.14	157.94	177.69	174.50
1984	167.73	164.67	184.18	181.12	175.24	172.18	191.68	188.63
1985	183,34	179.79	202.33	198.78	192.03	188.48	211.01	207.47

	SOUTH				WEST			
	URBAN		RURAL		URBAN		RURAL	
YEAR	WHITE	NONWHITE	WHITE	NONWHITE	WHITE	NONWHITE	WHITE	NONWHITE
1979	3.90	3.62	5.28	4.99	2.99	2.70	4.36	4.08
1980	16.80	15.46	22.32	20.98	13.20	11.85	18.71	17.37
1981	72.94	70.77	85.37	83.21	64.20	62.03	76.64	74.48
1982	115.30	113.12	129.38	127.21	105.24	103.06	119.33	117.15
1983	160.10	156.90	176.65	173.45	148.97	145.77	165.53	162.33
1984	174.45	171.39	190.90	187.84	163.15	160.09	179.61	176.55
1985	191.11	187.56	210.09	206.54	178.09	174.54	197.08	193.53

TABLE 5

EQUIVALENT VARIATIONS

1979 Income $8,000

	NORTHEAST				NORTH CENTRAL			
	URBAN		RURAL		URBAN		RURAL	
YEAR	WHITE	NONWHITE	WHITE	NONWHITE	WHITE	NONWHITE	WHITE	NONWHITE
1979	2.05	1.91	2.70	2.56	2.37	2.23	3.01	2.88
1980	8.87	8.24	11.46	10.83	10.30	9.67	12.89	12.26
1981	38.19	37.17	44.04	43.02	40.77	39.75	46.61	45.60
1982	60.36	59.33	66.98	65.95	63.14	62.11	69.76	68.73
1983	78.57	77.06	86.35	84.85	82.24	80.74	90.03	88.52
1984	85.63	84.19	93.37	91.93	89.16	87.73	96.90	95.46
1985	93.94	92.27	102.87	101.20	98.03	96.36	106.96	105.29

	SOUTH				WEST			
	URBAN		RURAL		URBAN		RURAL	
YEAR	WHITE	NONWHITE	WHITE	NONWHITE	WHITE	NONWHITE	WHITE	NONWHITE
1979	2.32	2.19	2.97	2.84	1.89	1.76	2.54	2.41
1980	10.03	9.40	12.62	11.99	8.33	7.70	10.93	10.30
1981	40.49	39.47	46.33	45.32	36.38	35.36	42.23	41.21
1982	62.78	61.75	69.40	68.37	58.05	57.02	64.67	63.65
1983	81.75	80.25	89.54	88.03	76.52	75.01	84.31	82.80
1984	88.79	87.36	96.53	95.09	83.48	82.04	91.22	89.78
1985	97.59	95.93	106.52	104.85	91.47	89.80	100.40	98.73

In Table 6 we give the negative of the net equivalent variation for households with $17,000 of income in 1979, having four members and age of head of household in the range from 35-44 years, as before, Similarly, in Table 7 we give the negative of the net equivalent variation for households with $8,000 in income in 1979 with the same demographic characteristics. As before, we provide results for consuming units in each of four regions of the United States, for Urban versus Rural residents, and for White versus Nonwhite racial groups.

Net equivalent variations are a measure of individual welfare losses. The change in individual welfare under oil price decontrol reflect both losses in welfare due to higher prices and gains in welfare due to higher incomes. The benefits of decontrol are proportionately greater for consumer groups with higher incomes. Second, at a given level of income the benefits for Urban groups generally exceed those for Rural groups. Nonwhites benefit more than Whites at a given level of income. Finally, households in the Northeast and West regions of the United States benefit more than households in the North Central and South regions. Among the groups we have examined, Rural White households in the North Central and South regions, with 1979 incomes of $8,000 benefit the least from oil price decontrol.

4 Conclusion

We have succeeded in bringing the implications of the theory of individual consumer behavior to bear on a model of aggregate consumer behavior without resorting to the restrictive framework required by the theory of the representative consumer. This has made it possible to incorporate nonlinearities in total expenditure and differences among households in consumer expenditure patterns observable in cross section budget studies into our model. It has also make it possible to incorporate the response of aggregate consumption patterns to changes in relative prices observable in time series demand studies.

Using our model of aggregate consumer behavior we have developed projections of changes in expenditure patterns resulting from changes in economic policy. We have also

TABLE 6

NET EXPENDITURE GAINS

1979 Income $17,000

	NORTHEAST				NORTH CENTRAL			
	URBAN		RURAL		URBAN		RURAL	
YEAR	WHITE	NONWHITE	WHITE	NONWHITE	WHITE	NONWHITE	WHITE	NONWHITE
1979	-3.32	-3.04	-4.70	-4.41	-4.00	-3.71	-5.37	-5.09
1980	20.17	21.51	14.65	15.99	17.14	18.48	11.62	12.96
1981	38.54	40.70	26.10	28.26	33.06	35.22	20.62	22.78
1982	49.67	51.85	35.58	37.76	43.75	45.93	29.67	31.85
1983	17.92	21.12	1.36	4.56	10.10	13.30	-6.45	-3.25
1984	26.45	29.51	10.00	13.06	18.94	22.00	2.50	5.55
1985	57.32	60.87	38.33	41.88	48.63	52.18	29.65	33.19

	SOUTH				WEST			
	URBAN		RURAL		URBAN		RURAL	
YEAR	WHITE	NONWHITE	WHITE	NONWHITE	WHITE	NONWHITE	WHITE	NONWHITE
1979	-3.90	-3.62	-5.28	-4.99	-2.99	-2.70	-4.36	-4.08
1980	17.71	19.05	12.19	13.53	21.31	22.66	15.80	17.14
1981	33.65	35.81	21.21	23.38	42.39	44.55	29.95	32.11
1982	44.52	46.70	30.44	32.62	54.58	56.76	40.50	42.67
1983	11.15	14.35	-5.41	-2.21	22.27	25.48	5.72	8.91
1984	19.73	22.79	3.28	6.34	31.02	34.08	14.57	17.63
1985	49.55	53.10	30.57	34.12	62.57	66.12	43.58	47.13

TABLE 7

NET EXPENDITURE GAINS

1979 Income $8,000

	NORTHEAST				NORTH CENTRAL			
	URBAN		RURAL		URBAN		RURAL	
YEAR	WHITE	NONWHITE	WHITE	NONWHITE	WHITE	NONWHITE	WHITE	NONWHITE
1979	-2.05	-1.91	-2.70	-2.56	-2.37	-2.23	-3.01	-2.88
1980	7.37	8.00	4.78	5.41	5.94	6.57	3.35	3.98
1981	11.97	12.99	6.12	7.14	9.39	10.41	3.54	4.56
1982	14.85	15.88	8.23	9.26	12.07	13.10	5.45	6.48
1983	2.02	3.52	-5.77	-4.26	-1.66	-0.15	-9.44	-7.94
1984	5.74	7.18	-1.99	-0.55	2.21	3.65	-5.52	-4.08
1985	19.31	20.98	10.38	12.05	15.22	16.89	6.30	7.96

	SOUTH				WEST			
	URBAN		RURAL		URBAN		RURAL	
YEAR	WHITE	NONWHITE	WHITE	NONWHITE	WHITE	NONWHITE	WHITE	NONWHITE
1979	-2.32	-2.19	-2.97	-2.84	-1.89	-1.76	-2.54	-2.41
1980	6.21	6.84	3.62	4.25	7.91	8.54	5.31	5.94
1981	9.67	10.69	3.82	4.84	13.78	14.80	7.93	8.95
1982	12.44	13.46	5.82	6.84	17.17	18.19	10.54	11.57
1983	-1.17	0.34	-8.95	-7.45	4.07	5.57	-3.72	-2.22
1984	2.58	4.02	-5.15	-3.71	7.90	9.34	0.16	1.60
1985	15.66	17.33	6.73	8.40	21.78	23.45	12.85	14.52

developed measures of individual welfare that make it possible to evaluate the impact of alternative economic policies. In our illustrative example of the response of expenditure patterns to the decontrol of petroleum prices in the United States, we have seen that the impacts of economic policy differ substantially among demographic groups at the same income level and among different income levels for the same demographic groups.

Perhaps our most important conclusion is that the theory of exact aggregation opens up a wide range of new research possibilities. First, we can provide a more detailed model for allocation among commodities. We have disaggregated our five commodity groups into thirty-six groups, assuming that individual preferences are homothetically separable in the five groups. We assume, for example, that the share of energy in total expenditure depends on household characteristics, while the share of, say, electricity in expenditures on energy does not. The share of electricity in total expenditure depends on household characteristics only through its dependence on the share of energy.

The second research objective suggested by our results is to imbed the system for expenditure allocation into a model that includes labor supply and savings decisions. The essential complication is that the labor-leisure choice depends on a price of leisure, the wage rate after taxes, that varies among consuming units. We must aggregate over wages in the same way as we have aggregated over income and consumer attributes, using the theory of exact aggregation. This is an additional example of the problem of determinants of demand, like income, that vary among consumers. Quantity-constrained allocation patterns provide another illustration of the same general problem. The theory of exact aggregation provides a general solution for this problem.

The third research objective suggested by our work is to incorporate our model of aggregate consumer behavior into a complete general equilibrium model including production as well as demand. This work is now underway and will be completed within the next year. An econometric general equilibrium model of the U.S. economy has been constructed by Hudson and Jorgenson (1974). However, this model was based on a much simpler approach to consumer behavior. The final problem for research is to integrate measures of individual welfare into a social welfare function. This will make it possible to summarize policy impacts by means of a single measure of social welfare. This work is still in an experimental phase.

REFERENCES

Berndt, E.R., M.N. Darrough, and W.E. Diewert (1977), "Flexible Functional Forms and Expenditure Distributions: An Application to Canadian Consumer Demand Functions," *International Economic Review*, Vol. 18, No. 3, October, pp. 651-676

Blackorby, C., R. Boyce, and R.R. Russell (1978), "Estimation of Demand Systems Generated by the Gorman Polar Form: A Generalization of the S-Branch Utility Tree," *Econometrica*, Vol. 46, No. 2, March, pp. 345-364

Bureau of the Census (various annual issues), *Current Population Reports, Consumer Income, Series P-60*, Washington, D.C., U.S. Department of Commerce

Carlson, M.D. (1974), "The 1972-1973 Consumer Expenditure Survey," *Monthly Labor Review*, Vol. 97, No. 12, December, pp. 16-23

Christensen, L.R., D.W. Jorgenson, and L.J. Lau (1975), "Transcendental Logarithmic Utility Functions," *American Economic Review*, Vol. 65, No. 3, June, pp. 367-383

Diewert, W. Erwin (1977), "Generalized Slutsky Conditions for Aggregate Consumer Demand Functions," *Journal of Economic Theory*, Vol. 15, No. 2, August, pp. 353-362

Faucett, Jack and Associates (1977), *Development of 35 Order Input-Output Tables, 1958-1974*, Final Report, Washington, Federal Emergency Management Agency, October.

Gorman, W.M. (1953) "Community Preference Fields," *Econometrica*, Vol. 21, No. 1, January, pp. 63-80

Houthakker, H.S. (1957), "An International Comparison of Household Expenditure Patterns Commemorating the Centenary of Engel's Law," *Econometrica*, Vol. 25, No. 4, October, pp. 532-551

(1960), "Additive Preferences," *Econometrica*, Vol. 28, No. 2 April, pp. 244-257

Hudson, E.A., and D.W. Jorgenson, "U.S. Energy Policy and Economic Growth, 1975-2000," *Bell Journal of Economics and Management Science*, Vol. 5, No. 2, Autumn 1974, pp. 461-514

Jorgenson, D.W., and L.J. Lau (1975), "The Structure of Consumer Preferences," *Annals of Economic and Social Measurement*, Vol. 4, No. 1 January, pp. 49-101

Klein, L.R., and H. Rubin (1947-1948), "A Constant-Utility Index of the Cost of Living," *Review of Economic Studies*, Vol. 15 (2), No. 38, pp. 84-87

Lau, L.J. (1977a) "Complete Systems of Consumer Demand Functions through Duality," in M.D. Intriligator, ed., *Frontiers of Quantitative Economics*, Vol. III A, Amsterdam, North-Holland, 1977, pp. 59-86

(1977b), "Existence Conditions for Aggregate Demand Functions," Technical Report No. 248, Institute for Mathematical Studies in the Social Sciences, Stanford University, Stanford, California, October, (Revised, February 1980).

Lesser, C.E.V. (1963), "Forms of Engel Functions," *Econometrica*, Vol. 31, No. 4, October, pp. 694-703

Muellbauer, J.S. (1975), "Aggregation, Income Distribution, and Consumer Demand," *Review of Economic Studies*, Vol. 42, No. 132, October, pp. 525-543

(1976a), "Community Preferences and the Representative Consumer," *Econometrica*, Vol. 44, No. 5, September, pp. 979-999

(1976b), "Economics and the Representative Consumer," in L. Solari and J.N. Du Pasquier, eds., *Private and Enlarged Consumption*, Amsterdam, North-

Holland, pp. 29-54

Pollak, R.A., and T.J. Wales, "Comparison of the Quadratic Expenditure System and Translog Demand Systems with Alternative Specifications of Demographic Effects," *Econometrica*, Vol. 48, No. 3, April 1980, pp. 595-612

Prais, S.J., and H.S. Houthakker (1955), *The Analysis of Family Budgets*, Cambridge, England, Cambridge University Press (2nd ed., 1971).

Roy, R. (1943), *De l'Utilitie: Contribution a la Theorie des Choix*, Paris, Herman

Samuelson, P.A. (1956), "Social Indifference Curves," *Quarterly Journal of Economics*, Vol. 70, No. 1, February, pp. 1-22

Schultz, H. (1938), *The Theory and Measurement of Demand*, Chicago, University of Chicago Press

Sonnenschein, H. (1973), "The Utility Hypothesis and Market Demand Theory," *Western Economic Journal*, Vol. 11, No. 4, December, pp. 404-410

Stoker, T.M. (1979), *Aggregation Over Individuals and Demand Analysis*, Ph.D. Dissertation, Harvard University

Stone, Richard (1954a), "Linear Expenditure Systems and Demand Analysis: An Application to the Pattern of British Demand," *Economic Journal*, Vol. 64, No. 255 September, pp. 511-527

(1954b), *Measurement of Consumers' Expenditures and Behaviour in the United Kingdom*, Vol. 1, Cambridge, Cambridge University Press

Wold, H.O.A., with L. Jureen (1953), *Demand Analysis: A Study in Econometrics*, New York, John Wiley

FOOTNOTES

1. This paper was presented at the Frank Paish Lecture at the Durham Conference of The Association of University Teachers of Economics by Dale W. Jorgenson. We are indebted to Daniel Slesnick for expert research assistance. Financial support from the Office of Planning and Policy Evaluation, Assitant Secretary of Conservation and Solar Applications, U.S. Department of Energy, is gratefully acknowledged.

2. See, for example, Houthakker (1957) and the references given there.

3. Evidence on demographic variations in consumer expenditures is presented by Prais and Houthakker (1955); additional evidence and more recent references are given by Pollak and Wales (1980).

4. See, for example, Prais and Houthakker (1955) and Leser (1963).

5. See, for example, Blackorby, Boyce, and Russell (1978) and the references given there.

6. See Samuelson (1956) for details.

7. See Christensen, Jorgenson and Lau (1975) and Jorgenson and Lau (1975)

8. See Roy (1943); a detailed review of econometric models of consumer behavior based on Roy's Identity is given by Lau (1977a)

9. For details, see Lau (1977b).

10. Our time series are based on data prepared by Jack Faucett Associated (1977) for the Federal Emergency Management Agency. For details on the estimation procedure, see Stoker (1979).

4. A REVIEW OF RECENT WORK ON TESTING FOR AUTO-CORRELATION IN DYNAMIC SIMULTANEOUS MODELS

T.S. Breusch and L. Godfrey

1. INTRODUCTION[1]

There has been a great deal of research carried out recently into the construction of tests for the various kinds of misspecification that are sometimes encountered in applied econometric analysis. The problem of testing for autocorrelation has received particular attention because of its well established and important role in checking model specification, and new results have been obtained for both single equation models and simultaneous equation systems. These results indicate the possibility of a single flexible and simple approach to testing for autocorrelation in regression equations, complete simultaneous equation models and individual structural relationships of such systems. The results also reveal that the tests can be easily calculated without modifications to existing estimation programmes. It, therefore, seems important to present these results in a way which is readily accessible to the non-specialist, and to discuss in some detail the implementation of tests for various statistical models now commonly employed in applied economic work.

The example of testing for first order autocorrelation in the errors of a simple regression model is used in Section 2 to develop and illustrate the general approach. The construction of tests against more complex forms of autocorrelation for general dynamic regression equations is also outlined, and some Monte Carlo evidence is discussed. Section 2 concludes with an examination of tests of the adequacy of assumed autocorrelation models to cover cases in which regression equations have been estimated allowing for serial correlation of the errors.

The discussion of testing for serial correlation in dynamic economic systems contained in Section 3 is also based upon a simple (two equation) model. It is shown that the essential features of the results reported in Section 2 for a single regression equation are still applicable whether a complete simultaneous system or one of its equations is being considered. Finally, some concluding remarks are offered in Section 4.

Since the primary purpose of this paper is expository, relatively little emphasis is placed upon technical matters and attention is instead focussed on those aspects of greater relevance to applied researchers (some theoretical material is provided in two appendices).

2. *TESTING FOR AUTOCORRELATION IN DYNAMIC REGRESSION MODELS*

Although economists have long recognised the importance of testing for serial correlation when estimating dynamic regression equations, they have usually relied solely upon Durbin's (1970) h-test (or the inappropriate Durbin-Watson statistic). Since the h-test was designed specifically for the alternative of a first order autoregressive error, this practice seems ill advised in many cases. For example, Wallis (1972) has put forward persuasive arguments that researchers should test for fourth order autocorrelation when fitting quarterly relationships. Moreover, given that regression equations with lagged dependent variables can often be regarded as transformed versions of some rational distributed lag model, the moving average error model is frequently a more plausible alternative than an autoregressive scheme (see Nicholls, Pagan and Terrell (1975, Section 2)). The lack of consideration of autocorrelation schemes which are more complex than the first order autoregression may have arisen from the fact that empirical researchers had not been provided with a wide range of easily implemented and flexible tests for such misspecification. Recent research, however, suggests that the Lagrange multiplier (LM) approach to hypothesis testing is most useful in filling this gap in the applied econometrician's toolkit.

In the first of the section's four subsections, a simple outline of the derivation of some LM tests for autocorrelation is presented[2]. Comments are made upon some practical considerations in the second subsection which contains a description of various approaches which can be used to compute LM test statistics for situations commonly encountered in applied work, and Monte Carlo evidence is reviewed in the third subsection. In the fourth and final subsection, it is supposed that an economic relationship has been estimated allowing for some form of autocorrelation, e.g. a first order autoregression, and tests which enable the researcher to check the adequacy of his assumed error model are discussed.

Finally, although the theory underlying this section was developed for dynamic regression models, it is also applicable when the regressors do not include lagged values of the dependent variable.

2.1 The Lagrange Multiplier approach and testing for autocorrelated errors

Serial independence of the regression errors is just one of the assumptions often made in empirical work in order to simplify the econometric problems of estimation and hypothesis testing. It is important that such assumptions should be tested against the available evidence and a thorough programme of checks for specification error is required in any empirical study. Such tests can frequently be carried out by viewing the specified relationship as a special case of a more general model, and then investigating the acceptability of the restrictions which yield the required specialisation. Since the emphasis is on testing the validity of the specified model, it would clearly be useful to construct tests from the results obtained from estimation of that model alone. The LM test and its variants are often ideally suited to this purpose.

In order to illustrate the basic ideas of the LM approach to testing for autocorrelation, consider the following simple regression model with autocorrelated errors:

$$y_t = \beta x_t + u_t, \quad t=1, 2, \ldots, n, \tag{2.1}$$

and

$$u_t = \rho u_{t-1} + \varepsilon_t, \qquad |\rho| < 1 , \tag{2.2}$$

where the ε_t are normally and independently distributed with mean zero and variance σ_ε^2 (more briefly, ε_t $NID(0,\sigma_\varepsilon^2)$). The disturbances u_t are independent if $\rho=0$ and are otherwise autocorrelated. The problem of testing the assumption of independent errors can, therefore, be formulated as testing the null hypothesis $H_o : \rho=0$ against the two sided alternative $H_1 : \rho\neq 0$.

It will sometimes be useful to regard ε_t and u_t as being functions of the observed values of y_t and x_t, and the parameters β and ρ. In such cases, the following notation will be employed:

$$u_t(\beta) = y_t - \beta x_t$$

and

$$\begin{aligned}\varepsilon_t(\beta, \rho) &= u_t(\beta) - \rho u_{t-1}(\beta)\\ &= y_t - \beta x_t - \rho y_{t-1} + \beta\rho x_{t-1}\\ &= (y_t-\rho y_{t-1}) - \beta(x_t-\rho x_{t-1}).\end{aligned}$$

Thus, the ordinary least squares (OLS) estimate of β is obtained by minimising $\sum_t u_t(\beta)^2 = \sum_t \varepsilon_t(\beta, 0)^2$.

A test of $H_o : \rho = 0$ could be carried out by obtaining autoregressive least squares (ALS) estimates by minimising

$$\begin{aligned}S(\beta, \rho) &= \Sigma_1^n [\varepsilon_t(\beta, \rho)]^2\\ &= \Sigma_1^n [(y_t-\rho y_{t-1}) - \beta(x_t - \rho x_{t-1})]^2 ,\end{aligned} \qquad (2.3)$$

with respect to β and ρ, and then either carrying out a test of the significance of the ALS estimate of ρ by dividing it by its estimated asymptotic standard error, or by comparing the maximised log likelihood associated with the ALS estimates with that obtained using OLS under the restriction $\rho=0$.[3] The first of these tests is known as a Wald (W) test and the second is, of course, the likelihood ratio (LR) procedure. These two procedures are, however, unattractive from the point of view of the researcher wishing to check his estimated model since they require him also to estimate its more complicated generalisation. Fortunately, a third procedure, namely the LM test, is available which, while sharing the asymptotic properties of the LR and W tests, requires only the estimation of the model under the null hypothesis (in the above example, this simply involves the OLS estimation of equation (*2.1*)).

The LM test is derived by regarding estimation under the null hypothesis is being an example of constrained optimisation. An objective function, namely $S(\beta, \rho)$ of (*2.3*), is minimised subject to the constraint $\rho=0$. The estimation problem can, therefore, be set up as a classical constrained optimisation problem as follows:

$$\text{minimise } S(\beta, \rho) = \Sigma_1^n [(y_t - \rho y_{t-1}) - \beta(x_t - \rho x_{t-1})]^2$$

subject to $\rho=0$.

The associated Lagrangean can then be written as

$$S^*(\beta, \rho, \lambda) = S(\beta, \rho) + 2\lambda\rho,$$

where λ is the usual multiplier.[4] If the first partial derivatives of $S^*(\beta, \rho, \lambda)$ vanish at $(\hat{\beta}, \hat{\rho}, \hat{\lambda})$, i.e.

$$\partial S^*(\hat{\beta}, \hat{\rho}, \hat{\lambda})/\partial\beta = \partial S(\hat{\beta}, \hat{\rho})/\partial\beta = 0$$

$$\partial S^*(\hat{\beta}, \hat{\rho}, \hat{\lambda})/\partial\rho = \partial S(\hat{\beta}, \hat{\rho})/\partial\rho + 2\hat{\lambda} = 0 ,$$

and

$$\partial S^*(\hat{\beta}, \hat{\rho}, \hat{\lambda})/\partial\lambda = 2\hat{\rho} = 0 ,$$

then $\hat{\rho} = 0$ and $\hat{\beta}$ is the OLS estimate of β of (*2.1*) since it satisfies $\partial S(\hat{\beta}, 0)/\partial\beta = 0$ with $S(\beta, 0)$ being $\Sigma_t u_t(\beta)^2$.

The LM procedure is simply a test of the significance of $\hat{\lambda}$. If the null hypothesis $\rho=0$ is correct, imposing it as a constraint in estimation can be expected to have little effect relative to unrestricted estimation. In an interpretation that will be familiar to economists, $\hat{\lambda}$ can be viewed as the shadow price of the constraint. When the implicit cost is too high, i.e. when λ is significantly different from zero, the constraint is to be rejected.

The estimated multiplier $\hat{\lambda}$ is given by

$$\hat{\lambda} = -\tfrac{1}{2}\partial S(\hat{\beta}, 0)/\partial\rho \qquad \text{(from } \partial S^*(\hat{\beta}, 0, \hat{\lambda})/\partial\rho = 0 \text{ (2.4)}$$

$$= -\Sigma_1^n [\varepsilon_t(\hat{\beta}, 0)\,\partial\varepsilon_t(\hat{\beta}, 0)/\partial\rho] \quad \text{(from equation (2.3))}$$

$$= \Sigma_1^n [\varepsilon_t(\hat{\beta}, 0)\,u_{t-1}(\hat{\beta})] \qquad \text{(from equation (2.2))}$$

$$= \Sigma_1^n \hat{u}_t\hat{u}_{t-1},$$

where $\hat{u}_0 \equiv 0$ and $\hat{u}_t = \varepsilon_t(\hat{\beta}, 0) = u_t(\hat{\beta}) = y_t - x_t\hat{\beta}$ is the OLS residual in period t ($t=1, 2, \ldots, n$). The test of the significance of $\hat{\lambda}$ leads, in this application, to a test of the significance of the estimated first order autocovariance of the OLS residuals, or, equivalently, of their estimated first order autocorrelation.[5] This result ties up rather well with the notion of λ as the shadow price of the constraint.

Equation (2.4) illustrates another interpretation of the LM approach by revealing that it is equivalent to testing the significance of $\partial S(\hat{\beta}, 0)/\partial\rho$. If $H_0 : \rho = 0$ is true, then the constrained estimates $\hat{\beta}$ and $\hat{\rho}=0$ will tend to be close to the corresponding unrestricted ALS estimates. As $\partial S(\beta, \rho)/\partial\rho$ equals zero when evaluated at the ALS estimates, it follows that $\partial S(\hat{\beta}, 0)/\partial\rho$ will tend to be close to zero when $\rho=0$. If, however, the errors are autocorrelated ($\rho\neq 0$), there is no reason why $\partial S(\hat{\beta}, 0)/\partial\rho$ should be small. Thus, the validity of the assumption of independent errors can be investigated by testing whether $\partial S(\hat{\beta}, 0)/\partial\rho$ is significantly different from zero.

The results above are easily generalized. If the alternative to independence is the p *th* order autoregression

$$u_t = \rho_1 u_{t-1} + \ldots + \rho_p u_{t-p} + \varepsilon_t,\ \varepsilon_t\ NID(0, \sigma_\varepsilon^2), \qquad (2.5)$$

then the estimated multipliers for testing $\rho_1 = \ldots = \rho_p = 0$ are given by

$$\hat{\lambda}_i = \Sigma_1^n \hat{u}_t\hat{u}_{t-i}, \quad i=1, \ldots, p,$$

where presample values $\hat{u}_j$, $j \leqslant 0$, are set equal to zero.

The above analysis provides the basis for testing against

autoregressive error schemes. Although most applied workers restrict their attention to such error models, it is important to examine tests against moving average processes, especially when dealing with dynamic regression relationships. The relevance of moving average schemes derives from the fact that many dynamic regression models are transformed versions of rational distributed lag models of one kind or another. For example, it is customary to transform a Koyck model

$$y_t = \beta\,[\Sigma_{i=0}^{\infty}\bar{\mu}^{\,i} x_{t-i}] + \varepsilon_t, \qquad 0 < |\bar{\mu}| < 1\ , \tag{2.6}$$

to obtain an estimating equation

$$y_t = \beta x_t + \bar{\mu} y_{t-1} + u_t, \tag{2.7}$$

where

$$u_t = \varepsilon_t - \bar{\mu}\varepsilon_{t-1} = \varepsilon_t + \mu\varepsilon_{t-1} \text{ where } \mu \equiv -\bar{\mu}. \tag{2.8}$$

Equation (2.8) implies that it is very likely that the u_t of (2.7) will be autocorrelated, and that the u_t are first order moving average if the ε_t are independent.[6]

If the assumption of the serial independence of the disturbances of the regression equation (2.1) is tested against a first order moving average alternative written as (2.8), then the LM approach leads to a test based upon

$$\hat{\lambda}_{MA} = -\Sigma_1^n [\varepsilon_t(\hat{\beta}\ ,\ 0)\,\partial\varepsilon_t(\hat{\beta}\ ,\ 0)/\partial\mu\,], \tag{2.9}$$

where ε_t is now defined as a function, $\varepsilon_t(\beta\ ,\ \mu)$, of β and μ by equations (2.1) and (2.8). But equation (2.8) can be rewritten as

$$\varepsilon_t = u_t - \mu\varepsilon_{t-1} = u_t - \mu u_{t-1} + \mu^2\varepsilon_{t-2}\ ,$$

so that

$$\partial\varepsilon_t(\beta\ ,\ \mu)/\partial\mu = -u_{t-1}(\beta) + 2\mu\varepsilon_{t-2}(\beta\ ,\ \mu) + \mu^2\partial\varepsilon_{t-2}(\beta, \mu)/\partial\mu.$$

Evaluation at $(\beta = \hat{\beta}\ ,\ \mu = \hat{\mu} = 0)$ yields

$$\partial \varepsilon_t(\hat{\beta}\ ,\ 0)/\partial \mu \ = -u_{t-1}(\hat{\beta}) \ = -\hat{u}_{t-1}\ ,$$

and, as $\varepsilon_t(\hat{\beta}\ ,\ 0) = \hat{u}_t$, $\hat{\lambda}_{MA}$ is given by

$$\hat{\lambda}_{MA} = \Sigma_1^n\ \hat{u}_t\hat{u}_{t-1} = \hat{\lambda} \text{ of equation } (2.4).$$

It follows that the same LM test statistic will be obtained whether the alternative is a first order autoregression or a first order moving average scheme, and this remarkable result can be easily generalised to the *p th* order case (see Breusch (1978a) and Godfrey (1979b)). Thus, when testing the assumption that regression disturbances are independent, one need only decide upon the order of the autocorrelation model under the alternative and not upon its form.

Although the analysis above involves only the simple regression model (*2.1*), the results on LM autocorrelation tests are applicable to general linear regression equations with lagged values of the dependent variable appearing as regressors. Methods for computing the sample values of LM test statistics will be discussed in the next subsection along with some other practical issues.

2.2 On the Implementation of LM Tests

Now that the values of the multipliers for testing serial independence have been derived, it is necessary to discuss how tests of their significance can be obtained. For the LM tests to be attractive to applied workers, it is also necessary to show that their implementation is simple and easily modified to take account of interesting restrictions on the alternative model. (It is also important to demonstrate that such tests are effective for finite samples and this issue will be examined in the next subsection). It will be shown below that LM tests for autocorrelation can be viewed as least squares tests of the joint significance of a subset of estimated regression coefficients, requiring only the estimation of an additional regression equation by OLS.

Suppose that the regression equation specified by the researcher is written as

$$y_t = \Sigma_{i=1}^{k} x_{ti}\beta_i + u_t, \qquad t=1,2, \ldots, n, \qquad (2.10)$$

where the x_{ti} includes lagged values of y_t, and the assumption that the u_t are independent is to be tested against a *p th* order autocorrelation alternative, e.g. the autoregressive scheme of (*2.5*). Breusch (1978a) and Godfrey (1978c) show that the appropriate LM statistic can be calculated as the product of the sample size, *n*, and the R^2 statistic from the regression of the OLS residual $\hat{u}_t$ on its first *p* lagged values $\hat{u}_{t-1}, \ldots, \hat{u}_{t-p}$ and the original regressors x_{ti}. If the assumption of independent errors is correct, then the LM statisic is asymptotically distributed as $\chi^2(p)$, so that its sample value should be compared to the selected critical value of that distribution with significantly large values leading to the rejection of the null hypothesis.

Since the OLS residual $\hat{u}_t$ is uncorrelated with (orthogonal to) each of the regressors x_{ti}, elementary regression theory implies that the LM test of $H_o : \rho_1 = \ldots = \rho_p = 0$ in the autoregression (*2.5*) is asymptotically equivalent to a standard large sample test of H_o when the alternative model is

$$\hat{u}_t = \Sigma_{i=1}^{k} x_{ti}\gamma_i + \Sigma_{i=1}^{p} \hat{u}_{t-i}\rho_i + \eta_t, \quad t=1, 2, \ldots, n.\text{[7]} \qquad (2.11)$$

Further, the same test of the assumption that the ρ_i coefficients all equal zero will be obtained if (*2.11*) is replaced by

$$y_t = \Sigma_{i=1}^{k} x_{ti}\delta_i + \Sigma_{i=1}^{p} \hat{u}_{t-i}\rho_i + \eta_t, \quad t=1, 2, \ldots, n. \qquad (2.12)$$

The null hypothesis of independent errors may, therefore, be tested against *p th* order autoregressive or moving average models by adding the first *p* lagged values of $\hat{u}_t$ to the regressors of the economic model (*2.10*) and then applying any asymptotically valid form of the usual test of the joint significance of the estimated ρ_i-coefficients.

For example, one could compare p times the conventional F statistic for testing $H_o : \rho_1 = \ldots = \rho_p = 0$ to the desired $\chi^2(p)$ critical value.

Procedures of this type are very simple to implement since all that is needed is the saving of the least squares residuals $\hat{u}_t$ and then the least squares estimation of a second regression equation such as (2.12). They are also easily modified to allow for restricted alternatives. For example, if quarterly data are being employed and the researcher wishes to test the validity of the independent errors assumption against a seasonal model of the form

$$u_t = \rho_4 u_{t-4} + \varepsilon_t , \qquad (2.13)$$

then all that is required is a test of $\rho_4=0$ in the model

$$y_t = \Sigma_{i=1}^{k} x_{ti}\delta_i + \rho_4 \hat{u}_{t-4} + \eta_t . \qquad (2.14)$$

If the alternative is either

$$u_t = \rho_1 u_{t-1} + \rho_4 u_{t-4} + \varepsilon_t$$

or

$$u_t = \rho_1 u_{t-1} + \rho_4 u_{t-4} - \rho_1 \rho_4 u_{t-5} + \varepsilon_t ,$$

then the augmented regression equation (2.14) should be replaced by

$$y_t = \Sigma_{i=1}^{k} x_{ti}\delta_i + \rho_1 \hat{u}_{t-1} + \rho_4 \hat{u}_{t-4} + \eta_t , \qquad (2.15)$$

and the joint contribution of $\hat{u}_{t-1}$ and $\hat{u}_{t-4}$ must be assessed.[8]

It should be noted that although the example given above have been for purely autoregressive schemes, the LM tests are also appropriate for the corresponding moving average models, e.g. testing $\rho_4=0$ in (2.14) yields the LM test against the simple fourth order moving average scheme

$$u_t = \varepsilon_t + \rho_4 \varepsilon_{t-4}, \qquad \varepsilon_t \; NID(0, \sigma_\varepsilon^2).$$

Further, tests of the type described in this subsection can be used to test against certain restricted mixed autoregressive-moving average error models although the standard results on LM, LR and W procedures cannot be employed when the alternative is an unrestricted mixed autoregressive-moving average error model: see Breusch (1978a) and Godfrey (1978b). For example, testing the validity of the restrictions $\rho_1=\rho_4=0$ in equation (*2.15*) is equivalent to

to testing the assumption of independent errors against the restricted mixed alternative

$$u_t = \rho_4 u_{t-4} + \varepsilon_t + \mu_1 \varepsilon_{t-1}, \qquad \varepsilon_t \; NID(0, \sigma_\varepsilon^2) .$$

2.3 Some Monte Carlo Evidence

It is important to investigate the finite sample performance of any asymptotic test proposed for use in empirical work. If samples have to be unacceptably large before a test achieves a reasonable degree of success, then it is of little value to the applied researcher. Moreover, since the LM test of serial independence seems to be neglecting an important piece of information about the alternative model (namely, whether it is autoregressive or moving average), it might be thought that it would be markedly less powerful than the corresponding LR and W tests. It, therefore, seems worthwhile to review some Monte Carlo evidence on the usefulness of LM tests for autocorrelation.

Some Monte Carlo results on the behaviour of "nxR^2" variants of the LM test have been reported by Mizon and Hendry (1980). These authors set up a dynamic regression model with first order autoregressive errors in order to study the LM statistic calculated from the regression of

$\hat{u}_t$ on $\hat{u}_{t-1}$ and the original regressors, and also the appro-

priate LR and W tests. On the basis of their estimates of the rejection frequencies of these three asymptotically equivalent tests, they conclude that "the evidence favours the use of the easily computed Lagrange multiplier test for residual autocorrelation".

Despite this favourable evidence, it could be thought that the finite sample behaviour of the "nxR^2" forms of LM tests might be adversely affected by the fact that they do not omit some asymptotically negligible terms, e.g. covariances between lagged residuals and exogenous regressors; see Breusch (1978a). If, for example, the residuals obtained by estimating the regression equation (*2.10*) are to be examined for first order autocorrelation, then dropping terms which vanish as $n\to\infty$ transforms the "nxR^2" LM statistic into the square of Durbin's (1970) h-statistic which can be written as

$$h^2 = n\, r_1^2 /(1-n\hat{\nu}), \text{ where } r_1 = \Sigma_2^n \hat{u}_t \hat{u}_{t-1} / \Sigma_2^n \hat{u}_{t-1}^2 \text{, and } \hat{\nu} \text{ is}$$

the estimated asymptotic variance of the OLS estimator of the coefficient of y_{t-1} in (*2.10*).[9] There are, however, many asymptotically equivalent forms for autocorrelation tests, e.g. h^2 is asymptotically equivalent to

$$(h')^2 = n(1-\tfrac{1}{2}d)^2/(1-n\hat{\nu}),$$

where d is the Durbin-Watson statistic. Although differences such as those between h^2 and $(h')^2$ are unimportant as $n\to\infty$, it will be important to compare the small sample performances of alternative forms.

An example of the small sample relevance of asymptotically negligible terms is provided in a paper by Godfrey and Tremayne (1979). These authors are concerned with the problem of testing for fourth order autocorrelation in quarterly dynamic relationships, and carry out Monte Carlo experiments using a model consisting of

$$y_t = \beta_1 + \beta_2 x_t + \beta_3 y_{t-1} + u_t \qquad (2.16)$$

and

$$u_t = \rho_4 u_{t-4} + \varepsilon_t,\ \varepsilon_t\ NID(0,\ \sigma_\varepsilon^2). \qquad (2.17)$$

The tests of $\rho_4=0$ corresponding to the h and h' tests can be shown to be

$$h_4 = \sqrt{n}\, r_4/(1-n\hat{\beta}_3^6\hat{\nu})^{\frac{1}{2}}$$

and

$$h_4' = \sqrt{n}(1-\tfrac{1}{2}d_4)/(1-n\hat{\beta}_3^6\hat{\nu})^{\frac{1}{2}}$$

where $r_4 = \Sigma_5^n \hat{u}_t \hat{u}_{t-4} / \Sigma_5^n \hat{u}_{t-4}^2$ and d_4 is the generalisation of the Dubin-Watson statistic proposed by Wallis (1972).[10] After investigating the sign of the difference between $(1-\frac{1}{2}d_4)$ and r_4, Godfrey and Tremayne suggest that h_4 is likely to be superior to h_4' (in terms of rejecting false null hypotheses) when $\rho_4 < 0$ and inferior when $\rho_4 > 0$. Their Monte Carlo results reveal that: (a) the small sample differences between h_4 and h_4' can be quite large for moderate values of ρ_4; and (b) the widespread practice of relying solely upon the *h*-test when estimating dynamic quarterly regression models cannot be recommended. Some typical results which illustrate these findings are reported in Table 1.[11]

TABLE 1

SOME RESULTS FOR LM TESTS FOR THE CASE OF A SIMPLE FOURTH ORDER AUTOREGRESSION

Value of ρ_4	*Sample size = 40*			*Sample size = 60*		
	h	h_4	h_4'	h	h_4	h_4'
-0.9	35.1	99.9	99.5	40.1	100.0	100.0
-0.6	14.4	96.2	79.2	14.2	99.8	96.1
-0.3	6.3	49.9	19.9	5.3	67.6	40.1
0.0	5.8	5.8	3.8	5.7	5.4	5.2
0.3	6.5	24.5	42.7	6.6	49.3	65.4
0.6	13.1	88.1	94.6	15.3	98.3	99.1
0.9	22.8	100.0	100.0	34.2	100.0	100.0

Note: This table is constructed from Table II of Godfrey and Tremayne (1979). The entries are the percentages of rejections of $H_o : \rho_4=0$ with a nominal type I error of 5 *per cent*. Estimates for $\rho_4=0$ cases are based upon 6000 replications, while all others are based upon 1000 replications. These results are for a case in which $\beta_1 = 0.0$, $\beta_2 = 1{,}0$, $\beta_3 = 0.6$,

$x_t = 0.4x_{t-4} + \zeta_t$, $\zeta_t NID(0.0,\ 1.0)$, and σ^2_ε is

chosen so that the model of (*2.16*) and (*2.17*) has a signal-noise ratio of 5.0.

Godfrey and Tremayne argue that the differences between h_4 and h'_4 are too important to ignore in empirical work and suggest that the two sided test of $H_o : \rho_4=0$ be carried out by using $H^2_4 = max[h^2_4, (h'_4)^2]$. It must, of course, be borne in mind that H^2_4 is asymptotically distributed as the maximum of two $\chi^2(1)$ variables when $\rho_4=0$, and so, if it is compared to 3.84 (the 5 *per cent* value for the $\chi^2(1)$ distribution), then the large sample probability of a type I error of the H^2_4 test is between 5 and 10 *per cent*.

There is a clear need for further Monte Carlo investigations of LM tests, but they do appear to offer a cheap, effective and flexible approach to testing for autocorrelation.

2.4 Testing for Misspecification of an Autocorrelation Model

Empirical workers who find that LM tests lead to the rejection of the assumption of independent errors will have to decide how to treat the residual autocorrelation. Two courses of action open to researchers are: (a) to re-estimate the original regression equation using a technique designed to take account of some specified form of autocorrelation; and (b) to re-specify the regression model until there is no significant evidence of autocorrelation.[12] If the re-estimation strategy is adopted, then the error model must be specified and this specification is a non-trivial task, especially since the LM test depends only on the order of the autocorrelation model of the alternative and not upon its form. It, therefore, seems worthwhile to examine tests of the adequacy of assumed error structures in order to have some guard against using an incorrect autocorrelation model and/or a misspecified economic relationship.

In order to provide a framework for the discussion of tests for misspecification of the error model it will be assumed that the economic relationship (*2.10*) has been estimated allowing for autocorrelated errors. In empirical work, autocorrelation is usually modelled by low order autoregressive processes, but, for the purpose of discussing available test procedures, a general mixed autoregressive-moving average model of order (p,q) can be considered and written as

$$u_t = \rho_1 u_{t-1} + \dots + \rho_p u_{t-p} + \varepsilon_t + \mu_1 \varepsilon_{t-1} + \dots + \mu_q \varepsilon_{t-q},$$
$$\varepsilon_t \; NID(0, \sigma_\varepsilon^2) \; . \qquad (2.18)$$

Models of the form (*2.18*) have yet to gain wide acceptance in applied econometrics, but clearly it is possible to obtain more popular models by setting p and/or q equal to zero.

The conventional time series approach to testing the adequacy of an autocorrelation model is to estimate the model, calculate some of the autocorrelations of the estimated residuals $\hat{\varepsilon}_t$, and then to test their joint significance. If the assumed error model is correct, then the ε_t are independent and one would expect the residual autocorrelations to be low. The significance of the (squared) autocorrelations can be assessed by using the Ljung-Box (1978) modification of the Box Pierce (1970) Q-statistic. The power of the Ljung-Box test has, however, been studied by Davies and Newbold (1979) who conclude that it only achieves a high level of success when the sample size is fairly large (100 or 200). In particular, when $n=50$, the test often fails to detect severe misspecification of time series models.

Whatever the merits of the Box-Pierce and Ljung-Box tests for time series models, it is not valid to apply these tests to the residuals obtained by estimating a regression equation when the regressors include both exogenous variables and lagged dependent variables and alternative tests must be derived; see Breusch and Pagan (1980, p. 245). If the adequacy of (2.18) is checked by testing it against a more general formulation, e.g. the $(p+r,\ q)$ scheme

$$u_t = \rho_1 u_{t-1} + \ldots + \rho_{p+r} u_{t-p-r} + \varepsilon_t + \mu_1 \varepsilon_{t-1} + \ldots + \mu_q \varepsilon_{t-q},$$

or the $(p,\ q+r)$ process

$$u_t = \rho_1 u_{t-1} + \ldots + \rho_p u_{t-p} + \varepsilon_t + \mu_1 \varepsilon_{t-1} + \ldots + \mu_{q+r} \varepsilon_{t-q-r},$$

then LM tests can be developed which use only the results from estimating (2.10) and (2.18).[13] In fact, it can be shown that the LM test of the $(p,\ q)$ model of (2.18) against the $(p+r,\ q)$ model is also the test against the $(p,\ q+r)$ alternative. (The method of proof of this result is a straightforward generalisation of that used in the latter part of Section 2.1 above for the particular case $p=q=0$.) It can also be shown that a test of the appropriate estimated multipliers is equal to a test of the significance of the first r autocorrelations of the $\hat{\varepsilon}_t$ residuals, so that there is a close link between the LM procedure and the time series analysis tests of Box and Pierce (1970) and Ljung and Box (1978) (see Breusch (1978a) and Hosking (1979) for a discussion of this relationship).

Although LM tests for general error models have been obtained (see Godfrey (1978c)), only the case of a pure autogregression ($q=0$) will be discussed in detail here since this is the model most commonly employed in applied work.[14]

If the model consisting of (2.10) and (2.5) is estimated by some appropriate ALS method to obtain estimates $\hat{\beta}_i$ $(i=1,\ \ldots,\ k)$ and $\hat{\rho}_i$ $(i=1,\ \ldots,\ p)$ and associated sets of residuals

$$\hat{u}_t = y_t - \Sigma_{i=1}^{k} x_{ti} \hat{\beta}_i \quad ,$$

and

$$\hat{\varepsilon}_t = \hat{u}_t - \hat{\rho}_1 \hat{u}_{t-1} - \dots - \hat{\rho}_p \hat{u}_{t-p} ,$$

then the LM test against the alternative that the u_t are generated by a $(p+r)$ *th* order autoregression (or by a mixed autoregressive moving average (p,r) model) can be calculated as the product of the sample size, n, and the R^2 from the OLS estimation of

$$\hat{\varepsilon}_t = \Sigma_{i=1}^{k} x^*_{ti}\gamma_i + \Sigma_{i=1}^{p} \hat{u}_{t-i}\rho_i + \Sigma_{i=1}^{r} \hat{\varepsilon}_{t-i}\alpha_i + \eta_t \qquad (2.19)$$

where x^*_{ti} is the estimated autoregressive transform of x_{ti}, i.e.

$$x^*_{ti} = x_{ti} - \hat{\rho}_1 x_{t-1,i} - \dots - \hat{\rho}_p x_{t-p,i}.$$

Alternative forms of the LM test statistic can be obtained in much the same way as in the earlier discussion of testing the assumption of independent disturbances. For example, it would be possible to calculate the test statistic as r times the usual least squares regression F-statistic for testing $H_o : \alpha_1 = \dots = \alpha_r = 0$ in the model

$$y^*_t = \Sigma_{i=1}^{k} x^*_{ti}\delta_i + \Sigma_{i=1}^{p} \hat{u}_{t-i}\rho_i + \Sigma_{i=1}^{r} \hat{\varepsilon}_{t-i}\alpha_i + \eta_t \qquad (2.20)$$

where $y^*_t = y_t - \hat{\rho}_1 y_{t-1} - \dots - \hat{\rho}_p y_{t-p}$. The sample value of the test statistic should be compared to the selected critical value of the $\chi^2(r)$ distribution, with significantly large values leading to the rejection of the specification of the error autocorrelation model (2.5).[15]

3. *TESTING FOR SERIAL CORRELATION IN DYNAMIC SIMULTANEOUS EQUATION MODELS*

Despite the importance of dynamic systems in current economic modelling, only a limited amount has been published on testing for serial correlation in simultaneous equation models. Guilkey (1975) applied Durbin's (1970) general procedure to obtain a test suitable for cases in which a complete system had been estimated by some full information estimation technique, e.g. three stage least squares (3SLS) or full information maximum likelihood (FIML). Unfortunately, as Maritz (1978) has pointed out, Guilkey's analysis is marred by errors which invalidate his expression for the test statistic.[16] In any case, it is not clear that tests based upon full information estimates will be widely used, since many applied workers estimate simultaneous equation models equation by equation using two stage least squares (2SLS) or some other instrumental variable (IV) technique.[17]

Tests for serial correlation which can be calculated from single equation IV estimates have been proposed by Godfrey (1976, 1978a), but the discussion of these tests was in some ways incomplete. One aim of this section is to provide a fuller discussion of these tests in order to assist the applied worker to carry out tests of the assumption of independent errors against plausible (and possibly complex) serial correlation alternatives.

The plan of this section is as follows: first, a simple illustrative model is set out and some basic concepts are discussed; next, tests based upon complete systems estimators like FIML and 3SLS are outlined and are shown to be closely related to the autocorrelation tests proposed in Section 2 for single regression equation models; and finally, tests calculated from 2SLS or IV estimates of individual equations from the system are examined. Tests for the misspecification of an assumed serial correlation model corresponding to those developed in Subsection 2.4 can be obtained by straightforward generalisation.

3.1 An Illustrative Model and Some Preliminary Remarks

The discussion of tests of the assumption of serially independent disturbances will be based upon the following simple model:

$$y_{t1} + \beta_{12} y_{t2} + \gamma_{11} y_{t-1,1} + \gamma_{13} z_{t1} = u_{t1} , \qquad (3.1)$$

$$\beta_{21} y_{t1} + y_{t2} + \gamma_{22} y_{t-1,2} + \gamma_{24} z_{t2} = u_{t2} , \qquad (3.2)$$

where the y_{ti} are the current endogenous variables of the system, the $y_{t-1,i}$ are their one period lagged values, and the z_{ti} are exogenous variables. Needless to say, none of the results presented below rely upon either the simplicity or the particular specification of the two structural equations (3.1) and (3.2). This model is, however, adequate for the purpose of outlining the main points of relevance to empirical workers.

As before, the approach adopted to constructing tests of the serial independence of the disturbances u_{ti} is to assume some form of serial correlation model as the alternative. The natural systems generalisation of the simple first order autoregressive scheme of (2.2) is a vector autoregressive process which can be written as

$$u_{t1} = \rho_{11}u_{t-1,1} + \rho_{12}u_{t-1,2} + \varepsilon_{t1} \qquad (3.3)$$

$$u_{t2} = \rho_{21}u_{t-1,1} + \rho_{22}u_{t-1,2} + \varepsilon_{t2} \qquad (3.4)$$

where the ε_{ti} are normally distributed with zero means, constant variances and covariance, and all serial correlations are zero (i.e. $E(\varepsilon_{si}\varepsilon_{tj}) = 0$ if $s \neq t$ for $i, j=1, 2$). Note that in this *vector* serial correlation model a disturbance term depends not only upon its own lagged value, but also upon the lagged value of the error of the other equation. If $\rho_{12} = \rho_{21} = 0$, the serial correlation model of (3.3) and (3.4) reduced to two *scalar* processes in which each disturbance depends upon only its own past values. If all the ρ_{ij} are zero, then the model's errors are serially independent.

The presence of serial correlation in the errors of a dynamic system will rob conventional estimators such as 2SLS and 3SLS of the asymptotic properties usually claimed for them and will also invalidate the standard tests of hypotheses. One way to see the adverse effects of the errors being serially correlated is to note that many simultaneous equation estimators involve (explicitly or implicitly) "purging" the endogenous variables appearing as regressors in order to remove the parts of these variables which are correlated with the model's errors. If the ρ_{ij} of (3.3) and (3.4) are all zero, then such "purging" can be based upon the reduced form relationships derived from (3.1) and (3.2). The reduced form can be written as

$$y_{t1} = \pi_{11}y_{t-1,1} + \pi_{12}y_{t-1,2} + \pi_{13}z_{t1} + \pi_{14}z_{t2} + \nu_{t1} \qquad (3.5)$$

$$y_{t2} = \pi_{21}y_{t-1,1} + \pi_{22}y_{t-1,2} + \pi_{23}z_{t1} + \pi_{24}z_{t2} + \nu_{t2} \qquad (3.6)$$

where the π_{ij} are functions of the parameters of the structural system. Thus, 2SLS and 3SLS involve estimating (3.5) and (3.6) by OLS to obtain predicted values (estimated "systematic parts") for y_{t1} and y_{t2}. If, however, the ρ_{ij} are non-zero, then the reduced form errors ν_{ti} will be serially correlated and so will be asymptotically correlated with $y_{t-1,1}$ and $y_{t-1,2}$. It follows that when the errors are serially correlated the usual reduced form relationships (3.5) and (3.6) no longer split endogenous variables into asymptotically uncorrelated systematic ("purged") and non-systematic parts.

This problem can be overcome by using a simple extension of the device employed in the previous section to obtain an equation with serially independent errors. Recall that

$$y_t = \beta x_t + u_t \qquad (2.1)$$

and

$$u_t = \rho u_{t-1} + \varepsilon_t \qquad (2.2)$$

implied that

$$y_t = \rho y_{t-1} + \beta x_t - \rho\beta x_{t-1} + \varepsilon_t \,.$$

A similar sort of substitution to eliminate vector autoregression in (3.5) and (3.6) leads to equations of the form

$$y_{ti} = \psi_{i1}y_{t-1,1} + \psi_{i2}y_{t-1,2} + \psi_{i3}z_{t1} + \psi_{i4}z_{t2} + \psi_{i5}y_{t-2,1}$$
$$+ \psi_{i6}y_{t-2,2} + \psi_{i7}z_{t-1,1} + \psi_{i8}z_{t-1,2} + \alpha_{ti} ,$$
$$i=1,\ 2, \qquad (3.7)$$

where the ψ_{ij} are functions of the β_{ij}, γ_{ij} and ρ_{ij}, and α_{ti} is a serially independent error. The set of equations like (3.7) plays the role of the reduced form in simultaneous equation models with autocorrelated errors, see Hatanaka (1976). It should be noted that the transformation to eliminate the serial correlation has introduced four new variables to the analysis, namely ($y_{t-2,1}$, $y_{t-2,2}$, $z_{t-1,1}$, $z_{t-1,2}$).

3.2 *Testing for Serial Correlation Using Full Information Estimates*

The well known FIML approach gives as estimates of the coefficients of (3.1) and (3.2) the maximisers of the likelihood appropriate for the case in which u_{t1} and u_{t2} are serially independent. If follows that the FIML estimates can be viewed as being obtained in a constrained optimisation problem in which the likelihood for the model comprising (3.1)-(3.4) is maximised subject to the four restrictions $\rho_{11} = \rho_{12} = \rho_{21} = \rho_{22} = 0$. This interpretation immdiately suggests the use of the LM approach advocated for testing $H_o : \rho = 0$ in

$$u_t = \rho u_{t-1} + \varepsilon_t \qquad (2.2)$$

above. Given the assumptions of Section 2, minimising the error sum of squares function $S(\beta, \rho)$ of (2.3) is equivalent to maximising the likelihood $L(\beta, \rho)$ for the model consisting of (2.1) and (2.2), so that the test of the significance of the multiplier of (2.4) is equivalent to that of the estimated multiplier arising from consideration of the first order derivatives of the Lagrangean

$$L^*(\beta, \rho, \lambda) = L(\beta, \rho) + \lambda\rho$$

which is appropriate for the constrained optimisation problem:

maximise $L(\beta, \rho)$

subject to $\rho = 0$.

The estimated multipliers for testing $H_o : \rho_{11} = \rho_{12} = \rho_{21} = \rho_{22} = 0$ can be obtained by solving the first order conditions for a Lagrangean equal to the sum of the likelihood function for the alternative model (3.1)-(3.4) and, e.g. $(\lambda_1\rho_{11} + \lambda_2\rho_{12} + \lambda_3\rho_{21} + \lambda_4\rho_{22})$, where the λ_i are the multipliers. The derivation of the LM test statistic is straightforward and is presented in Appendix A.

The direct LM approach is, however, unattractive because it requires a special subroutine to be added to standard full information estimation programmes and this may pose (short run) problems. Fortunately, appropriate generalisations of the results of Subsection 2.2 can be obtained and it can be shown that the LM test is asymptotically equivalent to testing $H_o : \rho_{11} = \rho_{12} = \rho_{21} = \rho_{22} = 0$ when the alternative is the following augmented version of the original system:

$$y_{t1} + \beta_{12}y_{t2} + \gamma_{11}y_{t-1,1} + \gamma_{13}z_{t1} + \rho_{11}\hat{u}_{t-1,1} + \rho_{12}\hat{u}_{t-1,2} = \eta_{t1}, \tag{3.8}$$

$$\beta_{21}y_{t1} + y_{t2} + \gamma_{22}y_{t-1,2} + \gamma_{24}z_{t2} + \rho_{21}\hat{u}_{t-1,1} + \rho_{22}\hat{u}_{t-1,2} = \eta_{t2}, \tag{3.9}$$

where the $\hat{u}_{t-1,i}$ are the lagged values of the residuals obtained by estimating the original economic model by FIML (or by some other estimator which is asymptotically equivalent to FIML when H_o is true). This result corresponds to the fact that when testing for first order autocorrelation in the residuals of a single (non-simultaneous) regression equation, the null hypothesis $\rho=0$ can be tested by applying the usual significance test after estimating

$$y_t = \beta x_t + \rho \hat{u}_{t-1} + \eta_t$$

by least squares.

If the alternative model consisting of (3.8) and (3.9) is estimated using FIML or 3SLS, then $H_o : \rho_{11} = \rho_{12} = \rho_{21} = \rho_{22} = 0$ can be tested, e.g. by a LR test.[18]

This approach is obviously convenient since it does not require modifications of existing estimation programmes. Considerations of computational cost suggest that it would be unwise to apply FIML directly to alternative models like (3.8)-(3.9), and that it would be better to first concentrate the likelihood with respect to the ρ_{ij}.[19] This concentration simply leads to re-estimating the original economic model (3.1)-(3.2) by FIML with all variables replaced by their residuals from OLS regressions on the lagged FIML residuals $\hat{u}_{t-1,1}$ and $\hat{u}_{t-1,2}$. The maximised likelihood for this "residuals for variables" version of (3.1)-(3.2) is equal to that obtained by estimating the alternative system (3.8)-(3.9) by FIML.

Several of the other results reported in Subsection 2.2 can be generalised to cover the systems tests of this subsection. For example, the LM test of serial independence against the first order vector autoregressive model is also appropriate for the first order vector moving average alternative. Also, tests against *p th* order vector serial correlation schemes are obtained by adding the required extra lagged values of the FIML residuals $\hat{u}_{ti}$ to the alternative model (3.8)-(3.9). (Restricted alternatives, e.g.

$$u_{t1} = \rho_{11} u_{t-4,1} + \rho_{12} u_{t-4,2} + \varepsilon_{t1}$$

$$u_{t2} = \rho_{21}u_{t-4,1} + \rho_{22}u_{t-4,2} + \varepsilon_{t2}$$

are handled in the obvious fashion.)

3.3 Testing for Serial Correlation Using Individual Structural Equation Estimates

As suggested above, it is unlikely that tests based upon estimates from full information methods like FIML and 3SLS will be widely used since many researchers use 2SLS or some other single equation IV technique to estimate the parameters of dynamic models. Being aware of the dangers of ignoring serial correlation when estimating dynamic simultaneous systems, some applied workers have tried to test the serial independence assumption by means of Durbin's (1970) *h*-test. Unfortunately, this test is not valid when the estimated relationship belongs to a simultaneous equation model (see Godfrey (1978a)). It is, therefore, important to develop valid tests which can be calculated from 2SLS or IV estimates, and which can be fairly easily used against a variety of alternative models. The purpose of this subsection is to discuss the problem of deriving such tests.

If the ρ_{ij} of (3.3) and (3.4) are all zero, the structural disturbances u_{ti} will be serially independent and the usual 2SLS/IV estimators will be consistent. These consistent estimators can in fact be used to construct tests of $H_o : \rho_{11} = \rho_{12} = \rho_{21} = \rho_{22} = 0$ which are asymptotically equivalent to the LM procedure mentioned in the previous subsection. The complexity of these alternatives to the LM approach is, however, probably sufficient to deter most researchers from using them (e.g. see the discussion of the $C(\alpha)$ test in Appendix A).

The *unrestricted* vector autoregressive scheme of (3.3)-(3.4) will, therefore, no longer be used as the alternative and attention will instead be focussed on the restricted process obtained by putting $\rho_{12} = \rho_{21} = 0$, i.e.

$$u_{ti} = \rho_{ii}u_{t-1,i} + \varepsilon_{ti} \quad (i=1,\ 2) \qquad (3.10)$$

The specification (3.10) reflects the emphasis on estimation of an individual structural equation as opposed to complete systems.[20]

Suppose that the first equation has been estimated and that the assumption of serially independent errors is to be tested against the appropriate member of (3.10). The null hypothesis of interest is then $H_o : \rho_{11} = 0$. It might be thought that the treatment of ρ_{22} (the coefficient of the error model of the second equation) is unimportant, but if ρ_{22} is not zero, then the transformed reduced form relationship (3.7) will include the variables $y_{t-2,2}$ and $z_{t-1,2}$ which are not in the original structural model (3.1)-(3.2). If these additional variables are not used in the instrument set when estimating the first structural equation (3.1), then the LM type test of $H_o : \rho_{11} = 0$ will not be asymptotically equivalent to the appropriate LR test.

One solution to this problem would be to assume $\rho_{22} = 0$ when testing $H_o : \rho_{11} = 0$, but this seems arbitrary and, in any case, it would appear illogical to stick to this strategy when testing $H_o : \rho_{22} = 0$ if significant evidence of serial correlation had been found in the first equation's residuals. Another solution would be to take account of the alternative when estimating models under the null hypothesis of serial independence by using the regressors of transformed reduced form relationships like (3.7) as the set of available instruments. This solution is, however, not in the spirit of the diagnostic check approach discussed in Section 2 which would involve restricting the instruments to be regressors of the original reduced form (3.5)-(3.6).

If estimation is to be based only upon instruments appearing in the specified economic model, then modified LM (MLM) tests can be derived which are asymptotically valid, but which need not be asymptotically equivalent to the LR test of $\rho_{11} = 0$. The derivation of MLM procedures is quite similar to that of the LM autocorrelation tests of Section 2. Sargan (1959) has proposed an autoregressive instrumental variable estimator which bears the same relationship to the standard instrumental variable procedure as does ALS to OLS. The MLM test is then designed to be asymptotically equivalent to a test of the significance of the autoregressive instrumental variable estimate of ρ_{11}.[21]

It can be shown that if the first structural equation (3.1) is estimated by 2SLS or IV to obtain

$$y_{t1} + \hat{\beta}_{12} y_{t2} + \hat{\gamma}_{11} y_{t-1,1} + \hat{\gamma}_{13} z_{t1} = \hat{u}_{t1} \qquad (3.11)$$

where " ^ " now denotes the 2SLS or IV estimate and $\hat{u}_{t1}$ is the residual, then the MLM test of $\rho_{11} = 0$ (based upon the set of instruments used for (3.11)) can be calculated as a test of the significance of the estimated coefficient of $\hat{u}_{t-1,1}$ in the alternative model

$$y_{t1} + \beta_{12} y_{t2} + \gamma_{11} y_{t-1,1} + \gamma_{13} z_{t1} + \rho_{11} \hat{u}_{t-1,1} = \eta_{t1}. \qquad (3.12)$$

(Under H_o, the "t-ratio" of this estimated coefficient will be asymptotically distributed as a normal variable with zero mean and unit variance.)

This result is clearly very similar to those obtained in Subsections 2.2 and 3.2. Furthermore, the main results for MLM tests are exactly what might be expected from the discussion above:

(a) the MLM tests of the serial independence of the u_{t1} errors against the p *th* order autoregression alternative

$$u_{t1} = \sum_{i=1}^{p} u_{t-i,1} \rho_{1i} + \varepsilon_{t1}$$

and the p *th* order moving average alternative

$$u_{t1} = \varepsilon_{t1} + \sum_{i=1}^{p} \varepsilon_{t-i,1}\mu_{1i}$$

are the same;

(b) this common test statistic can be calculated by means of a test of $H_o : \rho_{11} = \ldots = \rho_{1p} = 0$ in the alternative model

$$y_{t1} + \beta_{12}y_{t2} + \gamma_{11}y_{t-1,1} + \gamma_{13}z_{t1} + \sum_{i=1}^{p} \rho_{1i}\hat{u}_{t-i\ 1} = \eta_{t1} \qquad (3.13)$$

with the instrumental variables used in the estimation of (3.13) being the same as those employed when estimating the original model (3.1);

and

(c) restricted alternatives, e.g. corresponding to the seasonal model of equation (2.13), can be dealt with in the way described in Section 2.2.[22]

The test of the joint significance of the estimated ρ_{1j} of (3.13) can be calculated very simply. If the residuals obtained by estimating (3.13) are denoted by η_{t1}, then the test statistic can be expressed as

$$\pi(p) = n(R_1^2 - R_2^2), \qquad (3.14)$$

where R_1^2 is the R^2 statistic of the least squares regression of $\hat{u}_{t1}$ on the instruments used to estimate (3.1) and (3.13), and R_2^2 is the R^2 statistic when the regressors are again these instruments, but the regressand is $\hat{\eta}_{t1}$. This test statistic is asymptotically distributed as $\chi^2(p)$ under the null hypothesis with significantly large values indicating that the sample evidence is not consistent with the assumption of serial independence.

It should be noted that the choice of the instruments used to generate the MLM tests is not entirely unrestricted. Firstly, the instruments cannot consist entirely of exogenous variables since these would be asymptotically uncorrelated with the $\hat{u}_{t-i,1}$ regressors of (3.13) under H_o and so would not satisfy one of the usual conditions for the validity of an instrumental variable. Secondly, the number of variables in the instrument set used in estimating (3.1) must not be less than the number of coefficients in the alternative model (3.13), since this set is also used to estimate the latter model. In some cases, the number of regressors in the original reduced form (3.5)-(3.6) may be too small to satisfy this second restriction, but some of their lagged values can be used to overcome this problem.[23]

Since the MLM test need not be asymptotically equivalent to a LR test, there may be other procedures which are superior to it in large samples. One obvious alternative to the MLM approach is simply to examine the significance of the estimated autocorrelations of the IV residuals $\hat{u}_{t1}$ which have the general form

$$r_{11}(j) = \Sigma_{j+1}^{n}\hat{u}_{t-j,1}\hat{u}_{t1}/\Sigma_{1}^{n}\hat{u}_{t1}^{2} .$$ [24]

Godfrey (1978a) has derived an asymptotic test of the significance of the first order autocorrelation coefficient $r_{11}(1)$ and Sargan (1976) has provided a more general analysis. Unfortunately, it does not seem possible either to derive a general relationship between this sort of test and the MLM procedure, or to find a simple approach to computing a test, say $\theta(p)$, of the significance of the first p autocorrelations.[25]

A large sample test of the significance of a set of residual autocorrelations can be obtained using Sargan's (1976) results and an expression for such a test is given in Appendix B.

4. CONCLUSIONS

It is hoped that the discussion above has demonstrated that the LM approach (or some modification of it) provides easily implemented and versatile tests for various types of autocorrelation. Given that these tests are derived from asymptotic theory, their performance in finite samples deserves further investigation to provide applied workers with information about their practical value. The available Monte Carlo evidence is encouraging, but much remains to be done, especially in the area of testing for serial correlation in dynamic simultaneous equation models.

It is suggested that tests for autocorrelation of the type outlined above should be employed as part of the routine testing of economic models estimated using time series data. It should, however, be stressed that in the event of the assumption of serial independence being rejected, serious consideration should be given to the problem of how to react to this evidence of misspecification. Omitted variables, incorrect functional form and many other deficiencies in the specification of the economic model can lead to residual serial correlation. Even if it were possible to know that a significant value of a test statistic reflected the presence of autocorrelation in the errors of a correctly specified economic relationship, there would still remain the problem of choosing the autocorrelation model. This kind of choice will not be easy given that LM tests are usually the same for several alternatives, and will probably have some degree of power whenever the specified alternative is contained within the true model.[26] It follows that researchers must be prepared to respond to residual serial correlation by estimating a number of alternative models and applying various tests for misspecification to these estimated models in an attempt to reject inadequate specifications.[27] It seems very likely that the general LM procedure will be valuable in this context since it can be employed to construct simple tests for heteroskedasticity, functional form and other types of misspecification.

REFERENCES

Aldrich, J. (1978). An alternative derivation of Durbin's *h*-statistic. *Econometrica* 46, 1493-4.

Box, G.E.P. and D.A. Pierce (1970). Distribution of residual autocorrelations in autoregressive integrated moving average time series models. *Journal of the American Statistical Association* 65, 1509-26.

Breusch, T.S. (1978a). Testing for autocorrelation in dynamic linear models. *Australian Economic Papers* 17, 334-55.

Breusch, T.S. (1978b). *Some aspects of statistical inference for econometrics.* Unpublished Ph.D. thesis, Australian National University, Canberra.

Breusch, T.S. and A.R. Pagan (1980). The Lagrange multiplier test and its application to model specification in econometrics. *Review of Economic Studies* 47, 239-53.

Davies, N. and P. Newbold (1979). Some power studies of a portmanteau test of time series model specification. *Biometrika* 66, 153-5.

Durbin, J. (1970). Testing for serial correlation in least squares regression when some of the regressors are lagged dependent variables. *Econometrica* 38, 410-21.

Fisk, P.R. (1967). *Stochastically dependent equations.* (London: Griffin.)

Godfrey, L.G. (1976). Testing for serial correlation in dynamic simultaneous equation models. *Econometrica* 44, 1077-84.

Godfrey, L.G. (1978a). A note on the use of Durbin's *h*-test when the equation is estimated by instrumental variables. *Econometrica* 46, 225-8.

Godfrey, L.G. (1978b). Testing against general autoregressive and moving average error models when the regressors include lagged dependent variables. *Econometrica* 46, 1293-1302.

Godfrey, L.G. (1978c). Testing for higher order serial correlation in regression equations when the regressors include lagged dependent variables. *Econometrica* 46, 1303-10.

Godfrey, L.G. and A.R. Tremayne (1979). A note on testing for fourth order autocorrelation in dynamic quarterly regression equations. Unpublished paper, University of York.

Guilkey, D.K. (1975). A test for the presence of first-order vector autoregressive errors when lagged endogenous variables are present. *Econometrica* 43, 711-8.

Hatanaka, M. (1976). Several efficient two-step estimators for the dynamic simultaneous equations model with autoregressive disturbances. *Journal of Econometrics* 4, 189-204.

Hendry, D.F. (1976). The structure of simultaneous equations estimators. *Journal of Econometrics* 4, 51-88.

Hendry, D.F. (1977). On the time series approach to econometric model building, in: *New methods in business cycle research*, ed. C.A. Sims, (Federal Reserve Bank of Minneapolis).

Hendry, D.F. (1979). Predictive failure and econometric modelling in macroeconomics: the transactions demand for money, in: *Economic modelling*, ed. P. Ormerod (London: Heinemann).

Hosking, J.R.M. (1979). Lagrange mutliplier tests of time series models. Unpublished paper, University of Southampton.

Koopmans, T.C. and W.C. Hood (1953). The estimation of simultaneous linear economic relationships, in: *Studies in econometric method*, ed. W.C. Hood and T.C. Koopmans (New York: Wiley).

Ljung, G.M. and G.E.P. Box (1978). On a measure of lack of fit in time series models. *Biometrika* 65, 297-303.

Maritz, A. (1978). A note of correction to Guilkey's test for serial independence in simultaneous equations models. *Econometrica* 46, 471.

Mizon, G.E. (1977). Inferential procedures in nonlinear models: an application in a UK industrial cross section study of factor substitution and returns to scale. *Econometrica* 45, 1221-42.

Mizon, G.E. and D.F. Hendry (1980). An empirical application and Monte Carlo study of tests of dynamic specification. *Review of Economic Studies* 47, 21-45.

Newbold, P. and N. Davies (1978). Error misspecifcation and spurious regressions. *International Economic Review* 19, 513-9.

Neyman, J. (1959). Optimal asymptotic tests of composite statistical hypotheses, in: *Probability and statistics, the Harald Cramer volume*, ed. U. Grenander (New York: Wiley).

Nicholls, D.F., A.R. Pagan and R.D. Terrell (1975). The estimation and use of models with moving average disturbance terms: a survey. *International Economic Review* 16, 113-34.

Rothenberg, T.J. and C.T. Leenders (1964). Efficient estimation of simultaneous equation systems. *Econometrica* 32, 57-76.

Sargan, J.D. (1959). The estimation of relationships with autocorrelated residuals by the use of instrumental variables. *Journal of the Royal Statistical Society, Series B* 21, 91-105.

Sargan, J.D. (1976). Testing for misspecification after estimating using instrumental variables. Unpublished paper, London School of Economics.

Silvey, S.D. (1959). The Lagrangian multiplier test. *Annals of Mathematical Statistics* 30, 389-407.

Wallis, K.F. (1972). Testing for fourth order autocorrelation in quarterly regression equations. *Econometrica* 40, 617-36.

APPENDIX A. *Some asymptotic tests for vector serial correlation in dynamic simultaneous equation models*

An expression for the direct LM test of the serial independence of the errors of a system against the alternative of a first order vector autoregression will be provided in this appendix.[28] This appendix also contains a description of an asymptotically equivalent procedure which only requires the use of an estimator which is consistent under the null in contrast to the LM approach which involves maximum likelihood estimation subject to the restrictions of the null hypothesis. This second procedure is closely related to Neyman's (1959) $C(\alpha)$ test and, since the $C(\alpha)$ test has not been widely used in econometrics, it seems worthwhile to outline its derivation before obtaining the specific form for the problem under consideration.

Suppose that n^{-1} times the log of the likelihood function for an alternative model is $\ell(\theta)$, where the parameter vector θ consists of two subvectors θ_1(r by 1) and θ_2 (s by 1), and the null hypothesis to be tested is $H_o : \theta_2 = 0$. The null hypothesis could clearly be tested by obtaining the unrestricted MLE $\theta^* = (\theta_1^{*\prime}, \theta_2^{*\prime})'$, and then testing the significance of θ_2^*. The asymptotic properties of this (Wald) test would not be affected if θ_2^* were replaced by an estimator which was asymptotically equivalent to it under the null and a sequence of local alternatives $H_n : \theta_2 = n^{-\frac{1}{2}}\delta$, $\delta'\delta < \infty$; n being, as usual, the sample size. The $C(\alpha)$ approach simply involves using an estimator $\tilde{\theta} = (\tilde{\theta}_1', \tilde{\theta}_2')'$ which is consistent under H_n to construct such an asymptotically equivalent estimator.

Applying the Rothenberg-Leenders (1964) theorem on linearised maximum likelihood estimators yields the result that θ^* is, under H_n, asymptotically equivalent to

$$\bar{\theta} = (\bar{\theta}_1', \bar{\theta}_2')' = \tilde{\theta} + \tilde{G}^{-1}\tilde{g} \tag{A.1}$$

where

$$\tilde{G} = \{\tilde{G}_{i,j}\} = -\{ \partial^2 \ell(\tilde{\theta}) / \partial\theta_i \, \partial\theta_j\}, \; i, j=1, 2,$$

and

$$\tilde{g} = \{\tilde{g}_i\} = \{ \partial \ell(\tilde{\theta}) / \partial \theta_i\}, \qquad i=1, \; 2.$$

Thus, the estimator which is asymptotically equivalent to θ_2^* under H_n is

$$\bar{\theta}_2 = (\tilde{G}^{21}\tilde{g}_1 + \tilde{G}^{22}\tilde{g}_2), \tag{A.2}$$

where the $\tilde{G}^{ij}$ are defined by

$$\tilde{G}^{-1} = \{\tilde{G}^{ij}\}, \qquad i, j=1, 2.$$

Under H_o, $n^{\frac{1}{2}}\theta_2^*$ (and hence $n^{\frac{1}{2}}\bar{\theta}_2$) is asymptotically normally distributed with zero mean vector and asymptotic variance covariance matrix equal to plim G^{22}. Since $\bar{\theta}_2$ of (A.2) is asymptotically equivalent to θ_2^* and plim G^{22} equals plim $\tilde{G}^{22}$ when H_o is true, it follows that the standard Wald test of H_o is asymptotically equivalent to

$$\phi = n\bar{\theta}_2' \, [\tilde{G}^{22}]^{-1}\bar{\theta}_2 \tag{A.3}$$

$$= n[\tilde{G}^{21}\tilde{g}_1 + \tilde{G}^{22}\tilde{g}_2]' [\tilde{G}^{22}]^{-1} \, [\tilde{G}^{21}\tilde{g}_1 + \tilde{G}^{22}\tilde{g}_2]$$

$$= n[(\tilde{G}^{22})^{-1}\tilde{G}^{21}\tilde{g}_1 + \tilde{g}_2]' \, [\tilde{G}^{22}] \, [(\tilde{G}^{22})^{-1}\tilde{G}^{21}\tilde{g}_1 + \tilde{g}_2]$$

$$= n[\tilde{g}_2-\tilde{G}_{21}\tilde{G}_{11}^{-1}\tilde{g}_1]' \; [\tilde{G}^{22}] \; [\tilde{g}_2-\tilde{G}_{21}\tilde{G}_{11}^{-1}\tilde{g}_1] .$$

The final expression for ϕ in (A.3) is very similar to the form of Neyman's (1959) $C(\alpha)$ test (see Breusch and Pagan (1980) for further discussion of $C(\alpha)$ tests and their applications). When the null hypothesis is true, ϕ is asymptotically distributed as $\chi^2(s)$.

Note that when the constrained MLE $\hat{\theta} = (\hat{\theta}_1', 0)'$ is used to generate $\bar{\theta}_2$, then since

$$\hat{g}_1 = \partial \ell(\hat{\theta}) / \partial \theta_1 = 0,$$

(A.3) reduces to the expression for Silvey's (1959) LM test, i.e.

$$\phi_{LM} = n\hat{g}_2'\hat{G}^{22}\hat{g}_2 , \qquad (A.4)$$

where the $\hat{g}_i$ and $\hat{G}^{ij}$ are defined in the obvious fashion.

The above results can now be applied to the problem of testing for vector serial correlation in dynamic economic models. The simultaneous equation system will be written as

$$Y = YB + ZC + U \qquad (A.5)$$

$$= XA + U, \; (X = (Y,Z) \text{ and } A' = (B', C'))$$

where Y is a n by m matrix of observations on the current endogenous variables, Z is a n by k matrix of observations on lagged endogenous variables and current and lagged exogenous variables, U is a n by m matrix of error terms, B is a m by m coefficient matrix with $b_{ii} = 0$, $i=1, 2, \ldots, m$ and $det(I_m-B) \neq 0$, and C is a k by m coefficient matrix.

It will be assumed that the model is identified and stable, with plim $n^{-1}(Z'Z)$ being a finite non-singular matrix. The total number of variables in the dynamic model (A.5) is $f = m+k$.

The reduced form of (A.5) is

$$Y = ZC(I_m - B)^{-1} + U(I_m - B)^{-1} \tag{A.6}$$

$$= Z\Pi + V, \text{ where } \Pi = C(I_m - B)^{-1} \text{ and } V = U(I_m - B)^{-1},$$

$$= \bar{Y} + V, \text{ say.}$$

A typical equation of the system will be written in *unrestricted* form as

$$y_i = Y_i\beta_i + Z_i\gamma_i + u_i \qquad i=1, 2, \ldots, m, \tag{A.7}$$

where y_i is the i *th* column of Y, Y_i is the n by m_i matrix of current endogenous variables appearing as regressors, Z_i is a n by k_i matrix of predetermined regressors, β_i and γ_i are the unrestricted coefficient vectors and u_i is the i *th* column of U. The data matrix of "right hand side" variables in the i *th* structural equation is then $X_i = (Y_i, Z_i)$, and it will be useful to introduce a selection matrix T defined by

$$(I_m \otimes X)T = diag(X_1, X_2, \ldots, X_m); \tag{A.8}$$

compare Hatanaka (1976).

The error model under the alternative hypothesis is the vector autoregressive scheme

$$U = U_{-1}R + E, \tag{A.9}$$

where U_{-1} is the one period lagged value of U, R is the m by m coefficient matrix, and E is a n by m random matrix. The n rows of E are independently and normally distributed with zero mean vector and unrestricted variance-covariance matrix Σ. Since the errors of the system (A.5) are serially independent when $R=0$, the null hypothesis to be tested is H_o : $vec(R) = 0$ (a m^2 by 1 null vector). In terms of the earlier discussion, θ_2 is vec(R). It will be assumed that the likelihood function has been concentrated with respect to the unrestricted matrix Σ, and so the nuisance parameter vector θ_1 will consist of the unrestricted structural coefficients, i.e. the elements of θ_1 are made up of those of the β_i and γ_i of (A.7).

The concentrated log likelihood function for the alternative model comprising (A.5) and (A.9) is then

$$\ell(\theta) = const + \tfrac{1}{2}\, \ell n|(I_m-B)'W(I_m-B)| - \tfrac{1}{2}\, \ell n|E(\theta)'E(\theta)|, \quad (A.10)$$

where W is $Y'(I_n-Z(Z'Z)^{-1}Z')Y$ and $E(\theta)$ is $(Y-XA-Y_{-1}R+X_{-1}AR)$ regarded as a function of the unrestricted elements of A and the elements of R.

In order to develop $C(\alpha)$ tests for serial correlation, it is useful to obtain the first and second partial derivatives of $\ell(\theta)$ of (A.10) evaluated at $(\theta_1', 0')'$. It can be shown that, under H_o, the relevant partial derivatives are:

$$g_1 = n^{-1}T'(S^{-1}\otimes\bar{X}')vec(Y-XA) \quad (A.11)$$

$$g_2 = n^{-1}(S^{-1}\otimes(Y_{-1}-X_{-1}A)')vec(Y-XA) \quad (A.12)$$

$$G_{11} = n^{-1}T'(S^{-1}\otimes\bar{X}'\bar{X})T \quad (A.13)$$

$$G_{12} = n^{-1}T'(S^{-1}\otimes\bar{X}'(Y_{-1}-X_{-1}A)) = G_{21}' \quad (A.14)$$

and

$$G_{22} = (S^{-1}\otimes S), \quad (A.15)$$

where $\bar{X} = (\bar{Y}, Z) = (ZC(I_m-B)^{-1}, Z)$, and $S = n^{-1}(Y-XA)'(Y-XA)$.

The computation of the $C(\alpha)$ test requires a set of estimates obtained by the use of some procedure which is consistent when the errors of the system are serially independent. Under H_n, a m^2 by 1 null vector can serve as $\tilde{\theta}_2$, and 2SLS or any other IV estimator can be used to provide $\tilde{\theta}_1$. Given a suitable $\tilde{\theta}_1$, a consistent estimator of A, $\tilde{A} = (\tilde{B}', \tilde{C}')'$, can be obtained which can then be substituted in (A.11)-(A.15). Estimates of the g_i and G_{ij} can then be employed to calculate the sample value of the $C(\alpha)$ test statistic ϕ of (A.3).[29] When the errors of (A.5) are serially independent, ϕ of (A.3) is asymptotically distributed as $\chi^2(m^2)$, and if the sample value of the statistic exceeds the selected critical value for this distribution, then there is significant evidence of serial correlation.

The LM specialisation of (A.3) is obtained by using the FIML estimate $\hat{A}$ (or any other estimator which is asymptotically equivalent to FIML under H_o) in (A.12)-(A.15) and (A.4), and it is easy to show that the direct LM test is essentially the same as the appropriate generalisation of Durbin's (1970) *h*-test (see Breusch (1978b, Chapter 5)).

APPENDIX B. Testing the autocorrelations of instrumental variable residuals

The purpose of this appendix is to provide an asymptotic test of the significance of a set of residual autocorrelations calculated after estimating an individual equation of a simultaneous system by 2SLS or some other IV method. It will be convenient to adopt a notation which is different to that employed in the main body of the paper. Thus, the equation of interest will be written as

$$y = X\beta + u \tag{B.1}$$

where y is a n by 1 vector of observations on an endogenous variable, X is a n by k matrix of observations on endogenous, lagged endogenous, exogenous and lagged exogenous variables, β is k by 1 vector of unknown coefficients and u is a n by 1 vector of errors. Also, the n by m ($m \geqslant k$) matrix Z contains the observations on the instrumental variables used to obtain the IV estimator

$$\hat{\beta} = (\hat{X}'X)^{-1}\hat{X}'y = (\hat{X}'\hat{X})^{-1}\hat{X}'y, \tag{B.2}$$

where $\hat{X} = Z(Z'Z)^{-1}Z'X$. If Z is the observation matrix for all the predetermined variables of the complete system containing equation (B.1), then $\hat{\beta}$ is the 2SLS estimator. The residuals will be denoted by $\hat{u}_t$, so that

$$(\hat{u}_1, \ldots, \hat{u}_n)' = \hat{u} = y - X\hat{\beta} \tag{B.3}$$

and the implied estimates of the error variance and autocorrelations will be taken as

$$\hat{\sigma}^2 = n^{-1}\Sigma_1^n \hat{u}_t^2 \tag{B.4}$$

and

$$r(j) = \Sigma_{j+1}^n \hat{u}_t \hat{u}_{t-j} / \Sigma_1^n \hat{u}_t^2, \qquad j=1, 2, \ldots, \tag{B.5}$$

respectively.

Suppose that the significance of the first p residual autocorrelations is to be investigated in order to test the assumption that the errors of (B.1) are serially independent. The joint asymptotic distribution of $(r(1), \ldots, r(p))$ under the null hypothesis can be deduced from results derived by Sargan (1976). If W is a n by p matrix consisting of the p lagged values of the residual vector $\hat{u}$ (i.e. a typical element w_{ti} is equal to $\hat{u}_{t-i}$, $t=1, \ldots, n$ and $i=1, \ldots, p$), then Sargan's (1976) findings imply that

$$\theta(p) = \hat{u}'W[W'W - W'X(\hat{X}'\hat{X})^{-1}\hat{X}'W - W'\hat{X}(\hat{X}'\hat{X})^{-1}X'W + W'X(\hat{X}'\hat{X})^{-1}X'W]^{-1} W'\hat{u}/\hat{\sigma}^2 \tag{B.6}$$

is the appropriate criterion for testing the significance of $(r(1), \ldots, r(p))$. The statistic $\theta(p)$ is asymptotically distributed as $\chi^2(p)$ when the errors of (B.1) are serially independent.

Note that no alternative hypothesis has been specified,

so that $\theta(p)$ is a pure significance test in the spirit of the Box-Pierce (1970) procedure. It is, however, simple to modify this approach in order to restrict attention to some subset of the first p residual autocorrelations, e.g. if a quarterly relationship is being considered, then $r(4)$, $r(8)$ etc. might be of particular interest.

FOOTNOTES

1. The authors are grateful to Christine Godfrey, J.M. Malcomson, G.E. Mizon and the referee for their helpful comments.

2. See Silvey (1959) for a discussion of the general LM procedure, and Breusch (1978a) and Godfrey (1978b) for more detailed accounts of LM tests for autocorrelated errors.

3. It is assumed that the initial value u_0 is zero, but this assumption is unimportant as far as asymptotic properties are concerned. Moreover, the LM test statistic proposed below would not be affected if u_0 were treated as a random variable.

4. The factor of 2 appears in the expression for the Lagrangean $S^*(\beta, \rho, \lambda)$ in order to simplify later analysis.

5. The transformations required to convert $\hat{\lambda}$ of (2.4) into an autocovariance (division by n), or an autocorrelation (division by $\Sigma\hat{u}_t^2$) will not affect the form of the LM statistic.

6. Note that the coefficients of y_{t-1} in (2.7) and ε_{t-1} in (2.8) sum to zero. For the purpose of constructing tests of the assumption of serial independence, it will be assumed that the coefficients of the autocorrelation model of the alternative hypothesis are functionally independent of those in the regression equation.

7. A test against autoregressive errors based upon least squares estimation of (2.11) was proposed by Durbin (1970).

8. See Wallis (1972) for an interesting discussion of quarterly models and autocorrelation.

9. See Aldrich (1978) for a derivation of the h-test by means of the LM approach.

10. The form of the denominator of the test statistics depends upon the order of the systematic dynamics, see Godfrey and Tremayne (1979) for details.

11. Godfrey and Tremayne (1979) also examined the appropriate "$n \times R^2$" test and found that its small sample performance was very similar to that of h_4^2.

12. There are, of course, dangers associated with starting from very simple models and then trying to work towards more general ones using the results of tests for misspecification. Hendry (1979) provides a valuable discussion of this method of model building and of the alternative "general to specific" approach. It is, however, always possible that any specified "general" model is inadequate and so diagnostic checks are still important. Also see Mizon (1977, Section 3).

13. The Box-Pierce and Ljung-Box procedures do not require the specification of an alternative hypothesis and so are pure significance tests.

14. See Hendry (1977) for some evidence which supports the use of autoregressive schemes as approximations to more complex error models. It is, however, important not to restrict attention to low order autoregressive models, see Hendry (1977) and Newbold and Davies (1978).

15. The test statistic is, of course, only *asymptotically* distributed as $\chi^2(r)$ under the null hypothesis of correct specification.

16. It also seems that Maritz (1978) did not correct all the errors contained in Guilkey's derivation, see Breusch (1978b, Ch. 5).

17. A general analysis of testing for misspecification after estimation by the IV method is provided in an important unpublished paper by Sargan (1976).

18. The LR test involves comparing the maximised likelihoods from FIML estimation of the null model (3.1)-(3.2) and the alternative model (3.8)-(3.9).

19. See Koopmans and Hood (1953, Section 5.5) for a discussion of concentrating likelihood functions.

20. This specification does not imply that cross serial correlations between the equations' errors are zero, except in the special case when $E(\varepsilon_{t1}\varepsilon_{t2}) = 0$.

21. Godfrey (1976) has obtained the MLM test of $\rho_{11} = 0$ but his approach does not lead to simple implementation without modification of existing programmes. Godfrey's test is derived using Durbin's (1970) theorem, rather than the LM approach.

22. The p pre-sample residuals appearing in (3.13), i.e. $(\hat{u}_{01}, \ldots, \hat{u}_{1-p,1})$ can all be set equal to zero as suggested in Section 2.

23. Note that the researcher can choose which lagged variables to use and how many to add to the instruments of the original system, provided, of course, that the total number of instrumental variables is at least equal to the number of parameters of (3.13).

24. Fisk (1967) argues that it is unlikely that cross serial correlations will be non-zero when the autocorrelations of a series are zero and that, in most cases, it will be sufficient to test the serial independence assumption by examining autocorrelations of the latter type.

25. Breusch (1978b, Chapter 5) has obtained some results on the asymptotic relationship between the $\pi(1)$ and $\theta(1)$ tests. These results are, however, for fairly special cases in which both the ρ_{ij} and the instruments are restricted.

26. There is some evidence that the small sample performance of the LM procedure can be unsatisfactory if the selected alternative is greatly overspecified.

27. The importance of starting from general models is again to be emphasised.

28. This LM test is also appropriate when the alternative is the first order vector moving average process and the generalisations to higher order alternatives are straightforward.

29. The actual expression for the $C(\alpha)$ test against vector autoregression will, of course, be fairly complicated, but calculating the sample value of the test statistic will have a very small marginal cost once an appropriate subroutine has been added to the researcher's estimation programme.

DISCUSSION: DENISE R. OSBORN

This paper presents an admirable explanation of how the Lagrange multiplier (LM) technique can be used in practice to provide simple and flexible tests for autocorrelation in a wide variety of dynamic econometric models. Many of the results quoted in their paper are due to the two authors, and they are to be congratulated on making these so accessible to non-specialists.

In my view, one of the great advantages of LM tests is that they force us to think about the alternative hypothesis when we specify the null of zero autocorrelation: there is no longer any excuse for using the first-order autoregressive model as a dustbin into which we throw any model misspecification or autocorrelated error structure. When quarterly data are used, a joint test against first- and fourth-order autocorrelation is often appropriate, and such a test can now easily be carried out. There is, of course, a problem in that the LM statistics do not discriminate between autoregressive and moving average alternatives.

One case in which the appropriate hypothesis to be tested may not be clear is in the Koyck lag model, which leads to equations (2.7) and (2.8) of the paper. These equations may be written as

$$y_t = \beta x_t + \alpha y_{t-1} + u_t$$

$$u_t = \varepsilon_t + \mu\varepsilon_{t-1}$$

with the restriction $\alpha + \mu = 0$. From here the equation usually estimated is obtained by introducing the simplifications:

(i) $\alpha + \mu \neq 0$;

(ii) $\mu = 0$.

The first is then typically ignored, with any subsequent test for misspecification being based on the second simplification. Is, however, the appropriate test here simply a test for a moving average error process? Since the authors have introduced the Koyck model in order to motivate tests against moving average errors, I do not aim to criticise them for considering only a test of $\mu = 0$. My point is that where possible sources of misspecification are apparent, modelbuilders should seek appropriate statistics to test against these misspecifications.

Moving on to consider more technical matters, Section 2 of the paper introduces two LM tests for the regression model (2.10) with the alternative to independence of the u_t being given by equation (2.5). More compactly, the model is

$$y = X\beta + u$$

$$u = U_p\rho + \varepsilon$$

with y, u, ε all $n{\times}1$; the other dimensions are X $n{\times}k$, U_p $n{\times}p$, β $k{\times}1$, ρ $p{\times}1$. The ith column of U_p contains u_{t-i} $t = 1,\ldots,n$ where $u_s = 0$, $s \leq 0$. Under the null hypothesis that $\rho = 0$, the model is estimated by ordinary least squares to yield the residual vector $\hat{u}$ and lagged residual matrix $\hat{U}_p$. Now, the two variants discussed for the LM test of $\rho = 0$ both employ the regression (2.11), that is the regression

$$\hat{u} = X\gamma + \hat{U}_p\rho + \eta \tag{1}$$

The statistics are then obtained as:

1. $n{\times}R^2$ from this regression. That is,

$$LM_1 = \hat{u}'\hat{U}_p[\hat{U}_p'(I - N)\hat{U}_p]^{-1}\hat{U}_p'\hat{u}/\hat{\sigma}^2 \tag{2}$$

where $N = X(X'X)^{-1}X'$ and $\hat{\sigma}^2 = \hat{u}'\hat{u}/n$. In terms of the references of the paper, (2) is (16) of Godfrey (1978b).

2. p times the F statistic for testing $\rho = 0$. Using the restricted and unrestricted residual sum of squares (*RRSS* and *URSS* respectively) from the regression (1), we are interested in

$$LM_2 = \frac{RRSS - URSS}{URSS/(n-k-p)} \tag{3}$$

Now, since $X'\hat{u} = 0$

$$RRSS = \hat{u}'\hat{u} \tag{3a}$$

and hence

$$URSS = \hat{u}'\hat{u} - \hat{u}'\hat{U}_p[\hat{U}_p'(I - N)\hat{U}_p]^{-1}\hat{U}_p'\hat{u} \tag{3b}$$

Comparing LM_1 and LM_2, the numerators of the two statistics are identical and

$$LM_1 \gtrless LM_2 \text{ as } \frac{\hat{u}'\hat{u}}{n} \lesseqgtr \hat{u}'\{I - \hat{U}_p[\hat{U}_p'(I - N)\hat{U}_p]^{-1}\hat{U}_p'\}\hat{u}/(n-k-p)$$

Since $\hat{U}_p[\hat{U}_p'(I - N)\hat{U}_p]^{-1}\hat{U}_p'$ is positive semi-definite, $\hat{u}'\hat{u} \geq \hat{u}'\{I - \hat{U}_p[\hat{U}_p'(I - N)\hat{U}_p]^{-1}\hat{U}_p'\}\hat{u}$, but $n > n-k-p$ so that there is no simple inequality relationship between the two LM statistics. Also, the Monte Carlo studies have so far employed only LM_1, so there is no evidence on the relative finite sample performances of the LM_1 and LM_2 statistics. The differences could, clearly, be important.

Finally, I would like to point out that the authors' results on testing the null hypothesis of no autocorrelation against the alternative of a moving average model are more general than they have claimed. They derive the LM statistic assuming that the moving average estimation criterion is to minimise the residual sum of squares with "starting residuals" set to zero: the same statistic will, however, be obtained if the criterion is to maximise the exact likelihood function for the moving average process.[1]

Consider, first, the simple model (2.1) with u_t following the first-order process (2.8), using the equations of the paper. Assuming normality and after concentrating with respect to σ_ε^2, the log likelihood function is, excluding constants,

$$L(\beta,\mu) = -\frac{1}{2}\,log|K'K| - \frac{n}{2}\,log\,S(\beta,\mu) \tag{4}$$

where $S(\beta,\mu) = \sum_{t=0}^{n} [\varepsilon_t(\beta,\mu)]^2$

and $\varepsilon_t(\beta,\mu) = y_t - \beta x_t - \mu\varepsilon_{t-1}(\beta,\mu), \qquad t \geq 1.$

The matrix K depends only on μ, and in this first-order case

$$|K'K| = \frac{1-\mu^{2(n+1)}}{1-\mu^2}$$

Although $\varepsilon_0(\beta,\mu)$ in general depends on all the observations y_t and x_t as well as β and μ, $\varepsilon_0(\beta,0) = 0$. The exact likelihood function for the moving average process is derived by Box and Jenkins (1970, appendix A 7.4) and discussed by, among others, Osborn (1976). Clearly, maximum likelihood estimates may be obtained by minimising $-2L(\beta,\mu)$, so that the constrained optimisation problem can be solved using the first-order conditions for the Lagrangian function

$$L^*(\beta,\mu,\lambda) = log|K'K| + n\,log\,S(\beta,\mu) + 2\lambda\mu \tag{5}$$

Evaluating $\partial L^*(\hat\beta,\hat\mu,\hat\lambda)/\partial\mu$ at $\hat\mu = 0$, the term in $|K'K|$ drops out and

$$\frac{\partial L^*(\hat\beta,0,\hat\lambda)}{\partial\mu} = \frac{n}{S(\hat\beta,0)}\,\frac{\partial S(\hat\beta,0)}{\partial\mu} + 2\hat\lambda = 0 \tag{6}$$

where

$$\frac{\partial S(\hat\beta,0)}{\partial\mu} = 2\sum_{t=0}^{n} \varepsilon_t(\hat\beta,0)\,\frac{\partial\varepsilon_t(\hat\beta,0)}{\partial\mu}$$

$$= 2\sum_{t=1}^{n} \varepsilon_t(\hat\beta,0)\,\frac{\partial\varepsilon_t(\hat\beta,0)}{\partial\mu} \tag{7}$$

as $\varepsilon_0(\hat{\beta},0) = 0$. Except for the factor of $n/S(\hat{\beta},0)$ which does not affect the *LM* statistic, this gives $\hat{\lambda}$ as in the paper.

Generalising this likelihood discussion is not difficult: for a qth order moving average and k regressor variables, β is $k\times 1$ while μ,λ and $\varepsilon_0(\beta,\mu)$ are all $q\times 1$. The likelihood can still be written as in (4), with the summation in $S(\beta,\mu)$ now extending from $1-q$ to n and with the expression for $\varepsilon_t(\beta,\mu)$ appropriately generalised. The vector $\varepsilon_0(\beta,0) = 0$, while $K'K$ can be written as

$$K'K = I + A'A$$

where A involves only products and sums of the elements of μ. Suitably interpreted in vector terms (the lower limit of summation in $S(\beta,\mu)$ being amended), the logic follows through to reach again (7); hence the same *LM* statistic is obtained as when the criterion function of the paper is used.

REFERENCES

Box, G.E.P. and G.M. Jenkins (1970). *Time Series Analysis, Forecasting and Control*. San Francisco: Holden-Day.

Osborn, D.R. (1976). Maximum likelihood estimation of moving average processes. *Annals of Economic and Social Measurement*, 5, 75-87.

FOOTNOTE

1. This discussion is intentionally limited to the exact likelihood function for the error process: if the model contains lagged dependent variables among the regressors, the exact likelihood function for all the coefficients will be more complicated.

5. ESTIMATING CONTINUOUS CONSUMER EQUIVALENCE SCALES IN AN EXPENDITURE MODEL WITH LABOUR SUPPLY

Richard W. Blundell

1. Introduction[1]

In this paper we shall be concerned with the estimation of consumer equivalence scales using a single cross-section of data. We develop a model of household behaviour that considers both the labour supply and commodity demand decisions of the household. In particular we analyse male and female participation decisions jointly with the demand for goods. Incorporating the labour supply (leisure demand) decision into the analysis introduces a price (the marginal wage rate) which naturally varies over the cross-section and therefore aids the identification of the underlying composition parameters. Precisely how we specify this joint decision turns out to be crucially important. Recent additions to the literature on demand analysis, see for example, Barnett (1979), have stressed the restrictiveness of the traditional specification which assumes separability between goods and leisure. It is not difficult to see that if separability is assumed, all goods become substitutes for leisure. However, if separability is not *a priori* acceptable, demand systems and Engel curves that exclude the marginal price of leisure are misspecified. Indeed, it would be incorrect to assume the existence of a utility measure defined over goods alone, commonly used in welfare comparisons across households.

By providing detailed data on composition and labour supply for individual households, the U.K. Family Expenditure Surveys are ideal for the study of household composition effects in a leisure goods choice model. The composition data allows a close analysis of age effects in household decisions and in turn accurate estimation of the underlying equivalence scales. The labour supply data, apart from identifying these equivalence scales, allows us to test, and not impose *a priori*, separability between goods and leisure. We should, of course, always model female labour supply as well as male labour supply as it is likely that female participation is at least as responsive to price, income and demographic changes.

Incorporation of the female labour supply decision leads to certain complications since, if she is a secondary worker in a household, she will have the choice of whether to work or not. As we shall see, this implies that one dependent variable in our model, female labour income, although constrained to be non-negative may often take the value zero. Such limited dependent variable models are well known in the literature and were considered in detail by Tobin (1958) subsequently to be known as Tobit models. However, fully efficient estimation requires the maximisation of a 'non-standard' likelihood function and a computationally more tractable method of estimation may be preferred. The simple alternative of selecting only those observations for which the female participates produces inconsistent estimates of all the parameters, including the equivalence scales, when the usual joint least squares procedure is applied to the selected sample. Consistent estimation is nevertheless possible without resorting to the full Tobit procedure once it is seen, following Heckman (1976, 1979), that the sample selection bias can be corrected by the inclusion of an additional variable in each equation of the system.

In order to introduce equivalence scales into a system of household expenditure and labour supply equations and in order to test the separability hypothesis, a fully integrable model of household behaviour is essential. The model we choose is a generalisation of one suggested by Muellbauer (1980) and is described in Section 2 of this paper. It has the advantage of being quasi-homothetic (linear cost function) resulting in an essentially linear-in-variables expenditure system. Its disadvantage however, springs from its linearity, and in our empirical example we see it only as an approximation over some range of expenditure. For this example, we use a single cross-section of individual household data from the 1974 U.K. Family Expenditure Survey, and even though the price of goods is assumed constant over the cross-section, variation in the marginal wage is sufficient to identify all the parameters necessary for the purposes of this study. To specify the equivalence scales in such a way as to allow flexibility without over-parameterisation we use the cubic spline technique. This turns out to be a rather convenient method of imposing continuity on age effects and is described in detail in Section 3. Section 4 discusses the estimation problem and derives a consistent estimator. In Section 5 we present estimates of the model with and without the correction for the sample selection bias and provide a detailed analysis of the implied equivalence scales. Section 6 concludes the paper with a brief summary and evaluation of the empirical results.

2. *The Model of Household Behaviour*

Barten (1964) proposed that to compare households with different composition one should define the preferences of each household, by a strictly quasi-concave utility function,

$$U(q_1/m_1,\ q_2/m_2, \ldots, q_n/m_n) \tag{2.1}$$

where q_i is the quantity of good i consumed and the corresponding deflator m_i measures the specific effect on utility of household composition. Letting p_i denote the price of good i, the household cost function that solves:

$$min\ (\sum p_i q_i \mid U > \bar{U})$$

is given by:

$$C(\underline{p},\ U) = C(p_1 m_1,\ p_2 m_2, \ldots, p_n m_n,\ U) \tag{2.2}$$

The similarity between price and household composition effects in 2.2 imply very simple generalisations of the traditional individual demand models.

In this study, the cost function is specified directly as this leads immediately to both the demand equations and the true cost-of-living index useful to a study of equivalence scales. To begin with, let us specify the following quasi-homothetic form of 2.2 suggested by Gorman (1976),

$$C(\underline{p},\ U) = a(\underline{p}) + b(\underline{p})\ U \tag{2.3}$$

where $a(\underline{p})$ and $b(\underline{p})$ are concave, linear homogeneous functions in $\underline{p}$. In our model we shall only let the fixed cost $a(\underline{p})$ depend on household composition, in particular we shall write:

$$a(\underline{p}) = \sum_{i=1}^{n} p_i \gamma_i m_i \qquad 2.4$$

This form of the cost function corresponds to the translation method of incorporating composition effects developed by Pollak and Wales (1978). We note that choosing a Cobb-Douglas form for $b(\underline{p})$ would lead to equivalence between the Barten and translation methods.

In order to identify the parameters and to test the hypothesis of separability between goods and leisure, implicit in a form such as 2.2, we introduce the household labour supply decision. We suppose that each household has a male and female worker facing marginal wage rates w_m and w_f. The full income budget constraint for the household is given by:

$$p'q + w_m l_m + w_f l_f = w_m T_m + w_f T_f + y \qquad 2.5$$

where l_f and l_m represent leisure time, T_f and T_m the maximum time available for leisure activities and y unearned income. The supply of hours is then given by $h_i = T_i - l_i$ for $i = m, f$.

The cost function we choose to represent household preferences over goods *and* leisure is a generalisation of the form 2.3 suggested by Muellbauer (1980) and given by:

$$C(\underline{p}, w_f, w_m, U) = a(\underline{p}) + w_f d_f(\underline{p}) + w_m d_m(\underline{p})$$

$$+ b(\underline{p})^{1-\theta} w_f^{\theta_f} w_m^{\theta_m} U \qquad 2.6$$

where $\theta_f + \theta_m = \theta$ and U is a household utility measure similar to 2.1 but defined over leisure as well as goods. The functions $d_f(\underline{p})$ and $d_m(\underline{p})$ satisfy the usual homogeneity and concavity properties. If d_f and d_m are independent of prices p, then we shall see that leisure is separable from goods, otherwise this model allows for both substitutes and complements to leisure. The fixed cost $a(p)$ is defined as in 2.4 above, the other functions for simplicity are assumed to take the following forms:

$$d_i(\underline{p}) = \gamma_i \prod_j p_j^{\delta_{ij}} \quad , \quad \sum_j \delta_{ij} = 0 \quad \text{for } i = m,f \qquad \text{and}$$

$$b(\underline{p}) = \prod_j p_j^{b_j} \quad , \quad \sum_j b_j = 1.$$

These forms are not restrictive and are simply used for illustration. Prices are assumed constant in the cross-section and any second order flexible functions in prices will produce the same cross-section demand functions. In particular, we are not imposing separability between commodity groups in the resulting demand model. We would normally expect $d_f(p)$ to depend on household composition as this measures the necessary amount of female 'leisure' time. In particular we choose the form $d_f(p) = \gamma_f \prod_j p_j^{\delta_{fj}} + \gamma_a n_c$ where n_c is the number of children (0-18 years of age) in the household. This is a rather crude formulation and in Blundell and Walker (1980) it is extended to allow for differing age effects and economies of scale. Nevertheless, it does, as we shall see, lead to an interesting breakdown of composition effects on female participation.

The derivatives of the cost function with respect to w_m, w_f and the p_i will generate the labour income and goods expenditure equations for each household. For the cost function, 2.6, the implied labour income equations are given by:

$$w_f h_f = w_f(T_f - d_f(p))\ (1 - \theta_f) - \theta_f[y + (T_m - d_m(p))w_m - a(p)] \qquad 2.7$$

$$w_m h_m = w_m(T_m - d_m(p))\ (1 - \theta_m) - \theta_m[y + (T_f - d_f(p))w_f - a(p)] \qquad 2.8$$

Referring to the above discussion on composition effects in female participation, we see that in 2.7 the necessary leisure effect $d_f(p)$ has an opposite sign to the necessary expenditure effect $a(p)$. For households with young children we would expect $d_f(p)$ to dominate whereas for households with older children $a(p)$ would dominate. The goods expenditures are a generalisation of the familiar linear expenditure system and are given by:

$$p_i q_i = p_i \gamma_i m_i + \gamma_f \delta_{fi} w_f + \gamma_m \delta_{mi} w_m + (1 - \theta) b_i [y + (T_f - d_f(p))w_f + (T_m - d_m(p))w_m - a(p)] \qquad 2.9$$

The compensated substitution effects for goods and male leisure, for example, are given by:

$$S_{im} = \frac{\gamma_m \delta_{mi}}{p_i} + (1 - \theta)\ \frac{b_i}{p_i}\ ((T_m - d_m) - h_m) \qquad 2.10$$

for all $i = 1,\ldots.,n$.
We see that separability of goods from male leisure implies that $\gamma_m \delta_{mi}$ are zero for all i with a similar condition for female leisure. Given the form of the expenditure equations 2.9, this allows a simple test of separability.

3. *Specification of the Equivalence Scale Parameters*

In order to estimate equivalence scales from the composition variables m_i, we need to model explicitly the relationship between this variable and the demographic characteristics of the household. Let us suppose that there are D age groups and associated with each age group g, there are n_g members in the household. We then write:

$$m_i = \sum_{g=1}^{D} e_{ig} n_g \quad \text{for all } i = 1,\ldots,n \tag{3.1}$$

or

$$m_i = \underline{e}_i' \underline{n} \tag{3.2}$$

where the e_{ig} are the specific equivalence scales for good i.

If we have detailed age data, a parsimonious representation of the equivalence scales is required. We could set all $e_{ig} = 1$, then $m_i = N$ the total number of persons in each household. A slightly less restrictive alternative is that $e_{ig} = e_i$ for children and $e_{ig} = 1$ for adults, allowing a separate but constant child scale for each good. However, it seems more likely that age has a significant and continuously changing effect on consumption. We could suggest that structural changes in behaviour occur, in mid-teens and late twenties for example, but not so as to destroy the overall continuity of behaviour. We wish to impose a continuous, albeit fairly flexible, structure on e_i seen as a function of age.

The cubic spline technique satisfies these properties while allowing a significant reduction in the number of parameters estimated. We assume that between each point of structural change, the function is at most a cubic, but at these points a change in behaviour is represented by a jump in the third derivative, preserving continuity.

Suppose we can identify $k - 1$ such possible points at ages $\bar{g}_1, \bar{g}_2, \ldots, \bar{g}_{k-1}$, then our spline, for each good, is given by:

$$e(g) = \delta_k + \delta_{k+1} g + \delta_{k+2} g^2 + \delta_{k+3} g^3 + \sum_{j=1}^{k-1} \delta_j (g - \bar{g}_j)_+^3 \tag{3.3}$$

$$\text{where } (g - \bar{g}_j)_+^3 = \begin{cases} (g-\bar{g}_j)^3 & \text{if } g > \bar{g}_j \\ 0 & \text{if } g \le \bar{g}_j \end{cases}$$

and δ_i, $i=1,\ldots,k=3$ are unknown parameters.

From 3.3 we know the form of e_i for all g, so given observations at particular ages we could substitute $e_i(g)$ directly into our model. However, for practical application we follow Poirier (1976) and derive an alternative expression below. For this study we also restrict the second derivative of e_i at $\bar{g}_0$ to be zero and the first derivative at $\bar{g}_k$ to be zero, imposing a certain stability of behaviour with age, which seems *a priori* reasonable. These two restrictions reduce the number of equivalence scale parameters for each commodity to $k+1$.

In particular, we choose to write these cubic spline restrictions on our equivalence scale parameters as:

$$\underset{\sim}{e}_i = W \underset{\sim}{c}_i \qquad \text{for all } i=1,\ldots,n \tag{3.4}$$

where $\underset{\sim}{c}_i$ is a $k \times 1$ vector of coordinates corresponding to $\bar{g}_0, \bar{g}_1,\ldots,\bar{g}_k$ and W is a known transformation matrix, details of which are given in Appendix A1. Given $\underset{\sim}{c}_i$ we can use 3.4 to generate estimates of $\underset{\sim}{e}_i$ that satisfy the smoothness conditions outlined above. For estimation purposes we therefore combine 3.2 and 3.4 to write:

$$m_i = \underline{n}' W \underset{\sim}{c}_i$$

which after substitution into our expenditure equations 2.9, provides an essentially linear-in-variables expenditure and income system for each household.

Identification of the equivalence scale parameters in this model derives from the introduction of the labour supply decision. The coefficients of the wages rates that now appear on the right hand side of each equation allow us to find unique estimates of the $\gamma_f\delta_{fi}$ and $\gamma_m\delta_{mi}$ parameters. Given these, the composition terms $p_i\gamma_i m_i$ can be identified from the composition parameters in the expenditure equations. This is to be contrasted with the more traditional model where we exclude the labour supply equations and treat labour income as exogenous. In this case, as pointed out by Muellbauer (1974), the $p_i\gamma_i m_i$ terms are not identified in a single cross-section due to the adding up restrictions. We can only identify $n-1$ terms and a suitable restriction has to be placed on one of them. Finding such a plausible restriction is rather difficult and unsatisfactory. In our model the equivalence scale parameters are identified whether d_f and d_m depend on composition or not. We choose d_m to be independent of composition for *a priori* reasons and *not* in order to identify the equivalence scale parameters.

4. *Estimation*

We are now in a position to write a stochastic version of the whole system 2.7 - 2.9 as:

$$Y_i = X'\beta_i + \varepsilon_i \qquad \text{for all } i=1,\ldots\ldots,n,f,m \qquad 4.1$$

where the β_i are non-linear functions of the underlying parameters, $Y_i = p_i q_i$ for $i=1,\ldots\ldots,n$, $Y_f = w_f h_f$ and $Y_m = w_m h_m$. All dependent variables in this or any other expenditure system are constrained to be non-negative, but as we shall see, this is unimportant provided the probability of attaining the zero limit is very small. For female labour income this is not the case since we often observe a zero value.

The inconsistency that arises when estimating a system like 4.1 using joint least squares on a selected sample where $Y_f > 0$, can be seen from an examination of the expectation of the disturbances conditioning on $Y_f > 0$. We have:

$$E(\varepsilon_f \mid Y_f > 0) = E(\varepsilon_f \mid \varepsilon_f > - X'\beta_f) \neq 0 \qquad 4.2$$

and similarly

$$E(\varepsilon_i \mid \varepsilon_f > - X'\beta_f) \neq 0 \qquad \text{for all } i=1,\ldots\ldots,n,m \qquad 4.3$$

provided $E(\varepsilon_f \varepsilon_i) = \sigma_{fi} \neq 0$.

Following Tallis (1961) we can be more precise about these conditional expectations. First we note that the probability of $\varepsilon_f > - X'\beta_f$ is given by $1 - F(L_f)$ where $L_f = - X'\beta_f/\sigma_f$, F being the cumulative standard normal distribution function and $\sigma_f = \sqrt{\sigma_{ff}}$. Given this, the conditional expectation 4.2 can be written:

$$E(\varepsilon_f \mid \varepsilon_t > - X'\beta_f) = \sigma_f \lambda_f \qquad 4.4$$

where $\lambda_f = \dfrac{f(L_f)}{1 - F(L_f)}$ and f is the standard normal density function. Similarly, we may write:

$$E(\varepsilon_i \mid \varepsilon_f > - X'\beta_f) = \frac{\sigma_{fi}}{\sigma_f} \lambda_f \quad \text{for all } i=1,\ldots,n,m \qquad 4.5$$

In most empirical work both $f(L_f)$ and $F(L_f)$ are close enough to zero for λ_f, and therefore the conditional expectations 4.4 and 4.5, to be taken as zero. However, in the case of female labour supply, λ_f may be quite different from zero for many observations. Consistent estimation on the selected sample is possible provided we include the variable λ_f in each equation of the system. We have:

$$Y_i = X'\beta_i + \frac{\sigma_{fi}}{\sigma_f} \lambda_f + v_i \quad \text{for all } i=1,\ldots,n,m,f \qquad 4.6$$

and we note that $E(v_i \mid Y_f > 0) = 0$ for all i.

It is important to notice that the covariance structure of the v_i's is heteroskedastic. The exact form is derivable from the results on the second moments of truncated multivariate normal random variables and is given by:

$$E(v_f^2 \mid \varepsilon_f > -X\beta_f) = \sigma_{ff}\,(1 + L_f\lambda_f - \lambda_f^2)$$

$$E(v_f v_i \mid \varepsilon_f > -X\beta_f) = \sigma_{fi}\,(1 + L_f\lambda_f - \lambda_f^2) \qquad 4.7$$

$$E(v_i^2 \mid \varepsilon_f > -X\beta_f) = \sigma_{ii}\,\left(1 + \left(\frac{\sigma_{if}}{\sigma_i\sigma_f}\right)^2 (L_f\lambda_f - \lambda_f^2)\right)$$

for all i.

If λ_f was known for each household, then consistent estimation would be possible. If λ_f is replaced by a consistent estimate, then consistent estimation of all the parameters is again available. Such an estimator for λ_f is given by:

$$\hat{\lambda}_f = \frac{f(\hat{L}_f)}{1 - F(\hat{L}_f)} \qquad 4.8$$

where $\hat{L}_f = X'\left(\frac{\hat{\beta}_f}{\sigma_f}\right)$

and $(\hat{\beta}_{f/\sigma_f})$ is a consistent estimate.

The problem then is to consistently estimate $(\hat{\beta}_{f/\sigma_f})$ without prior knowledge of λ_f. Two possibilities seem open. We could use probit analysis on the whole sample and this would provide our consistent estimate (see for example Heckman (1979)). Alternatively, we could extend Amemiya's (1973) suggestion and use an instrumental variable estimator. The distinct advantage of this estimator over the probit estimator is that it only requires data on the selected sample. A more detailed discussion of the estimator is given in Appendix A2.

Given the estimator of λ_f, with a known limiting distribution, we can substitute back into system 4.6 and derive consistent (although not fully efficient) estimates of all the parameters of the model. In the following section we present the empirical estimates of this model concentrating in particular on the separability hypothesis and the implied equivalance scales.

5. *Empirical Results*

Estimation of the models with and without the correction for selection bias was carried out using a single cross-section from the 1974 Family Expenditure Survey. Each model required the use of non-linear least squares (non-linear in parameters only) and this was performed using the routine of Wymer (1973). Only those households with two married adults in employment were selected and their marginal wage rates were constructed using normal gross hourly earnings and multiplying this by one minus the basic tax rate (including an adjustment for national insurance contributions). Unearned income was then defined by the linear budget identity.

To make the assumption of quasi-homotheticity more palatable we selected only those households within a low expenditure range of £35-£55 per week.[2] This also enabled us to make the assumption that all household workers faced the same basic tax rate. Finally, to remove to some extent, the important possibility of heteroskedasticity in models with selectivity, all dependent variables were defined in share form. The resulting sample of 103 household observations was used to estimate the underlying parameters of the model.

The estimates of the two models are given in Tables 1 and 2. Overall, the parameter estimates look quite plausible. We note that in both tables, the crucial assumption of separability between commodity groups can be rejected. We cannot in this model say anything about the separability between commodity groups as we are deliberately assuming constant prices in the cross-section. Services and transport tend to be strong substitutes for male leisure whereas clothing, food, energy and our definition of durables[3] tend to be complements to male leisure. It is interesting to note that clothing is generally a substitute for female leisure! The values of $T-d$ for male and female household members which measure the maximum hours available for work (with zero children) are quite reasonable, even if a little low in Table 1. The correction for the selection bias has the expected effect of increasing both $T_f - d_f$ and d_f since we expect both of these parameters to be biased downwards by the selection process. The composition parameter entering into the female labour supply is highly significant and of the expected sign.

Turning now to the equivalence scales the FES data provides yearly age groups for all household members. Referring to Section 3 above, we choose k to be 4 which taking possible structural breaks at ages 15, 30 and 50 seemed to allow sufficient flexibility in the form of the equivalence scales. The parameter estimates of the fixed cost terms, corresponding to the coordinates of the spline functions, are given in Table 3. From equation 3.4 of Section 3, we can use these estimates to generate continuous commodity specific age scales which after normalisation become the specific equivalence scales. However, if we sum these estimates before normalisation across commodities, we can generate a total equivalence scale. This is presented in Table 4 and it tells us the total (utility constant) commodity cost for an additional household member of any age group. Together with the loss of potential female earnings, through a change in $w_f d_f$, this could be used to construct appropriate Hicksian compensating variations for horizontal equity across households with differing composition. Such compensation would, however, be biased in as much as composition enters directly into the household utility function (see Pollak and Wales (1979)).

The specific equivalence scales for the six commodity groups are presented in Table 5. It is interesting to note that not all scales start close to zero and neither do all scales for adults completely dominate those for children. As one would expect, this is especially true for goods such as energy and clothing. In contrast, for those goods that are essentially public goods to the household, for example durables and services, the scales stay relatively close to zero for children. Again, for such goods there is a significant decline after middle-age possibly reflecting life cycle expenditure patterns.

6. *Conclusions*

In this paper we have developed a model of composition effects in household decisions over goods and leisure which introduces smooth equivalence scales, using the spline technique, into a theoretically consistent model of behaviour. Incorporating the labour supply decision into a traditional expenditure system allowed us to both identify the equivalence scales and to test the assumption of separability between goods and leisure. Having rejected this assumption we may conclude that Engel Curve or demand studies that exclude the wage rate are misspecified and may therefore be subject to bias.

By modelling the female participation decision as well as the male labour supply decision, we were left with a model containing a limited dependent variable. Consistent estimation was achieved by selecting a sample of households with females in employment and correcting for the resulting sample selection bias. Consistent estimates of all the parameters of the model including the underlying equivalence scales were then produced for the particular sample of U.K. Family Expenditure Survey data.

Household composition effects are only allowed to enter preferences through the fixed cost element in the cost function. This assumption seems particularly restrictive and should be relaxed. However, the overriding consideration here is the necessity for a reasonably linear structure in order that estimation is computationally tractable. To this end, a model that is only non-linear in parameters is of considerable advantage and we hope to have struck a reasonable balance between realism and simplicity. Other extensions that could be made to this model are the allowance for household size effects over and above the equivalence scales considered and the allowance for possible rationing in the (male) labour supply market (see Blundell and Walker (1980)).

TABLE 1

Parameter Estimates of the Leisure-Goods Model*

Commodity Group	$(1-\theta)b_i$	$\gamma_m\delta_{mi}$	$\gamma_f\delta_{fi}$
Food	0.0815 (0.0283)	-0.9128 (1.3961)	-0.9681 (1.4136)
Energy	0.0149 (0.0104)	-0.4708 (0.5914)	0.5746 (0.6134)
Clothing	0.0966 (0.0242)	-0.9515 (1.3464)	2.0889 (1.0798)
Durables	0.0777 (0.0221)	-2.8952 (1.0174)	-0.7932 (1.1964)
Transport	0.0837 (0.0280)	2.4424 (1.2050)	-0.1472 (1.4216)
Services	0.1399 (0.0323)	2.7881 (1.3567)	-1.0493 (1.6863)

θ_f = 0.2058 (0.0316) $(1-\theta)$ = 0.4945 (0.0484) $\theta = \theta_n + \theta_f$

$(T-d_m)$ = 45.6655 (2.3412) (T_f-d_f) = 34.3421 (2.3445) γ_a = 9.2736 (1.0346)

*Asymptotic Standard Errors in Parentheses.

TABLE 2

Parameter Estimates of the Leisure-Goods Model with Correction for Selection Bias

Commodity Group	$(1-\theta)b_i$	$\gamma_m\delta_{mi}$	$\gamma_f\delta_{fi}$	σ_{fi}/σ_f
Food	0.0635 (0.0384)	-0.7426 (1.5185)	-1.1268 (1.9021)	0.0547 (0.0451)
Energy	0.0043 (0.0101)	-0.2975 (0.6437)	0.8374 (0.8250)	(0.0219) (0.0179)
Clothing	0.0755 (0.0343)	-1.1902 (1.4654)	1.9691 (1.0554)	0.0203 (0.0365)
Durables	0.0590 (0.0102)	-2.6465 (1.2665)	1.4697 (1.5964)	0.0865 (0.0348)
Transport	0.0553 (0.0379)	2.7325 (1.3309)	0.7785 (1.9129)	0.0695 (0.0442)
Services	0.1403 (0.0450)	2.1444 (1.3895)	-3.9279 (2.2473)	-0.0043 (0.0530)

θ_f = 0.2929 (0.0381) $(1-\theta)$ = 0.3981 (0.0512) σ_f = 0.1599 (0.0510)

$(T-d_m)$ = 50.1279 (2.7018) $(T-d_f)$ = 41.0009 (3.2216) γ_a = 4.5495 (1.2101)

TABLE 3

Equivalence Scale Parameter Estimates

Commodity Group	$p\gamma c_0$	$p\gamma c_1$	$p\gamma c_2$	$p\gamma c_3$	$p\gamma c_4$
Food	0.5664 (0.3533)	2.6069 (0.4270)	4.1432 (0.7411)	4.5857 (0.6451)	3.8188 (0.6342)
Energy	0.7026 (0.2287)	0.3476 (0.1434)	0.7727 (0.2607)	0.9072 (0.2288)	0.9952 (0.2301)
Clothing	0.3398 (0.2621)	0.9226 (0.3564)	1.0844 (0.6182)	1.0461 (0.5399)	0.9962 (0.5518)
Durables	0.7176 (0.5479)	0.9007 (0.3431)	2.2019 (0.5797)	2.1864 (0.5027)	0.8289 (0.5270)
Transport	0.7449 (0.7002)	0.9154 (0.4385)	2.7766 (0.7226)	1.9621 (0.6237)	1.8035 (0.6643)
Services	0.4791 (0.4385)	0.7212 (0.7226)	1.8271 (0.6237)	1.9259 (0.6643)	0.8571 (0.8687)

TABLE 4

Total Equivalence Scale (1974 £'s)

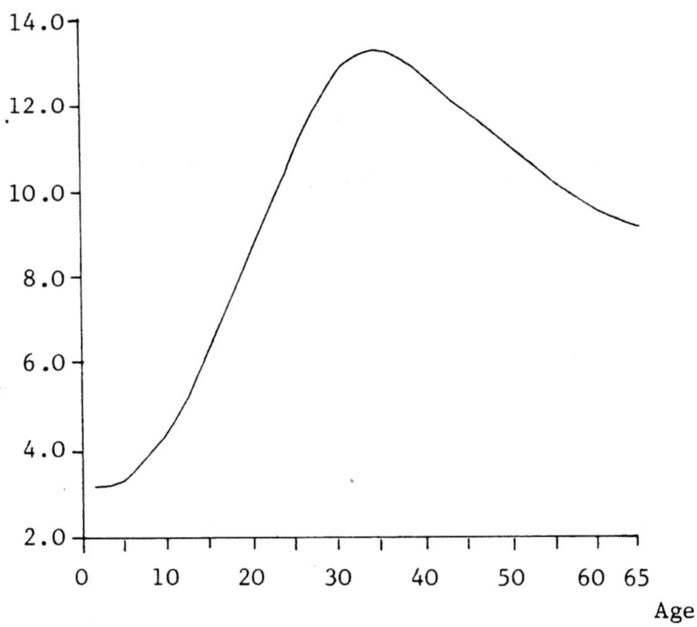

TABLE 5

Specific Equivalence Scales

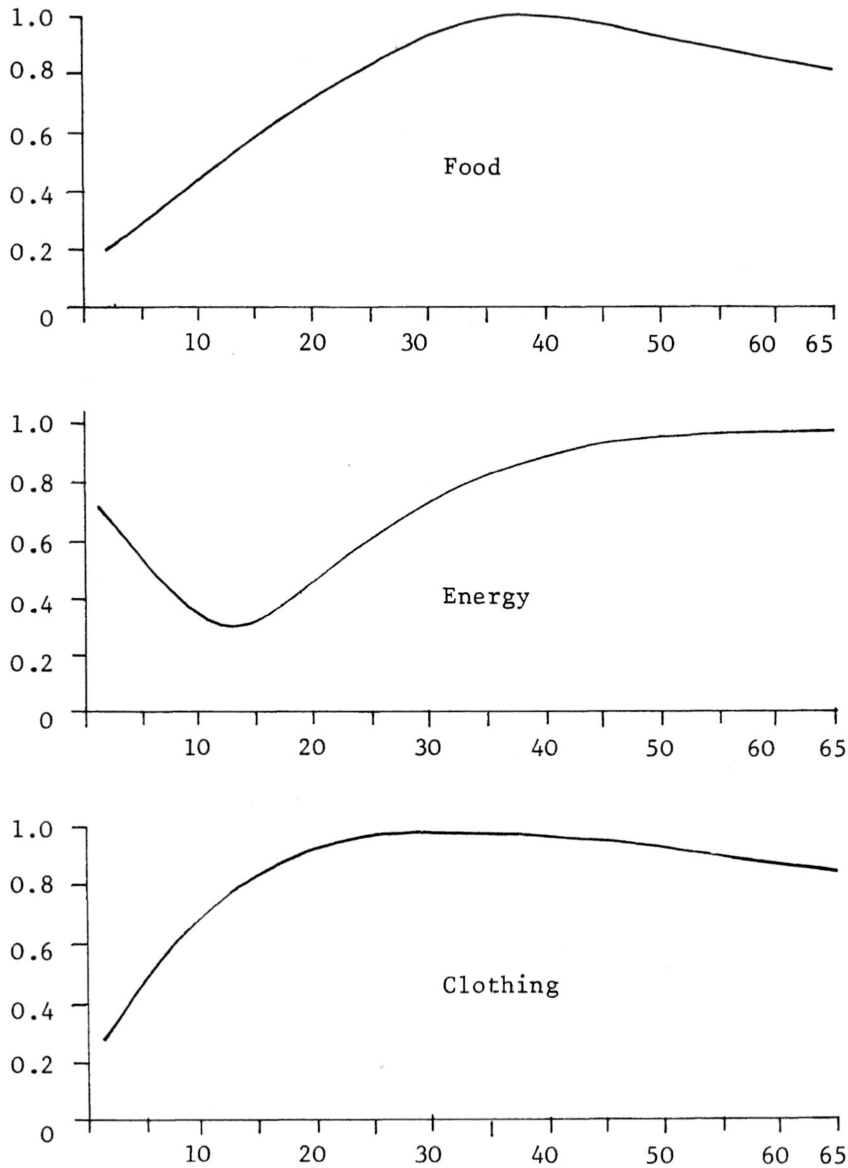

TABLE 5 (continued)

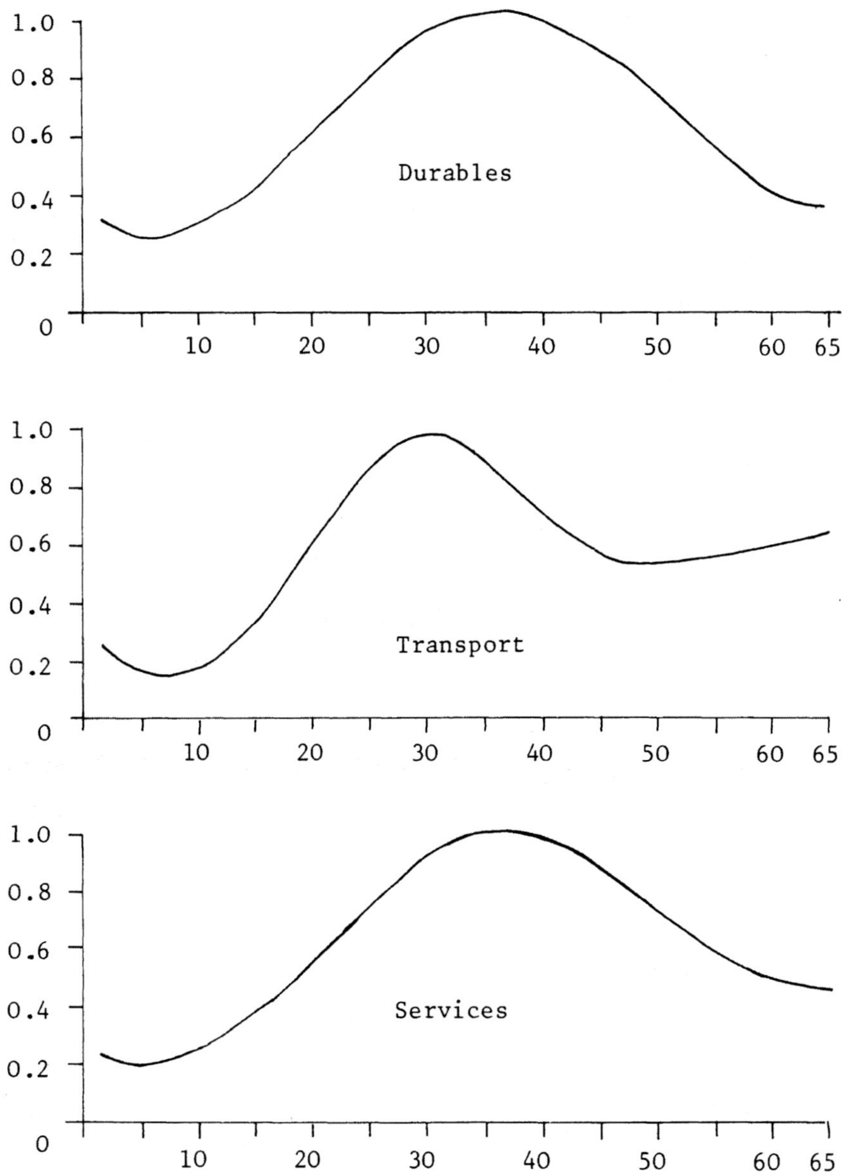

APPENDIX A1

Generation of the Cubic Spline Restrictions

Let us associate with the set of points (knots):

$$\Delta = \{\bar{g}_0 < \bar{g}_1 < \bar{g}_2 < \bar{g}_3 < \bar{g}_4\}$$

the ordinates $c_0,\ldots,c_4$. The cubic spline on Δ interpolating to $c_0,\ldots,c_4$ is denoted by $e_\Delta(g)$, and will satisfy the following conditions:

(i) $e_\Delta(g)$ and its first two derivatives, $e'_\Delta(g)$ and $e''_\Delta(g)$ are continuous over Δ.

(ii) $e_\Delta(g)$ coincides with a polynomial of degree at most three between knots.

(iii) $e''_\Delta(\bar{g}_j) = 0$ for $j=0$ (natural cubic spline).

(iv) $e'_\Delta(\bar{g}_j) = 0$ for $j=4$ (stability of consumption with age).

These four conditions may be seen as a set of restrictions on the second derivatives of $e_\Delta(g)$, given by (see Poirier (1976))

$$\Lambda \underline{q} = \theta \underline{c} \qquad \text{A1.1}$$

where $\underline{q}$ is the 5×1 second derivative vector of e_Δ evaluated at the knots,

$$\Lambda = \begin{bmatrix} 2 & 0 & 0 & 0 & 0 \\ 1-\lambda_1 & 2 & \lambda_1 & 0 & 0 \\ 0 & 1-\lambda_2 & 2 & \lambda_2 & 0 \\ 0 & 0 & 1-\lambda_3 & 2 & \lambda_3 \\ 0 & 0 & 0 & 1 & 2 \end{bmatrix}$$

and

$$\Theta = \begin{bmatrix} 0 & 0 & 0 & 0 & 0 \\ \frac{6}{h_1(h_1+h_2)} & \frac{-6}{h_1h_2} & \frac{6}{h_2(h_1+h_2)} & 0 & 0 \\ 0 & \frac{6}{h_2(h_2+h_3)} & \frac{-6}{h_2h_3} & \frac{6}{h_3(h_2+h_3)} & 0 \\ 0 & 0 & \frac{6}{h_3(h_3+h_4)} & \frac{-6}{h_3h_4} & \frac{6}{h_4(h_3+h_4)} \\ 0 & 0 & 0 & \frac{6}{h_4^2} & \frac{-6}{h_4^2} \end{bmatrix}$$

The last row of Λ and θ impose the additional restriction, to those of a natural cubic spline, that

$$e'_\Delta(\bar{g}_4) = 0,$$

where

$$h_j = \bar{g}_j - \bar{g}_{j-1}, \qquad \text{and}$$

$$\lambda_j = \frac{h_{j+1}}{h_j + h_{j+1}} \qquad j=0,\ldots.,4.$$

Between each knot, $e''(g)$ is linear,

$$e''_\Delta\ g = \left[\frac{\bar{g}_{j-1} - g}{h_j}\right] q_{j-1} + \left[\frac{g - \bar{g}_{j-1}}{h_j}\right] q_j$$

integrating twice and evaluating the constants of integration we can derive an expression for $e_\Delta(g)$. Given any vector $g = [g_1,\ldots,g_D]$ of data points on a we can then express the vector of spline interpolants $e_\Delta(g)$ as a linear function of the ordinate vector $\underline{c}$. First defining matrices P and Q as,

$$P_{i\ell} = \begin{bmatrix} (\bar{g}_j - g_i)\left[(\bar{g}_j - g_i)^2 - h_j^2\right]/6h_j, & \text{for } \ell=j-1 \\ (g_i - \bar{g}_{j-1})\left[(g_i - \bar{g}_{j-1})^2 - h_j^2\right]/6h_j, & \text{for } \ell=j \\ 0, \text{ otherwise} & \end{bmatrix}$$

$$q_{i\ell} = \begin{cases} (\bar{g}_j - g_i)/h_j & \text{for } \ell=j-1 \\ (g_i - \bar{g}_{j-1})/h_j & \text{for } \ell=j \\ 0, \text{ otherwise} & \end{cases}$$

we have

$$\underline{e} = P\underline{q} + Q\underline{c}.$$

Using restrictions A1.1 we have

$$\underline{e} = W\underline{c}$$

where $W = P\Lambda^{-1}\theta + Q$ is a known D × 5 matrix.

APPENDIX A2

In Section 4 we saw that:

$$E(Y_f \mid \varepsilon_f > -X'\beta_f) = X'\beta_f + \sigma_f\lambda_f \qquad \text{A2.1}$$

and we can show using the results of Tallis (1961) that:

$$E(Y_f^2 \mid \varepsilon_f > -X'\beta_f) = X'\beta_f(X'\beta_f + \sigma_f\lambda_f) + \sigma^2_f$$

$$= X'\beta_f(E(Y_f \{\varepsilon_f > -X'\beta_f)) + \sigma^2_f \qquad \text{A2.2}$$

For our selected sample we have:

$$Y_f^2 = \beta_f' X Y_f + \sigma^2_f + n_f \qquad \text{A2.3}$$

where

$$n_f = \beta_f' X \varepsilon_f + (\varepsilon_f^2 - \sigma_f^2) \qquad \text{A2.4}$$

has moments:

$$E(n_f \mid \varepsilon_f > - X'\beta_f) = 0$$

and

$$E(n_f^2 \mid \varepsilon_f > - X'\beta_f) = \sigma^2_{ff}(2 - L_f\lambda_f + L_f^2) \qquad \text{A2.5}$$

Now equation A2.3 could be used to estimate β_{f/σ_f} but we see that the explanatory variables $X Y_f$ are not independent of n_f. However, using the predictions $\hat{Y}_f$ from the OLS estimation of Y_f on X, we can use the set of instruments $(X \hat{Y}_f : 1)$ to provide a consistent estimator of β_f and σ_f in A2.3. This estimator can be shown to have a limiting normal distribution, see Amemiya (1973), whose moments can be found using A2.5 above. Using this estimator, we can find λ_f and derive its limiting distribution given that

$$\frac{\partial \lambda_f}{\partial L_f} = \lambda_f^2 - L_f\lambda_f.$$

REFERENCES

Amemiya, T. (1973). Regression analysis when the dependent variable is a truncated normal. *Econometric*, pp. 997-1017.

Amemiya, T. (1974). Multivariate regression and simultaneous equation models when the dependent variables are truncated normal. *Econometrica*, pp. 999-1012.

Barnett, W.A. (1979). The joint allocation of leisure and goods expenditure. *Econometrica*, pp. 539-564.

Barten, A.P. (1964). Family composition, prices and expenditure patterns. In P. Hart (ed.) *Colston Papers*, No. 16, Butterworths.

Blundell, R.W. and Walker, I. (1980). Demand for goods and leisure with female labour supply and rationing: testing for separability. Presented at the World Meeting of the Econometric Society, Aix-en-Provence.

Gorman, W.M. (1976). Tricks with utility functions. In M. Artis and R. Nobay (eds.) *Essays in Economic Analysis*.

Heckman, J. (1976). The common structure of statistical models of truncation, sample selection and limited dependent variables and a simple estimator for such models. *Annals of Economic and Social Measurement*, 475-492.

Heckman, J. (1979). Sample bias as a specification error. *Econometrica*, 153-162.

Muellbauer, J. (1974). Household composition, Engel Curves and welfare comparisons between households. *European Economic Review*, 103-122.

Muellbauer, J. (1980). Linear aggregation in neoclassical labour supply. *Review of Economic Studies*, Vol. 97, forthcoming.

Phlips, L. (1978). The demand for leisure and money. *Econometrica*, 1025-1044.

Poirier, D.J. (1976). *The Econometrics of Structural Change*, North Holland.

Pollak, R.A. and Wales, T.J. (1978). Estimation of Complete Demand Systems from Household Budget Data: The Linear and Quadratic Expenditure Systems. *American Economic Review*, 68, 348-359.

Pollak, R.A. and Wales, T.J. (1979). Welfare comparisons and equivalence scales. *American Economic Review* (Papers and Proceedings), 216-221.

Tallis, G.M. (1961). The moment generating function of the truncated multinormal distribution. *J.R.S.S.*,

Series B, 223-229.

Tobin, J. (1958). Estimation of relationships for limited dependent variables. *Econometrica*, 24-36.

Wymer, C.R. (1973). Computer Programs: *Resimul Manual*, Mimeo.

FOOTNOTES

1. I would like to thank Ian Walker for many helpful comments and also the Social Science Research Council Archive at the University of Essex for providing the necessary data for this study.

2. This in itself is a form of endogenous selection and may indeed lead to inconsistent parameter estimates. Here we have not corrected for the possibility of such inconsistency.

3. Energy covers fuel, light and power; clothing includes footwear; transport includes vehicles; we have excluded housing expenditure and we treat expenditure on durables as current consumption. Note that the durables definition includes items which are 'time saving' as well as 'time using' so that it would clearly be more appropriate to disaggregate this group.

DISCUSSION: A. INGHAM

I would like to address my remarks on this paper to a comment made in the last paragraph concerning what a reasonable balance between realism and simplicity is. This paper uses the enormous amount of data provided by the Family Expenditure Survey to answer important questions first raised by Henderson[1] and Prais and Houthakker[2] concerning the economic effects of differing family composition. Unfortunately as this is not panel data, its use is limited in answering the question one would like to raise, but this paper is clever in the way in which it makes use of what is available. However in avoiding data limitation, certain costs have to be borne, and it is these costs I wish to draw attention to.

The first problem is whether the length of workday is a true decision variable. It is true that certain housewives will be able to choose whether to work or not, and some individuals may have the choice of working overtime, but in general the working day for a particular occupation is fixed within a particular year and the individual will be unable to alter it, except by changing occupation. Of course, the working day will vary across occupation and so across the sample, which means that an effect picked up will be the distribution of occupations in the economy. Whilst one would not want this to influence the estimated parameters it does allow the problems first noticed by Forsyth[3] to be solved, enabling the family composition effects to be estimated. However, certain restrictions are implicit, the first being the quasihomothetic cost function. This depends on family composition only through $a(\underline{p})$, and so is particularly severe as it implies that the additional cost of a child (or any other change for that matter) is independent of the household utility level. Whilst this means that the cost of an additional child can be calculated when the household utility level is unknown, it is a strong and inhibiting assumption. The second restriction is the particular cost function chosen and whilst the Muellbauer form appears reasonably flexible, it is somewhat paradoxical that a functional form chosen for its desirable aggregation properties should be chosen when a considerable amount of micro data is available.

The use of the spline technique means that a great deal

of age-related consumption behaviour can be introduced at the cost of relatively few parameters. Sudden changes in expenditure patterns which were imposed by the age grouping method do not occur and the age at which children adopt adult consumption patterns is determined here by the data rather than externally imposed. However, certain problems do remain. Firstly, sudden changes in consumption according to age may occur, for example expenditure on motor cycles at 16, and a continuous scale may be unable to pick this up. Other discontinuities may occur at the transition between school and university and at retirement. For an aggregate model these discontinuities could be smoothed out by the distribution of households, but this is not available for this micro sample. One solution would be to locate the knots in the spline function so as to take account of these problems, and a next step in the analysis could be to have the knots determined by the data.

Finally, some features of the estimation procedure deserve comment. Non negativity constraints, usually not problematical in these models, become so here as the inclusion of female labour as a separate variable means that within the sample the value zero will sometimes be observed. In the paper this problem is avoided by restricting the sample to households with two married employed adults. Whilst the paper takes great care to properly estimate the model from this restricted data set, one should still be cautious about inferences for the entire population. The second problem is concerned with dropping the expenditure on housing from the model. This has become rather fashionable, and whilst one can understand the difficulties involved in treating housing expenditure properly, estimating only $n - 1$ equation does not impose the theoretical restrictions of Engel Aggregation and Adding up. A further point of interest is that one of the strongest effects of differing family composition will be on the demand for housing.

In interpreting the results, it should be remembered that the final version is rather restrictive, both in specification and in terms of the sample over which it has been estimated. This could perhaps explain the slightly curious result that all the equivalence scales are close to a maximum in the 30 - 35 age band.

REFERENCES

1. Henderson, A.M. (1949-50). The Cost of a Family, *Review of Economic Studies*.

2. Prais, S.J. and Houthakker, H.S. (1955). *The Analysis of Family Budgets*. Cambridge University Press, London.

3. Forsyth, F.G. (1960). The Relationship Between Family Size and Family Expenditure. *Journal of the Royal Statistical Society*, A.

6. CONSISTENT ESTIMATION OF A LARGE GENERALISED STRONGLY SEPARABLE DEMAND SYSTEM

P. Simmons

Many of the commonly estimated demand systems are either directly or indirectly separable and frequently additive, e.g. linear expenditure system, addilog systems, s-branch systems. Such systems have the following theoretical limitations:

(a) additive and some strongly separable systems involve strong a priori restrictions on the nature of price elasticities in the form of Pigou's law [4]. Occasionally it has been argued that this is in fact an advantage since the price data is often collinear; this view is not universally valid since there is a difference between the number of parameters in a system and the number of theoretical restrictions between elasticities, for example compare a Cobb-Douglas $u = \Sigma\alpha_i log\ x_i$ with a pure CES $u = \Sigma x_i^b$.

(b) the two-stage budgeting process implicit in any directly separable system itself is open to criticism. The clearest case might be that in which particular commodities within a group have strongly divergent income elasticities. For example, suppose that prices of various foodstuffs are constant but other prices and income change in such a way as to keep spending on food constant overall. Then with any directly separable system expenditure on all individual foodstuffs must remain unchanged although one might expect substitutions between say bread and meat;

(c) if the maintained hypothesis is always that demands correspond to separable preferences then it is not possible to test for separability. In fact tests of separability that have been conducted are usually in the context of some local approximation to an unknown demand system e.g. Rotterdam and translog models [18]; [3] so that one is frequently testing a very narrow structure of substitution effects against the hypothesis that they have quite a general structure. A more powerful testing procedure may emerge from testing separability against a narrower alternative.

It follows that a useful class of preferences to consider are those yielding demand systems that can be written in the form

$$x_i = f^i\ (p_r,\ m_r,\ m) \qquad i \in r \tag{1}$$

$$m_r = g^r\ (p,\ m)$$

or even $m_r = g^r(p^1(p_1)\ \ldots\ p^R(p_R),\ m)$

for some grouping of the commodities $i=1,\ \ldots,\ n$ into R groups $r=1,\ \ldots,\ R$. Here x_i and p_i refer to quantity and price of the ith good respectively; m to income or total spending and m_r to spending on group r. Pollak [13] has referred to this class (1) as exhibiting weak decentralisation.

A related issue concerns the size of the system to be estimated in terms of the number of commodities to be distinguished. For several reasons it is as well to estimate as disaggregated a system as the data and computing resources permit. Firstly the conditions under which commodity aggregation is possible with the usual forms of aggregate that time series data provides (e.g. simple weighted sums) are extremely restrictive. Essentially preferences must either be homothetically separable or additively separable with a Gorman polar form [7] in which the price functions have a linear structure. Moreover empirically in a simulation experiment Anderson [1] found that estimation of a misspecified aggregate demand system involved relatively large inaccuracies in parameter estimation. Secondly there is some justification in the argument that an aggregated demand system conceals large differences in the behaviour of the different items within the aggregate. Indeed once the restrictions of constrained utility maximisation have been imposed on a demand system with n commodities, there still remains $\frac{n(n+1)}{2} - 1$ independent price and income elasticities in general. This is, of course, a quantity which increases with n. Thirdly some particular microeconomic policies, e.g. public transport pricing or fuel policy, require estimates of price and income elasticities for quite detailed items of expenditure. If provided within a demand systems framework such estimates will be automatically corrected for failures of the usual ceteris paribus assumption of partial equilibrium analysis at least on the demand side.

The purpose of this paper is to provide consistent and asymptotically efficient parameter estimates of a large demand system consisting of some 80 commodities which is consistent with weak decentralisation and also generalised strong separability. Moreover the actual system selected exhibits nonlinear Engel curves.

Functional Specification

Pollak [14] cites several forms of indirect utility function corresponding to generalised strongly separable preferences. However to preserve nonlinear Engel curves and avoid budget shares of different goods being in a linear relation independent of prices and income, the most useful case to work with is

$$v(p, m) = \Sigma\phi^r(\log \gamma^r(z_r) + A(R), \tilde{z}_r) + C(R)$$

where $\Sigma\phi_r'(\cdot) = R$, $C'(R) = -RA'(R)$, $\phi_r' = \dfrac{d\phi_r}{d(\log \gamma^r + A(R))}$.

Here $z_i = p_i/m$ and z_r is a subvector of $z = (z_1, \ldots, z_n)$ corresponding to price-income ratios belonging to the rth group; $\gamma_r(\cdot)$ is a function homogeneous of degree one in z_r. The notation $\tilde{z}_r$ indicates that the function in which z_r appears as an argument is homogeneous of degree zero in this argument. In this case the demand functions and group spending functions are given by

$$x_i = \frac{\phi_r(\cdot)}{R(\cdot)}\frac{\gamma_i^r(\cdot)}{\gamma^r(\cdot)} + \frac{\phi_i^r(\cdot)}{R(\cdot)} = \frac{m_r}{m}\frac{\gamma_i^r(\cdot)}{\gamma^r(\cdot)} + \frac{\phi_i^r(\cdot)}{R(\cdot)}$$

and $m_r = \dfrac{m\phi_r'(\cdot)}{R(\cdot)}$ respectively. Since $\dfrac{\gamma_i^r(\cdot)}{\gamma^r(\cdot)}$ is homogeneous

of degree -1 in z_r, this system of conditional demands can equivalently be written as

$$x_i = m_r \frac{\gamma_i^r(p_r)}{\gamma^r(p_r)} + \frac{\phi_i^r(z)}{R(z)}$$

In fact in view of the specifications below it is much more convenient to take $\gamma^r(\cdot)$ to be homogeneous of degree -1, so that the demand functions become

$$x_i = \frac{\phi_r'(\cdot)\,\dfrac{\gamma_i^r(\cdot)}{\gamma^r(\cdot)} + \phi_i^r(\cdot)}{-R(\cdot)} \qquad R = \Sigma\phi_r' \qquad RA' + C' = 0. \tag{2}$$

$$m_r = \frac{m\phi_r'(\cdot)}{R}.$$

Combining systems (1) and (2) gives $\dfrac{\partial}{\partial p_j}\left(\dfrac{\phi_i^r(\cdot)}{R}\right) = 0;\ i \in r$ $j \in s$ or for R not a constant

$$\frac{\phi_i^{r\,\prime}(\cdot)}{\phi_i^r(\cdot)} = \frac{1}{A'R(\cdot)}.$$

Defining $w = \log \gamma_r + A(R)$ and integrating over w yields

$$\log \phi_i^r + a_{ri}(p_r) = \frac{1}{A'R}\log \gamma_r + \log R.$$

Taking antilogs and integrating over p_i gives

$$\phi_r = \gamma_r^{\frac{1}{A'R}} R\, a_r(p_r) + B_r(w) = a_r(p_r)\, e^{\frac{1}{A'R}\log(\gamma^r R^{A'R})} + B_r(w).$$

Then for $\phi_r(\cdot)$ to be a function of only w_r and z_r requires that for some function $f(w_r)$

$$\frac{1}{A'R}\left[\log \gamma^r + A'R \log R\right] = f(w_r).$$

However as an identity $\dfrac{\partial f}{\partial \log \gamma_r} = \dfrac{\partial f}{\partial R}\dfrac{1}{A'}$. Substituting in values for the partials of $f(\cdot)$ from the above equation yields

$$\frac{1}{A'R} = \frac{1}{A'}\left[\frac{1}{A'R}(A''R \log R + A' \log R + A') - \frac{(A''R+A')}{(A'R)^2}(\log \gamma^r + A'R \log R)\right]$$

leading to

$$0 = (A''R + A')\left[\log R - \frac{1}{A'R}\ (\log \gamma^r + A'R \log R)\right]$$

or

$$A''R + A' = 0.$$

This leads to $A(R) = \alpha \log R$; $c = -\alpha R$ and $\phi^r(\cdot) = \tilde{a}_r(z_r)e^{1/\alpha\ w_r} + B^r(w)$. Now consider adding the restriction $m_r = G^r(P^1 \ldots P^R\ m)$ where P^r is a function only of z_r and is homogeneous of some degree. This has the interpretation of group spending being determined only by total spending and a price index for each group. Then there must exist some function $F^r(P^1 \ldots P^R, m)$ such that

$$\frac{\phi^r}{\sum_s \phi^s} = \frac{\frac{a^r}{\alpha}\gamma^{r^{1/\alpha}} R + B^{r'}(\log \gamma^r + \alpha \log R)}{\frac{1}{\alpha}\ \Sigma a^s \gamma^{s^{1/\alpha}}\ R + \Sigma B^{s'}(\log \gamma^s + \alpha \log R)} = F^r(\cdot).$$

From which it follows that $B^{r'} = b_r$ a constant.

Defining $\beta_r = br/\Sigma b_s$, taking monotonic transformations of utility and using the homogeneity properties of the functions involved leads to

$$R = \frac{\Sigma b_r}{1 - 1/\alpha \Sigma a^s \gamma^{s^{1/\alpha}}}$$

and to indirect utility

$$v^* = \Pi \gamma^r(p_r)^{\beta_r} \left[m^{-1/\alpha} - \frac{1}{\alpha}\ \Sigma a_r(p_r)\gamma^r(p_r)^{1/\alpha}\right]^{-\alpha} \tag{3}$$

To complete the specification a functional form must be selected for $\gamma^r(\cdot)$ and $a_r(\cdot)$. Taking

$$\gamma^r(p_r) = \Pi p_i^{-\gamma i} \qquad \Sigma\gamma_i = 1$$

$$a_r(p_r) = k_r \Pi p_i^{a_i} \qquad \Sigma a_i = 0$$

then for indirect utility to be increasing in income and decreasing in prices requires

$$\alpha k_r > 0 \quad k_r[a_i - \gamma_i \alpha] < 0 \qquad i \varepsilon r$$

$$\gamma_i > 0 \quad \beta_r > 0 \text{ and } m^{-1/\alpha} - \frac{1}{\alpha}\Sigma a_r \gamma^{r^{1/\alpha}} > 0.$$

We also require that (3) should be strictly quasiconvex in p. Taking logs of (3) and imposing the selected functional forms

$$v^{**} = -\sum_r \beta_r \sum_{i\varepsilon r} \gamma_i \log p_i - \alpha \log\left[m^{-1/\alpha} - \frac{1}{\alpha}\sum k_r \prod_{i\varepsilon r} p_i^{a_i - \gamma_i/\alpha}\right]. \tag{4}$$

Since β_r, $\gamma_i > 0$ $\sum_r \beta_r \sum_{i\varepsilon r} \gamma_i \log p_i$ is strictly quasiconcave. Similarly

$$\prod_{i\varepsilon r} p_i^{a_i - \gamma_i/\alpha}$$

is strictly quasiconcave if $0 < a_i - \gamma_i \alpha < 1$ so for $\alpha k_r > 0$,

$-\frac{1}{\alpha}\Sigma k_r \prod_{i\varepsilon r} p_i^{a_i - \gamma_i/\alpha}$ is strictly quasiconvex. Then for $\alpha < 0$ the second term of (4) is strictly quasiconvex since log is a strictly increasing function. For $\alpha > 0$, $a_i - \gamma_i/\alpha < 0$ since then $k_r > 0$. But $\prod_{i\varepsilon r} p_i^{a_i - \gamma_i/\alpha}$ is then strictly quasiconvex. A similar argument then shows that the second term of (4) is strictly quasiconvex in p. However the sum of strictly quasiconvex functions is quasiconvex.

The utility function (3) is also related to Muellbauer's price independent generalised linear system [10]. Define

$$P(p) = \left[\frac{1}{\alpha}\Sigma a_r \gamma_r^{1/\alpha}\right]^{-\alpha}$$

and $Q(p) = \Pi\gamma_r^{-\beta r}$ so that the cost function corresponding to (3) can be written as

$$m = \left[P(p)^{-1/\alpha} + u^{-1/\alpha} Q(p)^{-1\alpha}\right]^{\alpha}. \tag{5}$$

With the functional specifications adopted, $Q(p)$ and $P(p)$

are positive valued and homogeneous of degree one; hence they can be interpreted as price indices. The form (5) corresponds to the P.I.G.L. system when $Q(p)$ and $P(p)$ are increasing and concave [10].

Properties of the Demand Functions

Under this specification the system of demand functions becomes

$$p_i x_i = \gamma_i m_r - a_i m^{1+1/\alpha} k_r \prod_{j \varepsilon r} p_j^{a_j - \gamma_j/\alpha} \qquad i \varepsilon r \tag{6}$$

$$m_r = \frac{1}{\alpha} m^{1+1/\alpha} k_r \prod_{j \varepsilon r} p_j^{a_j - \gamma_j/\alpha} + \beta_r \left[m - \frac{1}{\alpha} \sum_s k_s \prod_{j \varepsilon s} p_j^{a_j - \gamma_j/\alpha} \right] \tag{7}$$

with the constraints $\alpha k_r > 0$; $k_r[a_i - \gamma_i \alpha] < 0 \quad i \varepsilon r$; $\Sigma a_i = 0$; $\Sigma \gamma_i = 1$; $\gamma_i = 0$, $\beta_r = 0 \quad \Sigma \beta_r = 1$.

These demand functions have some strong qualitative properties. Firstly they fail to be separable solely due to the influence which income exerts on the conditional demand functions. Secondly, within each group, spending on detailed commodities is determined as a constant proportion of group spending adjusted by a correction factor that sums to zero within the group and that depends on group prices and total income. The correction factor can be regarded as a proportional part of a real income index

$$\left[\frac{m}{\prod_{j \varepsilon r} p_j^{a_j - \gamma_j \alpha}} \right]^{1/\alpha} = m_r^*$$

defined from the viewpoint of the group. Put slightly differently conditional expenditures are a fixed linear combination of two independent functions m_r and m_r^* that differ by group. This permits any two commodities within each group to have relatively arbitrary behaviour and then conditional expenditure for other goods within that group are a fixed linear combination of these two. The group spending system has the form of a P.I.G.L. system; if $\alpha = -1$ it reduces to a relative of the linear expenditure system. It thus implies that there is a linear relation between the shares of spending on different groups that is independent of the level of income.

The comparative statics of demand behaviour is also clear. Income elasticities of group spending are given by

$$\frac{\partial \log m_r}{\partial \log m} = 1 + \frac{1}{\alpha}\,2\,\frac{m^{1+1/\alpha}}{m_r}\left(\Sigma k_s \prod_{j\varepsilon s} p_j^{a_j-\gamma_j/\alpha}\right)\left[\frac{k_r \prod_{j\varepsilon r} p_j^{a_j-\gamma_j/\alpha}}{k_s \prod_{j\varepsilon s} p_j^{a_j-\gamma_j/\alpha}} - \beta_r\right]$$

and for the detailed demands by

$$\frac{\partial \log x_i}{\partial \log m} = 1 + \frac{m^{1+1/\alpha}}{\alpha p_i x_i}\left[\left(\frac{\gamma_i}{\alpha} - a_i\right) k_r \prod_{j\varepsilon r} p_j^{a_j-\gamma_j/\alpha} - \frac{\gamma_i}{\alpha}\beta_r \Sigma k_s \prod_{j\varepsilon s} p_j^{a_j-\gamma_j/\alpha}\right]$$

It is then evident that commodities and groups may both be either inferior, normal or superior. Similarly for price effects

$$\frac{\partial \log m_r}{\partial \log p_j} = -\beta_r \frac{m^{1+1/\alpha}}{\alpha m_r} k_s (a_j-\gamma_j/\alpha)\Pi p_j^{a_j-\gamma_j/\alpha} \qquad j \varepsilon s$$

$$= (1-\beta_r)\frac{m^{1+1/\alpha}}{\alpha m_r} k_r (a_j-\gamma_j/\alpha)\Pi p_j^{a_j-\gamma_j/\alpha} \qquad j \varepsilon r$$

$$\frac{\partial \log x_i}{\partial \log p_j} = \frac{\gamma_i}{w_i}\frac{\partial \log m_r}{\partial \log p_j} \qquad i \varepsilon r \quad j \varepsilon s$$

$$= \frac{\gamma_i}{w_i}\frac{\partial \log m_r}{\partial \log p_j} - \frac{a_i k_r m^{1+1/\alpha}}{p_i x_i}(a_j-\gamma_j/\alpha)\Pi p_j^{a_j-\gamma_j/\alpha}$$

$$i, j \varepsilon r$$
$$i \neq j$$

where $w_i = \dfrac{p_i x_i}{m_r}$, $i \in r$.

The price effects are then quite heavily restricted. Between groups depending on the sign of α either all goods are gross complements or gross substitutes. On the other hand within groups considerably more variation is possible - the result essentially depending on the sign of a_i and the relative strength of price effects on group spending as compared with price effects on detailed commodity spending.

Estimation Methodology

The estimating model then has the form

$$m_{rt} = \beta k_r m_t^{1+\beta} \prod_{j \in r} p_{jt}^{a_j - \gamma_j \beta} + \beta_r \left[m_t - \beta m_t^{1+\beta} \Sigma k_s \prod_{j \in s} p_{jt}^{a_j - \gamma_j \beta} \right] + u_{rt} \tag{8}$$

$$p_i x_i = \gamma_i m_{rt} - a_i k_r m_t^{1+\beta} \prod_{j \in r} p_{jt}^{a_j - \gamma_j \beta} + \varepsilon_{it} \qquad i \in r \tag{9}$$

where $\beta = 1/\alpha$. The parameter restrictions are $\gamma_i, \beta_r > 0$

$\beta k_r > 0$, $k_r[a_i - \beta\gamma_i] < 0$, $\sum_{i \in r} \gamma_i = \Sigma\beta_r = 1$, $\sum_{i \in r} a_i = 0$ and

$m - \beta m^{1+\beta} \Sigma k_s \prod_{j \in s} p_j^{a_j - \gamma_j \beta} > 0$. The stochastic disturbances are

assumed to be independent and identically distributed with

$$E(u_{rt}) = E(\varepsilon_{it}) = 0 \qquad \sum_r u_{rt} = \sum_{i \in r} \varepsilon_{it} = 0$$

$E(\varepsilon_{it}, u_{rt}) = 0$ for all i and r

and to have finite fourth moments.

Denoting by u_t the vector of errors at t on all group spending equations except the last one and by ε_{rt} the vector of errors at t on all commodities $i \in r$ except for the last one then

$$E(u_t, u_t') = \Sigma = [\delta_{rs}] \qquad E(\varepsilon_{rt}, \varepsilon_{rt}') = \Omega_r = [\omega_{ij}]$$

where for each r Ω_r and Σ are symmetric positive definite matrices. The assumption that errors on different subsystems are uncorrelated has been used by Theil [18] and commented on by Anderson [1]. Under the interpretation of two stage budgeting as a sequential process in which, say, expenditure on food is first determined (possibly with error) and then the realised food expenditure allocated to individual foodstuffs, there may be little reason to suppose that errors in the level of food expenditure are correlated with errors in expenditure on, say, bread.

To achieve economy of computation, particularly for a system with a large number of commodities, it is desirable to exploit the block recursive structure of equations (8) and (9) in the estimation process. For a sample of size T, let A_{rT} be a symmetric positive definite matrix with dimension equal to the number of elements of ε_{rt} and A_T, a symmetric positive definite matrix with dimension equal to the number of elements of u_t.

Define $\theta = (\beta, k_1 \dots k_R, \beta_1 \dots \beta_R)$, $\phi_r = (a_i, \gamma_i; i \in r)$

$$\mu_r = (\beta, k_r, a_i \quad i \in r), \quad \gamma_r = (\gamma_i, i \in r)$$

and let θ^o, ϕ_r^o, μ_r^o and γ_r^o represent true parameter values. For brevity's sake rewrite (8) and (9) as

$$p_{it}x_{it} = h^i(m_{rt}, z_{rt}, \mu_r^o \gamma_r^o) + \varepsilon_{it}$$

$$m_{rt} = g^r(z_t, \theta^o, \phi^o) + u_{rt} \text{ where } \phi = (\phi_1 \dots \phi_R).$$

The estimation procedure employed is then as follows:

(i) generate estimates $\hat{\mu}_r$, $\hat{\gamma}_r$ minimising

$$Q_{RT} = \frac{1}{T}\sum_t \bar{\varepsilon}_{rt}' A_{rT}^{-1} \bar{\varepsilon}_{rt} \text{ where } \bar{\varepsilon}_{rt} = [p_{it}x_{it} - h^i(\cdot)];$$

(ii) Generate estimates $\hat{\theta}$ minimising

$$Q_T = \frac{1}{T}\sum_t \bar{u}_t' A_T^{-1} \bar{u}_t \text{ where } \bar{u}_t = [m_{rt} - g^r(z_t, \theta, \hat{\phi})].$$

This procedure has the obvious advantage that at any stage only one of the systems (8) or the system (9) has to be estimated. It is related to a procedure suggested by Pudney [15] partly for similar reasons of computational simplicity. The asymptotic properties of these estimators can be deduced, under suitable assumptions, by following the arguments of Jennrich [8] and Phillips [12]. Consider the following assumptions:

<u>A.1</u> $A_{rT} \xrightarrow{a.s.} A_r$. A_{rT}, A_r finite, positive definite.

<u>A.2</u> (γ_r, μ_r) are contained in a compact set and $g^r(\cdot)$ and $h^i(\cdot)$ are continuous and twice differentiable.

<u>A.3</u> $plim \frac{1}{T} \sum_t [h^i(m_{rt}, z_{rt}, \mu_r, \gamma_r] A_{rT}^{-1} [h^i(m_{rt}, z_{rt}, \mu_r, \gamma_r)]$ exists for all possible (μ_r, γ_r) and (ρ_r, γ_r).

<u>A.4</u> For all i and j

$$plim \frac{1}{T} \sum_t [h_t^i(\mu_r, \gamma_r) - h_t^i(\mu_r^o, \gamma_r^o)] [h_t^j(\mu_r, \gamma_r) - h_t^j(\mu_r^o \gamma_r^o)]$$

forms a positive definite matrix for all $(\mu_r, \gamma_r) \neq (\mu_r^o, \gamma_r^o)$ where

$$h_t^i(\mu_r, \gamma_r) = h^i(m_{rt}, z_{rt}, \mu_r, \gamma_r).$$

<u>A.5</u> $plim \dfrac{\partial^2 Q_{rT}}{\partial(\gamma_r, \mu_r)\partial(\gamma_r, \mu_r)}$ exists and is nonsingular.

Minor extension of Phillips' argument establishes the strong consistency of these estimators. Defining $h^i(\cdot) = \gamma_i \; m_{rt} + f^i(z_{rt}, \mu_r, \gamma_r)$ and expanding $-\sqrt{T}/2 \dfrac{\partial Q_{rT}}{\partial(\gamma_r, \theta_r)}$ about the true values eventually yields

$$-\frac{\sqrt{T}}{2}\begin{bmatrix}\dfrac{\partial Q_{rT}(\hat{\gamma}_r, \hat{\theta}_r)}{\partial \gamma} \\ \\ \dfrac{\partial Q_{rT}(\hat{\gamma}_r, \hat{\theta}_r)}{\partial \theta r}\end{bmatrix} = \begin{bmatrix}\dfrac{1}{\sqrt{T}} \sum \dfrac{\partial f^{r^{o}\,'}}{\partial \beta_r} A_{rT}\varepsilon_{rt} + \dfrac{1}{\sqrt{T}} \sum_t g^{o}_{rt} A_{rT}\varepsilon_{rt} \\ \\ \dfrac{1}{\sqrt{T}} \sum_t \dfrac{\partial f^{r^{o}\,'}}{\partial \gamma_r} A_{rT}\varepsilon_{rt}\end{bmatrix} +$$

$$\begin{bmatrix} a_{11} & a_{12} \\ \\ a_{21} & a_{22}\end{bmatrix}\begin{bmatrix}\sqrt{T}(\hat{\gamma}_r - \gamma^{o}_r) \\ \\ \sqrt{T}(\hat{\theta}_r \;\; \theta^{o}_r)\end{bmatrix} = \begin{bmatrix} 0 \\ \\ 0 \end{bmatrix} \tag{10}$$

where

$$a_{11} = -\frac{1}{T} \sum_t g^{o2}_{rt} A_{rT} - \frac{1}{T} \sum g^{o}_{rt} \frac{\partial f^{o\,'}_r}{\partial \gamma_r} A_{rT} - \frac{1}{T} \sum_t u^{2}_{rt} A_{rT} -$$

$$\frac{1}{T} \sum g^{o}_{rt} A_{rT} \frac{\partial f^{r^{o}\,'}}{\partial \gamma_r}$$

$$-\frac{1}{T} \sum \frac{\partial f^{o\,'}_r}{\partial \gamma_r} A_{rT} \frac{\partial f^{o}_r}{\partial \gamma_r}$$

$$a_{12} = -\frac{1}{T} \sum g^{o}_{rt} A_{rT} \frac{\partial f^{o}_r}{\partial \gamma_r} - \frac{1}{T} \sum_t \frac{\partial f^{o\,'}_r}{\partial \gamma_r} A_{rT} \frac{\partial f^{o}_r}{\partial \theta_r}$$

$$a_{21} = -\frac{1}{T} \sum g^{o}_{rt} \frac{\partial f^{or\,'}}{\partial \theta\;\; r} A_{rT} - \frac{1}{T} \sum_t \frac{\partial f^{r^{o}\,'}}{\partial \gamma_r} A_{rT} \frac{\partial f^{r^{o}}}{\partial \gamma_r}$$

$$a_{22} = -\frac{1}{T} \sum_t \frac{\partial f^{r^{o}\,'}}{\partial \gamma_r} A_{rT} \frac{\partial f^{r^{o}}}{\partial \gamma_r}$$

and $\dfrac{\partial f^{r}}{\partial \gamma_r} \quad \begin{bmatrix}\dfrac{\partial f^{1}}{\partial \gamma_1} & \cdots & \dfrac{\partial f^{1}}{\partial \gamma_{nr}} \\ \\ \dfrac{\partial f^{nr}}{\partial \gamma_1} & \cdots & \dfrac{\partial f^{nr}}{\partial \gamma_{nr}}\end{bmatrix}$, etc.

Asymptotically negligible terms have been neglected in (10). The asymptotic distribution of these estimates is given by

$$\sqrt{T}\begin{pmatrix} \hat{\gamma}_r - \gamma_r^o \\ \hat{\theta}_r - \theta_r^o \end{pmatrix} \sim N(O \quad A_r^{*-1} \; \Omega_r^* \; A_r^{*-1}{}') \text{ where}$$

$$\Omega_r^* = \begin{bmatrix} \Omega_{11}^* & \Omega_{12}^* \\ \Omega_{21}^* & \Omega_{22}^* \end{bmatrix} \tag{11}$$

with

$$\Omega_{11}^* = \lim_{T\to\infty} \left[\frac{\sum_t \left(\frac{\partial f_t^{r^o}}{\partial \gamma_r} + g_{rt}^o I \right)' A_r \Omega_r A_r \frac{\partial f_t^{r^o}}{\partial \gamma_r}}{T} \right]$$

$$\Omega_{12}^* = \lim_{T\to\infty} \left[\frac{\sum_t \left(\frac{\partial f_t^{r^o}}{\partial \gamma_r} + g_t^o I \right)' A_r \Omega_r A_r \frac{\partial f_t^{r^o}}{\partial \theta}}{T} \right]$$

$$\Omega_{21}^* = \lim_{T\to\infty} \left[\frac{\sum_t \frac{\partial f^{r^o{}'}}{\partial \theta_r} A_r \Omega_r A_r \frac{\partial f_t^{r^o}}{\partial \gamma_r} + g_{rt}^o I}{T} \right]$$

$$\Omega_{22}^* = \lim_{T\to\infty} \left[\frac{\sum_t \frac{\partial f_t^{r^o{}'}}{\partial \theta_r} A_r \Omega_r A_r \frac{\partial f_t^{r^o}}{\partial \theta_r}}{T} \right]$$

Again the arguments amount to a relatively minor modification of Phillips. To summarise so far; under the assumptions made, $\sqrt{T}(\hat{\gamma}_r, \hat{\theta}_r)$ is consistent and asymptotically normally distributed.

These results differ from the usual minimum distance formulae only in that the asymptotic covariance matrix of the estimators explicitly includes a term in the variance of

u_{rt}. A.3 and A.4 are analogous to the linear model assumption that plim $\frac{(X'\Omega^{-1}X)}{T}$ exist and be positive definite respectively. With prices and incomes amongst the exogenous variables, this might cause some concern.

A similar approach can be applied to the second stage estimators. Assume:

A.6 $A_T \xrightarrow{a.s} A \qquad A_T, A$ finite, positive definite.

A.7 θ is contained in a compact set.

A.8 $plim \frac{1}{T} \sum_t [g^r(z_t, \theta^o, \phi^o) - g^r(z_t, \theta, \hat{\phi})[{}'S_T]g^r(z_t, \theta^o, \phi^o) - g^r(z_t, \theta', \hat{\phi})]$ exists for all θ, θ'.

A.9 For all r and s

$$plim \frac{1}{T} \sum_t (g_t^r(\theta, \hat{\phi}) - g_t^r(\theta^o, \phi^o))(g_t^s(\theta, \hat{\phi}) - g_t^s(\theta^o, \phi^o))$$

forms a definite matrix for all $\theta \neq \theta^o$ where

$$g_t^r(\theta, \phi) = g^r(z_t, \theta, \phi).$$

A.10 $plim \dfrac{\partial^2 Q_T(\theta^o, \phi^o)}{\partial\theta \quad \partial\theta}$ exists and is nonsingular and

$plim \dfrac{\partial^2 Q_T(\theta^o, \phi^o)}{\partial\theta \quad \partial\phi}$ exists.

Following Phillips [12] so long as

$plim \frac{1}{T} \sum_t [g_t(\theta^o, \phi^o) - g_t(\theta^o, \hat{\phi})] A_T u_t = 0$, $\hat{\theta}$ is consistent.

However, since $\hat{\phi}$ is consistent and $g_t(\cdot)$ continuous, for all t $plim[g_t(\theta^o, \theta^o) - g_t(\theta^o \hat{\phi})] = 0$. The result then follows from Cramer's theorem.

It follows from A.10 that

$$plim \frac{\left(\frac{\partial g'^{o}}{\partial \theta}(A_T \otimes I_T)\frac{\partial g^{o}}{\partial \theta}\right)}{T} = G_{\theta o \theta o}$$

exists and is nonsingular and that

$$plim\left(\frac{\partial g^{o}}{\partial \phi_r}(A_T \otimes I_T)\frac{\partial g^{o}}{\partial \theta}\right) = G_{\phi_r \theta_o}$$

exists. (Here $\frac{\partial g}{\partial \theta}$ is the $RTxn$ Jacobian of the stacked group spending equations when there are $R+1$ group spending equations in all and n parameters in θ; similarly $\frac{\partial g}{\partial \phi r}$ is $RTxn_r$ where there are n_r elements in ϕ_r and u is the $RTx1$ stacked vector of group spending system errors.)

The asymptotic distribution of $\sqrt{T}(\hat{\theta}-\theta^{o})$ can be deduced by expanding $\sqrt{T}\frac{\partial Q_T}{\partial \theta}(\hat{\theta}, \hat{\phi})$ around θ^{o}, ϕ^{o} yielding

$$\left[\frac{\frac{\partial g^{*\prime}}{\partial \theta_o}(A_T \otimes I)\frac{\partial g^{*}}{\partial \theta_o}}{T} - \frac{D}{T}\right]\sqrt{T}(\hat{\theta}_o - \theta^{*}_o) = \frac{\frac{\partial g^{*\prime}}{\partial \theta_o}(I \otimes A_T)u}{\sqrt{T}} +$$

$$\sum_r \sum_{k\varepsilon r} \sqrt{T}(\hat{\phi}_k - \phi^{*}_k)\frac{\partial^2 g^{*}}{\partial \theta_o \partial \phi_k}(I \otimes A_T)u - \frac{\frac{\partial g^{*\prime}}{\partial \theta_o}(I \otimes A_T)\sum_r \frac{\partial g^{*}}{\partial \phi_r} T(\hat{\phi}_r - \phi^{*}_r)}{T}$$

The first square bracket on the LHS converges to the nonsingular matrix $G_{\theta_o \theta_o}$. The first term on the RHS converges to a multinormal vector with mean zero and covariance matrix

$$\lim_{T\to\infty}\left(\frac{\sum_t \frac{\partial g^{*}_t}{\partial \theta_o} A_T \Sigma A_T \frac{\partial g^{*}_t}{\partial \theta_o}}{T}\right);$$

the second term converges to zero since the asymptotic

covariance between $\hat{\phi}_k$ and u_{rt} is zero; the *rth* part of the third term converges to a multinormal vector with zero mean and covariance matrix

$$G_{\theta_o\theta_r} A_r^{*-1} \Omega_r^* A_r^{*-1}{}' G'_{\theta_o\theta_r}.$$

But then since all the nondegenerate terms on the RHS converge to random vectors that are mutually uncorrelated $\sqrt{T}(\hat{\theta}_o - \theta_o^*)$ converges to a multinormal variable with zero mean and covariance

$$G^{-1}_{\theta_o\theta_o}\left[\lim_{T\to\infty} \sum_t \frac{\partial g_t^{*\prime}}{\partial \theta_o} A'_T \Sigma A_T \frac{\partial g_t^*}{\partial \theta_o} + \sum_r G_{\theta_o\theta_r} A_r^{*-1} \Omega_r^* A_r^{*-1} G'_{\theta_o\theta_r}\right]$$

$$G^{-1}_{\theta_o\theta_o}{}'.$$

To endow these estimators with some efficiency properties, if joint normality of $(\varepsilon_{1t}, \ldots, \varepsilon_{Rt}, u_t)$ is assumed, the Rothenberg-Leenders [16] linearised maximum likelihood principle could be applied so that if $O = (\theta_o, \phi_1, \ldots, \phi_R)$ then efficient estimators $\tilde{\theta}$ are given by

$$\tilde{\theta} = \hat{\theta} - \left[\frac{\partial^2 L(\hat{\theta})}{\partial\theta\partial\theta}\right]^{-1} \frac{\partial L(\hat{\theta})}{\partial\theta}$$

with consistent estimates of its covariance matrix given by

$$-\left[\frac{\partial^2 L(\hat{\theta})}{\partial\theta\partial\theta}\right]^{-1}$$

for $\hat{\theta} = (\hat{\hat{\theta}}_o, \hat{\phi}_1, \ldots, \hat{\phi}_R)$.

Data and Application

This system has been applied to UK annual consumer expenditue over 1955-1973 on approximately 90 commodities aggregated into ten groups. The commodities distinguished are shown in the accmopanying tables. The data is taken from that made available to the Southampton Econometric Model Building Unit by the CSO and is compiled on a basis consistent with the National Accounts [10].

This gives a total of some 87 commodities; with this level of disaggregation it is debatable if all the individual commodities should be regarded as appropriate to the theory. Firstly there is the problem of durable commodities - should these be treated in the same way as any other commodity? Some researchers include them while others exclude them; from the empirical point of view one would expect to get relatively poor explanation of commodities closely associated with durables e.g. fuels if they are excluded. Moreover from the empirical point of view with U.K. data as compared with U.S. data the variation in durable expenditures and prices is of a similar order of magnitudes to that of say foodstuffs so that if a demand model can explain one then it should equally be able to explain the other. As against this it must be stressed that the correlogram of the residuals of the durables equation might be expected to have distinct properties from those of other goods. The second major feature which emerges from this classification of commodities concerns the treatment of public sector provided services. The major items affected here are television licenses, motor tax, driving tests, national health service payments, local authority fees, stamp duty, central government fines and rates. Some of these commodities - motor tax, television licenses, rates and stamp duty are in the nature of expenditure that is necessarily incurred in the acquisition of some other privately supplied commodity, e.g. televisions, motor cars, houses, stocks and shares. However they are also a recurrent toll on the ownership of assets (with the exception of stamp duty) and a case could be made for arguing that expenditure on these items in the aggregate reflects both consumer acquisition decision and decisions to continue to hold the relevant assets rather than scrapping or realising them. Note also that virtually all demand systems estimated from U.K. data implicitly include these items in consumer expenditure since they are generally conducted at a much higher aggregation level. The two alternatives to treating these items as commodities would firstly be to just exclude them or secondly to use them to calculate some measure of effective price that the consumer actually has to pay to acquire the relevant associated private good. The problem with the first approach is clear - the effects of variation in the level of these 'fixed costs' on the acquisition of the relevant private goods is lost. The difficulty with the second approach lies in finding an appropriate adjustment to the implicit deflator of the public good; such adjustments will depend on such factors as the depreciation of the private asset involved which has little role to play in the static system here. Local authority fees and national health service payments typically represent payments for actual services provided, e.g. prescription charges. The two problems here are firstly that the range of services provided by the government for which the consumer directly pays at least in part has varied rather widely over time; thus in 1964-5 the series of current expenditure per capita for national health service payments showed a jump from 61.075m to 6.599m. Secondly, some of the expenditure under these items is of the nature of a public good - consumers have no discretion over their payments. It is evident that in so far as there is no consumer choice over these commodities they should not be treated in a demand system. From the published data it is very difficult if not impossible to determine the proportion of such expenditure that is discretionary.

Current expenditure are deflated by midyear home population and prices are taken as implicit deflators based on 1970.

The matrices A_{rT} and A_T are assumed to take the following forms:

$$A_{rT} = [a_{ij}^{rT}] \quad [\delta_{ij} w_{iT} - w_{iT} w_{jT}]$$

$$A_T = [a_{rs}^{T}] \quad [\delta_{rs} \mu_{rT} - \mu_{rT} \mu_{sT}]$$

where δ_{ij}, δ_{rs} are Kronecker deltas, $w_{iT} = \dfrac{\sum_t p_i x_{it}}{\sum_t m_{rt}}$ $i \varepsilon r$

and $\mu_{rt} = \dfrac{\sum_t m_{rt}}{\sum_t m_t}$. This structure has been previously used and given some interpretation by Deaton [5] and Barten [2].

Estimation Results

The accompanying tables give consistent parameter estimates and their associated standard errors together with selected price and income elasticities evaluated at the price base period. The columns labelled s_i, $p_i x_i$ (63) and R^2 give the standard deviations of the residuals, the value of the dependent variable in the price base year and R^2 defined by $1 - \frac{SSE}{SST}$.

Commodity	γ_i	a_i	s_i	$p_i x_i(63)$	R^2	Income Elasticity	Gross Own Price Elasticity	Compensated Own Price Elasticity
Group 1: Household Services			β -2.396 (1.0991)		k_r	-18336.7 (954)		
Soap	.075 (.024)	.244 (.1138)	.081	2.25	.9990	-.457	-.749	-.752
Other Cleaning	.047 (.007)	.070 (.0363)	.052	1.19	.9985	-.140	-.904	-.904
Matches	.0007 (.012)	.125 (.057)	.024	.411	.9970	-1.931	-.961	-.962
Chemists	.460 (.102)	-1.05 (.479)	.223	5.49	.9990	1.251	-.921	-.902
Domestic Service	.195 (.011)	.102 (.059)	.108	2.09	.9998	-.052	-.829	-.829
N.H.S.	.049 (.009)	-.054 (.062)	.173	.964	.9694	.634	-.947	-.946
Laundry	.019 (.021)	.220 (.100)	.037	1.09	.9989	-1.135	-.830	-.833
Dry Cleaning	.022 (.011)	.102 (.056)	.096	.82	.9878	-.630	-.921	-.922
Repair	$.197 \times 10^{-7}$ (.079)	.789 (.375)	.349	2.22	.9834	-2.024	-.233	-.243
Miscellaneous	.022 (.003)	.029 (.018)	.035	.50	.9967	-.023	-.890	-.890

Hairdressing	.2103	-.577		2.57	.9896	1.579	-.925	-.915
Group 2: Recreation		-2.510 (1.5)		-54754 (4686)				
Books	,081 (.008)	-,077 (.179)	.122	1,070	,9939	1,276	-1.129	-1.125
Newspapers	.161 (.077)	.061 (.143)	.148	3.005	.9986	1.006	-.859	-.850
Magazines	.050 (.006)	.057 (.132)	.056	1.141	.9982	.897	-.884	-.881
CODI items	.251 (.014)	-.136 (.318)	.177	3.661	.9990	1.177	-.994	-.981
Horticulture	.066 (.005)	,041 (.096)	.090	1,414	,9976	-.970	-.881	-.878
Caravans	.014 (.002)	-.020 (.046)	.024	,174	,9898	1,386	-1,150	-1,149
Pet Food	.146 (.007)	-,059 (,137)	.127	2,277	.9985	1.147	-1.000	-,992
Other misc.	,231	-.134		4.782	,9550	1.148	-,805	-.791

Commodity	γ_i	a_i	s_i	$p_i x_i (63)$	R^2	Income Elasticity	Gross Own Price Elasticity	Compensated Own Price Elasticity
Group 3: Travel		-1.947 (.679)		-8179.	(320.)			
British Rail	.068 (.019	.063 (.043)	.077	2.39	.9993	.969	-.514	-.508
Light Rail	.042 (.021)	-.0048 (.036)	.032	.568	.9982	1.128	-1.173	-1.171
Buses	.114 (.068)	.222 (.155)	.226	6.46	.9991	.927	-.319	-.316
Taxis	.047 (.072)	.002 (.065)	.154	.693	.9788	1.081	-.971	-.969
Sea	.037 (.068)	.011 (.091)	.123	.855	.9858	1.033	-.792	-.790
Air	.292 (.048)	-.155 (.108)	.229	1.240	.9930	1.455	-2.338	-2.331
Car ferry	.015 (.020)	-.006 (.042)	.016	.123	.9922	1.286	-1.821	-1,820
Postal Service	.056 (.011)	.028 (.020)	.133	1,444	.9948	1.006	-.665	-.661
Phone Service	.329	-.1602		1.704	.9948	1.392	-.2072	-2.064

Group 4: Financial Services			β -2.053 (1.081)	k_r -1609.5 (106.)				
Insurance	.468 (.022)	-.352 (.348)	.225	4.15	.9988	1.696	-1.119	-1.096
Private Medical	.021 (.010)	.169 (.167)	.083	.667	.9872	1.274	-.465	-.463
Private Education	.069 (.009)	.159 (.156)	.050	1.061	.9990	1.475	-.779	-.775
Burial	.023 (.010)	.168 (.165)	.027	.672	.9988	1.288	-.487	-.485
L.A. Fees	.178 (.007)	-.093 (.095)	.140	1.68	.9971	1.647	-1.043	-1.035
Stockbroking	.101 (.013)	-.205 (.206)	.197	.598	.9708	1.892	-1.427	-1.422
Stampduty	.030 (.009)	.130 (.129)	.130	.626	.9730	1,367	-.610	-.607
Bank Charges	.037 (.002)	-.028 (.029)	.039	.373	.9942	1.704	-1.135	-1.133
Government Fines	.023 (.002)	-.014 (.017)	.045	.217	.9808	1.691	-1.115	-1.113
Domestic Hire	$.413 \times 10^{-4}$ (.003)	.057 (.057)	.037	.108	.9371	.979	-.014	-1.377
Misc. Services	.05	-.009		.573	.9905	1.585	-.946	-.943

Commodity	γ_i	a_i	s_i	$p_i x_i (63)$	R^2	Income Elasticity	Gross Own Price Elasticity	Compensated Own Price Elasticity
Group 5: Rent, Fuel, Light			β -2.347 (3.288)		k_r -16656.7 (3138.)			
Rent, rates	.676	-1.563	1.227	33.057	.9994	1.683	-1.092	-.913
	(.067)	(1.587)						
Maintenance	.115	.225	.571	7.289	.9970	1.555	-.894	-.860
	(.011)	(.254)						
Coal	$.713\text{X}10^{-3}$	1.291	.974	6.192	.9710	.984	-.009	-.001
	(.056)	(1.308)						
Electricity	.125	-.166	.635	7.178	.9957	1.650	-1.042	-1.008
	(.010)	(.205)						
Gas	.070	-.084	.446	3.226	.9934	1.642	-1.029	-1.010
	(.005)	(.112)						
Coke	$.76810^{-3}$	.175	.239	.887	.9240	1.034	-.096	-.094
	(.008)	(.180)						
Paraffin	.008	.072	.128	.902	.9823	1.424	-.695	-.692
	(.003)	(.078)						
Oil Fuel	.003	.007	.030	.256	.9751	1.474	-.766	-.765
	(.0005)	(.010)						
Wood	.00512	.043		.127	.9544	1.451	-.770	-.770

Group 6: Food	β -2.036			κ_r -3893.2 (813.)				
Bread	.115 (.006)	.211 (.116)	.348	11.76	.9993	.034	-.848	-.847
Meat	.324 (.018)	-.660 (.338)	.601	23.29	.9996	1.208	-.838	-.767
Fish	.040 (.002)	-.071 (.045)	.203	2.97	.9970	1.109	-.863	-.854
Oils, fats	.021 (.010)	.368 (.183)	.217	4.44	.9980	-1.955	-.986	-1.004
Sugar	.076 (.007)	.273 (.138)	.224	8.60	.9995	-.349	-.880	-.887
Dairy Produce	.150 (.003)	-.017 (.046)	.331	13.12	.9995	.556	-.872	-.855
Fruit	.059 (.002)	.024 (.028)	.177	5.23	.9992	.409	-.940	-.935
Vegetables	.127 (.007)	-.194 (.107)	.382	9.96	.9990	1.019	-.866	-.842
Beverages	.052 (.004)	.132 (.069)	.178	5.46	.9992	-.122	-.970	-.971
Other	.036	-.066		2.75	.9978	1.130	-.854	-.847

Commodity	γ_i	a_i	s_i	$p_i x_i(63)$	R^2	Income Elasticity	Gross Own Price Elasticity	Compensated Own Price Elasticity
Group 7: Drink, Tobacco		β -2.117	(1.135)	k_r -16664.8 (1009.)				
Beer	.369 (.030)	-.195 (.116)	1.022	13.39	.9974	.862	-.943	-.908
Spirits	.219 (.035)	-.253 (.136)	.383	6.63	.9984	1.068	-1.232	-1.211
Imp. wine	.142 (.042)	-.301 (.160)	.265	2.17	.9961	1.676	-1.800	-1.786
UK Wine	.010 (.001)	-.006 (.003)	.037	.396	.9948	.886	-1.083	-1.082
Cider, Perry	.008 (.001)	.001 (.002)	.034	.420	.9922	.735	-.926	-.925
UK Cigarettes	.207 (.097)	.697 (.372)	1.119	21.06	.9978	.387	-.335	-.316
UK Tobacco	.029 (.013)	.091 (.049)	.142	2.82	.9981	.402	-.671	-.668
Imported Tobacco	.016	-.034		.144	.8348	1.953	-2.529	-2.527

Group 8: Durables	β -1.989 (1.118)		k_r -6308.6 (3368.)					
Footwear	.062 (.009)	.100 (.137)	.258	6.108	.9988	1.036	-.840	-.825
Mens wear	.107 (.011)	.132 (.181)	.332	9.657	.9992	1.075	-.850	-.824
Womens wear	.215 (.021)	.243 (.333)	.645	19.221	.9993	1.087	-.808	-.757
Cars	.263 (.045)	-.524 (.717)	1.159	11.955	.9950	1.672	-1.322	-1.264
Furniture	.112 (.006)	.059 (.082)	.473	8.835	.9983	1.236	-.983	-.955
Electrical	.121 (.003)	-.001 (.018)	.467	8.873	.9983	1.219	-.967	-.978
Textiles	.048 (.001)	.002 (.007)	.178	3.362	.9984	1.227	-.988	-.988
Hardware	.072	-.011		4.278	.9970	1.262	-1.025	-1.008

Group 9: Entertainment	γ -1.133 (.590)		k_r -18.76 (8.036)					
Cinema	.017 (.106)	.078 (.349)	.708	1.130	.7626	-.013	-.726	-.726
Other Admissions	.056 (.003)	.063 (.046)	.148	1.943	.9968	.306	-.831	-.829

Commodity	γ_i	a_i	s_i	$p_i x_i(63)$	R^2	Income Elasticity	Gross Own Price Elasticity	Compensated Own Price Elasticity
Group 9: continued								
T.V. Rental	.118 (.118)	-.134 (.301)	.764	2.335	.9514	-.847	-1.088	-.726
T.V. Licenses	.013 (.027)	.124 (.130)	.179	1.018	.9860	-.178	-.617	-.618
Meals	.772 (.126)	-.579 (.594)	.739	20.043	.9991	.710	-.676	-.640
Betting	.024	.448		3.067	.9826	-.325	-.384	-.387
Group 10: Running Cost of Motor Vehicles β -1.996 (4.704) k_r -226.89 (55.59)								
Petrol, Oil	.528 (.034)	-1.054 (3.243)	.195	5.778	.9997	1.639	-1.063	-1.020
Car Spares	.274 (.098)	.269 (.811)	.139	3.848	.9995	1.510	-1.002	-.980
Garage	.018 (.012)	.359 (1.094)	.030	.411	.9967	.925	-.881	-.880
Car Insurance	.032 (.012)	.329 (.962)	.107	.643	.9857	1.180	-.928	-.925
Car Tax	.132 (.006)	-.003 (.342)	.265	1.752	.9925	1.550	-1.038	-1.028

Driving Lessons	.013 (.003)	.095 (.287)	.047	.233	.9015	1.277	-.994	-.995
Driving Tests	.003	.005		.032	.9060	1.609	-1.312	-1.311

Consistent Estimates and Elasticities 1970: Group Spending System

	b_r	$k_r/\Sigma k_s$	k_r	s_r	$m_r(63)$	β	Σk_s	R^2	Income Elasticity
Household Services	.034 (.0059)	.106	-172825.3 (5930.6)	.346	19.6	-2.742 (.6251)	$-.163\text{x}10^7$	.9998	.229
Recreation	.051 (.0023)	.044	-72268.6 (2480.9)	.542	17.5			.9995	1.070
Travel	.045 (.0021)	.037	-61166.6 (1967.6)	.851	15.5			.99974	1.089
Financial Services	.040 (.0024)	.0005	-899.15 (207.9)	.757	10.7			.9977	1.617
Rent, Fuel	.211 (.0114)	.001	-1655.46 (1707.1)	2.256	59.2			.9992	1.622
Food	.168 (.0105)	.364	-594424.6 (20112.8)	3.019	87.6			.9992	.512
Drink, Tobacco	.117 (.0061)	.182	-297094.6 (10143.7)	1.483	47.0			.9994	.774
Durables	.205 (.0092)	.119	-194238.5 (6324.1)	2.968	72.3			.9990	1.232
Entertainment	.063 (.0065)	.137	-224584.3 (7348.5)	1.704	29.5			.9979	.506
RCMV	.066	.0095	-15063.0 (741.3)		12.7			.9512	1.524

The most startling aspect of these estimates is just how well they explain the data. The range of estimates for from different groups is relatively small and the simultaneous increase in the absolute values of β and k_r in passing from the conditional demands to the group spending system leaves the predictions of the conditional demand systems relatively unaffected since to some extent the two increases are self-compensating. Given these consistent estimates, the next step would be to attempt to find relatively efficient estimates by linearised maximum likelihood. This was not done here, primarily because of the difficulties of inverting the Hessian of the full likelihood function - a 174,174 matrix. Instead the consistent estimates were treated as final estimates with the value of β and k_r from the group spending system: caution must then be applied to any inferences or hypothesis testing. However the point estimates themselves have considerable interest. Since $\beta < 0$, $k_r < 0$ spending on any group increases with the prices of that group but decreases with the prices of other groups: in elasticity terms

$$\frac{\partial\, log\, m_r}{\partial\, log\, p_j} = -b_r \beta m^{1+\beta} k_s (a_j - \gamma_j \beta)\frac{1}{m_r} < 0 \qquad j \in s \quad r \neq s$$

$$= (1-b_r)\beta m^{1+\beta} k_r (a_j - \gamma_j \beta)\frac{1}{m_r} > 0 \qquad j \in r$$

where units are selected so that prices are unity at the point at which the elasticity is taken. On the other hand groups can be either inferior, normal or superior

$$\frac{\partial\, log\, m_r}{\partial\, log\, m} = 1 + \frac{\beta^2 m^{1+\beta}}{m_r} \Sigma k_s \left[\frac{k_r}{\Sigma k_s} - b_r\right]$$

(again when prices are taken as unity). In this limited sense there is then gross complementarity between groups. To some extent, given the conditions $\beta < 0$, $k_r < 0$, $(a_i - \gamma_i \beta) > 0$, these relations carry over to the elasticities for individual commodities. When prices are unity

$$\frac{\partial\, log\, x_i}{\partial\, log\, p_j} = \gamma_i \frac{m_r}{x_i p_i} \frac{\partial\, log\, m_r}{\partial\, log\, p_j} < 0 \qquad i \in r \quad j \in s \quad r \neq s$$

$$\frac{\partial\, log\, x_i}{\partial\, log\, p_j} = \gamma_i \frac{m_r}{p_i x_i} \frac{\partial\, log\, m_r}{\partial\, log\, p_j} - \frac{a_i k_r m^{1\ \beta}}{p_i x_i}(a_j - \gamma_j \beta) > 0$$

$i, j \varepsilon r, i \neq j$

so that between groups individual goods are gross complements, while within groups they are gross substitutes. This conforms in a sense with the early theoretical arguments of Morishima [9] on intrinsic complementarity and substitutability. It is then rather remarkable that in a system which does not enforce gross complementarity or substitutability, the parameter estimates should be such that between groups there is gross complementarity in accord with almost all previous work. The summary tables of elasticities show the income elasticities for group expenditure for 1970 and for each of the 87 commodities its income elasticity and own price elasticities. No groups are inferior but food and household services together with entertainment are the least income elastic. Rather surprisingly rent, fuel and light is strongly a luxury; this may well be due to the complementarity of some of the group components with other luxuries, e.g. durables. There is considerable diversity of income elasticities within groups; for example there are both inferior and luxury items amongst foodstuffs. On the other hand none of the groups which are strongly luxuries contain inferior goods. Pigou's law does not appear to be empirically substantiated at this point; the ranking of commodities by their income elasticity does not coincide with that by price elasticity and the accompanying diagram reveals a relatively weak association between the two. There is a greater variation in income than in price elasticities. From the detailed elasticity results not presented here there is no very clear pattern of net complementarity or substitutability - both within and between groups there are both net complements and net substitutes. The extent to which the model can "pick up" some of the detailed commodity interactions that armchair speculation would indicate can be judged by examination of the magnitudes of the cross price elasticities. The major such interactions that one might expect would be complementarities between durables and their associated running costs (cars and running costs of motor vehicles; electricity and electrical appliances) and substitution relationships between alternative sources of the same service (electrical appliances and television rental; cars and public transport; durables and domestic hire; alternative types of fuels). At a slightly broader level one might also expect substitution between alternative forms of entertainment and recreation or alternative forms of public transport. In fact there are not strong complementarities between durables and their running costs - if anything at the net level there are substitute relations. This may merely reflect the fact that a static framework is of limited value in exploring the dynamic relationship between durable good stocks and non-durable flows. There is some evidence of relatively strong net substitution between the purchase of electrical appliances and television rental but it does not extend to the gross level. Similarly there is some evidence of net substitution between cars and public transport especially for buses and durables and domestic hire but it is not as strong as one would have expected. There are strong net substitution relations between alternative forms of fuel.

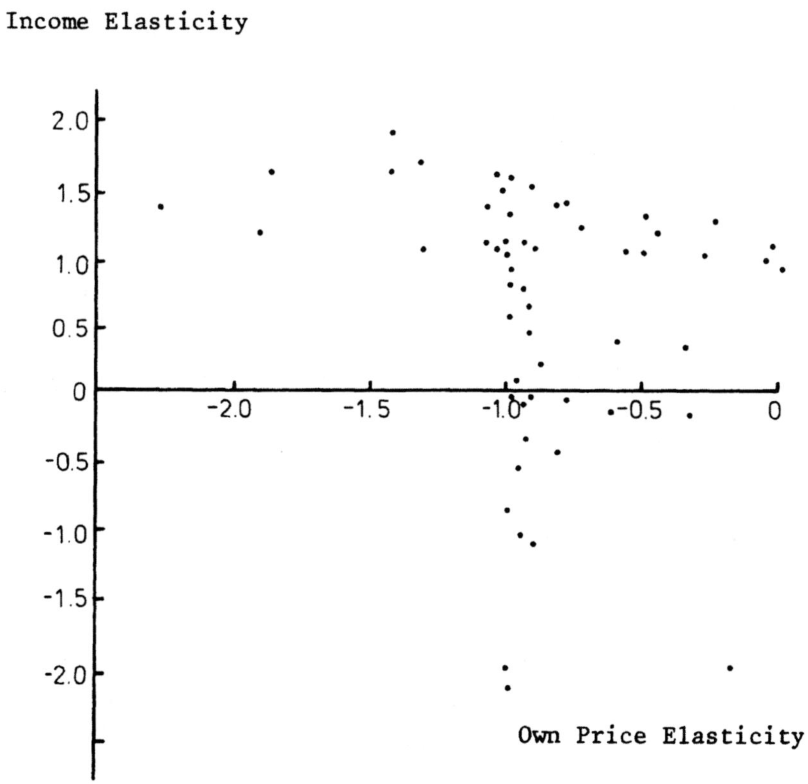

REFERENCES

[1] Anderson, R., Perfect Price Aggregation and Empirical Demand Analysis, *Econometrica* 47, pp. 1209-1230, (1979).

[2] Barten, A. and Theil, H., *Simultaneous Estimation of a Complete System of Demand Equations* (1964), Netherlands, School of Economics.

[3] Christansen, L., Jorgenson, D., and Lau, L., Transcendental Logarithmic Utility Functions, *The American Economic Review* 65, pp. 367-383 (1975).

[4] Deaton, A., A Reconsideration of the Empirical Implications of Additive Preferences, *Economic Journal* 84, pp. 338-348 (1974).

[5] Deaton, A., *Models and Projections of Demand in Postwar Britain* (Chapman Hall, 1975).

[6] Gallant, A.R., Seemingly Unrelated Nonlinear Regressions, *Journal of Econometrics* 3, pp. 35-50.

[7] Gorman, W., Separable utility and aggregation, *Econometrica* Vol. 28, pp. 469-481.

[8] Phillips, P.C.B., "The Iterated Minimum Distance Estimator and The Quasi-Maximum Likelihood Estimator", *Econometrica,* 44, 1976.

[9] Morishima, M., The Problem of Complementarity and Separability of Goods, *Metroeconomica* 11, pp. 188-202 (1959).

[10] Muellbauer, J., Community Preferences and the Representative Consumer, *Econometrica* 44, pp. 979-999 (1976).

[11] *National Income and Expenditure*, C.S.O. (London).

[12] Jennrich, R.I., "Asymptotic Properties of Nonlinear-least Squares Estimators", *Annals of Mathematical Statistics,* 40, 1969.

[13] Pollak, R., Budgeting and Decentralisation, Discussion Paper 157, Department of Economics, University of Pennsylvania (1970).

[14] Pudney, S., *The Estimation of a Class of Large Nonlinear Demand Systems*, L.S.E. (mimeo, 1978).

[15] Rothenberg, T.J., and Leenders, C.T., Efficient Estimation of Simultaneous Equation Systems, *Econometrica* 32, pp. 57-76 (1964).

[16] Sargan, J.D., The Estimation of Relationships with Auto-correlated Residuals by the Use of Instrumental Variables, *J.R.S.S.*, Series B, Vol. 21 (1959).

[17] Theil, H., *Theory and Measurement of Consumer Demand*, Vol. 1, 2 (North Holland, 1976).

DISCUSSION : J. E. SPENCER

Two major theoretical problems arise in the estimation of demand functions. Firstly, as is well known, standard demand theory is insufficiently restrictive to permit the useful estimation of consumer demand functions. The second problem, usually ignored in empirical work, concerns difficulties of aggregation, especially over consumers. Aggregation of demand functions which are based on individual utility maximisation lead to aggregate demand functions which do not appear to be subject to much a priori restriction.

Simmons' paper is not concerned with the second problem but specifies demand functions based on a certain indirect utility function. The demand functions therefore satisfy the standard restrictions of demand theory and it is assumed that they can be applied at the aggregate level. Much of the previous empirical work of this type has involved assumptions on the form of the utility function which leads to peculiarly specific and restrictive forms of the demand functions. For example, the linear expenditure system with constant positive base quantities involves constant marginal budget shares, does not permit goods to be price elastic or inferior and rules out complementarity.

Recent theoretical work on various notions of separability is suggestive of several possibilities for suitable restrictions and Simmons accordingly appeals to Pollak's work on generalized strong separability. A demand system exhibits this property if the goods may be partitioned into mutually exclusive and exhaustive subsets so that the demand for each good belonging to the r'th partition depends only on the normalized prices of all goods in the subset and a scalar function of all normalized prices. This specification indeed permits concentration on own price and income effects but is by no means fully motivated or fully characterized in terms of preferences. He chooses a particular form of utility function which satisfies generalized strong separability and this is combined with the intuitively quite attractive weak decentralization assumption (with the partitioning assumed the same as for the separability). Further assumptions on certain functional forms leads after some manipulation, to demand functions suitable for estimation.

In order to appraise the generality of the demand functions estimated in the paper and in order to try to increase the intuitive content, it is perhaps instructive to compare their properties with those generated by the S-Branch utility function (Brown and Heien (1972), for example). This function has utility as a CES function of CES functions of translated variables $x_i - d_i$ where the d's play the same role as the base quantities of the LES system. To ease discussion, assume the d's are zero so that the utility function is homothetically separable into m groups one of which contains, say, x-goods only, another z-goods etc. This specification has most attractive aggregation and indexation properties, allows a two stage budgeting strategy and permits reasonably general price responses both within and between groups depending on the elasticities of substitution within groups (σ_x, σ_z, etc.) and on the overall elasticity (σ). The S-Branch system is restricted to an income elasticity of unity for each good.

Write expenditure on x-goods as M_x, $S_i(X)$ = share of M_x spent on X_i, $S(X)$ = share of total spending (M) devoted to M_x.

Then own-price elasticity of X_i may be written:

$$\sigma_x + (\sigma - \sigma_x)S_i(X) + (1 - \sigma)S_i(X)S(X)^1$$

Further,

$$\frac{\partial \log X_i}{\partial \log P_{x_j}} = \sigma_x S_j(X) - S_j(X)[\sigma + (1 - \sigma)S(X)]$$

$$\frac{\partial \log X_i}{\partial \log P_{z_j}} = (\sigma - 1)S_j(z)S(z), \text{ constant for all } X_i,$$

sign depending on σ.

$$\frac{\partial \, \log M_x}{\partial \, \log P_{x_i}} = (1 - \sigma)S_i(X)(1 - S(X))$$

$$\frac{\partial \, \log M_x}{\partial \, \log P_{z_j}} = \pi_z^{-\sigma_z}(1 - \sigma)(\sigma_z - 1)S_j(z)S(z),$$

π_z = price index of z-goods.

These expressions are reported in this manner to aid hopefully suggestive comparison with the analogous expressions in Simmons' paper. Broadly speaking Simmons' specification is considerably less restrictive thereby giving the data more freedom but there are some interesting similarities. Thus, for example, in both systems, depending on the sign of $\sigma - 1$ in one case or on β in the other, all goods are either gross substitutes or gross complements between groups. Empirically Simmons finds β negative suggesting intergroup complementarity (interestingly consistent with Brown and Heien who estimated, with US data, σ at about one half). Again, given $\beta < 0$, spending in a group must fall with prices rising in other groups. This compares with $\sigma < 1$ when spending in the x-group falls with rising prices in the z-group only if $\sigma_z < 1$.

Simmons uses a two-stage estimation procedure as is not unusual in this kind of work. Clearly the estimation has been a major exercise in its own right - 87 commodities divided into 10 groups indicates considerable disaggregation compared to the 28 commodities and 5 groups of the Brown and Heien study. The theoretical justification is via the asymptotic distribution and one feels somewhat churlish in mentioning that some 200 parameters are estimated from a sample of 19 observations. The assumptions used to guarantee asymptotic normality could perhaps be motivated more strongly but this is often problematical in empirical studies. How does one justify, for example, a claim that a disturbance term has finite fourth moment? The assumption that the covariance matrices are independent of t does seem dubious, however, especially as the dependent variables are levels of money expenditure rather than say shares.

In conclusion, this is a useful paper which has clearly involved a great deal of careful work by the author. The demand system examined is interesting, avoids obviously unacceptable restrictions in contrast with much previous work and despite some arbitrariness in its motivation must take its place as a serious attempt to measure the intricate interrelationships of consumer expenditure data.

REFERENCES

Brown, M. and Heien, D. (1972). The S-Branch Utility Tree. A Generalization of the Linear Expenditure System. *Econometrica*, Vol. 40, No. 4, 737-747.

Deaton, A. (1974). A Reconsideration of the Empirical Implications of Additive Preferences. *Economic Journal*, Vol. 84, No. 334, 338-348.

FOOTNOTES

1. Deaton (1974) recently claims this as unrealistically restrictive essentially because it is approximately equal to σ_x (Pigou's Law). Clearly this need not be so as σ, σ_x are not restricted beyond being positive. While Deaton stresses the empirical accuracy of the approximation rather than its theoretical accuracy, a priori estimates of the σ's would not seem sufficiently secure to warrant the conclusion.

7. ON THE STRUCTURE OF THE THEORY OF MONETARY POLICY

Victoria Chick

I THE NEED TO EXAMINE "DEEP STRUCTURE"[1]

The theory of monetary policy as it exists at present, represented by the "Monetarist-Keynesian Debate", is, from a methodological point of view, degenerate. The cause of the trouble is that the subject is perceived in terms of an inappropriate classification. The two opposing opinions around which the debate supposedly revolves are defined at too superficial a level, and the fact that only two claim attention (allowing for variations within each camp), follows the tradition of Western thought to analyse by dichotomisation (good and evil, nature and culture, mind and body), which has been known to cause trouble before. In this case, to see the extremely rich set of ideas which constitute the theory of monetary policy in terms of two opposing camps requires a good deal of Procrustean engineering.

This paper is concerned to demonstrate the weakness of this dichotomy and to provide an alternative. Thus its topic is not the content of the debate but about the fashion in which it is being conducted.

At present, the Keynesian and Monetarist camps are identified, broadly speaking, by whether money is supposed to work its magic on the "real sector" through interest rates or whether the link between money and income is paramount. The transmission mechanism

$$M \rightarrow r \rightarrow I \rightarrow Y$$

identifies the Keynesian and

$$M \rightarrow Y$$

is associated with Monetarism. The proliferation of theories flying the "Keynesian" or "Monetarist" banners has served to blur this sharp outline, but not to obliterate it.

How sharp the distinction is, is not, however, the issue. The point is that these postulated "transmission mechanisms" are not *theories* but manifestations of underlying theoretical structures. Surely it is at the level of *theory* that opposing views should be evaluated. That job, I argue, has not yet been done in this field of enquiry.

If there were a one-to-one mapping between the underlying theoretical structure and the transmission mechanism which is supposed to follow from it, there would be nothing lost in characterising the two camps by their transmission mechanisms, but this is not the case. I have already shown (Chick, 1973) that a variety of theories and their permutations reduce to one or other of these two mechanisms - indeed the book's *leitmotif* was the robustness of the conclusions to the variety of theories adduced to support them.[2]

This fact gives rise to paradoxes. For example, Tobin's approach (as in e.g. (1961, 1969), Tobin and Brainard (1963)) is a portfolio framework not dissimilar from that of Friedman (1956, 1958, 1968, 1972), yet Tobin serves as a representative Keynesian and if Friedman does not count as a monetarist I should be quite lost. One could go on: Friedman claims the Quantity Theory[3] as his antecedent, while Patinkin (1972) argues that Friedman's work is a development of Keynes's liquidity preference, and Brunner (1968, p.18) states that the antecedents of the "weak monetarist" general portfolio approach are Keynes, Fisher and Wicksell. There is also a need to reconcile the coexistence of Radcliffe theory and Tobin in the Keynesian camp; the one is concerned with adjustment to a portfolio of assets - no one ever seems to go into debt - while the other theory revolves around the problems of access to credit. Does Friedman's characterisation of "credit" and "monetary" theories help? And where does Keynes fit in all this?

The paradoxes arise from the method, used before now by me as well as other commentators, of evaluating each theory as a total package. When the theories are pulled apart into their components, their "deep structure", a way to resolve some of these paradoxes is found. The Table provides a suggested structural scheme. It does not pretend to be exhaustive or definitive; it is offered as provisional and suggestive.

TABLE

STRUCTURE OF THE THEORY OF MONETARY POLICY

Theoretical Issues (Postulated Responses)

- effect on interest, output, prices
  - neutrality
- role of interest rate in transmission mechanism
- efficacy of monetary policy

Analytical Structure

- money circulating v. money held
  - commodity and financial circulations
- income-wealth schema
  - Fisherian v. Keynesian
  - "rationality" and the treatment of debt
  - consolidation and the treatment of debt
  - "aggregative detail"
- treatment of time
  - impact effect v. equilibrium
  - Marshallian periods: market period, production period, investment period, accumulation
  - the unit period, temporary equilibrium
  - the "long run" - satisfaction of expectations
- method
  - statics, "pseudodynamics", differential-equation dynamics
  - sequence analysis

Stimuli

- change in outside money
  - through foreign trade
  - through government policy
    - open market operations
    - fiscal deficits
    - "helicopter"
- change in inside money
  - change in bank reserves
  - increased private sector demand

continued overleaf

The Environment (Changeable Aspects)

- institutional framework
  - credit
    - direct - stock and bond markets
    - indirect - intermediaries
  - money
    - circulating metallic money
    - convertible paper
    - inconvertible paper
- cyclical phases

Assumed States of Nature

- degree of stability inherent in the private sector
- inherent optimality of the outcome of private sector behaviour
- role of government
- individualism v. behaviour determined by economic class
- nature of long term trend (stationary state or growth)

It begins with the *results* of theorising, listing the main issues in the monetary debate, encompassing questions such as "how will interest rates respond to an increase in the money supply?" The idea that answers might differ because of the assumed source of new money is explored in Chick (1978) and the fiscal policy counterpart has also now been treated explicitly (see especially the papers in Stein, 1976). But there are many other potential sources of differences. The answer may depend on the institutional environment and the current state of the economy, the way the monetary increase occurs, what is assumed about the "normal" long term state of the economy, as well as the more obviously theoretical aspects listed under "Analytical Structure". Friedman might reply to the above that as an impact effect interest rates would go down, thus appearing to agree with Keynesians. However, because his income-wealth scheme is Fisherian, he describes services of durable goods as providing a return akin to interest on those durables. Thus he may have in mind something a Keynesian would describe as a direct effect, leaving what the Keynesian understands by rate of interests - the observable money-rates - unchanged.

This example is fairly typical of the sort of problem generated by lack of explicit treatment of analytical structure, much less a full statement of the assumptions about the environment or the nature of the stimulus whose effects are being analysed. In addition, there is evidence of an anachronistic carryover of ideas devised in and for, e.g., metallic-money economics.

Apart from minimising the amount of talk at cross-purposes which so bedevils this field, there is another potential benefit from the explicit concern with deeper structure: if we dismantle the theories carefully, we stand to gain possession of serviceable building-blocks with which to construct new theories suited to new problems or a changed universe, consciously deciding which pieces to use and which to discard.

A full analysis of theories of monetary policy according to their structure obviously cannot be attempted here. I have given one example of the potential usefulness of the approach. The body of the paper will explore one element of "analytical structure" in detail: namely, whether money is modelled as being in continual circulation or held as an asset.

II MONEY CIRCULATING, MONEY HELD

1. Introduction

It will be argued in this part of the paper that an important source of difference between theories of monetary policy lies in their implicit modelling of money's role. This may seem a curious concern, for surely nearly everyone would agree that in actual fact "no asset is in action as a medium of exchange except in the very moment of being transferred from one ownership to another ... Between transactions all money is idle." (Sayers, 1960, p.712.)

The accuracy of that statement is the beginning, not the end, of one's woes. Is the money held on Monday and designated for expenditure on Tuesday "held" in the same sense as money accumulated and held in anticipation of an annual holiday? One knows that no rational person intends to hold money forever; do we therefore say all money circulates? This question is entirely bound up with *time*; the essential problem is how best to model money's indisputable movement between agents through time, in the context (almost always) of a static model. Even if the model is dynamic the problem is not solved, for plainly money circulates in different spheres at different speeds, and at different speeds under different circumstances.

Concentration on one or other aspect of money results in theories which explain why one can expect money to be continually changing hands (it has only exchange value, is a barren asset, etc.) or why it is held (uncertainty about prices or interest rates, transactions costs, etc.). I shall argue that classical theory was almost entirely concerned with the first and modern theory almost exclusively with the second, with Keynes perhaps serving as a bridge between.

Uncovering the underlying view of money is a difficult enterprise, for at least two reasons. Firstly, the view is almost always mixed (correctly reflecting how money behaves): elements of "money on the wing" are hidden away in portfolio theory and even theories of circulating money allow it to rest for a time. Secondly, the view is usually implicit. Discussing what is implicit is by necessity highly subjective, for it involves inferring what lies behind what is written. The authors may or may not have *consciously* taken the view that I shall ascribe to them; still less have they discussed it openly. And one can never be sure that something which is not said has been omitted precisely because it was taken for granted.

That said, let us proceed, for the only alternative is to leave the question alone, and that is not right if one believes that these differences of vision are important. I shall begin with the present consensus.

2. *Portfolio Theories*

a. *In general*

Portfolio theory has become the accepted framework for the analysis of monetary policy, as demand-for-money theory has been transformed into a theory of wealth allocation.[4] There is wide agreement that the only questions with which the theory of monetary policy need be concerned are the relative substitutability amongst assets and which ones should be on the choice list. The rest is detail. This view is endorsed by, *inter alia*, Tobin (1972), Patinkin (1978). This is the evaluation in a thorough survey of the literature:

> The general view that has been emerging from the writings of both neo-Keynesians and monetarists stresses the impact of monetary policy changes on the composition of assets held by the public and the influence of these changes on interest rates on these assets and ultimately on the rate of return from investing in the production of new physical assets. There is, however, considerable disagreement as to the major variables and interest rates that must be defined in order to take account of all the ways in which monetary policy works out its effects. (Park, 1972, pp. 11-12.)

The characterisation of Keynes by Tobin (1969) and Leijonhufvud (1968) is also widely accepted. Keynes is supposed, in their lights, to have lumped all non-money assets together and called them "bonds"; the "portfolio" was thus restricted to two assets, money and bonds. It follows that monetary policy can only work through the bond rate. The significance of Tobin's own framework is said to be that by including real capital in the "portfolio", the margin of substitution between money and real goods is "re-opened",[5] as if it had previously been closed. Friedman claims still greater generality; his framework (1956) includes consumer durables (and possibly also non-durables) and human capital. Indeed the scope of Friedman's "portfolio" is the entire range of alternatives to holding money.

Are we to understand by this characterisation that there has been a steady progression toward greater realism, from the *simpliste* notion of Keynes through Tobin to the full majesty of Friedman's framework in which money impinges on all areas of economic life, and monetary policy stops not at the borders of the City but goes all the way to training college and university, where the demand to add to human capital must be backed by money? It is surely correct to say that money can buy a wide range of things, but is that adequate reason for claiming superiority for the theory which encompasses the broadest range of assets, and for regarding the developments from Keynes to Tobin to Friedman as one of progressive improvement?

I shall argue that the view that these theories differ only in their scope or in their elasticities of substitution is quite misguided. Though both the Yale and Friedman approaches share a certain superficial affinity with Keynes's treatment of money, they are far closer to each other than Keynes. The fundamental difference is often masked by the descriptive language chosen, but the fact remains that the portfolio approach treats money entirely as an asset to be *held*. Keynes, on the other hand, was concerned with money both circulating and held (though he seems at times to forget the former [6]).

Portfolio theory is comparative-static in method[7] and based on the device of the unit period[8]. Asset demands are specified as end-of-period stocks. It is an obvious but rarely remarked feature of theory based on these foundations, whether "Keynesian" or "monetarist", that once the equilibrium portfolio is reached, holdings will be maintained unless there is some exogenous change in the data. Money, gilts, looms, aircraft and dining room chairs find their place in individuals' optimal portfolios and *stay there* until something new happens. Thus portfolio theory precludes the kind of equilibrium which characterises the classical conception of money, an equilibrium in which money is continuously circulating from hand to hand in an ever-recurrent pattern. Despite the seas of ink that have been spilled on the subject of the inadmissibility of money in a world where one tatonnement settles everything, Friedman-and-Tobin portfolio theory belongs to just such a world. Once portfolio equilibrium is reached, no further exchange takes place - and there is no need to hold money, even to avoid "risk", for capital gains and losses are irrelevant if not *realised* by sale - i.e. a further exchange.

The logic of the model offers two possibilities: either the equilibrium holds only for the unit period and no-one knows what will happen next (temporary equilibrium), or as protection against a quite spurious risk people hold some money 'till Kingdom come:

> So we are told, without a smile on the face.
> But ... what an insane use to which to put it!
> For it is a recognised characteristic of money as
> as store of wealth that it is barren; whereas
> practically every other form of storing wealth
> yields some interest or profit. Why should any-
> one outside a lunatic asylum wish to use money

as a store of wealth? (Keynes, 1937a, pp.115-16.)

Money in these models only has a chance to circulate in disequilibrium, to restore equilibrium after a monetary increase. It is commonly assumed that the response to a monetary increase is to lower the yield on money relatively to whatever else is included in the portfolio and thus to encourage the "substitution" of those other things for money in the portfolio. For some strange reason, commonsense language is never used at this point: why is it not said that people or firms will *buy* securities or real assets?

This reticence to speak of expenditure and portfolio readjustment in the same breath has been going on for quite a time. Keynes (1911) took Fisher to task for it in his review of the first edition of *The Purchasing Power of Money*. Fisher's rejoinder in the preface to the second edition (1931) is that this means of achieving substitution was, in effect, too obvious to state.

It is not as obvious as all that. Indeed, it is entirely possible for relative rates of return to change *without* any money changing hands. Dealers set security prices in response to their perceptions of the state of the market; they often change without any trading taking place. Similarly the yield on real capital is not entirely objective; it varies as much with the expectations of the owner as with the assets' market prices. And the market prices of assets vary with the expectations held by their suppliers, who may change prices as much in anticipation of demand as in response to it.

The allegation that portfolio theory does not model money as circulating (in disequilibrium) is reinforced when one looks at the same theories in the context of an excess *demand* for money. In the opposite, customary context, that of excess supply, it is easy to imagine excess balances being spent on assets, even if this expenditure need not follow logically. However, the indivisibility and poor marketability of many assets makes it quite implausible to suggest converting these things back into money when one's putty turns to clay. Durable goods can be sold at knock-down prices, to be sure, and the fall in prices will increase the real value of the existing money stock, but people are unlikely to do this every time they want a bit more money, reversing the decision when the situation changes - "as if a farmer, having tapped his barometer after breakfast, could decide to remove his capital from the farming business between 10 and 11 in the morning and reconsider whether he should return to it later in the week." (Keynes, 1936, p.151.)[9]

b. *Tobin in particular*

Tobin gets around this absurdity by equating shares to real capital, for one can sell equities easily. As individuals try to realise them for money, their value falls - but at least money actually circulates in the process. This device of treating equities as if they were of the same form and substance as the real capital they supposedly represent is, however, nothing but a sleight of hand. In the real world when a business firm is faced with a cash flow problem the solution is hardly to be found in "substituting real capital for money", nor would the firm be heartened or helped by the knowledge that its shares are falling on the market.[10]

So the story that money circulates in asset markets is not convincing. If further evidence is needed, we have Tobin's explicit statement (1969, p.334) that the significance of money in capital-account adjustment owes nothing to its medium-of-exchange function.[11]

Furthermore, any circulation of money which may be occurring in the consumption sphere is implicit and inconsequential. In Tobin's models, quite explicitly, the dichotomy between the "portfolio", however rich, and flows of income and expenditure is absolute. An early model (Tobin 1961) is concerned with the capital account only. Where the income account is included in the model (e.g. Brainard and Tobin, 1968), the capital account is insulated from it: changes in the rate of saving do not disturb portfolio balance, because of the assumption of homogeneity of degree one in wealth of the asset demands. Similarly, while real assets might be "substituted for money" to restore portfolio equilibrium, substitution between money and consumer goods is not permitted. Consumption belongs to the flow sector of the model and is insulated from capital-account events.

The assumption of the dichotomy of saving and portfolio balance is, of course, truly Keynesian. So, for that matter, is the insulation of consumption from the direct effect of a money-supply change. In Keynes's model, however, the rate of interest is important because it indicates the incentive required to bring idle money into circulation as it is borrowed to finance investment.[12] In portfolio theory, this circulation is missing - as it must be, for the circulation which might occur amongst members of the private sector is debarred by the consolidation of that sector into a single aggregate.[13] So we have the irony that the Keynesian result - money works by affecting interest and investment - is derived from a theory with a very un-Keynesian view of money, by the device of restricting the assets for which money is a substitute for capital goods.

c. The "New Quantity Theory"

In claiming the Quantity Theory as his antecedent, Friedman sees the link to Fisher, Ricardo, Thornton and Keynes (whom he cites specifically) in that they "pay no attention to the effect on the rate of interest of shifts in the demand for money" and "minimize changes in market interest rates as the primary channel through which changes in the quantity of money affect spending, output and prices" (1972, p.945).

These properties are either conclusions, which tell us nothing about the nature of the theories which generate them, or they are properties which are simply assumed (to protect "neutrality") rather than derived. (The use of the terms "pay no attention" and "minimize" suggest this.) Friedman's claim is a prime example of the kind of superficial association of which I complained in the Introduction.

Friedman's "Restatement of the Quantity Theory" (1956), which is the basis of a major strand of Monetarist theory, presents a paradox: while the hallmark of Old Quantity Theory is that money is modelled as continually circulating, Friedman's Quantity Theory is a model of money held. Friedman himself stresses the portfolio character of his model, distinguishing it from that of the Keynesians by claiming greater breadth and generality.

It is not obvious what is to be gained by the monetarists in taking up the portfolio approach. It would be easy to accede to the proposition that if people are given[14] more money, or if their money-incomes rise, they are likely to spend a larger amount of money than formerly. That is what one might call Commonsense Monetarism. But it is far from obvious that this is what Monetarists have in mind. In their use of the portfolio approach, the circulation of money in exchange, even for assets, is hard to find, and the link between money and expenditure is, to say the least, indirect.

As before, common sense suggests that "substitution" entails the use of money as a medium of exchange in the *purchase* of assets. Confirmation that this is the meaning intended is offered, e.g. by Friedman (1972, p.910):

> We, on the other hand, stress a much broader and more "direct" impact on spending, saying ... that individuals seeking to dispose of what they regard as their excess money balances ... will try to pay out a larger sum for the purchase of securities, goods and services, for the repayment of debts, and as gifts than they are receiving from the corresponding sources.

If this is the mechanism intended, it would be well to say so, for many have complained that the monetarists do not explain "the mechanism" by which money affects the economy, and faced with a description like the following, from Friedman and Meiselman (1963, p.218), one can see why:

> The ... "monetary" view can be expressed in terms of interest rates and balance sheets only by taking a much different, and broader view. It is necessary to regard households as themselves enterprises holding physical assets which they use to produce services that they consume themselves. An interest rate is a pure number relating the price of services acquired by households as being connected by an interest rate to the source that yields it.
>
> ... On this ... view, the conception of assets is as broad as the conception of expenditures ... That is why there is such a close link between the "monetary" view and the quantity-theory approach.

Common sense interprets this passage as a way of bringing in consumption expenditure. But once again it is entirely possible for all the effects on relative rates of return to go through *without* any money changing hands. There is, indeed, an additional reason for suspecting this:

Friedman's definition of consumption follows Fisher[15] - it is identified as the services yielded by goods. Insofar as goods are durable, therefore, and already owned by households, consumption can take place without any expenditure at all. Clearly all that Friedman and Meiselman's household-enterprises need do to restore portfolio equilibrium is convene a meeting and revalue their assets.

3. *Old Quantity Theory*

Old Quantity Theory, in contrast, generates its link between money and expenditure from its theory of the properties of and the demand for money. While Quantity theorists differ in many respects, money is always modelled as *circulating*. This follows from the theory's first premise: that money has no use-value[16] and is, therefore, only held as a means to an end. Holdings of money balances in this theory are akin to what accountants call a "suspense account" - an account which serves as a way-station for funds destined for other uses.

In the modern expositions of Old Quantity Theory the "other uses" tend to be exclusively goods and services: Quantity Theory is represented as the simplest form of the transactions demand for money.

Make the reasonable assumption that the purchase of goods (which equals consumption if (i) the goods are not very durable or (ii) if we take Keynes's definition - consumers' expenditure) goes on virtually continously, whether in a steady stream or irregularly, but in an amount which is stable and predictable over the period between receipts of income. Inflows of cash, chiefly from the sale of labour, are also predictable both in amount and in interval: the interval defines the "income period".[17] In these circumstances the individual holds a fluctuating balance of cash for transactions purposes: it rises to equal the whole of his weekly or monthly income and falls to the bedrock of his precautionary balances, held in case the regularities which we have assumed, fail to hold in practice. His average balance over the income period will depend on the size of his income and the timing of payments. Increase the moneyflow to all individuals and - assuming they are satisfied with their precautionary balances - each will spend more, for there is no point in holding the extra money, as it has no utility except for what it will buy.

That is the foundation for the "direct effect" of increases in the quantity of money on the volume of expenditure.

This model of circulating money has implications for the specification of the transactions demand for money. As Tsiang (1966) insisted, in opposition to the treatment in *Value and Capital* (Hicks, 1939), in the absence of perfect knowledge of the timing of receipts and payments, the amount of money held for transactions purposes by an individual at any particular point of time is just an accidental consequence of the timing of receipts and expenditures. It does not follow, however, that transactions balances are not volitional, that is, not demanded;[18] the concept of transactions demand is perfectly cogent when specified as an average over time, even though the level of those balances is continually fluctuating.

The important thing to notice is that unless the exact timing of all purchases and receipts is known, so that each day's transactions balances may be planned and held intentionally, transactions demand cannot be formulated as a *stock* demand at a *point* of time. An appeal to the literature, which is full of stock demand functions, leaves me unmoved.

The fact that the concept of transactions demand only makes sense over time is part of the reason why it has been treated so badly in the neo-classical systhesis, which does its best to abolish time: a stock approach reduces time to a point. There seems to be a difficulty in comprehending or accepting a *demand* for something which is relinquished so readily; nor, despite all those diagrams of circular flow, are we comfortable with an equilibrium in which there is continual movement - the circulation of money.[19] In modern theory, income is a flow and money a stock; the fact that income *comes in* as a cash flow is not allowed to affect thinking on this matter.

It is the stock approach to transactions demand which *ought*, in fact, to make one uneasy, for the end-of-period demand (if we knew where the end was) is zero for an individual and equal to expected outpayments for firms. What do the aggregate empirical estimates measure?

As a result of the shift from a flow to a stock conception of the role of money, the quantity theory became associated with the idea, embodied in the static treatment of the real balance effect in Patinkin (1956), that expenditure was uniquely related to the *stock* of money in existence. One finds that several of those who gave evidence to the Radcliffe Committee (1958)[20] felt the need to refute this idea.

The stock conception is I think also partly responsible for recent emphasis amongst monetarists on the rate of *growth* of the money supply: it is a way of ensuring that money is seen as continually entering the private sector, even if its movement thereafter is doubtful. It also goes some way to explaining the extreme view that Friedman takes of Keynes and Keynesians over "absolute liquidity preference":[21]

> I [Friedman] believe that only a finding of near-absolute liquidity preference would raise "fundamental" issues [in monetary] theory and that any other finding would not. (1966, p.144.)

Absolute liquidity preference prevents any new money from circulating, absolutely: changes in M have no effect - on r *or* Y - whereas if the elasticity of demand for speculative balances is less than infinite, at least *some* of that money circulates, however sluggishly, and money matters, however little.

Before turning to Keynes, a moment should be spent on the Quantity Theory view of the circulation of money which was not held for current purchases. Quantity theorists assumed that it was not rational to hold money idle except for the short time between receipt and expenditure. The rest would be put at interest, either directly or through banks and other intermediaries, which also do not hold money idle. Thus in the classical conception, money saved passes through the capital markets to borrowers, who spend it immediately and return it to circulation in the commodity sphere.

This theory, which (with some looseness?) may be called a loanable funds theory, is over-optimistic,[22] for the act of purchasing financial claims does not necessarily constitute lending: only if *newly-issued* securities are purchased does money reach borrowers, and hence move from the financial to the commodity sphere. If existing securities are purchased by current savers from previous holders, the net effect on demand is nil where sellers of securities spend all their proceeds: their dissaving and current saving are matched. Usually, of course, some of the proceeds are re-invested, but to this negative effect on goods-demand there is the counter-weight of new borrowing, the proceeds of which are spent.

As mentioned earlier, there is no trace of the idea of borrowing or the issue of new securities in either Friedman's or Tobin's version of portfolio theory: indeed, there cannot be such within the private sector, as its members' balance sheets are consolidated for aggregate analysis. It must be concluded that neither theory shares the property of money circulating, either for goods or for financial assets. So much for Old Quantity Theory. Tobin might be relieved, but surely Friedman has something to explain.

4. Keynes

Now we come to Keynes - the Keynes of the *General Theory*.[23] As with so much else in that book his view is not entirely consistent, in a way that is itself revealing.

Looking first at his theory of the demand for money, we note that he took over Marshall's transactions demand[24] without fuss[25] and, as Marshall counts as a Quantity Theorist, we might as well accept that money was modelled as circulating in exchange for goods and labour services.[26] It is in the financial sphere that Keynes differs from the Quantity Theory, and for a purpose - to refute Say's Law. To do this, it had to be shown that money could be withdrawn from circulation and held idle, not just temporarily, while awaiting imminent use in the purchase of commodities or investments, but in significant volume for a significant period of time. The only justification for holding money idle which to him made sense was that there were times when the return to be obtained from putting money at interest was in danger of being destroyed by capital losses.

The interest rate influences the demand for money in Keynes not as its opportunity cost but as a proxy for the expectation of changes in the rate in the near future: the higher the current rate, the greater the preponderance of opinion that it is likely soon to fall. Those who hold securities which they expect to fall in value do not diversify - they "plunge" - into money, a capital-safe asset.[27] Since people's expectations differ, *some* money is likely to be thus held idle, in aggregate, over a wide range of interest rates. This demand for money is an unwillingness to hold financial assets whose value varied with the interest rate,[28] not an "unwillingness to hold the existing capital stock," as Tobin would have it.

The extent of this unwillingness determined the criterion which an investment project had to equal, but if the return or investment failed to meet the test, it was the entrepreneurs who were unwilling to expand the capital stock - or even, perhaps, maintain it. Alternatively, liquidity preference determines the cost of borrowing, as new securities must compete with those already existing. By this device of separating transactions from the flow of new demands for and supplies of loanable funds, Keynes sharpened the contrast with the then prevailing orthodoxy, in which saving was not a withdrawal but continued to circulate by providing loan capital.

If new securities did successfully compete, money would circulate through borrowing, back into the spending stream. Keynes, however, played this down, perhaps to maintain his sharp contrast with loanable-funds theory. In Chapters 11, 12, 13 and 17, he analyses money's role in an entirely portfolio-theoretic way, with the exception of the second sentence of Chapter 13, where borrowing breaks into the discussion. The whole treatment of the financing of investment is cursory: the finance motive for holding money does not appear in the book, but in a later article (Keynes, 1937 b).

Add to this playing-down of borrowing the concentration on the innovation in liquidity preference theory (speculation) at the expense of what Keynes could assume was old hat (transactions) and you have the foundations of the sort of "stagnant pool" theory of money of which I have been complaining.

The development of portfolio-theory out of Keynes, while understandable, is not, however, legitimate. The quotation cited earlier fully indicates Keynes's scorn for the idea that money had a *permanent* place in an individual's portfolio: he would have rejected totally the diversification demand of portfolio theory. No *individual* devotes funds to financial investments forever,[29] certainly not to money holdings. Speculative money balances are held until expectations change or the money is wanted for transactions in goods, whichever is earlier. To an individual, one of these two things will happen eventually. With enough time, interest rates do not even have to change for idle balances to be disgorged: if a given interest rate were to persist for a long period, it would come to be regarded by everyone as "normal" and the speculative demand for money would disappear. The only legitimate *full-equilibrium* demand for money is the demand for money which circulates - precisely what modern theory, despite its obsession with equilibrium, ignores!

Although Keynes regarded his additive specification of the demand for money as nothing but a simplification,[30] it was, perhaps quite a good idea, for the dimensions in which the transactions and speculative demands should be measured are not commensurate. Beyond the technical point of measurement, there are differences in the postulated *response* of transactions and speculative demands which also reflects conflicting time horizons: transactions balances, average holdings over time, respond gradually to changes in income, a flow which takes time to accrue, while speculative holdings, a stock demand, can move in and out of securities markets virtually instantaneously. Keynes's additive formulation avoided a direct confrontation of the different time horizons involved, but his theory of the transmission mechanism was much influenced by their existence.

Keynes's Transmission Mechanism

One cannot blame Keynes's interpreters for taking him at his uncompromising word:

> The primary effect of a change in the quantity of money on the quantity of effective demand is through its influence on the rate of interest. (1936, p.298.)

Let us see how he arrives at this conclusion. Unfortunately the relevant passage is quite long (1936, p.200):

> [If] changes in M are due to Government printing money wherewith to meet its current expenditure ... the new money accrues as someone's income. The new level of income, however, will not continue sufficiently high for the requirements of M_1
>
> [transaction and precautionary balances] to absorb the whole of the increase in M; and some

> portion of the money will seek an outlet in buying securities or other assets until r has fallen so as to bring about an increase in the magnitude of M_2 [speculative balances] and at the same time to stimulate a rise in Y to such an extent that the new money is absorbed either in M_2 or in the M_1 which corresponds to the rise in Y caused by the fall in r. Thus at one remove this case comes to the same thing as the alternative case, where the new money can only be issued in the first instance by a relaxation of the conditions of credit by the banking system, so as to induce someone to sell the banks a debt or a bond in exchange for the new cash.

On the face of it, this is a very strange passage. Although it begins with the statement "... [the] relation of changes in M to Y and r depends, in the first instance, on the way in which changes in M come about", Keynes ends by seeming to say it makes little difference. Plainly it makes a difference in the initial stages: in the first example, the printing of money enabled the government to make an income-generating expenditure; in the second, the banks lower lending rates to encourage borrowing. A concern with the impact effect yields the Monetarist or Keynesian transmission mechanism depending on the mode of introducing new money into the economy, but the passage following "at the same time" suggests that more than impact effects are involved.

Despite appearances, Keynes's first example does not allow of Monetarist interpretation, at least not that of Commonsense Monetarism. In the second sentence, the possibility arises that the now-larger money supply could stimulate spending. But no: M_1 balances adjust passively to the income change: even when money is exogenously supplied, income, not money, determines spending, and M_1 balances are acquired only as needed to *facilitate* spending.

It follows that with a direct effect of money on spending disallowed, the weight of money's influence on income falls on what happens when the excess of money over transactions needs finds its way into securities markets and affects r. The cases "come to the same thing" for the very reason that the money aspect of income is ignored when speaking of spending.

In one sense this way of thinking is fair enough. Whoever got the money had to work for it; it came into the system to pay for some income-creating transactions. So it can be analysed as equivalent to a rise in wages, employment, or profits, and the behavioural postulates involving expenditure are unaffected. And it forestalls such silliness as including an excess supply of money variable in expenditure functions along with income. But it is ironic that in a book which goes far to integrate money and the real sector, Keynes, in taking the hyphen out of money-income, began the separation of stocks and flows which in Tobin is explicit and complete, and encouraged discussions (and *implementations*) of "demand management" policies without regard to their financial consequences - a flaw we needed Monetarism to point out. It would not have happened if the *basis* of transactions demand in the fact of the circulation of money had been kept at the forefront of our thinking.

Circulation of funds through borrowing has survived rather better, if not at Yale. Despite the lack of emphasis Keynes gave to the interest rate as a cost of keeping funds moving in financial markets, some interpreters have placed such a strong emphasis on this aspect[31] that Friedman and Meiselman identify the "Keynesian" view as the "credit" approach. It is interesting to look at it through their eyes:

> The ... "credit" view ... typically concentrates attention on paper claims dealt in on reasonably well organized markets or created and held by recognized financial institutions: government securities, open market commercial paper, industrial bonds and equities; loans by commercial banks, insurance companies, and other financial intermediaries; real estate mortgages, and the like. These claims are as a class precisely the ones used to finance the kinds of expenditure that are generally included in autonomous expenditures: government deficits, residential construction, business investment in plant, equipment and inventories. This is why there is such a close link between the "credit" view and the income-expenditure approach. (1963, p.218.)

The gross unsuitability of some of the listed paper claims as vehicles for speculation shows that the portfolio aspect of Keynes has almost disappeared. Apart from that, however, the description is spot-on and brings us nicely to Radcliffe. Before going on, dare I make the obvious point that autonomous expenditures are autonomous partly because they, unlike consumption, are not financed out of money-income?

5. *Radcliffe, for a moment*

Compare the treatment of financial markets in the Radcliffe Report (1958). Rather than concentrate on existing financial assets as transmitters of monetary impulses, as Keynes did, Radcliffe denied any importance to the stock of money, while being passionately concerned with its velocity - velocity not in the commodity sphere, which would have been too suggestive of Quantity Theory, but, through credit institutions, in the financial sphere. Hence we have the irony that while vigorously anti-Quantity Theory in its orientation and conclusions, Radcliffe shares with it the explicit concern with money circulating: money flowing from lenders to borrowers finances expenditure which in the absence of these flows would not take place. There are portfolio elements in Radcliffe as well: the ability of financial institutions to grant credit depends ultimately on the willingness of the public to hold those institutions' liabilities.[32] Thus the portfolio choice in Radcliffe influences spending through its influence on the balance sheets of lending institutions - quite a different framework from the other theories we have discussed.

III SUMMARY AND CONCLUSION

As a Summary, the Figure gives a visual interpretation of the verbal presentation of Sections 2 to 5. Symbols should be obvious except L for lending, E for equities, FI for financial intermediaries, and C*, stocks of durable goods which produce the services called, in Friedman's scheme, consumption. Horizontal placements of symbols connected by arrows indicate portfolio choices; spheres of circulation are indicated by circuits linking vertically displaced variables. Important links are drawn bold.

In the (old) Quantity Theory, money-income circulates in

FIGURE

Quantity Theory
all flows

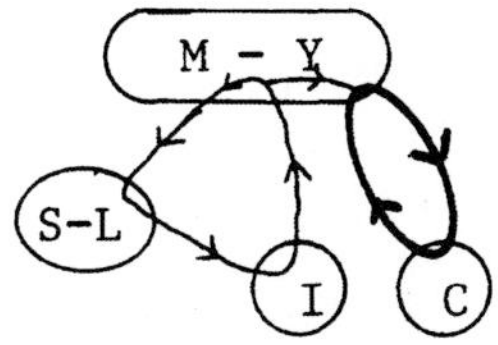

Keynes
stock-flow

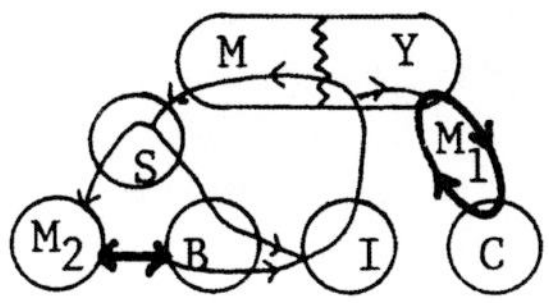

IS-LM
stock-flow

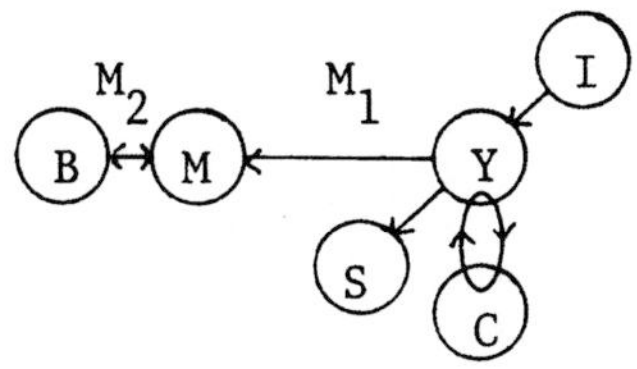

Tobin-Brainard
stock-flow

not in Tobin (1961)

Radcliffe
stock-flow

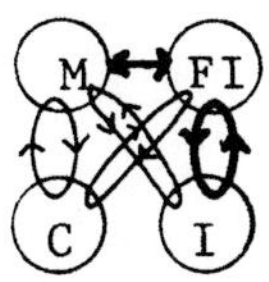

Friedman
all stock

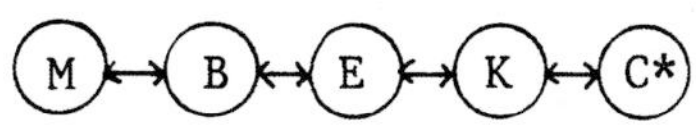

exchange for consumer goods and, circulating through financial markets, finances investment; it thus affects both interest and prices. Ultimately, only prices are affected, because the purchase of goods is the ultimate use of money.

Keynes's theory establishes a border between money and income. Their only direct link is the transactions demand for money. Expenditure is affected by money if and only if money comes into the system as income, and then the monetary aspect of the transaction is suppressed: the classical circulation of money becomes the circular flow of income facilitated by M_1 balances. Any effect of money, *as* money, on income is indirect, operating through its action in the financial sphere. Thus the Keynesian transmission mechanism emerges. Even *fiscal policy* financed by new money, has the $M \rightarrow r$ connection built into it, though it occurs as a post-impact effect. Money ceases to circulate and have its effects as and when *and for as long as* it is held as M_2 balances. The Keynesian transmission mechanism applies in a more obvious way to the case of open market operations. The difference with the Monetarists arises from Keynes's correct modelling of the holding of funds (M_2 balances *and* bonds) as consisting of a surplus of money-income over what was required for current purchases of goods, while Monetarists suggest that the money introduced by an open market purchase may find its way into the goods market.

In the ISLM version of Keynes, stocks and flows are further disconnected, as there is no relationship between saving and investment, and assets; this reflects the absence of money circulating by means of borrowing and lending, leaving only the implicit circulation of M_1 balances.

The Yale model, in the more complete version (e.g. Tobin and Brainard, 1968), shows complete bifurcation into stocks and flows. The primacy of investment in the transmission mechanism is maintained by the narrowness of the portfolio, though the possibility of its operating through equity prices rather than bond prices is "opened up". (It is argued in the body of the paper that this possibility was never absent in Keynes.)

Radcliffe is not a complete theory. Its chief elements are the portfolio choice between money and financial intermediaries' liabilities and the finance, chiefly through these intermediaries, of all types of expenditure. The Keynesian link to income via investment is retained by virtue of the fact that borrowed finance is more often required for investment than for consumption.

Friedman, like Tobin and Keynes, has generated many models. Here, as in the verbal analysis, I take the "Restatement" to be the underlying model. The transformation to a stock theory is complete: even C* is not consumption, for that needn't have much to do with whether one holds money or not. In Friedman, holding money is an alternative to holding the durables which *generate* consumption. Money in this model can go everywhere - if it goes anywhere at all. Thus money influences income as a whole, not just investment.

In conclusion: no theory is so simple as to be capable of description by a single attribute; the frequent need for reference to other elements of analytical structure than the one discussed here is proof enough of that. It is not claimed that this detailed examination of one element is an adequate basis for understanding in full how the theories of transmission are generated. But the exercise would be pointless if the distinction between money circulating and resting tells us nothing. The conclusion that I draw is one which should make biologists happy: namely that hybrids are usually more robust animals. The weakness of classical pure-flow loanable funds theory is probably better understood and more widely accepted than what I believe to be the equally extreme weakness of pure-stock portfolio theory. Yet I am not convinced that Keynes's hybrid is quite the right mixture: his construction is tailored too closely, perhaps, to the need to refute classical theory and to take account of the turbulent stock market behaviour which had immediately preceded the writing of the *General Theory*, and the inadequate integration of the financing of investment into a full macroeconomic theory still needs remedying. Of the theories discussed here, Radcliffe is an alternative hybrid, but it may in fact be time to breed another.

REFERENCES

Brainard, W.C. and J. Tobin (1968). Pitfalls in Financial Model Building. Reprinted in Tobin (1971).

Brunner, K. (1968). The Role of Money and Monetary Policy. Federal Reserve Bank of St. Louis *Review*, July; 9-14.

Brunner, K. and Meltzer, A.H. (1972). Money, Debt and Economic Activity; *Journal of Political Economy* 80; pp. 951-977.

Chick, V. (1973). *The Theory of Monetary Policy*. Gr y-Mills, London (2nd edition Basil Blackwell, Oxford 1977).

Chick, V. (1978). Keynesians, Monetarists and Keynes: The End of the Debate - or a Beginning? *Thames Papers in Political Economy*, Thames Polytechnic, London.

Fisher, I. (1931). *The Purchasing Power of Money*. 2nd edition, Macmillan, New York.

Foster, J. (1978). The Demand for Money: A Critique of the Theory and a Reinterpretation of the Evidence. Mimeographed, University of Glasgow.

Friedman, M. (1956). The Quantity Theory of Money: A Restatement. Reprinted in Friedman (1969).

Friedman, M. (1958). The Supply of Money and Changes in Prices and Output. Reprinted in Friedman (1969).

Friedman, M. (1966). Interest Rates and the Demand for Money. Reprinted in Friedman (1969).

Friedman, M. (1968). The Role of Monetary Policy. Reprinted in Friedman (1969).

Friedman, M. (1969). *The Optimum Quantity of Money*. Macmillan, London.

Friedman, M. (1972). Comments on the Critics. *Journal of Political Economy* 80, September/October; 906-950.

Friedman, M. and D. Meiselman (1963). The Relative Stability of Monetary Velocity and the Investment Multiplier in the United States. In Commission on Money and Credit, *Stabilization Policies*. Prentice-Hall, Englewood Cliffs, N.J.

Friedman, M. and A.J. Schwartz (1963). Money and Business Cycles. Reprinted in Friedman (1969).

Hahn, F.H. (1980). Monetarism and Economic Theory. *Economica* 80, February; 1-17.

Hicks, J.R. (1939). *Value and Capital*. The Clarendon Press, Oxford.

Hicks, J.R. (1967). *Critical Essays in Monetary Theory*. The Clarendon Press, Oxford.

Hume, D. (1752). Of Money. In E. Rotwein, ed., *David Hume: Writings on Economics*. Nelson, London, 1955.

Johnson, H.G. (1962). Monetary Theory and Policy. *American Economic Review* 52, June; 335-84.

Johnson, H.G. (1970). Recent Developments in Monetary Theory - A Commentary, in D.R. Croome and H.G. Johnson, eds., (1970), *Money in Britain, 1959-1969*. Oxford University Press.

Keynes, J.M. (1911). Review of I. Fisher, *The Purchasing Power of Money*, *Economic Journal* 21, September; 393-8.

Keynes, J.M. (1936). *The General Theory of Employment, Interest and Money*. Macmillan, London.

Keynes, J.M. (1937a). The General Theory of Employment. Reprinted in *The Collected Writings of J.M. Keynes*, Volume XIV; 108-123. Macmillan, London, 1973.

Keynes, J.M. (1937b). Alternative Theories of the Rate of Interest. Reprinted in *The Collected Writings*, *op.cit.*, Volume XIV; 201-223.

Laidler, D.E.W. (1978). Money and Money-Income: An Essay on the Transmission Mechanism. *Journal of Monetary Economics* 4; 151-191.

Leijonhufvud, A. (1968). *On Keynesian Economics and the Economics of Keynes*. Oxford University Press, London.

Mann, M. (1968). How Does Monetary Policy Affect the Economy? *Federal Reserve Bulletin*, October; 803-814.

Marshall, A. (1923). *Money, Credit and Commerce*. Macmillan, London.

Mayer, T. (1978). *The Structure of Monetarism*. Norton, London.

Morgan, B. (1978). *Monetarists and Keynesians: Their Contribution to Monetary Theory.* Macmillan, London.

Modigliani, F. (1977). The Monetarist Controversy, or Should We Forsake Stabilisation Policy. *American Economic Review* 67, March; 1-19.

Park, Y.C. (1972). Some Current Issues in the Transmission Process of Monetary Policy. *International Monetary Fund Staff Papers* 19, March; 1-45.

Patinkin, D. (1956). *Money, Interest and Prices.* Harper and Row, New York.

Patinkin, D. (1972). Friedman on The Quantity Theory and Keynesian Economics. *Journal of Political Economy* 80, September/October; 864-882.

Radcliffe Committee (Committee on the Working of the Monetary System) (1959). *Report* (Cmd. 837), and *Memoranda of Evidence.* HMSO, London.

Robertson, D.H. (1922). *Money.* Cambridge University Press.

Robertson, D.H. (1940). Mr. Keynes and the Rate of Interest. Chapter 1 of *Essays in Monetary Theory.* P.S. King & Son, London.

Sayers, R.S. (1960). Monetary Thought and Monetary Policy in England. *Economic Journal* 70, December; 710-724.

Spencer, R.W. (1974). Channels of Monetary Influence: A Survey. Federal Reserve Bank of St. Louis *Review,* November; 8-26.

Stein, J. (1976). *Monetarism.* North-Holland, Amsterdam.

Termini, V. (1978). Keynes on Finance. Mimeographed.

Tobin, J. (1961). Money, Capital and Other Stores of Value. Reprinted in Tobin (1971).

Tobin, J. (1969). A General Equilibrium Approach to Monetary Theory. Reprinted in Tobin (1971).

Tobin, J. (1971). *Essays in Economics,* Volume 1: *Macroeconomics.* North-Holland, Amsterdam.

Tobin, J. (1972). Friedman's Theoretical Framework. *Journal of Political Economy*, Volume 80.

Tobin, J. and W.C. Brainard (1963). Financial Intermediaries and the Effectiveness of Monetary Controls. Reprinted in Tobin (1971).

Townsend, M.I. (1968). The Quantity Theory of Money. Mimeographed, University of Southampton.

Tsiang, S.C. (1966). Walras' Law, Say's Law and Liquidity Preference in General Equilibrium Analysis. *International Economic Review* 7, September; 329-345.

FOOTNOTES

1. The author wishes to thank Michael Danes for helpful discussions and anonymous referees for their comments, and to acknowledge the usefulness, in a way too general for specific citations within the paper, of unpublished papers by John Foster (1978), Maurice Townsend (1968) and Valeria Termini (1978).
2. Many believe, or at any rate say, that there are *no* genuine theoretical differences, that everyone, despite superficial differences, subscribes to the same model (e.g. ISLM plus an expectations-augmented Phillips curve). Those who hold that view can only conclude that the differences to be resolved are purely empirical. If that is the case, theoretical controversy is wasteful; energy should be directed entirely to empirical work based on agreed criteria. Others have argued that the issue is the role of government (e.g. Modigliani, 1977) or that what divides the two camps is their world-view (e.g. Mayer, 1978). Hahn (1980), however, is still looking to theory for explanation.
3. Just what the Quantity Theory was or has become, is, I think, not at all clear.
4. For a survey of this development see Johnson (1962).
5. Cf. Park (1972, p.5.): "... the Keynesian analysis considers only substitution between money and bonds important, but ignores entirely the substitutability between money and real assets or real expenditures."
6. Robertson (1940, p.12.): "... Mr. Keynes was so taken up with the fact that people sometimes acquire money to *hold* it that he had apparently all but forgotten

the more familiar fact that they often acquire it in order to *use* it." (only "often"? - VC)

7. Here we impinge on other elements of analytical structure. It cannot be helped, as they are not entirely independent.
8. Multi-period portfolio theory exists, but it is not used in monetary policy discussions.
9. And how does one cash in one's stock of human capital? One can pay money to take a training course, but one cannot unlearn something to realise its value. One may re-value one's "present value" - that is, regret having taken the course; but one is not paid for regret.
10. The usual defence of the asymmetry brought about by assets' poor marketability is to say that one borrows on the strength of future income or uses durable assets as collateral. This is, assuredly, more realistic than supposing that portfolio reorganisation must involve forced sales, but there are problems with this defence, nonetheless. Firstly, it is the only place in the story where borrowing and lending are allowed to enter (activity on securities markets is apparently in already-existing assets), and a theory that you borrow to realise the cash value of assets but never to buy them is hardly satisfactory. Secondly, if capital markets were as perfect as a symmetrical application of the theory would require, it is difficult to imagine the need for money at all.
11. It is interesting that money's medium of exchange function is so played down by both Tobin (*op.cit.*) and Brunner and Meltzer (e.g. 1972) despite their earlier contributions to the theory of transactions demand.
12. This is beautifully analysed in terms of "monetary" and "credit" mechanisms by Friedman and Meiselman (1963).
13. This fact is particularly jarring (though true nonetheless) in a model which places the entire weight on the "supply price of capital". This phrase seems (and certainly ought) to mean the price at which loanable funds can be obtained.
14. The "helicopter" ensures that as a consequence of getting more money no one has less of something else - or has to work.
15. In raising this point we again touch on another element of analytical structure from that currently under discussion.
16. Some seem to find this assumption odd, given that the theory was current in the time of metallic money. Surely, they say, gold and silver have use-value in industry

and the arts. Precisely. When not being used as money, the monetary metals do have use-value; when they are minted, and become money, their utility lies not in their metallic properties but in their ability to command other commodities - their exchange-value. The utility of liquidity services is the modern term for exchange value, although it is used in an attempt to restore a sense of use-value to money, for reasons too deep to explore here.

17. In the reverse pattern experienced by firms, the date of wage payments defines the period.
18. This conclusion is in answer to a quite different question to that raised by Hicks (1967, Chapter 1) in his challenge to the volitional content of transactions demand. Hicks's question was not whether balances are held by accident or by design, but rather whether they are held by choice or by necessity.
19. Somewhat to my astonishment, the objection has been put to me that since money *is* a stock and is *measured* as a stock, both the demand for money and monetary equilibrium must be of a stock dimension. Now, the water in one's central heating system is also a stock and measured as a stock, but one would not, I think, say that the system was in equilibrium only when the water stopped flowing and was all "willingly held" by various radiators and the tank. It is easy to agree that the system is not in equilibrium when the stock of water is rising, but that was not, I think, my objector's point.
20. See, e.g. the evidence of Dow, Kahn and Kaldor.
21. See also Friedman (1972).
22. Though perhaps not for its time, when secondhand markets in claims were not highly developed.
23. There is quite enough to do without exploring the *Treatise* or the *Tract*.
24. Marshall (1923), Chapter 14.
25. He made a slight but potentially significant alteration in separating the transactions demand for money from the precautionary motive. Transactions needs are regular and predictable. Thus money demanded for transactions purposes is continuously circulating and being run down to zero at the end of each income period. (Therefore the notion of an average balance demanded can be applied quite strictly.) Precautionary balances are held against less regular cash flows and enter the commodity circulation sporadically. Thus they are

typically positive even at the end of the income period. For those who define equilibrium in terms of end-of-period stocks this feature is very comforting. Apparently only Robertson (1940, p.p. 25-6) has made use of this point.

26. Marshall's exposition *can* be seen as portfolio-theoretic, but not in the sense of this paper.
27. Much has been made of the fact that speculators would be better advised to hold interest-bearing deposits and short-term assets. I urge those who find this a telling criticism to keep in mind that the significance of the speculative demand lies in its implications for long-term interest rates, which influence investment; then to have a look at Keynes (1936), p.167, n.1; and also to consider whether the rates of interest on short term assets at the time Keynes was writing (3 month Treasury bills ran at an annual rate of considerably less than one per cent from 1933 to 1938) were worth chasing, or even safe from capital loss themselves, given the speculator's time horizon.
28. Equities could (I think should) be included along with "bonds". Keynes analysed them along marginal efficiency lines, as if they were real capital, a retrogression from the *Treatise*. The change of method is explained in Keynes (1936), p.151.
29. To account for the behaviour of the rich, call a bequest an expenditure.
30. "Money held for each of the three purposes forms, nevertheless, a single pool ... The same sum can be held primarily for one purpose and secondarily for another. Thus we can - equally well and perhaps better - consider the individual's aggregate demand for money in given circumstances as a single decision, through the composite result of a number of different motives." (Keynes 1936, p.195.)
31. Some have even been accused, for their pains, of ignoring the effects of changes in r on asset valuations - a reflection of the separation in thinking between the portfolio approach to asset choice and the flow-of-funds approach to the investment decision, though they are the same when properly formulated.
32. This aspect was confusing; it led to Radcliffe being thought a variant of portfolio theory. See, e.g., Johnson (1970).

8. PROBLEMS AND RESOLUTIONS OF PROBLEMS CONCERNING THE SHORT RUN DEMAND FOR MONEY

George A. Akerlof

This paper is a discussion of the conventional demand for money. It points out that there are problems both with the standard Keynesian view and the standard monetarist view of the demand for money. A framework is posited for considering the demand for money quite generally; this framework is then applied in four separate ways to solve the problems both of Keynesians and monetarists. These solutions leave yet a final problem of their own concerning the demand for money; this final problem is the subject of current research. The direction of that research, which is implicit in our general approach to money demand, will be indicated. This paper summarises one paper of my own (1979) and four papers which I have written jointly with Ross Milbourne (1978, 1979, 1980a, 1980b). As such it makes no original contribution; but as a general summary it gives the unifying thoughts behind these papers: it indicates the problems with conventional theory which caused these papers to be written and the sense in which these papers can be considered a direct outgrowth of these problems.[1]

Part I: Problems with Conventional Demands for Money

A. Problems with Keynesian Demand for Money in Short Run

I begin with problems with the Keynesian demand for money. Nothing stops me from defining money to be M_1. Governments which wish to control the money supply have very specific definitions of M_1 such as currency plus demand deposits, and they must consider such issues as whether vault cash is considered part of M_1 or not. For the level of generality of the discussion in this paper I shall define M_1 to be noninterest bearing forms of assets which are normally used for transactions purposes. The question arises: what determines how much money people hold? or, in the economist's jargon, what is the demand for money?

There has never been any doubt that the demand for money depends on nominal income, although prior to the use of aggregate income as a common concept, this thought was expressed in slightly different ways. If the demand for money depends only on nominal income but on no other variable, and if demand equals supply, a central bank capable of controlling the money supply will also be capable of controlling nominal income; and furthermore, in this regard, no other policy matters.

To the Keynesians, who felt that nominal income depended not only on the money supply, but potentially also on other factors such as government expenditure and taxes, it was a prime necessity to explain why some variable other than nominal income might affect money demand. The Keynesian choice for the second variable was the nominal rate of interest. This is indeed a natural choice since money, as I have defined it, is M_1; anyone who holds M_1 is giving up interest returns on alternative assets, or perhaps borrowing at the rate of interest in order to hold more money. So the rate of interest reflects the opportunity cost of holding money and, as such, can be considered the "price" of money holding; and, as any economist knows, the demand for almost any good is most naturally written as a function of income and its own price (with the prices of other goods perhaps also added).

The Keynesians have given three specific justifications why the demand for money depends on the rate of interest. I will discuss all three of these justifications, and show the problems with all of them, at least for money as I have defined it, as M_1.

Problems with Speculative Demand

First, we have the Keynesian speculative demand. According to Keynes persons have normal long-run expectations regarding the rate of interest; thus, if the rate of interest is low, it will be expected to rise. If the rate of interest is high, it will be expected to fall. In both cases it will tend toward a normal level. The argument continues, the lower the rate of interest the more people expect the rate of interest to rise; and if they expect the rate of interest to rise, they will expect to take capital losses on bonds and other long term assets whose prices vary inversely with the rate of interest. Relatively small increases in the nominal rate of interest will cause capital losses which more than offset premium returns; and thus at low interest rates persons will prefer to hold money to bonds, so as to avoid capital losses, even though the yield on money is absolutely zero. There are at least two faults with this argument; one is absolutely trivial but nevertheless it poses a major difficulty. As long as money is defined as M_1, the argument may explain why persons might hold building society deposits rather than long-term assets (as long as those deposits have positve returns). The argument does not explain why persons prefer noninterest-bearing deposits to interest-bearing deposits of whatever form. As an asset interest-bearing near-monies dominate M_1. Furthermore, it can be noted that the preceding argument applies equally to Tobin's (1958) explanation of money-holding as "behaviour towards risk". As long as there are interest bearing deposits which are riskless and which can be withdrawn at will, they dominate M_1 in any optimal portfolio, irrespective of whether returns are risky or not.

There is another major difficulty with the speculative demand for money. According to the textbook Keynesian story, if the interest rate is low, persons will expect it to rise and therefore they *will* expect to take capital losses on assets. On the contrary, with rational expectations and risk neutrality, the current price of assets will be low reflecting the future expected rises in interest rates - the price of long-term assets falling relative to the price of short-term assets to the point where the expected return on all bonds, long and short is exactly equal.

This point is illustrated with the Pure Expectations Hypothesis of the term structure of interest rates, (whereby the rate of discount on returns received *n* periods in the future is the product of the expected short-term rates of discount in each of the *n* intervening periods.)

Consider an asset with expected payoff of R_1^e in period 1 and R_2^e in period 2. The price of the asset $p(0)$ under the pure expectations hypothesis in period 0 is

$$p(0) = \frac{R_1^e}{1+r_1} + \frac{R_2^e}{(1+r_1)(1+{}_1r_2^e)} \tag{1}$$

where r_1 is the short-term rate of interest from period 0 to period 1 and ${}_1r_2^e$ is the expected short-term rate of interest occurring in period 1 from period 1 to period 2. Consistent with these expectations about payoffs and rates of return, the expected price of this asset in the next period, period 1, is

$$p^e(1) = \frac{R_2^e}{1+{}_1r_2^e} \tag{2}$$

Only a small bit of juggling of (1) and (2) is needed to show that the expected return to holding this asset, which is the sum of the expected coupon R_1^e and expected capital gain $(p^e(1) - p(0))$, is $r_1p(0)$. Thus, as long as the short-term rate of interest is positive, as can be easily observed if true, the expected return on money is less than that on long-term bonds, provided the pure expectations hypothesis describes the term structure of interest rates. Similar conclusions obtain with more complicated term structure hypotheses.

The Integer Constraint Problem

Because of the failure of the speculative demand to explain the interest elasticity of M_1, Keynesians, mindful of the necessity either to scrap their macroeconomics or find an alternative explanation for interest elasticity, have turned to the transactions demand. The most famous papers in this regard are those of Baumol (1952) and Tobin (1956), which derive the interest elasticity of transactions demand in an inventory-theoretic approach. It is commonly believed that the Baumol and Tobin papers are all but identical, both deriving the famous so-called Baumol-Tobin square root formula for the demand for money.

$$M^D = (aY/2r)^{1/2} \qquad (3)$$

where a is transactions cost, Y is nominal income and r is the nominal rate of interest. A glance at Tobin's paper shows that he does not derive a formula, but instead specifies how the demand for money will depend on the parameters a, r and Y, taking into careful account that the number of transactions must be an integer number; either 0 or an integer greater than or equal to two. (In the Tobin framework one transaction is made from money into bonds in the beginning of the period with subsequent withdrawals occurring over the course of the period; for that reason the minimum number of positive transactions is two - one into bonds, one out of bonds.)

It is natural to suppose, as most critics have done, that the "integer-constraints" would make negligible difference to the Baumol formula. In fact, however, if transactions costs are high or interest rates are low, it makes a considerable difference. To illustrate, if the payments period is one month and the interest rate is 6 per cent per year, as used to be the case before the current inflation, and if the cost per transaction is £1, the breakeven level of income for making two transactions is £1,600 per month. In any economy with all households earning less than £1,600 per month, there will be no interest elasticity to the demand for money in the Tobin model in this case; household demand for money is exactly proportional to household income. At current rates of interest, say 16 per cent per year, the income threshold for positive transactions is £500 per month; with current UK incomes and interest rates many persons would be close to a threshold where they should change the number of transactions if interest rates rise or fall. Barro (1976) has discussed conditions which cause Tobin's exact integer approach to give a good approximation to Baumol's square root formula. This occurs only if a significant proportion of the population is above the 0-transaction level of income. It can be concluded that the "Baumol-Tobin" formula gives a good approximation to optimal inventory behaviour in their model so long as interest rates are fairly high and transactions costs are fairly low. On the other hand the Baumol-Tobin model fails to explain the interest elasticity of the demand for money with low interest rates and high transactions costs.

The Long-Run/Short-Run Problem

There is yet another, and in my view more fundamental, difficulty with the Baumol-Tobin interest elasticity of transactions demand. According to Baumol persons choose the optimum number of transactions n to maximize revenue of holding "bonds" net of transactions costs. The formula for this net revenue is

$$R = \tfrac{1}{2}\ ((n-1)/n)rY - na \qquad (4)$$

where R is net revenue.

Consider the consequences for a person at the optimum (or close to it) who fails to change the number of his transactions n in response to changes in the rate of interest. For a person with £2,000 per month at an annual rate of interest of 15 per cent per year and a transactions cost of £1 per transaction, the optimum nonintegral number of transactions is approximately 3.54. (It is given by the formula $(rY/2a)^{1/2}$). The net revenue from engaging in these transactions is £5.43 per month. Suppose the interest rate rises from 15 per cent to 18 per cent. Net revenue, continuing to make the same transactions rises to £7.22 per month at the higher interest rate. Suppose the person exactly adjusted his transactions according to the "Baumol-Tobin" formula to the optimum $(rY/2a)^{1/2}$. My pocket calculator shows that with the optimum number of transactions, approximately 3.87 per month, his net revenue will be £7.25 per month instead of £7.22.

Economics is said to explain human behaviour in terms of natural human greed. In view of the low returns to optimal behaviour in the Baumol model (approximately 3p per month being lost by suboptimality in our example), I conclude that the appeal to greed will not be very strong.

The Baumol formula may serve well to explain the long-run interest elasticity of the demand for money at high interest rates, but in view of the low returns from complete (as opposed to partial) optimisation it does not give a convincing explanation why the demand for money will respond *quickly* - in the short run - to changes in the rate of interest.

The Traditional Quantity Theory

The case just outlined against a short-run interest elasticity to the transactions demand for money was well understood by pre-Keynesians and Keynes himself. According to Irving Fisher, who I consider to be the exemplar of pre-Keynesian monetary theory, persons had habits of payment; from these habits derived an average lag between inpayments and outpayments. Fisher (1911) made a long list of factors which might cause these habits to change. Among these factors was a change in the cost of holding money, and, presumably, the interest lost by not holding alternative assets was one important element in these costs. Fisher's use of the word *habits* implies that although the demand for money may well respond to changes in interest in the long run, it will not respond much in the short run; in the short run the demand for money will be proportional to transactions, the average lag of inpayment following outpayment being fixed by sluggish habits. Aside from difference in style the section of *The General Theory* on the transactions demand for money and the constant relation between income and transactionsdemand could well have been written by Fisher. Basically, neither Fisher nor Keynes felt that the incentives from changing interest rates was sufficiently great to change payments habits noticeably in the short run, and thus the ratio of transactions demand to income would be constant.

Nonconstant Velocity

Following Fisher and Keynes leads to a transactions demand for money which is proportional to income. The additional denial of a speculative demand yields a short-run quantity theory. A short-run quantity theory predicts that velocity changes slowly. On the other hand persons who have examined velocity, Milton Friedman (1959) included, have found that velocity varies with income over the course of the business cycle. Indeed Friedman's chart of velocity in his famous *JPE* article (1959)shows this covariant behaviour for U.S. long-term time series of M_2 and Y. My definition of M is M_1 but that makes little difference in this very robust finding. The simple correlation between detrended velocity and detrended income by almost any definition for these variables is one of the best established facts in economics.

The Coinage Problem

There is yet another difficulty with the constant velocity theory. Consider alternative definitions of money. Suppose that money is defined as *coins*. (Monetary theorists used to debate whether the definition of money should include paper notes, then later bank deposits). The quantity theory logic about "habits" and average lag between receipt and expenditure applies as well to coins as it does to money more broadly defined. Consider the argument of any elementary textbook in its explanation why the demand for money should be proportional to income. The logic seems to fit just as well with the word *coins* substituted for the word *money*. To be concrete the following paragraph is Samuelson's explanation of the quantity theory with my substitution of the word *coins* where the word *money* was used in his text (Samuelson (1967)).

"*Demand for Money*: The higher their annual income, the more dollars of business people will want to transact: with various allowances for economies of scale, men hold [coins] at any time about in proportion to their *income* rate per year or per month. This transaction demand for [coins] will be a little lower when the interest rate offered on good bonds, savings deposits and other close substitutes rises above the 1 or 2 percent level; but once people are holding minimal balances at each income level for transactions, the demand for [coins] becomes rather inelastic to interest rate changes."

Indeed, Goldfeld (1973) has estimated an equation for currency, if not for coins. He finds, as might be expected, that currency demand depends on income and there is quite a low interest elasticity. The goodness of fit in terms of standard error is as good as the goodness of fit of his preferred money demand function for M_1. No one would conclude from the preceding "theory" or even from Goldfeld's "evidence" that one should have a quantity theory of *coins* or a quantity theory of *currency* whereby a decrease in coins or currency causes an almost proportionate decline in income. Nor does anyone believe that a small coin or currency shortage will seriously raise interest rates. But the logic is isomorphic to the logic for a quantity theory for money more broadly defined.

Indeed, if we can put our finger on the way in which a coin shortage is "solved" *ie.* the mechanisms whereby a coin shortage does not cause a proportionate reduction in money income, we may also discover mechanisms whereby a shortage of money more broadly defined will also be solved. It is just possible, and we shall discuss this at greater length, that the mechanisms which cause velocity to rise with income over the course of the business cycle, are the same mechanisms which cause coinage velocity to rise if there is a coin shortage.

Anyone who has been to the corner grocer often enough will, after a few moment's reflection, figure out why a coin shortage, while a nuisance, is not likely to cause a proportionate decrease in money GNP, but instead "cause" an increase in "coin-velocity" *ie.* the ratio of GNP to coins. Typically, in a coin shortage a trip to the grocer is apt to involve some trivial negotiation over who will give change and who will make it. In terms of the general statement of the model of the demand for money, it can be said that in the given transactions, payments flows, in this case of coins, change due to the coin shortage. The importance of this conclusion, which relative to coins is a triviality, will become clear in Part II of this paper, where a model is proposed paralleling the nature of coinage flows, in which the demand for money adjusts to the supply of money, not through price-theoretic interest changes, but rather through quantity-theoretic changes in payments flows. But this is getting ahead of the story. For the moment it is to be recorded that Irving Fisher's logic cannot apply equally to coins, currency and M_1; his model does not discriminate between the type of money being used. Clearly, some description of behaviour, important in the case of coins and currency has been left out with respect to money more broadly defined. Conceivably this omitted aspect of behaviour is of no empirical importance for M_1 demand, although crucial in description of coin and currency demand. But certainly at this stage of the argument such a conclusion would be premature.

Trade Credit

Finally, in addition to the Coinage Problem and the nonconstant observed velocity, there is a third problem with the quantity theory. This is the problem of trade credit. Credit can serve as a substitute for money. This substitutability of money and trade credit is the subject of a number of papers, most notably that of Brechling and Lipsey (1963), who show that the availability of trade credit may cause restrictive monetary policy to be "frustrated". In general the quantity theory must deal with the ways in which this "frustration" might occur.

Friedman's 'Restatement'

It may be objected that I have left out of my account Friedman's quantity theory "Restatement" (1956) . Insofar as Friedman refers to the *permanent* as opposed to the *current* demand for money nothing I have said is in conflict. And indeed the explanations for the short-run procyclic behaviour of velocity which are offered in Part II of this essay are exactly consistent with (indeed they form a microfoundations for) Friedman's restatement.

Summary of Part I

To summarise, for Keynesian policies to work in the short run there must be a significant interest elasticity to the demand for money if there is also a significant income elasticity. Keynesians have attempted to show such an interest elasticity, but they have not been entirely convincing that it is of large magnitude in the short run. On the contrary, there are reasons why the short-run elasticity might be quite small.

However, the leading alternative to the Keynesian demand for money, the quantity theory in the style of Irving Fisher, poses problems of its own. Observed velocity is pro-cyclical rather than constant as predicted, and the simple theory whereby money holdings are proportional to income breaks down with respect to certain definitions of money *eg.* coins and currency. This augurs possible breakdown in the theory of money more broadly defined. Finally, trade credit is a money substitute; it should therefore have a place, as should all money substitutes, in the theory. This is yet a third difficulty with the simple quantity theory. A resolution to these questions will be given in Part II of this paper. The key to this resolution is a low short-run income elasticity to the demand for money which roughly matches the low short-run interest elasticity.

Part II Resolutions of Problems

Most of the problems mentioned in the last section would be solved if the demand for money could be shown to have a low short-run income elasticity. Fiscal policy would be effective because the LM curve, whose slope is $-\partial L/\partial Y/\partial L/\partial r$, need not be very steep even with a low interest elasticity of demand. The procyclic behaviour of velocity would be consistent with such a low income elasticity, and M_1 would then, at least in the short-run, behave very much like coins and currency, of which a shortage is presumed to cause little change in income. Yet to most economists a low income elasticity to the demand for money has been unthinkable. This section will demonstrate, on the contrary, that there are several reasons why a low income elasticity to the demand for money is natural. Four simple models will be described which yield exactly this result. Furthermore, it will be noted that most empirical estimates of the demand for money have used functional forms which make precisely this assumption.

Autonomous and Induced Payments

Before describing these four models and these empirical results I would like to introduce some terminology which I find useful in thinking about the demand for money. This terminology is useful because it conveys an idea of the generality, or lack thereof, of particular models of money demand,

An *autonomous payment* is defined as a payment which is made, which both in timing and amount, is independent of the level of a bank account. For example, wage receipts to wage earners might be considered autonomous inpayments.

In contrast to an *autonomous* payment is an *induced* payment, either whose timing or whose amount depends on the level of the bank account. We say that *induced* payments are made to *monitor* the level of bank accounts.

All inventory models of the demand for money can be written in the following form:

$$L = L(P,S) \tag{5}$$

where P describes autonomous payments and S describes the rules whereby bank accounts are monitored. Both P and S may be quite complicated objects; for example P may be a description of payments which may be a random variable differing over different persons. S may vary likewise over all bank accounts. And both P and S may depend upon endogenous variables, such as income and interest.

Irving Fisher's monitoring rule consisted of outpayments following inpayments with a constant average lag. The Baumol-Tobin monitoring rule consists of withdrawals from bonds in amounts Y/n, n times per month; according to Baumol n is $(rY/2a)^{1/2}$. Yet a third rule has been specified by Miller and Orr (1966) in their stochastic model of payments and money holding. According to Miller and Orr if money holdings exceed a threshold h, the balance is returned to a target z; if money holdings fall below a lower threshold, which in their model is 0, again the balance is returned to the target z. Both the target h and the threshold z are functions of autonomous payments and interest rates, chosen to minimise the interest lost from holding money plus transactions costs. Thus the standard inventory models of monetary demand can be expressed in terms of autonomous payments and monitoring rules.

It is the claim of the Fisher quantity theory that the gains from an optimal, as opposed to suboptimal, rule are sufficiently small that in the short run S can be considered constant. In that case it appears natural that if payments depend only on income (suppose they are proportionate) so will the demand for money also be proportionate, S being fixed. This conclusion does not follow, as the four models which will be described presently attest.

Model I: Constant Target-Threshold Monitoring, Stochastic Payments

Suppose that money holdings are monitored in the short run, not by a constant lag rule, as in Fisher's story, but instead by a constant target-threshold rule. By constant target-threshold I mean that if money holdings exceed an upper threshold h they are returned to a target z; if they fall below a lower threshold, which I take to be 0, they are again returned to the target z. (The lower threshold need not be zero, and in general the upper return target may be different from the lower return target. No violence will be done to our conclusions.) Suppose that nonzero autonomous payments occur with various probabilities, and these probabilities are constant. Money holdings are then described by a Markov system, determined totally by the targets and thresholds and the probabilities of autonomous payments in various amounts. In the long run the probability distribution of money balances is determined totally by the probabilities of autonomous payments and the thresholds and targets, independent of the initial value of money holdings for any individual bank account. In this long run steady state the expected value of money holdings is constant. This is equivalent to the usual statement that there is a "stock" demand for money. It must therefore be the case that the net expected value of additions to money holdings, which is the sum of expected autonomous and of expected induced payments, equals zero. Suppose that an increase in income causes a proportionate increase in the probability of all (nonzero) autonomous payments. Such an increase will cause no change in the probability of holding any given amount of money as long as the thresholds and targets are fixed, a result which makes intuitive sense.

Consider the money balance as a flea bouncing up and down in a box with lid at height h and floor at height 0. The increase in the probabilities of autonomous payments could be considered to increase the "speed" at which the flea moves up and down. But in no way should the speed at which the flea travels affect the probability that it be in any given position at a fixed time. Indeed the expected value of the position of the flea in the box is independent of any equiproportionate change in the probability of its jump from one place in the box to another. In terms of autonomous and induced payments, the expected value of autonomous flows increases proportionately with an equiproportionate increase in the probabilities. Nor is there a change in the probability that the "flea" is at a given position in the box. The expected value of induced flows is the probability of their occurrence (ie. the probability that a threshold is pierced) times their respective amounts. An equiproportionate increase in the probabilities of nonzero autonomous payments causes an equiproportionate increase in the probability that a threshold is pierced, given the position of the "flea"; the amount of the induced payment in this event remains unchanged; the probability that the "flea" is in any position is unchanged. The net result therefore of an equiproportionate increase in the probabilities of nonzero autonomous payments is likewise an equiproportionate increase in the probabilities of all induced payments. If expected autonomous payments and expected induced payments all summed to zero prior to the increase in probabilities, so they will continue to sum to zero afterwards. The net result therefore of an increase in income which causes an equiproportionate increase in the probabilities of all nonzero autonomous payments is no increase in money holdings as long as thresholds and targets are fixed. Of course these targets and thresholds will respond to the increase in income; but following the spirit, if not the letter, of Irving Fisher's argument, these changes will occur in the long run, but not in the short run.

It may be useful to be a bit more precise in telling the story about the "flea". Let us follow the Miller and Orr model with slight modification. A bank account has an autonomous inpayment of £1 with probability p and an autonomous outpayment of £1 with probability q; no payment occurs with probability s. The threshold h and the target z are defined. The net result is a long-run distribution of money holdings determined by p,q,h and z. This distribution f, which is pictured in Figure 1, can be computed algebraically. It depends on the value of p relative to q; but it is independent of s. Thus an equiproportionate change in p and q causes no change in this distribution.

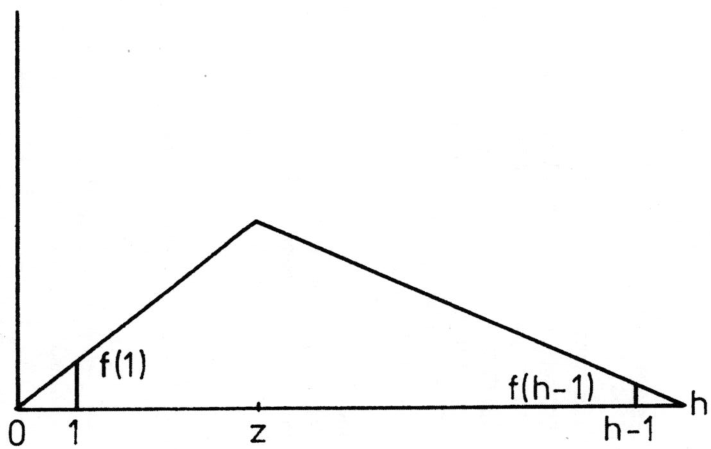

Figure 1

Probability Distribution of Money Holdings with Threshold h and Target z in Miller and Orr Model

The expected value of change in money holdings is the sum of expected autonomous payments, which is p-q plus the expected value of induced payments. These induced payments can be calculated as follows: with probability $f(h-1)$ the bank account holds h-1. With probability p, £1 is received, which triggers an outpayment in amount h-z pounds. Similarly with probability $f(1)$ the bank account holds £1. With probability q, £1 is lost, in which case an induced payment is made in amount z pounds. Thus the expected sum of autonomous plus induced payments is

$$p - q - pf(h-1)(h-z) + qf(1)z \tag{6}$$

In steady state this sum is zero, as can be checked from the steady-state formulae for $f(h-1)$ and $f(1)$, given p, q, h and z. An equiproportionate change in p and q causes no change in $f(h-1)$ and $f(1)$ either in the long run or in the short run. As a result all terms of (6) change in the same proportion. Their sum being zero prior to the change, their sum is also zero afterwards.

Thus in this model a change in income will produce no change in money holdings until the targets and thresholds respond to the change in income. Insofar as that response is slow, so will the short-run income elasticity of the demand for money be low.

Model II: Constant Target-Thresholds, Periodic Payments

The preceding model makes the assumption that autonomous payments occur with constant probability. It might be argued that this assumption violates the spirit of the Fisher quantity theory, if the average lag with which outpayments follow inpayments is considered due to such institutional arrangements as monthly pay days and billing cycles. The model in this section analyses the extent to which the 0-income elasticity of money demand is preserved even where there is a monthly payments cycle.

The usual picture in the textbooks explaining the quantity theory is of the time pattern of money holdings of an individual who receives an income Y at the beginning of each month and exactly spends this income, finishing with 0 balances at the end of the month. The average balance of such a person is *Y/2*. His money holdings are proportional to his income.

A slight modification of his behaviour, which in my opinion makes it a bit more realistic, causes this person's money holdings to be almost independent of income. Suppose, rather than the individual's autonomous expenditures exactly matching his income, that the individual's autonomous expenditures are all but a small fraction of his income, so that in the absence of any induced transaction, his money balance would increase from one period to the next by an amount *S*. Clearly the individual will not continue accumulating money indefinitely; his bank account must be monitored in some way. Let us assume, as before, that the bank account is monitored if it exceeds the threshold *h*, at which point the individual purchases bonds to reduce his holdings to his immediate consumption needs of the period in which the excess occurs.

Figure II illustrates. Each month that the individual fails to make an induced transaction his bank account increases by an amount *S*. Over the course of the month his expenditure is *Y-S*. Figure II shows large triangles which represent the expenditure of *Y-S* each period. It also shows the stepwise increase in money holdings for *n* periods, the steps being each of height *S* and *n* being the number of months between the monitoring of the bank account; *n* is the number of months it takes a bank account periodically to exceed the threshold *h*.

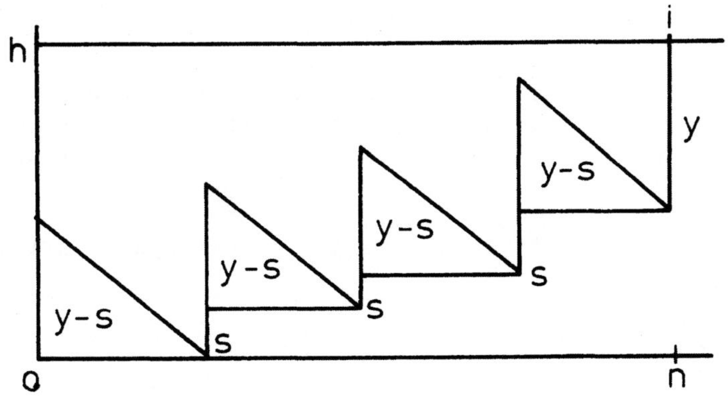

Figure II

Money Holdings as Described in text

A simple calculation shows the average level of money holdings. On monitoring the bank account, which only occurs on the receipt of income, the individual retains enough for his expenditure for that period. This is an amount $Y-S$. That expenditure occurs evenly over the period, so his average holdings in that period are $(Y-S)/2$; in the second period his average holdings are higher by S; therefore they are $(Y-S)/2+S$, and so on, up to the final, nth period, when his average holdings are $(Y-S)/2 + (n-1)S$. Average money holdings for all n periods are thus

$$M^D = \frac{1}{n}\sum_{j=1}^{n}\left\{\frac{Y-S}{2} + (j-1)s\right\} = \frac{Y-S}{2} + \frac{(n-1)S}{2} \tag{7}$$

It remains to calculate n. n is determined as the smallest integer n such that

$$(Y-S) + nS \geqslant h \tag{8}$$

As an approximation (ignoring the integer constraint)

$$n \cong \frac{h - (Y-S)}{S} \tag{9}$$

Substituting in (7) the approximate value of n yields

$$M^D \cong h/2 - S/2 \tag{10}$$

Thus, with the exception of the small term $-S/2$, as long as autonomous expenditure does not exactly balance income, we find that the demand for money is almost independent of income in the short run in which the threshold h is fixed. The result of Model I, rather than being dependent on the nonperiodicity of payments, is perhaps surprisingly, robust.

Model III Endogenous Timing of Payments Relative to Expenditure

The equation $L = L(P,S)$ is helpful in at least one mnemonic way. It forces the realisation that the demand for money depends on *payments* and the *monitoring rule*;

there are many different payments schemes possible as well as many different possible monitoring rules. The formula is thus helpful in pointing out the great particularity of the standard models of the demand for money and the possible range of models which are perfectly natural.

In particular, the standard inventory models assume a one-to-one relation between payments and expenditures. Clearly this need not be the case. An expenditure may be made at quite a different time from its corresponding payment. The recent six-month delays in telephone bills should serve as a reminder of this fact. Furthermore, persons have some considerable discretion over the timing of their payments relative to their expenditures. It is simply too expensive to police to a very fine degree of accuracy the payment of all bills on the exact dates due, except of course for very large payments. The timing of these large payments tend to be negotiated rather than habitual and therefore are themselves endogenous.

It is the view of Ross Milbourne and myself that persons have in the short run some discretion in the timing of payment of their bills, although there is a cost to persistent late payments in terms either of a reduced credit rating or anxiety on the part of the late payer. Nevertheless, in response to a temporary shortfall of ready cash relative to expenditure, the easiest possible remedy is often a juggling of the timing of payments. If this juggling is complete, as I shall demonstrate in a moment, it means again that the income elasticity of the demand for money is zero.

Picture an economy in which agents periodically monitor their bank accounts, at which times they set them at target levels, which in the short run are fixed. Between these periodic monitorings persons make autonomous expenditures independent of their bank accounts. Insofar as money in their bank accounts is not sufficient for payment of their bills on their due date, instead of borrowing to pay these bills, instead the agents in this economy juggle the payment of their bills. The net result is that at the times of monitoring aggregate money holdings is the sum of the targets of all bank accounts. Between these times the demand for money must be constant since, considering all money holders, no money is brought in from outside agents: insufficient money for persons to pay their bills does not result in outside borrowing but instead in delayed payment. In this way the demand for money depends only on the targets; the targets respond to changes in income and/or interest. But the short-run response may be slow for the same reasons that Fisher pictured habits of money holding as responding slowly to changes in the costs.

An analogy with a game of poker exactly fits this model. According to this analogy a group of friends plays a weekly game of poker. To the game each player brings a sum of money with which to pay his potential losses. There are two polar theories as to how an unexpected increase in the stakes of the game might affect the players. The quantity theory predicts that an increase in the stakes of the game will cause the players to quit early unless they have brought more money commensurate with the increase in the stakes, or unless the players can borrow money from elsewhere. Our theory says that with an increase in the stakes the game continues as usual; the winners, however, bankroll the losers. Sometime after the increase in the stakes the players begin to remember that they must bring more money with them to the game to pay for their increased nominal losses. By analogy, the short-run demand for money has a zero income elasticity. It should be noted that the same basic mechanism which causes coin velocity to rise in a coin shortage here causes M_1 demand to be unresponsive to changes in income: that basic mechanism is a temporary change in payments flows to compensate for the low level of M_1 relative to income.

Model IV: Endogenous Timing of Expenditures Relative to Receipts

The final consideration which again produces a low income elasticity of money demand is that the timing of purchases may be dependent on the timing of receipts if money is scarce. It does not take much imagination for the money-short person to wait until the beginning of the month to make an expenditure. And it may be more convenient than borrowing money or selling an asset or even going to the savings account. Ross Milbourne and I have written a paper which models the endogenous timing of expenditures relative to receipts. The model works in much the same way as the endogenous timing of payments relative to expenditures and produces the same results. If the cost of delay is small relative to the transactions cost in obtaining funds from other sources, the short-run income elasticity of demand for money is 0.

Empirical Agreement with Theory

There remains, among other issues, the question of agreement of our prediction of a zero short-run income elasticity with the empirical evidence. First, I must be careful not to overinterpret my findings. The models show a zero short-run income elasticity. By this it is meant that only as the targets and thresholds respond to changes in income will the demand for money also change; thus the demand for money may be expected to react slowly to changes in Y.

In fact almost all recent estimates of the demand for money have been made with a stock adjustment form in which the demand for money adjusts slowly to changes in income and interest. Three examples of such estimates are by Chow (1966), Laidler (1966) and Goldfeld (1973). The stock adjustment can be written in differential form as

$$\dot{m} = \alpha(m^*(y,r) - m) \qquad (11)$$

where m^* is long-run desired money holdings dependent on income and interest. In terms of our models we could view m^* as dependent on the targets and thresholds, which themselves are determined optimally given y and r. m adjusts slowly to m^* (ie. at rate α) because the thresholds and targets themselves are slow to adjust. In this way our models are exactly consistent with a stock adjustment form for the demand for money. And in the short-run, even though such equations show a low interest elasticity (because thresholds and targets are slow to adjust to changes in r), it also happens symmetrically that such equations show a comparable low income elasticity.

Conclusions and Directions of Current Research

In conclusion, the three major problems of the traditional quantity theory are solved by our 0-income elasticity approach. The theory is consistent with the procyclical behaviour of velocity; it equally well applies to coins, currency and money more broadly defined; trade credit is not ignored in the theory (see Model III). At the same time, the short-run interest elasticity of the demand for money need not be high to explain, for example, the pro-cyclical behaviour of velocity.

There are yet two difficulties with our approach. In the first instance, many estimates of money demand show rather rapid adjustment to the long run demand. If this is the case, our theory does not lead astray, since in our prediction the long-run and short-run slopes of the LM curve are not all that different. Nevertheless, no estimate of the demand for money to date has been totally convincing. Even Goldfeld's very careful estimation, within four years spawned the famous "case of the missing money". In view of the lack of robustness of such estimates, it is useful to know (if true) that the efficacy of fiscal policy does not depend on the speed of adjustment of money demand.

There is yet a second theoretical problem. I will sketch my solution to that problem. If the demand for money is insensitive to short-run changes in income and interest, how does the quantity of money change? In this essay we have been examining the transactions demand for money. Persons who take out loans have a finance motive for holding money. Their average holdings amount to virtually nothing if they hold the cash for a very short period of time. But expenditure of these funds causes flows to change. In models I, III and IV the demand for money is "spongy". "Spongy" means that an increase in autonomous inpayments causes an increase in average balances, the way a faster flow of water into a gigantic sponge causes it to hold more water. Reductions in the rate of interest, by causing agents to take credit, in turn causes shifts in autonomous payments which cause increases in money demand. Thus an expansive open market operation increases the loanable funds available to investors, who in spending these funds cause more money to be held. The exact process of this mechanism is the topic of current research.

REFERENCES

Akerlof, G.A. (1979). 'Irving Fisher on His Head:The Consequences of Constant Target-Threshold Monitoring of Money Holdings.' *Quarterly Journal of Economics,*

93, May, 169-187.

Akerlof, G.A. and R.M. Milbourne, (1978) 'New Calculations of Income and Interest Elasticities in Tobin's Model of the Transactions Demand for Money', *Review of Economics and Statistics,* 60, November, 541-546 .

Akerlof, G.A. and R.M. Milbourne, (1979) 'The Consequences of Changes in the Timing of Purchases for the Demand for Money', *Institute for Business and Economic Research*, mimeo, September.

Akerlof, G.A. and R.M. Milbourne, (1980a) 'The Short-Run Demand for Money', *Economic Journal*, 90, December.

Akerlof, G.A. and R.M. Milbourne, (1980b) 'Irving Fisher on His Head II: The Consequence of the Timing of Payments for the Demand for Money', *Quarterly Journal of Economics*, 95 , August.

Baumol, W.J., (1952) 'The Transactions Demand for Cash:An Inventory Theoretic Approach', *Quarterly Journal of Economics*, 66 (November) 545-556.

Brechling, F.P.R. and Richard G. Lipsey (1963), 'Trade Credit and Monetary Policy', *Economic Journal*, 73, 618-41.

Chow, G.C., (1966) 'On the Long-Run and Short-Run Demand for Money', *Journal of Political Economy*, 74 (April), 11.131.

Fisher, I., (1911), *The Purchasing Power of Money*, (New York: Macmillan).

Friedman, M., (1956) 'The Quantity Theory of Money - A Restatement', in Milton Friedman, editor, *Studies in the Quantity Theory of Money*. (Chicago: University of Chicago Press), 3-21.

Friedman, M., (1959) 'The Demand for Money: Some Theoretical and Empirical Results', *Journal of Political Economy*, 67, (August) 327-351.

Goldfeld, S.M., (1973) 'The Demand for Money Revisited', *Brookings Papers on Economic Activity*, 3, 577-638.

Goldfeld, S.M., (1976) 'The Case of the Missing Money', *Brookings Papers on Economic Activity* 3, 577-638.

Keynes, J.M. (1936), *The General Theory of Employment, Interest and Money* (New York: Macmillan).

Laidler, D., (1966), 'The Rate of Interest and the Demand for Money: Some Empirical Evidence', *Journal of Political Economy*, 74, (December) 543-555.

Miller, M.H. and Orr, D. (1966) 'A Model of the Demand for Money by Firms', *Quarterly Journal of Economics*, 80, (August), 413-435.

Samuelson, P.A., (1967), *Economics*, Seventh Edition, (New York: McGraw-Hill).

Tobin J., (1956), 'The Interest Elasticity of the Transactions Demand for Cash', *Review of Economics and Statistics*, 38, (August), 241-247.

Tobin J., (1958) 'Liquidity Preference as Behaviour toward Risk', *Review of Economic Studies* 25, February, 65-86.

FOOTNOTES

1. Paper presented at Conference of Associated University Teachers of Economics, Durham, England, 27 March 1980. The author would like to thank Janet L. Yellen for helpful comments. He would also like to thank the National Science Foundation for generous financial support under Research Grant Number SOC 79-05562.

9. THE ROLE OF ECONOMIC POLICY AFTER THE NEW CLASSICAL MACROECONOMICS

Willem H. Buiter

Summary

The paper considers the implications of the rational expectations - New Classical Macroeconomics revolution for the "rules versus discretion" debate. The following issues are covered 1) The ineffectiveness of anticipated stabilization policy, 2) Non-causal models and rational expectations, 3) optimal control in non-causal models -- the inconsistency of optimal plans. I establish the robustness of the proposition that contingent (closed-loop or feedback) rules dominate fixed (open-loop) rules. The optimal contingent rule in non-causal models - the innovation or disturbance-contingent feedback rule - is quite different from the state-contingent feedback rule derived by dynamic stochastic programming.[1]

1. *Introduction*

The stagflation of the past 15 years appears to have undermined conventional neo-Keynesian economics in the same way the Great Depression undermined neoclassical economics in the 1930's. The economic collapse of the thirties destroyed the faith of many in the self-regulating properties of the "unaided" decentralized market economy and motivated a major increase in the role of government in economic affairs. The worsening economic muddle of the late sixties and the seventies has seriously undermined neo-Keynesian optimism about the ability of government to select attractive combinations of output, employment, inflation and external balance through the judicious use of fiscal, monetary, financial and exchange rate policy. "Fine tuning," the sensitive response of monetary and fiscal instruments to even minor disturbances in economic activity, has acquired an especially bad name.

The skepticism about the ability of governments to use *stabilization policy* wisely has been matched by an increasingly vocal criticism of *structural policy*. By structural policies I mean policies that alter the level and composition of full employment output and employment, both in the short run - for a given capital stock and state of technology - and in the long run, when the size and composition of the capital stock and the state of technology are endogenous. *Stabilization policies* are policies that influence (and, one hopes, minimize) deviations of output and employment from their full employment ("natural" or "equilibrium") levels. The view advanced by Bacon and Eltis (1978) that the nonmarket sector has encroached unduly on the market sector represents a criticism of past and present structural policies. Policies aimed at altering the relative size of the public and private sectors or at changing a nation's consumption-investment mix are structural policies, as are policies designed to favor the primary, secondary or tertiary sectors. The Laffer curve is the conceptual foundation of structural tax policy proposals. Policies that influence the "natural" rate of unemployment (*e.g.* minimum wage laws) are structural policies.

If stabilization policies were defined to include only those policies that affect the fluctuations of output and employment around their "natural" levels without having any short-run or long-run effects on these "natural" levels themselves, the stabilization policy set would be the empty set. In virtually every macroeconomic or macroeconometric model that is not strictly for classroom use only, the distinction between the two kinds of policies is quite arbitrary. Certainly, every real-world economic policy action has both stabilization and structural consequences. This is, of course, quite consistent with ill-informed policymakers considering only either the stabilization, or the structural consequences of their actions and ignoring half the implications of their policies. Some of the most serious dilemmas in economic policymaking occur when a policy that is desirable for its short-run stabilization effects has undesirable long-run structural implications or vice versa. Cutting government spending to reduce demand pressures in an overheated economy may lead to painful changes in the composition of output away from the provision of public consumption goods or from investment in social overhead capital. A desire to reduce the (relative) size of the public sector may result in a slump when the cut in public spending is not immediately matched by an equivalent expansion of private domestic or external demand.

The practical impossibility of indentifying a pure stabilization policy that does not have any structural implications is of some importance when the policy conclusions of the New Classical Macroeconomics School are discussed below. A plausible interpretation of some of the writings of this school is that (at least) two pure stabilization policies exist. The first is monetary policy - the control of the nominal stock of high-powered money. The second is deficit financing - the substitution of borrowing (and sometimes also money financing) for lump-sum tax financing of a given level and composition of real exhaustive public spending. This view is incorrect: both these policies have structural consequences.

I consider the retreat from neo-Keynesian policy optimism both understandable and appropriate. In the light of the accumulated empirical evidence of the last 15 years some critical revaluation of the conventional wisdom of the fifties and the early sixties is clearly required. What is harder to understand is how, for so many, this retreat from the neo-Keynesian mainstream and from policy optimism has taken the form of a return to the neoclassical dogmas and modes of analysis that received such a battering in the thirties. The most convincing explanations for this curious phenomenon are the gradual passing of the generations whose consciousness was shaped during the Great Depression and the failure to teach economic history at all seriously in many contemporary graduate economics programs.

The revival of pre-thirties macroeconomics which is now widely referred to as the *New Classical Macroeconomics* is associated historically with Milton Friedman (1968) but has achieved its recent prominence as a result of the work of Edmund Phelps (1970), Robert Lucas (1972*a*, *b*, 1975, 1976), Thomas Sargent and Neil Wallace (1975, 1976), Robert Barro (1974, 1976, 1979), Edward Prescott (1975, 1977), Finn Kydland and Edward Prescott (1977), Bennett McCallum (1977, 1978), Robert Hall (1970, 1979), and a host of others. The major improvement of the modern variant over the original, as represented, *e.g.*, in the works of Hayek (1932, 1939), Knight (1941), Douglas (1932, 1935), Hawtrey (1926), Haberler (1932) and Fisher (1933), reflects the considerable progress made since the thirties in the technical aspects of economic analysis. We know now how to formally analyze simple, preferably linear, stochastic processes. A not entirely facetious characterization of the New Classical Macroeconomics is to regard it as a formalization of certain aspects of the old classical macroeconomics with white noise added. The new version compares unfavorably with the old one, however, in its unsophisticated treatment of the money supply process and of financial markets in general. The old classical macroeconomics was also more flexible in recognizing the possibility of departures from ideal competitive behavior in goods, factor and financial markets during cyclical upswings or downturns, although no formal characterization of such departures was ever provided.[2]

The New Classical Macroeconomics relies heavily on the application of the efficient markets hypothesis to all markets, real and financial. This means that prices in all markets are competitive, market-clearing prices that "fully reflect" all available information. They adjust instantaneously to current and anticipated future disturbances so as to balance notional demand and supply in each market. All agents are price takers. Households' notional demands and supplies are derived from expected utility maximization subject only to the contraint of the household endowment valued at market prices that are viewed as parametric by each individual agent. The notional demands and supplies of firms are derived from market value maximization subject only to the constraint of the production possibility set, with all planned sales and purchases valued at prices that are viewed as parametric by each individual firm. Households and firms (and the government?) act as if, at the prevailing set of market prices, they can buy or sell any amount of any good or service. An industrious and costless auctioneer instantaneously and continuously sets prices in all markets at levels that make these notional demands and supplies mutually consistent.[3]

Compelling empirical evidence to support this extreme view of the way in which markets operate is seldom offered. This is not surprising, as it bears very little relation to the modus operandi of many labor, goods and financial markets in contemporary developed capitalist or mixed economies, as described in the labor economics, industrial organization and financial literature. Instead of careful studies of market organization, a priori arguments are advanced that purport to identify privately rational behavior and the useful concept of equilibrium with Walrasian, competitive, market-clearing equilibrium. This "equilibrium approach" is then contrasted favorably with selected ad hoc neo-Keynesian approaches (Barro (I979), Lucas and Sargent (I978)).

The characterization of the New Classical Macroeconomics as *equilibrium economics* does not suffice to generate the New Classical invariance or policy neutrality propositions. It is also insufficiently precise because of the universality of the concept of equilibrium. *Equilibrium* refers to a state in which optimizing agents have no incentive to alter their behavior because, conditional on their expectations, their current plans are mutually consistent and can be executed. An *expectations equilibrium* is a slightly stronger concept, because it also requires that agents formulate plans or strategies on the basis of optimal inferences and forecasts of current and future exogenous and endogenous variables, that are consistent with the stochastic processes actually generating these variables. Until the constraints subject to which agents optimize, including their information sets, are specified, the assumption of equilibrium and optimizing behavior is essentially vacuous, because it does not impose refutable restrictions on observable behavior. The most general version of the Walrasian competitive equilibrium model represents only a very small move towards potential falsifiability: the equilibrium values of all real variables should be homogeneous of degree zero in all current and anticipated future money prices and nominal endowments, and Walras' Law should be satisfied.

One can have optimizing, privately rational behavior and equilibrium without this equilibrium being competitive. Monopolistic competition, oligopoly and monopoly are familiar market forms. More generally, game theory, and especially its dynamic extension, differential games, offers a wide variety of equilibrium concepts, many of which are more appropriate as approximations to actual market configurations than the Walrasian competitive equilibrium (Intriligator (I97I), Kydland, (I975), Bacharach (I976)). Even if a competitive equilibrium concept is preferred for certain markets, this competitive equilibrium need not be an efficient, Walrasian, market-clearing equilibrium.

Stiglitz *et.al.* have developed theories of nonmarket-clearing, quantity-constrained competitive equilibria for markets with costly, imperfect and asymmetric information (Stiglitz (1977, 1979), Grossman (1976), Grossman and Stiglitz (1976), Akerlof (1970), Riley (1979), Wilson (1977, 1979), Salop (1978, 1979) . For a somewhat different approach see Negishi (1960), Hahn (1979) and the recent survey by Drazen (1980)). Inefficient markets, *e.g.*, those characterized by a partial (or no) immediate response of prices to innovations in cost or demand, create opportunities for known monetary and deficit financing rules to have real effects (*e.g.* Buiter (1980*b*)). Noncompetitive game-theoretic equilibria and competitive but inefficient non-Walrasian equilibria will be the cornerstones of a "New Keynesian Macroeconomics." The Walrasian, efficient competitive market-clearing equilibrium remains a useful special case that may characterize a limited number of commodity markets and financial markets.

This paper analyses the implications of the New Classical Macroeconomics for the conduct of economic policy. The focus of the analysis is on what used to be called "rules versus discretion" but should be called fixed rules (rules without feedback or open-loop rules) versus flexible rules, *i.e.* rules with feedback, contingent rules or closed-loop rules. With open-loop policies the values of the actual time paths of the policy variables are specified at the beginning of a planning period and are functions only of the information available at the beginning of the planning period. These paths are not future information-dependent: they are to be followed by the policymaker without regard to future events or to any new information that may accrue as time passes. Milton Friedman's advocacy of a fixed growth rate for some monetary aggregate is an example of a very simple kind of open-loop rule. Closed-loop, contingent or feedback policies specify the values of the policy variables in period t as known functions of the information that will be available when a value will actually have to be assigned to the policy instruments, but may not yet be available in earlier periods. Thus future policy instruments are known functions of observations yet to be made. There is no serious disagreement that policy should be determined by rules. Views differ as regards the desirability of open-loop rules vis-a-vis closed-loop rules.

The application of stochastic dynamic programming to dynamic models in state-space form or 'causal' models leads to optimal contingent (feedback) rules that in models with uncertainty dominate any open-loop rule. In view of this, how can anyone argue that open-loop rules should be adopted? The common-sense reason for the superiority of contingent rules over fixed rules - that one can never do worse by permitting a flexible (but known) response to new information - seems robust.

There are three distinct foundations for the view that open-loop policies are superior to closed-loop rules. The first argument does not contest the proposition that monetary, fiscal and financial policies, anticipated and unanticipated, have important real effects, short run and/or long run. However, these effects come with lags that are often long and are always variable and uncertain. In such an environment, even a well-informed and well-intentioned policy maker is likely to have a difficult time determining the optimal feedback rule. Real-world governments are frequently neither well-informed nor well-intentioned. It is therefore preferable to constrain the policy authorities' options by committing them to simple fixed rules such as a constant growth rate for the money supply or a balanced budget - if necessary by constitutional amendment. This general position appears to be the one adopted by Milton Friedman. It reflects a very practical concern about the wisdom of leaving powerful instruments with uncertain effects in the hands of persons or agencies with limited ability and sometimes dubious motives. Although I consider it to be the most powerful of the three arguments in favor of fixed rules, I shall not discuss it any further, as it ante-dates the New Classical Macroeconomics.

The second argument is that economic policy - mainly stabilization policy and often only monetary policy - is irrelevant for the behavior of the real economy to the extent that it is anticipated. Known, deterministic policy rules, open-loop or feedback, have no effect on the joint probability density functions of real economic variables. Applications of this view to monetary policy can be found in Sargent and Wallace (1975) and Barro (1976), who also applied it to deficit financing: the substitution of bond financing (and money financing?) for (lump-sum) tax financing of a real spending program has no real consequences (Barro (1974)).

McCallum (1977) argued that it held for all forms of stabilization policy. This second argument does not question the wisdom of attempts at stabilization policy, it questions the very possibility of stabilization policy. Since any known policy rule will have no real effects, the only contribution of the government to economic stabilization consists in not introducing additional uncertainty into the economy by having an unknown, stochastic policy rule. In principle any known feedback rule is as neutral as any known open-loop rule. In practice, however, instrument uncertainty is likely to be minimized by the selection of the simplest possible fixed rule. Some aspects of this second argument, that only unanticipated (stabilization) policy has real effects are analyzed in Section III after a brief discussion of rational expectations in Section II.

The third argument takes aim at the application of traditional optimal control techniques based on dynamic programming to the derivation of optimal economic policies in models with optimizing agents endowed with rational expectations of the future.

Kydland and Prescott (1977) have shown that feedback rules derived by dynamic programming, which they call "consistent" policies, are sub-optimal in models with optimizing agents endowed with rational expectations of the future because such consistent policies fail to allow for the effect of anticipated future instrument values on current (and past) states. The optimal policy in such 'non-causal' models, they argue, is an open-loop rule.

To lay the groundwork for an analysis of this proposition, Section IV considers causal and non-causal solutions of dynamic systems and other non-uniqueness problems arising in models with rational expectations of future endogenous variables. Section IV then analyses the derivation of optimal policies in non-causal systems.

The conclusion reached by Kydland and Prescott that the consistent policy is suboptimal is confirmed. However, it is also shown that, in models with uncertainty, there always exists a feedback policy (called an "innovation-contingent" feedback policy) that dominates the optimal open-loop policy. Only in models without uncertainty is the optimal open-loop policy truly optimal.

I conclude that, with the exception of the demonstration of the inapplicability of traditional dynamic programming methods in non-causal models, the open-loop versus closed-loop debate stands where Milton Friedman left it. Further progress has to wait for the development of substantive economic models out of an emerging New Keynesian Macroeconomics.

II Rational Expectations

In the development of the New Classical Macroeconomics, rational expectations modelling has played an important part. It is however possible and in my opinion desirable to distinguish clearly between the insights gained from the rational expectations revolution per se and the contribution of the rest of the New Classical package. The other building blocks of the New Classical Macroeconomics - identical public and private sector opportunity sets or "Modigliani-Miller" of the public sector vis-a-vis the private sector, identical public and private information sets and efficient markets (see Buiter (1979*a*,*b*, (1980*a*,*b*), Buiter and Tobin (1979), Tobin and Buiter (1980)) - can be jettisoned without sacrificing the crucial contribution of the rational expectations revolution. This is the "principle of policy - dependent structural parameters" and its corrollary that in any model, New Classical or Old Keynesian, there is no scope for governments to use unanticipated policy in a systematic manner.

The expression "rational expectations" represents a minor abuse of language. Standard practice in economics commands that the label rational expectations be reserved for forecasts generated by a rational, *i.e.*, expected utility maximizing decision process in which the uncertain costs of acquiring, processing and interpreting additional information are balanced against the uncertain anticipated benefits from further refinement of the forecast. As used by the New Classical Macroeconomists, rational expectations shortcut the actual process of information gathering and forecasting and focus on the long-run equilibrium outcome of a "Bayesian" sequential prediction process, when forecasting has become a fairly simple and mechanical procedure: the subjective probability distribution of future economic variables held at time t coincides with the actual, objective conditional distribution based on the information assumed to be available at time t.[4] In many applications only the first moments of these distributions are assumed to be relevant. In Muth's original contribution, *e.g.*, (Muth (1961)), it was hypothesized that the mean expectation of firms with respect to some phenomenon, *e.g.*, the future price of a commodity, was equal to the prediction that would be make by the relevant, correct and universally agreed upon economic theory. Future variables anticipated at time t are "true mathematical expectations of the future variables conditional on all variables in the model which are known to the public at time t" (Shiller (1978), p. 3). Analytical tractability often compels the use of linear models in which case rational expectations become least squares forecasts.

The specialization of rational expectations to best linear unbiased predictors conditional on an information set that includes the true, objective structure of the model is a powerful simplification that greatly facilitates practical applications. It also begs a number of crucial questions. The issue of how economic agents acquire their knowledge of the true structure of the economy which is used in making their rational forecasts is not addressed. The appeal of rational expectations lies in the fact that any forecasting scheme that is not rational in the sense of Muth will be consistently wrong: it will result in systematic, predictable forecast errors. Sensible economic agents will detect unexploited arbitrage opportunities which will force the abandonment of the forecasting scheme and the adoption of a new one. Economic theory has very little to say about the learning process by which unsatisfactory forecasting schemes are revised. Ultimate convergence of the revision process to a rational expectations mechanism is neither self-evident nor inevitable (De Canio (1979)). Unless the forecasting mechanism has converged to the rational expectations scheme and economic agents know the true structure of the model, the crucial error-orthogonality property does not hold.[5] Analytical tractability is a necessary but not a sufficient condition for a model to be economically interesting. Since rational expectations is such a crucial assumption,[6] it would be most useful to have some direct tests of its validity. Unfortunately this behavioral hypothesis is seldom tested in isolation. Most applied econometric work incorporating the rational expectations hypothesis only permits the testing of composite hypotheses: natural rate of unemployment plus rational expectations, term structure of interest rates plus rational expectations, the market model of asset pricing plus rational expectations, international interest parity plus rational expectations, etc. Survey data, such as the Livingston price index, while subject to all the problems associated with measuring unobservables through questionnaires, provide direct test of such rational expectations implications as the error orthogonality property (see Brown and Maital (1979)). They have not been exploited to their full extent.

It is a commonplace that the behavior of private agents depends in many ways on estimates of imperfectly observed past and present variables and on expectations of future variables. If changes in public sector behavior alter these estimates and expectations, models that ignore links from (anticipated) government behavior via private expectations to private behavior are misspecified. Such misspecification may lead to poor conditional forecasts and to erroneous conclusions being drawn form policy evaluation using simulation methods.

The rational expectations approach offers a simple solution to the problem of the link between private sector behavior, private sector expectations and government behavior: the private sector is assumed to know the true structure of the model, including the parameters that describe government behavior. The lesson of the rational expectations view for macroeconomic and macroeconometric modeling is the requirement to solve simultaneously for the currently anticipated future value of an endogenous variable and its future value calculated from the model that incorporates these anticipations of the future. Once this is done the models include the response of the private sector to current and anticipated future government actions and fully respect the "principle of policy-dependent structural parameters." Policy simulations that are immune to the "Lucas Critique" can then be carried out.

III Real Effects of Anticipated and Unanticipated Money

In this Section of the Paper I discuss briefly some of the foundations and implications of the view that only unanticipated stabilization policy can have real effects. This proposition has been advanced seriously for only two kinds of policies: changes in the nominal supply of (outside) money balances and substitution of government borrowing for lump-sum taxation, keeping constant the size and composition of the government's real spending programme. The second one, "debt neutrality" has been dealt with at length in a number of recent papers (Barro (1974), (1978*a*), Buiter (1977, 1979*a*,*b*,*c*) Buiter and Tobin (1979), Tobin and Buiter (1980)). These demonstrated that the conditions for complete debt neutrality to hold are so extreme that they are certain to be violated in any real-world economy. Empirical attempts to quantify the degree of debt-neutrality have so far been completely inconclusive. In what follows attention is confined to the issue of the short-run and long-run neutrality of anticipated and unanticipated money.

Most channels through which changes in the nominal money stock can potentially affect real variables such as output and employment are represented in the "portmanteau" reduced form equation (1) which is a generalization of of an equation used in empirical work by Barro (1977*a*, 1978*b*) and Attfield, Demery and Duck (1979*a*,*b*).

$$\begin{aligned} y_t = Ax_t &+ \sum_{i=0}^{T_1}\sum_{j=0}^{S_1} b_{ij}\,[\dot{m}_{t-i} - E(\dot{m}_{t-i}/I_{t-i-j})] + \sum_{i=0}^{T_1} c_i\,\dot{m}_{t-i} \\ &+ \sum_{i=0}^{T_2}\sum_{j=0}^{S_2} d_{ij}\,E(\dot{m}_{t+i}/I_{t-j}) \qquad (1) \\ &+ \sum_{k=1}^{R_1}\sum_{i=-T_4}^{T_3}\sum_{j=0}^{S_3} e_{ijk}\,[E(\dot{m}_{t+i}/I_{t-j}) - E(\dot{m}_{t+i}/I_{t-j-k})] \\ &+ u_t \end{aligned}$$

For concreteness let y_t denote the logarithm of real output. x_t is a vector of regressors, possibly including lagged values of y_t, as well as those policy variables (public spending, tax rates) that are generally recognized to have real effects whether anticipated or unanticipated. These effects may of course differ with the extent to which the policies are anticipated and the degree to which they are perceived as transitory or permanent. $\dot{m}_t$ is the first difference of the logarithm of the nominal money supply. For our purposes it is not essential whether the levels or the rates of change of the money supply should be on the *r.h.s* of (1). u_t is an *i.i.d* random disturbance term.

Four kinds of channels through which money affects real variables can be distinguished

a) The inflation tax channel or *Tobin effect*. Anticipated future money growth, to the extent that it is associated with anticipated future inflation, will move desired portfolio composition away from assets that are poor hedges against inflation. *E.g.* in many money and growth models money and capital are the only two stores of value. With no market-determined interest rate attached to outside money balances, an increase in the anticipated future rate of inflation will reduce the demand for money, stimulate capital formation and thus over time boost productive capacity and actual output. Whenever output is a function of some anticipated real rate of return variable, either in the short run (via the supply of labour) or in the long run (via the capital stock), anticipated future money will have real effects unless money is super-neutral. This effect is captured by

$$\sum_{i=0}^{T_2} \sum_{j=0}^{S_2} d_{ij} \quad E(\dot{m}_{t+i}/I_{t-j})$$

. It has not been considered in the empirical work on anticipated and unanticipated money.

b) The multi-period non-contingent nominal contract channel or *Fischer-Phelps-Taylor effect*. One of the key assumptions required for anticipated monetary (and other) policy to have no real effects is that the private sector can respond to new information by changing all of its controls (labor supply, consumption, portfolio allocation, sales, etc.) at least as fast as the public sector can alter any of its controls. If the public sector can change at least one of its instruments (e.g., the money supply) continuously, while the private sector is locked into predetermined nominal contracts for finite periods, deterministic money supply rules will have real effects (Fischer (1977), Phelps and Taylor (1977), Taylor (1980) and Buiter and Jewitt (1980)). E.g., models incorporating overlapping multi-period nominal wage contracts exhibit very "Keynesian" behavior. In any given period, the majority of the labor force is covered by pre-existing nominal wage contracts. Each contract can in principle incorporate all relevant information on the behavior of the general price level and average wages over the life of the contract, that was available at the date the contract was entered into. It is not contingent on any new information that may become available over the life of the contract. As new information becomes available in period t, it is reflected only in the contracts that are up for renegotiation that period. The majority of the labor force is still covered by unexpired pre-existing contracts. Management responds to "innovations" in demand by altering output and employment at these precontracted wages. If the money supply can respond to demand innovations before each and every labor contract is up for renewal, output stabilizing monetary feedback rules exist. The *information sets* of the monetary authorities and the private sector may be identical, but the difference in *opportunity sets* - in this case in the speed of response to demand innovations - creates scope for beneficial or detrimental monetary feedback rules. The microfoundations of such multiperiod nominal wage contracts are still quite unsatisfactory (Barro (1977*b*, 1979)). In the U.S economy, at any rate, they are a fact of life and it seems unwise to deny their existence unless they can be fitted into an a prioristic paradigm of how the economy ought to work.

The Fischer-Phelps-Taylor effect is represented by

$$\sum_{i=0}^{T_1} \sum_{j=0}^{S_1} b_{ij} [\dot{m}_{t-i} - E(\dot{m}_{t-i}/I_{t-i-j})] \text{ with } S_1 > 0.$$

In the empirical work of Barro et.al. referred to earlier, only current period (or one period ahead) forecast errors were included *i.e.* it was implicitly assumed that $b_{ij} = 0$ for $j > 0$. This precludes a search for the presence of Fischer-Phelps-Taylor effects. These require that current outputbe influenced by forecast errors from forecasts of money growth at a given date ($t-i$) made at one or more dates before $t-i$; *i.e.*, at dates $t-i-j$ with $0 \leqslant j \leqslant S_1$

where S_1 represents the longest forecast horizon

If monetary policy in period $t-i$ can be determined on the basis of information more recent than I_{t-i-S_1}, it can influence at least one monetary forecast error and thus real output.

c) The expectation revision channel or *Turnovsky-Weiss effect*. This effect is most easily demonstrated using the macro model of equations (2) and (3) which is a simplified version of a model of Turnovsky (1980).

$$m_t - P_t = \alpha_1 y_t - \alpha_2 [E(P_{t+1}/I_t) - P_t] + \dot{u}^m_t \qquad \alpha_1, \alpha_2 > 0 \quad (2)$$

$$y_t = \beta\,[P_t - E(P_t/I_{t-1})] + u^y_t \qquad \beta > 0 \quad (3)$$

Equation (2) is a monetary equilibrium condition equating the real money supply to a Cagan-type demand for real money balances which is a function of real income and the expected future inflation rate. Equation (3) is a Sargent-Wallace (1975) supply function that makes output an increasing function of the gap between current price and last period's anticipation of the current price level. I_t includes current and past observations on y_t, P_t and m_t and the correct model of the economy as specified in (2) and (3). Assuming stability we can solve for the price forecast error as in (4).

$$P_t - E(P_t/I_{t-1}) = \frac{1}{1+\alpha_1\beta+\alpha_2}[m_t - E(m_t/I_{t-1})]$$

$$+ \frac{\alpha_2}{(1+\alpha_1\beta+\alpha_2)(1+\alpha_2)} \sum_{i=0}^{\infty} \left(\frac{\alpha_2}{1+\alpha_2}\right)^i [E(m_{t+1+i}/I_t) - E$$

$$(m_{t+1+i}/I_{t-1})] - \frac{1}{1+\alpha_1\beta+\alpha_2}(\alpha_1 u^y_t + u^m_t) \quad (4)$$

Thus the current price forecast error is a function of the revision in the forecasts for all current and future money stocks between period t and $t-1$. Consider a monetary feedback rule that makes the current money supply a function of (in principle) all current and past disturbances.

$$m_t = \sum_{i=0}^{\infty} [\mu_{i,1} u^y_{t-i} + \mu_{i,2} u^m_{t-i}] \tag{5}$$

substituting this into (4) yields

$$P_t - E(P_t/I_{t-1}) = \frac{1}{1 + \alpha_1\beta + \alpha_2} (\mu_{0,1} u^y_t + \mu_{0,2} u^m_t) \tag{6}$$

$$+ \frac{\alpha_2}{(1+\alpha_1\beta + \alpha_2)(1+\alpha_2)} \sum_{i=0}^{\infty} \left(\frac{\alpha_2}{1+\alpha_2}\right)^i [\mu_{1+i,1} u^y_t + \mu_{1+i,2} u^m_t]$$

$$- \frac{1}{1 + \alpha_1\beta + \alpha_2} (\alpha_1 u^y_t + u^m_t)$$

This shows that the government can completely eliminate the price forecast error $P_t - E(P_t/I_{t-1})$, either by responding only currently ($\mu_{1+i,1} = \mu_{1+i,2} = 0$, $i \geqslant 0$, $\mu_{0,1} = \alpha_1$ and $\mu_{0,2} = 1$)

or by responding currently and in the future or even by responding only in one or more future periods, to current disturbances. All that is required is that the $\mu_{1,i}$ and $\mu_{2,i}$ be chosen in such a way that

$$\mu_{0,1} + \frac{\alpha_2}{(1+\alpha_2)} \sum_{i=0}^{\infty} \left(\frac{\alpha_2}{1+\alpha_2}\right)^i \mu_{1+i,1} - \alpha_1 = 0 \tag{7a}$$

and

$$\mu_{0,2} + \frac{\alpha_2}{(1+\alpha_2)} \sum_{i=0}^{\infty} \left(\frac{\alpha_2}{1+\alpha_2}\right)^i \mu_{1+i,2} - 1 = 0 \qquad (7b)$$

E.g., if the government cannot respond currently to current disturbances (say, because unlike the private sector it receives this information with a one period lag) *i.e.*

$\mu_{0,1} = \mu_{0,2} = 0$ and chooses to respond only with a one period lag, *i.e.* $\mu_{1+i,1} = \mu_{1+i,2} = 0,\ i \geq 1$, the price forecast error is eliminated by choosing and

$$\mu_{1,1} = \frac{\alpha_1(1+\alpha_2)}{\alpha_2} \qquad (8a)$$

$$\mu_{1,2} = \frac{1 + \alpha_2}{\alpha_2} \qquad (8b)$$

Therefore, even if the government has information that is inferior to that available to the private sector, in the sense that it receives information on current and past realizations of random disturbances later than the private sector, it can eliminate the effects of current disturbances on the price forecast error from last period's forecast of the current price level (and therefore on the deviation of output from its ex-post "natural" level u_t^y). It does this by committing itself to respond in a known way to these current disturbances during some future period when the relevant information has become known to it.

This equivalence of current or instantaneous policy response and future or lagged policy response only holds when the current state of the system (P_t in our example) is a function of anticipations of future states ($E(P_{t+1}/I_t)$ in our example). Consider *e.g.* the case when $\mu_{i,1} = \mu_{i,2} = 0$ for all i except $\mu_{1,1}$ and $\mu_{1,2}$. Changes in m_t

in response to u^y_{t-1} and u^m_{t-1} have no effect on $P_t - E(P_t/I_{t-1})$ because u^y_{t-1} and u^m_{t-1} belong to I_{t-1}. Anticipated future changes in m_{t+1} in response to u^y_t and u^m_t, however, will effect the anticipated future price level $E(P_{t+1}/I_t)$ and thereby P_t and $P_t - E(P_t/I_{t-1})$.

Turnovsky has pointed out (Turnovsky (1980)) that the ability of lagged monetary feedback policy to affect real output will disappear if $E(P_{t+1}/I_t)$ in (2) is replaced by $E(P_{t+1}/I_{t-1})$. Unless the expectations in (2) and (3) are conditioned at different dates, new information accruing to private agents between periods $t-1$ and t cannot be reflected in the price level established in period t: both portfolio allocation decisions and money wage decisions for period t are predetermined from period $t-1$. Policy that depends for its effectiveness on the aquisition of new information by the private sector, on consequent expectation revision and on the immediate reflection of these new expectations in current prices will become powerless. Buiter and Eaton (1980) note that policy rules that operate through current (and/or past) expectations of future policy actions are time-inconsistent, an issue addressed in greater detail in Section 5.

If there are more independent targets than instruments or if the private secor does not have complete contemporaneous information on all disturbances, it will not be possible to achieve perfect stabilization, as we did in the simple example.[7] Nevertheless, the qualitative proposition that monetary policy effectiveness can be achieved via the effect of anticipated future policy remains valid. (See Turnovsky (1980) and Weiss (1980)). This is one way in which rational expectations have increased the scope for stabilization policy beyond what is possible under ad-hoc expectations. The Turnovsky-Weiss effect is represented in (1) by

$$\sum_{k=1}^{R_1} \sum_{i=-T_4}^{T_3} \sum_{j=0}^{S_3} e_{ijk} [E(\dot{m}_{t+i}/I_{t-j}) - E(\dot{m}_{t+i}/I_{t-j-k})]$$

It was not incorporated in any of the empirical work on anticipated and unanticipated money.

d) Other channels. The only term left in (1) is $\sum_{i=0}^{T_1} c_i \dot{m}_{t-i}$ representing past and present actual monetary growth. This can affect real output for a variety of reasons. The three major ones are money illusion, absence of debt neutrality in the presence of nominal interest-bearing public debt and ad-hoc sticky money wages or prices. The last category does not include those multi-period, non-contingent nominal contract models like Fischer (1977), Phelps and Taylor (1977), Taylor (1980) and Buiter and Jewitt (1980) that incorporate rational expectations and have all real variables homogeneous of degree zero in anticipated money, nominal wages and prices. These were discussed under the Fischer-Phelps-Taylor effect. The necessity of debt neutrality for neutrality of anticipated money is argued in Buiter (1979*a*,*b*; 1980*b*) and Tobin and Buiter (1980).

It is important in empirical work on equations such as (1) to incorporate the assumption of homogeneity of degree zero of all real variables in all actual and anticipated money prices and nominal quantitities. As a special case of this if there is debt neutrality, anticipated money should be neutral in the long run. The "Keynesian" proposition that anticipated money can have real effects in the short run is not to be confused with the strawman of long run money illusion (Gordon 1979).

IV Causal and Non-Causal Solutions to Rational Expectations Models and Other Non-Uniqueness Problems

Traditional optimal control techniques for dynamic models are presented most thoroughly in Chow (1975). In order to be applicable to problems encountered in modern macroeconomic analysis, the traditional approach must be extended in two directions. The first extension is to allow for many independent controllers or "players" with distinct and possibly conflicting objectives. Each player is aware of and responds to the current and anticipated future actions of the other players. Thus, instead of modeling a single controller playing a game against "nature," we need the approach of multiplayer dynamic game theory or differential games. This issue is considered in a longer version of this paper (Buiter (1980*a*)).

The second extension is to develop optimization techniques for noncausal models. Both single-player and many-player solution techniques need to be developed. The distinction between causal or backward-looking and noncausal or forward-looking models is a familiar one in the control engineering literature. In a causal system the state of the system at time τ, y_τ, is completely determined once a past state $y_{\tau-i}$, $i = 1,2, \ldots$ is given together with the entire sequence of values of the forcing variables or inputs, v_t, between $\tau-i+1$ and τ, i.e., $(v_{\tau-i+1}, v_{\tau-i+2}, \ldots, v_{\tau-1}, v_\tau)$. If the system is stable, the influence of the initial state will ultimately vanish and the current state will be a function only of all past and present inputs. Inputs are the exogenous variables, the instruments and the random disturbances. Causal system are solved forward in time from a given initial condition. Noncausal systems are systems for which it is not sufficient for determining y_τ to know an initial condition $y_{\tau-i}$, $i > 0$, and the values of the forcing variables or inputs between $\tau - i$ and τ(inclusive). In addition, knowledge of (expected) future inputs $v_{\tau+j}$, $j = 1,2, \ldots$, is required. Noncausal models have been argued to arise frequently in the context of rational expectations models, although some rational expectations models--those incorporating only current or past expectations of the present or the past--have generally been solved as causal models.

It is probably better to talk of causal and noncausal solutions to dynamic models than of causal and noncausal models. Every dynamic model, with or without rational expectations, has a causal (or "backward-looking") and a noncausal (or "forward-looking") solution. This is most easily demonstrated with the linear difference equation model of equation (9)

$$y_t = Ay_{t-1} + Cx_{t-1} \tag{9}$$

y_t is a vector of state variables and x_t a vector of

exogenous variables or policy instruments. The matrix A is assumed to be invertible. The causal or backward-looking solution y_t^b of (9) is

$$y_t^b = \sum_{k=0}^{\infty} A^k Cx_{t-1-k} + \lim_{N\to\infty} A^N y_{t-N} \tag{10a}$$

The non-causal or forward looking solution y_t^f of (9) is

$$y_t^f = -\sum_{k=1}^{\infty} A^{-k} Cx_{t-1+k} + \lim_{M\to\infty} A^{-M} y_{t+M} \tag{10b}$$

Indeed, as Blanchard (1978) has pointed out, any linear combination of the backward and the forward solutions with weights that sum to unity, such as y_t^m in (11), is also a solution to (9).

$$y_t^m = \alpha y_t^b + (1-\alpha)\, y_t^f \tag{11}$$

The mathematics are quite silent on which one of the continuum of solutions given in (11) to pick. Economic theory must narrow down the possible range. If y_t is an asset price determined in an efficient market the noncausal solution (10b) may be the natural one. In terms of equation (9), momentary equilibrium is represented by an equation relating the asset price, y_t, to its (actual and expected) future value y_{t+1} and an exogenous variable or policy instrument x_t. Such a noncausal solution was proposed by Sargent and Wallace (1973) for a money-and-growth model. If the price were determined in an inefficient market and is viewed as predetermined at any given instant, the causal solution is the appropriate one.

It is sometimes argued that the choice between the causal and the non-causal solutions should be based on the principle that unstable solutions are inadmissable. Note that if the model in (9) has a stable backward-looking solution for a constant path of the forcing variables ($x_t=x$), its forward-looking solution will be unstable and vice versa. If the characteristic roots of A are λ_i, $i=1,..,n$, the characteristic roots of A^{-1} are given by $\mu_i = \lambda_i^{-1}$.

There is of course nothing uniquely interesting about constant paths for the forcing variables. While they permit us to analyse the stability of the homogeneous equation system, the behaviour of the complete system cannot be determined until the actual trajectories for the forcing variables have been specified. Assume e.g. that all characteristic roots of A are unstable and that C is square and of full rank. Let x_t satisfy $x_t = C^{-1}(A^{-1}-A)y_t$. Equation (9) then evolves according to $y_t = A^{-1}\, y_{t-1}$. The causal solution is now stable and the non-causal solution is unstable.

If a random disturbance term u_t were added to equation (9), the causal solution would involve current and lagged disturbances and the non-causal solution actual, realized values of future random disturbances. While the mathematics are willing, economic sense does not accept the proposition that *actual* future realizations of random variables (as opposed to current and past estimates of future random variables or distribution functions of future random variables) can influence the current state. Non-causal models that arise in economic applications will have known future deterministic exogenous variables and estimates of future random variables as determinants of the current state vector.

Some further non-uniqueness problems that arise in stochastic models with rational expectations of future endogenous variables can be illustrated with the simple Cagan-type hyperinflation model of equation (12)

$$m_t - p_t = -\alpha[E(p_{t+1}/I_t)-p_t] + u_t \qquad \alpha > 0 \qquad (12)$$

u_t is an *i.i.d.* random disturbance term. I_t, the information set conditioning expectations formed in period t, includes the market fundamentals (m_t, p_t the structure of the model, including the correct values of α and therefore u_t) as well as past values of m_t, p_t and u_t. It may also include current and past observations on an extraneous, "sunspot" variable ε_t which is an *i.i.d.* random disturbance.

The non-causal or forward-looking solution of (12) is :

$$p_t^f = \frac{1}{1+\alpha} m_t + \frac{1}{1+\alpha} \sum_{i=1}^{\infty} \left(\frac{\alpha}{1+\alpha}\right)^i E(m_{t+i}/I_t) - \frac{1}{1+\alpha} u_t + \lim_{M\to\infty} \left(\frac{\alpha}{1+\alpha}\right)^M E(p_{t+M}^f/I_t) \quad (13)$$

The current price level is a function of the current money stock and the current "fundamental" disturbance u_t, all anticipated future money supplies and a transversality condition for

$\lim_{M\to\infty} \left(\frac{\alpha}{1+\alpha}\right)^M E(p_{t+M}^f/I_t) = \eta_t$. Even if we assume that $\left|\frac{\alpha}{1+\alpha}\right| < 1$, η_t does not necessarily vanish. In fact any η_t that satisfies (14) can be substituted into (13)

$$\eta_t = \frac{\alpha}{1+\alpha} E(\eta_{t+1}/I_t) \quad (14)$$

Consider e.g. the case in which η_t is an infinite distributed lag on the fundamental disturbance u_t and the extraneous disturbance ε_t.

$$\eta_t = \sum_{i=0}^{\infty} [\, a_i u_{t-i} + b_i \varepsilon_{t-i} \,] \quad (15)$$

Let the a_i and b_i satisfy

$$a_i = \frac{\alpha}{1+\alpha} a_{i+1} \qquad i \geqslant 0 \tag{16a}$$

$$b_i = \frac{\alpha}{1+\alpha} b_{i+1} \qquad i \geqslant 0 \tag{16b}$$

The general non-causal solution to (12) is therefore given by

$$P_t^f = \frac{1}{1+\alpha} m_t + \frac{1}{1+\alpha} \sum_{i=1}^{\infty} \left(\frac{\alpha}{1+\alpha}\right)^i E(m_{t+i}/I_t) - \frac{1}{1+\alpha} u_t + \eta_t \tag{17}$$

where η_t is defined by (14) in general and, given our assumptions about I_t, by (15) and (16a,b). Note again that we cannot say anything about the stability of (17) until we have specified the stochastic process governing m_t.

Using the same kind of reasoning, the causal or backward-looking solution of (12) can be found to be

$$P_t^b = -\frac{1}{\alpha} \sum_{i=0}^{\infty} \left(\frac{1+\alpha}{\alpha}\right)^i m_{t-1-i} + \frac{1}{\alpha} \sum_{i=0}^{\infty} \left(\frac{1+\alpha}{\alpha}\right)^i u_{t-1-i} + \eta_t \tag{18}$$

η_t again satisfies (14), while a specific example of a process satisfying (14) and consistent with our assumptions about I_t is given in (15) and (16a,b). Note that even if $\left|\frac{1+\alpha}{\alpha}\right| > 1$, as will be the case if $\alpha > 0$, it makes no sense to describe (18) as unstable until the stochastic process governing m_t has been specified. For constant m_t, (18) is unstable if $\alpha > 0$, but with e.g.

$m_t = \left(\frac{1+2\alpha}{1+\alpha}\right) P_t$ this instability would be eliminated.

With the non-causal solution, an equal proportional increase in period t in the current and anticipated future money supplies raises the price level immediately and by the same proportion. By contrast, the causal solution shows that a fully anticipated increase in the money supply in period t will have no effect at all on the price level in period t; it will only affect the price level in period $t+1$ and beyond. Unanticipated current money, $m_t - E(m_t/I_{t-1})$, could be included in η_t and could therefore have an immediate effect on the price level. As it can enter η_t with a coefficient of either sign, the direction of the effect is arbitrary. Both (17), a "New Classical" equation and (18), an "Old Keynesian" equation are consistent with financial equilibrium and rational expectations. The policy implications of the two solutions differ greatly. By direct computation it can also be shown that linear combinations,with weights that sum to unity,of the causal and non-causal solutions are also solutions to (12).

Thus with rational expectations models that include current (or past) anticipations of future endogenous variables there are two kinds of non-uniqueness problems. As in all dynamic models, there is the problem of choosing between the causal solution, the non-causal solution and mixtures of the two. Additional information from outside the formal model is in general required to make this choice. The choice of the non-causal solution appears, on a priori economic grounds, to be appropriate for variables such as asset prices determined in efficient markets. In such models current asset prices are a function of expected future asset prices, and current prices can respond instantaneously to changes in information. For prices determined in inefficient markets the choice of the causal solution would seem to be appropriate. To rule out a solution because it is explosive for a constant path of the forcing variables is incorrect. First, there exist, in general, non-constant paths of the forcing variables that will stabilize a system whose homogeneous solution is unstable. Second, at any rate for causal systems, there is no good economic reason to rule out unstable solutions unless they lead infinite time to violations of physical or behavioural constraints. There is no divine guarantee that economic systems are stable.

In addition, having resolved this non-uniqueness problem, there is the problem of what to do about η_t in either solution. Unless one imposes the condition that $\eta_t \equiv 0$, "irrelevant" lagged fundamental disturbances and current and lagged extraneous random disturbances can enter the solutions (17) or (18). Price level variance minimizing solutions are characterized by $\eta_t \equiv 0$. For the η_t process in (15) this is achieved e.g. by setting $a_0 = b_0 = 0$. Whether decentralized markets can achieve the collectively rational decision of ignoring extraneous information and irrelevant lagged fundamental disturbances is an issue that has not yet been resolved. There may be a role for a central policy maker in imposing the minimum variance solution.

V Optimal Feedback Rules in Non-Causal Models: The "Innovation Contingent" Policy

In a well-known paper Kydland and Prescott have argued that optimal control in rational expectations models is impossible (Kydland and Prescott (1977)). In more recent statements, this argument has been weakened to the proposition that the search for optimal policies should be limited to a comparison of alternative fixed operating rules in order to select the one with the most attractive operating characteristics. The most plausible interpretation of their view is that in non-causal rational expectations models optimal policies are of the *open-loop* type rather than of the *closed-loop* or *feedback* type. As stated before, an open-loop policy is a non-state-dependent policy announced at some initial date which specifies the values of the policy instruments for all future time as a function of the information set at the initial date. Closed-loop or feedback policies make the values of the instruments at the current moment and in the future a possibly time-varying but known (as of the initial date) function of the current (respectively the future) states of the economy. These future states will be random variables in a stochastic world.

Kydland and Prescott's proposition is quite distinct

from the New Classical proposition that only unanticipated (monetary) policy can have real effects. It applies with full force only if the anticipated future values of the policy instruments as well as innovations in the policy instruments affect the joint probability density functions of real variables. Traditional optimal control techniques such as stochastic dynamic programming do not allow for the impact of future policy measures on the current state through the changes in current behavior induced by anticipation of these future policy measures. Such "time-consistent" policies may be suboptimal. A time-consistent policy or plan is a sequence of rules, one for each period, which specifies policy actions contingent on the state of the world in that period. Each such rule has the property of being optimal given the subsequent elements of the sequence. (Prescott (1977)). In dynamic games with optimizing agents in which the current state depends on anticipated future states, the optimal plan in subsequent periods may not be the continuation of the first-period optimal plan over the remainder of the planning period: the optimal plan in a non-causal model may not be time-consistent.

In this section a linear-quadratic version of a simple two-period example due to Kydland and Prescott (1977) is analyzed that brings out the issues clearly. A deterministic model is considered first, followed by a stochastic version of the model.

A Certainty Model

The dynamic model is given in equations (19a,b,c), the objective function to be minimized in (20).

$$y_t = \alpha y_{t-1} + \gamma x_t + \delta x_{t+1} \qquad \alpha,\gamma,\delta \neq 0 \tag{19a}$$

$$y_0 = \bar{y}_0 = 0 \tag{19b}$$

$$x_3 = \bar{x}_3 = 0 \tag{19c}$$

$$W = k_1(y_1 - a_1)^2 + k_2(y_2 - a_2)^2 + k_3(x_1 - a_3)^2 \qquad k_1, k_2, k_3 > 0 \tag{20}$$

The model is non-causal because the current state depends on a future instrument value. An initial condition for y_0 and a terminal condition for x_3 are needed to make this a well-defined problem.

The optimal policy can be derived by minimizing (20) with respect to x_1 and x_2 subject to the constraints (19a,b,c). This optimal solution is open-loop and time-inconsistent, that is, it does not take advantage of the "time structure" of the model by deriving, in each period, the optimal policy choice for that period as a function of the state at the beginning of that period, taking into account that the same optimizing approach will be adopted in all subsequent periods.

The optimal policy is:

$$x_1{*} = \frac{\gamma^2[a_1(\alpha\delta + \gamma)-a_2\delta]k_1k_2 + a_3\delta^2k_1k_3 + a_3(\alpha\delta + \gamma)^2k_2k_3}{\gamma^4k_1k_2 + \delta^2k_1k_3 + (\alpha\delta + \gamma)^2k_2k_3} \tag{21a}$$

$$x_2{*} = \frac{\gamma^3[a_2-\alpha a_1]k_1k_2+\delta[a_1-\gamma a_3]k_1k_3 + (\alpha\delta + \gamma)[a_2-\alpha\gamma a_3]k_2k_3}{\gamma^4k_1k_2 + \delta^2k_1k_3 + (\alpha\delta + \gamma)^2k_2k_3} \tag{21b}$$

The time-consistent solution, in the sense of Kydland and Prescott, is the solution derived by traditional dynamic programming methods that attempt to exploit the time structure of the model. Starting from period 2, the value function for the last period $\underset{W}{=}$ is minimized with respect to x_2, taking as given the values of y_1 and x_1. *I.e.*, the dependence of y_1 on x_2, modeled in equation (19a), is ignored. The "optimum" value of x_2, $\hat{x}_2$ is then substituted into $\bar{\bar{W}}$ to yield $\hat{\bar{\bar{W}}}$. The optimization problem for period 1 consists in selecting the value of x_1 that minimizes W, given that $x_2 = \hat{x}_2$. Thus the time-consistent policy for period 2 is derived by choosing x_2 to minimize $k_2(y_2-a_2)^2$, treating y_1 as predetermined. This yields:

$$\hat{x}_2 = [a_2 - \alpha y_1]\gamma^{-1} \tag{22a}$$

Note that is implies $y_2 = a_2$.

The time-consistent policy for period 1 is derived by choosing x_1 to minimize

$k_1(y_1-a_1)^2 + k_3(x_1-a_3)^2$, given that x_2 is given by (22a).

This yields:

$$\hat{x}_1 = \frac{((\alpha\delta + \gamma)a_1 - \delta a_2)\gamma^2 k_1 + (\alpha\delta + \gamma)^2 a_3 k_3}{k_1\gamma^4 + k_3(\alpha\delta + \gamma)^2} \tag{22b}$$

Using $\hat{x}_2 = [a_2 - \alpha\gamma\hat{x}_1]\,[\alpha\delta + \gamma]^{-1}$, equation (22a) can be

rewritten as:

$$\hat{x}_2 = \frac{(a_2-\alpha a_1)\gamma^3 k_1 + (a_2-\alpha\gamma a_3)(\alpha\delta + \gamma)k_3}{k_1\gamma^4 + k_3(\alpha\delta + \gamma)^2} \tag{22a'}$$

Comparing (21a) with (22b) and (21b) with (22a') we note that in a model without uncertainty the "time-consistent" policy is suboptimal and the optimal policy is time-inconsistent. This conclusion needs to be qualified in a major way when uncertainty is introduced.

A Stochastic Model

The stochastic version of the optimization problem given in equations (19a,b,c) and (20) is given below:

minimize $W = \min E[k_1(y_1-a_1)^2 + k_2(y_2-a_2)^2 + k_3(x_1-a_3)^2/I_1]$

subject to:

$$y_t = \alpha y_{t-1} + \gamma x_t + \delta E(x_{t+1}/I_t) + u_t \tag{23}$$

$$y_0 = \bar{y}_o = 0$$

$$x_3 = \bar{x}_3 = 0$$

Without loss of generality we assume that I_t, the information set at the beginning of period t, does not contain y_t or u_t. When non-stochastic open-loop solutions are considered, $E(x_{t+1}/I_t) = x_{t+1}$. The optimal open-loop policy under uncertainty is the same as the optimal (open-loop) policy under certainty, given in (21a) and (21b). However, an open-loop policy cannot be truly optimal in a stochastic model. If $\alpha \neq 0$, y_t is a function of y_{t-1} (in our model y_2 is a function of y_1). When the optimal open-loop policy for periods 1 and 2 is chosen at the beginning of period 1, y_1 is unknown because it depends on the realization of the as yet unobserved disturbance u_1. After t=1, u_1 will be known. Any truly optimal policy rule for x_2 would enable it to respond to u_1. Conventional feedback policies that make x_t a function of y_{t-1} enable the policy instruments to respond to new information as it accrues. This advantage of feedback control in the presence of random disturbances has to be balanced against a disadvantage, highlighted in the certainty model: feedback control that makes x_t a function of y_{t-1} does not allow fully for the effect of future instrument values on the current state, both directly and indirectly through the effect of future instrument values on the optimal choice of current instrument values. Whether optimal open-loop control dominates or is dominated by feedback control can now only be determined on a case-by-case basis.

Note, however, that a more sophisticated kind of feedback control will not be subject to the Kydland-Prescott criticism. Optimal feedback control must permit a response of x_t to "news"; in our model this news consists of u_{t-1}, the random disturbance in the previous period. y_{t-1} is a function of $E(x_t/I_{t-1})$. To treat it as predetermined in the derivation of the "time-consistent" solution for x_t is suboptimal in almost all cases. u_{t-1} is not a function of x_t or $E(x_t/I_{t-1})$ but does convey useful information for the optimal choice of x_t. A truly optimal policy incorporates the dependence of y_{t-1} on x_t *and* allows a flexible response of future instrument values to future random disturbances. It can therefore be conveniently expressed as in "innovation" or "disturbance"-contingent policy. In a model with certainty the "innovation response" component of the optimal policy rule vanishes and the optimal rule is open-loop. Traditional time-consistent state-contingent feedback policies derived by dynamic programming may or may not be superior to the optimal open-loop policy, depending on the parameters of the model under consideration. There always exists an innovation-contingent feedback rule that is superior to the optimal open-loop policy. These points are illustrated with some simple examples.

The Time-Consistent or "State-Dependent" Feedback Policy

The time-consistent policy for period 2 is derived by choosing x_2 to minimize $E(k_2(y_2-a_2)^2/I_2)$,[9] treating y_1 as given. From the vantage point of period 2 we have $y_2 = \alpha y_1 + \gamma x_2 + u_2$. The solution for x_2 is:

$$\hat{x}_2 = [a_2-\alpha y_1]\gamma^{-1} \tag{24a}$$

Note that this choice of x_2 implies that $E(y_2-a_2/I_2) = 0$. The time-consistent solution for x_1 is found by choosing x_1 to minimize $E(k_1(y_1-a_1)^2 + k_2(y_2-a_2)^2 + k_3(x_1-a_3)^2/I_1)$ given that x_2 is set according to (24a). This implies that $E(y_2-a_2/I_1) = 0$

The solution for x_1 is:

$$\hat{x}_1 = \frac{((\alpha\delta+\gamma)a_1-\delta a_2)\gamma^2 k_1 + (\alpha\delta+\gamma)^2 a_3 k_3}{k_1\gamma^4+k_3(\alpha\delta+\gamma)^2} \tag{24b}$$

Comparing (24a) and (24b) with (22a) and (22b) we note that the time-consistent solution is the same with and without uncertainty, provided the solution is expressed in feedback form. Under certainty, however, the time-consistent solution is suboptimal and the (time-inconsistent) optimal open-loop solution is the truly optimal solution. With uncertainty the expected loss under the optimal open-loop policy may either be smaller or larger than the expected loss under the time-consistent policy. This is because the optimal open-loop policy is not truly optimal because it cannot respond to future random disturbances. The optimal open-loop policy may be dominated not only by the time-consistent policy but also by simple ad-hoc (linear) feedback rules that permit future instrument values to respond to new information. The ranking of the various policies depends on all the parameters of the model under consideration and can only be established on a case-by-case basis.

To compare the expected loss under the optimal open-loop policy and the time-consistent policy we must evaluate

$E[k_1(y_1-a_1)^2 + k_2(y_2-a_2)^2 + k_3(x_1-a_3)^2 | I_1]$ under the two regimes. Thus, for the open-loop policy we evaluate

$$W_u^* = E[k_1(\gamma x_1^*+\delta x_2^*+u_1-a_1)^2 + k_2(\alpha\gamma x_1^*+(\alpha\delta+\gamma)x_2^*+\alpha u_1+u_2-a_2)^2 + k_3(x_1^*-a_3)^2/I_1] \tag{25a}$$

while for the time-consistent policy we evaluate

$$\hat{W}_u = E[k_1(\gamma\hat{x}_1+\delta E(\hat{x}_2/I_1) + u_1-a_1)^2 + k_2(\alpha\gamma\hat{x}_1+\alpha\delta E(\hat{x}_2/I_1) + \alpha u_1+\gamma\hat{x}_2+u_2-a_2)^2 + k_3(\hat{x}_1-a_3)^2/I_1] \tag{25b}$$

Note that

$$E(\hat{x}_2/I_1) = [a_2-\alpha\gamma\hat{x}_1]\ (\alpha\delta+\gamma)^{-1} \tag{26a}$$

$$\hat{x}_2 = a_2\gamma^{-1}-\alpha\hat{x}_1-\alpha\gamma^{-1}\delta E(\hat{x}_2/I_1) - \alpha\gamma^{-1}u_1$$
$$= [a_2-\alpha\gamma\hat{x}_1](\alpha\delta+\gamma)^{-1}-\alpha\gamma^{-1}u_1. \tag{26b}$$

To simplify the calculations, it is assumed that $a_1 = a_2 = 0$. As regards the random disturbances it is assumed that $E(u_1) = E(u_2) = E(u_1u_2) = 0$ and $E(u_1^2) = E(u_2^2) = \sigma_u^2$. Substituting (21a) and (21b) into (25a) and (25b), (26a) and (26b) into (25b) we obtain:

$$W^*_u = E[k_1(\frac{a_3\gamma^2(\alpha\delta+\gamma)k_2k_3}{\gamma^4k_1k_2 + \delta^2k_1k_3 + (\alpha\delta+\gamma)^2k_2k_3} + u_1)^2$$

$$+ k_2(\frac{-a_3\delta\gamma^2k_1k_3}{\gamma^4k_1k_2 + \delta^2k_1k_3 + (\alpha\delta+\gamma)^2k_2k_3} + \alpha u_1 + u_2)^2$$

$$+ k_3(\frac{-a_3\gamma^4k_1k_2}{\gamma^4k_1k_2 + \delta^2k_1k_3 + (\alpha\delta+\gamma)^2k_2k_3})^2\ /I_1]$$

$$\hat{W}_u = E[k_1(\frac{a_3\gamma^2(\alpha\delta+\gamma)k_2k_3}{\gamma^4k_1k_2+(\alpha\delta+\gamma)^2k_2k_3} + u_1)^2$$

$$+ k_2(u_2)^2 + k_3(\frac{-a_3\gamma^4k_1k_2}{\gamma^4k_1k_2+(\alpha\delta+\gamma)^2k_2k_3})^2/I_1]$$

Therefore,

$$W^*_u-\hat{W}_u = k_1[(\frac{a_3\gamma^2(\alpha\delta+\gamma)k_2k_3}{\gamma^4k_1k_2+\delta^2k_1k_3+(\alpha\delta+\gamma)^2k_2k_3})^2 -$$

$$\left(\frac{a_3\gamma^2(\alpha\delta+\gamma)k_2k_3}{\gamma^4k_1k_2+(\alpha\delta+\gamma)^2k_2k_3}\right)^2] \qquad (27)$$

$$+ k_2\left(\frac{a_3\delta\gamma^2k_1k_3}{\gamma^4k_1k_2+\delta^2k_1k_3+(\alpha\delta+\gamma)^2k_2k_3}\right)^2 + k_2\alpha^2\sigma_u^2$$

$$+ k_3[\left(\frac{a_3\gamma^4k_1k_2}{\gamma^4k_1k_2+\delta k_1k_3+(\alpha\delta+\gamma)^2k_2k_3}\right)^2 - \left(\frac{a_3\gamma^4k_1k_2}{\gamma^4k_1k_2+(\alpha\delta+\gamma)^2k_2k_3}\right)^2]$$

Except for the term $k_2\alpha^2\sigma_u^2$, equation (27) also measures the difference between the loss under the optimal (open-loop) policy under certainty, W_c^* and the loss under the time-consistent policy in the case without uncertainty, $\hat{W}_c$. Therefore,

$$W_u^* - \hat{W}_u = W_c^* - \hat{W}_c + k_2\alpha^2\sigma_u^2 \qquad (28)$$

In the absence of uncertainty we know that $W_c^* - \hat{W}_c < 0$. With uncertainty however, it is quite possible that the minimum expected loss under the time-consistent policy is less than that under the optimal open-loop policy. A sufficiently large value of σ_u^2 will ensure this, if k_2 and α are not equal to zero.

An Innovation-Contingent Feedback Policy

It is easily established that the optimal open-loop policy given by x_1^* and x_2^* in (21a) and (21b) is dominated by an innovation-contingent feedback policy. Substituting the constraint given by (23) into the objective function yields:

$$W = E[k_1(\gamma x_1+\delta E(x_2/I_1)+u_1-a_1)^2+k_2(\alpha\gamma x_1+\alpha\delta E(x_2/I_1)+\gamma x_2+\alpha u_1 +u_2-a_2)^2 + k_3(x_1-a_3)^2/I_1] \tag{29}$$

Now the difference between x_2 and $E(x_2/I_1)$ can only be a linear function of the new information that has accrued between the beginning of period 1 when the expectation $E(x_2/I_1)$ was formed and the beginning of period 2 when x_2 is set (before y_2 and u_2 are observed). This new information consists only of u_1. We can therefore write:

$$x_2 = E(x_2/I_1) + Gu_1 \tag{30}$$

Here G is a linear function, to be chosen by the policy maker. Substituting (30) into (29) yields

$$W = E[k_1(\gamma x_1+\delta E(x_2/I_1) + u_1-a_1)^2 + k_2(\alpha\gamma x_1+(\alpha\delta+\gamma)E(x_2/I_1)+(\alpha+\gamma G)u_1-u_2-a_2)^2+k_3(x_1-a_3)^2/I_1] \tag{31}$$

We now minimize (31) with respect to x_1, $E(x_2/I_1)$ and G. This yields optimal values x_1^{**}, $E(x_2/I_1)^{**}$ and G^{**} given by

$$x_1^{**} = x_1^* \tag{32a}$$

$$E(x_2/I_1)^{**} = x_2^* \tag{32b}$$

$$G^{**} = -\alpha\gamma^{-1} \tag{32c}$$

The optimal innovation-contingent feedback policy is therefore given by:

$$x_1^{**} = x_1^* \tag{33a}$$

$$x_2^{**} = x_2^* - \alpha\gamma^{-1}u_1 \tag{33b}$$

The optimal innovation-contingent feedback policy has the optimal open-loop policy (x_1^*, x_2^*) as its open-loop component, that is, the component anticipated as of $t=1$. The optimal value of the feedback coefficient G is the one that exactly neutralizes the effect of u_1 on y_2.[10] The policy (x_1^{**}, x_2^{**}) dominates the optimal open-loop policy x_1^*, x_2^*, as can be seen by comparing W_u^* in (25a) with W_u^{**} below:[11]

$$W_u^{**} = E[k_1(\gamma x_1^{*}+\delta x_2^{*}+u_1-a_1)^2 + k_2(\alpha\gamma x_1^{*}+(\alpha\delta+\gamma)x_2^{*} + u_2-a_2)^2 + k_3(x_1^* - a_3)^2/I_1] \tag{34}$$

$$W_u^* - W_u^{**} = k_2\alpha^2\sigma_u^2 > 0 \tag{35}$$

The (x_1^{**}, x_2^{**}) policy is not "time-consistent" in the sense of Kydland and Prescott because it cannot be derived by the backward recursive optimization techniques of stochastic dynamic programming. It is therefore subject to all the well-known problems of inducing the policy-maker to adopt and stick with an optimal, time-inconsistent policy. This paper has nothing to say on how to adopt and enforce a time-inconsistent policy rule or "constitution". It does make clear that such a constitution should be a flexible, closed-loop constitution rather than a fixed, open-loop constitution. This is because (x_1^{**}, x_2^{**}) can only be specified as a feedback rule or contingent rule and because it dominates the time-inconsistent optimal open-loop rule except in the special case of no uncertainty, when the two policies coincide. It is easily checked that the innovation-contingent rule also dominates the time-consistent policy; from (35)

$$W^{**}_u = W^*_u - k_2\alpha^2\sigma^2_u < \hat{W}_u$$

Conclusion

There has been a "rational expectations revolution" in macroeconomics. The subject will never be the same again. The "principle of policy-dependent structural parameters" brings out the need to model simultaneously the expectation formation process and the stochastic processes governing the behavior of the variables whose values are being predicted or inferred - stochastic processes that may themselves be functions of the expectation formation process. There is an urgent need to relax the extreme informational requirements of most current macroeconomic rational expectations models and to reformulate the rational expectations hypothesis in terms of a more general optimal Bayesian prediction and inference theory. Such developments are within reach and will in no way diminish the importance of the contribution of Lucas.

The rational expectations revolution has also forced a fundamental rethinking of the dynamic programming approach to optimization in dynamic economic models. In causal models, differential game theory provides the appropriate analytical tool for modeling the interdependence of rational private sector and public sector agents. (See Buiter (1980a)). In noncausal models, Kydland and Prescott's demonstration of the suboptimality of "consistent" plans derived from traditional dynamic programming approaches alters, but does not eliminate the scope for beneficial feedback policy. In models with uncertainty, the optimal open-loop policy need not dominate the "consistent" policy or other, ad-hoc feedback policies that make the values of the current policy instruments some known (linear) function of the information set at the time that the policy instrument value must be set. The optimal open-loop policy is dominated by the optimal linear innovation-contingent feedback rule that sets the current values of the policy instruments equal to their optimal open-loop values plus a linear function of the "news". There is no presumption that a suboptimal, restricted open-loop policy such as a constant growth rate for the stock of money will generate desirable outcomes in macroeconomic models that incorporate a variety of internal and external disturbances.

Acceptance of the importance of the contribution of the rational expectations hypothesis should, however, be kept quite separate from one's view on the value of the remainder of the New Classical Macroeconomics package. That remainder - the general application of the efficient markets hypothesis to goods and factor markets, the monetary neutrality and super-neutrality postulates, the debt neutrality theorem and the other assumptions underlying what I have called the "public sector-private sector Modigliani-Miller theorem" (Buiter (1979a,b) - does not constitute a promising approach to the analysis and control of real-world economic systems. The theoretical case against debt neutrality and against monetary superneutrality is overwhelming. A strong case also can be made for short-run real effects of deterministic money supply rules. The microeconomic foundations of inefficient markets are in the process of being developed. Non-cooperative game theory, bargaining theory and the theory of production and exchange under asymmetric, imperfect and costly information are the starting point for the New Keynesian Macroeconomics.

REFERENCES

Akerlof, G. (1970) "The Market for 'Lemons': Qualitative Uncertainty and the Market Mechanism," *Quarterly Journal of Economics*, 84, August, pp. 488-500

Aoki, Masanao, and Matthew Canzoneri (1979) "Reduced Forms of Rational Expectations Models," *Quarterly Journal of Economics*, 93, February, pp. 59-71

Attfield, C.L.F., Demery, D. and Duck, N.W. "Unanticipated Monetary Growth, Output and the Price Level: U.K. 1946-77" University of Bristol *Mimeo*, July 1979a

"A Quarterly Model of Unanticipated Monetary Growth and Output in the U.K. 1963-70" University of Bristol *Mimeo*, September, 1979b

Bacharach, Michael, (1976) *Economics and the Theory of Games*, Macmillan, London

Bacon, Walter, and Eltis, Robert (1978) *Britain's Economic Problem: Too Few Producers. 2nd.* ed. Macmillan

Barro, Robert J. (1974) "Are Government Bonds Net Wealth?" *Journal of Political Economy* 82, November-December, pp 1095-117

Barro, Robert J. (1976) "Rational Expectations and the Role of Monetary Policy," *Journal of Monetary Economics*, 2, January, pp. 1095-1117

(1977a) "Unanticipated Money Growth and Unemployment in the United States," *American Economic Review*, March, pp. 101-115

"Long-Term Contracting, Sticky Prices and Monetary Policy," *Journal of Monetary Economics*, 3, July 1977b, pp 305-316

The Impact of Social Security on Private Saving. Evidence from the U.S. Time Series, A.E.I. Washington D.C. 1978a

(1978b) "Unanticipated Money, Output and the Price Level in the United States," *Journal of Political Economy*, August, pp. 549-580

(1979) "Second Thoughts on Keynesian Economics," *American Economic Review*, Papers and Proceedings, 69, May, pp. 54-9

Blanchard, Olivier (1979) "Backward and Forward Solutions for Economies with Rational Expectations," *American Economic Review*, 69, Papers and Proceedings, May, pp. 114-118

Brown, Bryan W. and Shlomo Maital, (1979) "What Do Economists Know? An Empirical Study of Experts' Expectations," Woodrow Wilson Working Paper, Princeton University

Buiter, Willem H "Crowding Out and the Effectiveness of Fiscal Policy," *Journal of Public Economics*, 7, June 1977, pp 309-328

(1979a) *Temporary and Long-run Equilibrium*, Garland Publishing Inc., New York, 1979

(1979b) "The Roles of Monetary, Financial and Fiscal Policy under Rational Expectations," NBER Working Paper No. 412, November

(1979c) "Government Finance in an Overlapping Generations Model with Gifts and Bequests" in George M.

von Furstenberg ed. *Social Security vs. Private Saving*, Ballinger 1980

(1980a) "The Role of Economic Policy after the New Classical Macroeconomics," Bristol University Discussion Paper No. 78/80. January 1980

(1980b) "The Macroeconomics of Dr. Pangloss; A Critical Survey of the New Classical Macroeconomics," *Economic Journal*, 90, March, pp. 34-50

Buiter Willem H. and James Tobin, (1979) "Debt Neutrality: A Brief Review of Doctrine and Evidence" in George M. von Furstenberg, ed. *Social Security vs. Private Saving*, Ballinger 1980

Buiter Willem H and Jonathan Eaton "Policy Decentralization and Exchange Rate Management in Interdependent Economies," University of Bristol Discussion Paper, August 1980

Buiter, Willem H and Ian D. Jewitt "Staggered Wage Setting Without Money Illusion: Variations on a Theme of Taylor," University of Bristol Discussion Paper August 1980

De Canio, Stephen, (1979) "Rational Expectations and Learning from Experience" *Quarterly Journal of Economics*, February, pp. 45-57

Chow, Gregory, (1975) *Analysis and Control of Dynamic Economic Systems*, John Wiley and sons, New York

Douglas, Paul, (1932) "Money, Credit and the Depression." *The World Tomorrow*, 15 March, pp. 78-80

(1935) *Controlling Depressions* New York: W.W. Norton and Co.

Drazen, Allan, (1980) "Recent Developments in Macroeconomic Disequilibrium Theory," *Econometrica*, 48, March, pp. 283-306

Fischer, Stanley, (1979) "Long-term Contracts, Rational Expectations and the Optimal Money Supply Rule,"

Journal of Political Economy, February. pp. 191-205

Fisher, I. (1933) "Debt Deflation Theory of Great Depressions," *Econometrica*, 1, October, pp. 337-357

Flood, Robert P and Peter M. Garber (1980) "Market Fundamentals vs. Price Level Bubbles: The First Tests," forthcoming in the *Journal of Political Economy*, 1980

Friedman B. (1979) "Optimal Expectations and the Extreme Information Assumptions of 'Rational Expectations' Macromodels." *Journal of Monetary Economics*, 5 January, pp. 23-41

Friedman, Milton, (1968) "The Role of Monetary Policy," *American Economic Review*, 58, March, pp 1-17

Gordon, Robert J, "New Evidence that Fully Anticipated Monetary Changes Influence Real Output After All," *NBER Working Paper* No. 361, June 1979

Grossman, Sanford, (1976) "On the Efficiency of Competitive Stock Markets Where Traders Have Diverse Information," *Journal of Finance*, 31, May, pp 573-85

Grossman, S. and J. Stiglitz, (1976) "Information and Competitive Price Systems," *American Economic Review*, May, pp. 246-253

Haberler, G. (1932) "Money and the Business Cycle" in *Gold and Monetary Stabilization*, Q. Wright ed. pp. 43-74. Chicago, University of Chicago Press

(1956) "Monetary and Real Factors Affecting Economic Stability: A Critique of Certain Tendencies in Modern Economic Theory." in *Banca Nazionale Del Lavoro. Quarterly Review*, Vol IX, September. Reprinted in *Readings in Business Cycles*, R.A. Gordon and L.R. Klein eds. Richard D. Irwin Inc. Homewood Illinois, 1965, pp. 130-149

Hahn, Frank H. (1977), "Exercises in Conjectural Equilibria," *Scandinavian Journal of Economics*, 79, pp. 210-226

Hall, Robert E. (1970) "Why is the Unemployment Rate so High at Full Employment?" *Brookings Papers on Economic Activity*, 3, pp. 369-402

(1979) "A Theory of the Natural Unemployment Rate and the Duration of Employment," *Journal of Monetary Economics*, 4, April. pp. 153-170

Hawtrey, Ralf G. (1926) "The Trade Cycle," *De Economist*, 1926, reprinted in *Readings in Business Cycles*, G. Haberler, ed. The Blakiston Co. 1944, Philadelphia pp. 330-349

Hayek, Friedrich A. (1932) *Monetary Theory and the Trade Cycle:* Harcourt, Brace and Co. New York

(1939) "Price Expectations, Monetary Disturbances and Malinvestments." First published in *Nationalokonomisk Tidsskrift*, vol 73, no, 3, 1935. Reprinted in *Readings in Business Cycles*, G. Haberler, ed. The Blakiston Co. 1944, Philadelphia, pp. 350-365

Intriligator, Michael D. (1971) *Mathematical Optimization and Economic Theory*, Prentice Hall, Inc. Englewood Cliffs, N.J.

Knight, Frank, (1941) "The Business Cycle, Interest and Money; A Methodological Approach," *Review of Economic Statistics*, 23, May, pp. 53-67

Kydland, F.E. (1975) "Noncooperative and Dominant Player Solutions in Discrete Dynamic Games," *International Economic Review*, 16, June, pp, 321-335

and Prescott, E.C. (1971) "Rules Rather than Discretion: The Inconsistency of Optimal Plans" *Journal of Political Economy*, 85, June, pp. 473-491

Lucas, Robert E. (1972a) "Expectations and the Neutrality of Money," *Journal of Economic Theory*, 4, April, pp. 103-124

(1972b) "Econometric Testing of the Natural Rate Hypothesis," in O. Eckstein ed. *The Econ-*

ometrics of Price Determination, a conference sponsored by the Board of Governors of the Federal Reserve System and the Social Science Research Council

(1975) "An Equilibrium Model of the Business Cycle," *Journal of Political Economy*, 83, December, pp. 1113-44

(1976) "Econometric Policy Evaluation: A Critique," in *The Phillips Curve and Labor Markets*, Karl Brunner and Allen H. Melzer, eds. Amsterdam, North Holland

and Sargent, T.J. (1978) "After Keynesian Macroeconomics," in *After the Phillips Curve: Persistence of High Inflation and High Unemployment*, Federal Reserve Bank of Boston, Boston, pp. 49-72

McCallum, Bennett T. (1977) "Price Level Stickiness and the Feasibility of Monetary Stabilization Policy with Rational Expectations." *Journal of Political Economy*, 85, June, pp, 627-634

(1978) "Price Level Adjustments and the Rational Expectations Approach to Macroeconomic Stabilization Policy," *Journal of Money, Credit and Banking*, 10, November, pp. 418-436

Muth, J. (1961) "Rational Expectations and the Theory of Price Movements," *Econometrica*, 29, July, pp. 315-335

Negishi, T. (1960) "Monopolistic Competition and General Equilibrium," *Review of Economic Studies*, 28, pp 196-201

Phelps, Edward S. et.al. (1970) *Microeconomic Foundations of Employment and Inflation Theory*, W.W. Norton, New York

and John B. Taylor, (1977) "Stabilizing Powers of Monetary Policy under Rational Expectations," *Journal of Political Economy*, 85, February, pp. 163-190

Prescott, Edward, (1975) "Efficiency of the Natural Rate,"

Journal of Political Economy, 83, December, pp. 1229-36

(1977) "Should Control Theory be used for Economic Stabilization?" in *Optimal Policies, Control Theory and Technology Exports*, eds. K. Brunner and A.H. Meltzer, Carnegie-Rochester Conference Series on Public Policy, Vol. 7

Riley, J. (1979) "Noncooperative Equilibrium and Market Signalling" *American Economic Review*, 69, Papers and Proceedings, May, pp. 303-307

Salop, S. (1978) "Parables of Information Transmission," in A. Mitchell, ed. *The Effect of Information on Consumer and Market Behavior*. Chicago

(1979) "A Model of the Natural Rate of Unemployment." *American Economic Review*, 69, March, pp. 117-125

Sargent, Thomas, and Neil Wallace, (1973) "The Stability of Models of Money and Growth with Perfect Foresight," *Econometrica*, 41, November, pp. 1043-48

(1975) "Rational Expectations, the Optimal Monetary Instrument and the Optimal Money Supply Rule," *Journal of Political Economy*, 83, April, pp. 241-254

(1976) "Rational Expectations and the Theory of Economic Policy," *Journal of Monetary Economics*, 2, April, pp. 1-44

Shiller, Robert J. (1978) "Rational Expectations and the Dynamic Structure of Macroeconomic Models: A Critical Review," *Journal of Monetary Economics*, 4 January, pp. 1-44

Stiglitz, Joseph E. (1977) "Monopoly, Non-linear Pricing and Imperfect Information: The Insurance Market." *Review of Economic Studies*, 44, October, pp. 407-430

(1979) "Equilibrium in Product Markets with Imperfect Information," *American Economic Review*, Papers and Proceedings, 69, March, pp. 339-345

Taylor, John, (1977) "Conditions for Unique Solutions in Stochastic Macoeconomic Models with Rational Expectations" *Econometrica*, 45, September, pp. 1377-85

Taylor, John B. (1980) "Aggregate Dynamics and Staggered Contracts," *Journal of Political Economy*, 88, February 1980, pp. 1-23

Tobin, James and Willem Buiter, (1980) "Fiscal and Monetary Policies, Capital Formation and Economic Activity," in George von Furstenberg ed. *The Government and Capital Formation*, Ballinger

Turnovsky, Stephen J. (1980) "The Choice of Monetary Instruments under Alternative Forms of Price Expectations," *Manchester School*, March 1980, pp. 39-62

Weiss, Laurence (1980) "The Role for Active Monetary Policy in a Rational Expectations Model," *Journal of PoliticalEconomy*, 88 April, pp. 221-233

Wilson, Charles A. (1977) "A Model of Insurance Markets with Incomplete Information," *Journal of Economic Theory*, 16, December, pp. 167-207

(1979) "Equilibrium and Adverse Selection," *American Economic Review*, Papers and Proceedings, March, pp. 313-317

FOOTNOTES

1. This paper was written while I was a consultant with the Financial Studies Division of the Research Department of the International Monetary Fund. The opinions expressed are my own. I would like to thank Mohsin Khan and Don Mathieson for discussions on causal and noncausal solutions to dynamic models, and George von Furstenberg for comments on an earlier draft. Sean Holly pointed out an error in an earlier version of the paper. An anonymous referee made extensive comm-

ents.

2. An excellent early survey of the role of monetary and real factors in the trade cycle is Haberler (1956). While emphasizing the importance of the money supply process and of financial factors in general, he also considers price and wage regidity to be necessary elements in the transmission mechanism. His emphasis on "large fixed monetary contracts" (p.139, p. 140) is also surprisingly "modern."

3. Price stickiness is consistent with only unanticipated policy having an effect on real output or employment as long as production and employment depend only on price surprises and not on the actual price. McCallum (1977, 1978) has sticky prices but equates the quantity produced to the notional supply of output which is a function of the price surprise only. One can even have a "disequilibrium" determination of production by assuming that actual output is the "min" of the effective demand for and the effective supply of output. As long as both effective demand and effective supply are functions of price surprises only, ineffectiveness of anticipated policy follows.

4. An early characterization of a "rational expectations equilibrium"can be found in Hayek (1939). "The main difficulty of the traditional approach is its complete abstraction from time. A concept of equilibrium which essentially was applicable only to an economic system conceived as timeless could not be of great value .... It has become clear that, instead of completely disregarding the time element, we must make very definite assumptions about the attitude of persons towards the future. *The assumptions of this kind which are implied in the concept of equilibrium are essentially that everybody foresees the future correctly and that this foresight includes not only the changes in the objective data but also the behavior of all the other people with whom he expects to perform economic transactions*" (Italics added).

5. This is the property that predictions of future variables differ from the actual future outcomes only by errors which are independent of the variables used to generate the predictions. Friedman (1979), p. 24

6. Crucial in the sense that major qualitative properties of the model depend on it.

7. Note that instead of minimizing deviations of output from the ex-post natural level u_t^y we could instead have minimized deviations of output from the ex-ante natural level, *0*.

8. See also Taylor (1977), Aoki and Canzoneri (1979), Flood and Garber (1980).

9. Note that it is assumed that y_t and u_t are not elements of I_t. x_t has to be chosen before y_t and u_t are observed. This assumption can easily be relaxed to include partial or complete contemporaneous observations on y_t and u_t.

10. Having derived the optimal policy, x_2** and x_1** , we can, using (23), express the optimal value of x_2 as a function of y_1. While it is always possible to reformulate any innovation-contingent policy as a state-contingent one (and vice-versa), the innovation-contingent description of the optimal policy rule is preferable because it emphasises the nature of its derivation and the way in which it differs from the time-consistent policy.

11. In a private communication, Mr. C. R. Birchenhall of Manchester University has shown that the linear innovation contingent policy not only dominates the open-loop policy but also is the global optimal policy for this linear-quadratic model.

DISCUSSION : SEAN HOLLY

In his paper Willem Buiter has achieved a tour de force of a technically demanding field. While this provides an excellent service to the reader it makes the task of the discussant very difficult. At the risk of giving an unbalanced discussion of the many issues he addresses I will confine my substantive comments to the question of *time-consistency* and use this as an opportunity to make some points about the role of optimality in economic policymaking.

The author identifies three main pillars upon which the argument against activist stabilisation policies rests. The first, associated with Milton Friedman, emphasises the long and variable lags between changes in instruments and resulting effects on targets. The second, the New Classical view asserts that any anticipated policy has no real effects on the economy. The rapidly equilibrating behaviour of the economy makes stabilisation policy unnecessary. Thirdly, Kydland and Prescott (1977) have shown that when expectations are forward-looking the pursuit of optimal economic policies will be "time-inconsistent". For whatever of these reasons fixed rules (or open-loop policies) are to be preferred to discretionary rules (or closed-loop or feedback policies).

I shall consider this last argument in more detail. Kydland and Prescott have made a significant contribution to our understanding of dynamic economic systems; and it is worth noting that the validity of the paradox they have revealed is not predicated on the strict form of rational expectations which as Buiter shows plays such an integral role in the new classical economics. It is sufficient that economic agents only have some regard to the way in which policymakers respond to the economy when they form their expectations. Nevertheless, my own feeling is that Kydland and Prescott were not entirely clear in how they distinguished between time-consistent and time-inconsistent policies and optimal policies. In particular their conclusion that one should eschew stabilisation policies in favour of more or less fixed rules was not a straight inference from the problem of time-inconsistency but arises out of some numerical experiments they carried out in which they found that attempting to implement a stabilisation policy under rational expectations tended to perform worse than some passive policy and in some instances was actually destabilising. Orthodox optimal control procedures, whether they use a dynamic programming solution or some direct nonlinear optimisation algorithm, will for a deterministic system give values for the selected policy instruments that will minimise a quadratic objection function for some interval of time. We know also that by Bellman's Principle of Optimality if we implement this policy for one half of this interval (assuming that the preferences reflected in the objective function are unchanged) the optimal policy for the remainder of the interval is identical to the policy first calculated at the beginning of the interval. It is in this sense that we mean that a policy is time-consistent. Equally when we have a linear system with Gaussian disturbances the Principle of Optimality holds for the optimal feedback law calculated for the interval. When, however, current behaviour is affected by expectations about the future the Principle of Optimality breaks down. One response to this have been to try to devise methods which take account of the dependence of current states on future states and policy instruments. For example Chow (I980) has proposed a dynamic programming method which uses the noncausal solution approach while Holly and Zarrop (I979a) have suggested a nonlinear optimisation algorithm which also uses the noncausal representation. Taylor (I979) on the other hand first derives the causal solution for estimation purposes and then uses if for policy optimisation. In each case the intention is to ensure that expectations of economic agents are consistent with the optimal policies. That is, at time period t the optimal (open-loop or closed loop) policy for the interval $[1,N]$ is what can be denoted 'expectations-consistent' (Holly and Zarrop (I979b)). If the policymaker now implements this policy (which is time-consistent) in a deterministic system (implying perfect foresight) the 'expectations' that agents have formulated will turn out to be confirmed. Note that if in this context the policymaker were to ignore the forward nature of expectations formation (assuming adaptive expectations for example) then the problem he is trying to solve may be seriously misspecified and the policy he calculated for even the current period may be far from optimal.

Buiter states that "..policies derived by dynamic programming, which (kydland and Prescott) call 'consistent' policies, are suboptimal in models with optimising agents endowed with rational expectations of the future because such consistent policies fail to allow for the effect of anticipated future instrument values on current and past states." (p.7). This naturally raises the question whether 'expectations-consistent' policies will meet this condition and thus ensure 'time-consistency'. This may not necessarily be the case. Let us suppose that in time period t the policymaker calculates his 'expectations-consistent' optimal policy for the interval $[1,N]$ and we assume that economic agents *believe* that the policymaker will stick to the announced policy (open-loop in a deterministic world, closed-loop in a stochastic). The policymaker then implements the current period policy and moves to time period $t+1$. He then finds, however, that it is to his advantage (in the sense of achieving a lower value for the objective function over the remainder of the interval $[2,N]$) to change his policies from what they were intended to be. It is 'optimal' for him to renege on his previous commitments. If he could then somehow convince agents that for the remainder of the interval he will pursue his new set of policies the optimal policy could be implemented for time period $t+1$. If it were conceivable that the policymaker could continue in this vein, period by period, he would be able to implement his own optimal, though time-inconsistent, policies. In practice, however, he would be unable to continuously inflict prediction errors on economic agents. Given our rational expectations assumption they could equally infer what the policymaker's sequential time-inconsistent optimal policy was and base their expectations upon that. If they did this then the resulting path for the economy over the interval $[1,N]$ would be from the point of view of the policymaker less preferable, in the sense of having a higher quadratic cost, than if he had stuck to his original expectations-consistent policy calculated in time period t. This must be so because in time period t among the feasible set of expectations-consistent paths over $[1,N]$ the one which minimises the quadratic objective function has already been selected.

Clearly there is an element of indeterminacy in the problem which depends upon the amount of credence agents will place in the policymaker's announced actions. This seems a natural starting point for a dynamic game theoretic treatment of the subject.

Given that time-inconsistency remains a problem, how significant should we regard it? Is it just a special case arising from the particular way in which expectations are formulated or is it of more general application? In the origianl paper on time-inconsistency Strotz (1955-6) examined the case of a consumer choosing at time t a plan of consumption over some interval of time $[1,N]$ so as to maximise the utility of the plan as evaluated at time t. Strotz's conclusion was that this optimal plan would be one which would not be pursued. An analogous case can be found for the economic policymaker who (in a non-rational expectations world) wants an optimal policy for the interval $[1,N]$. Suppose he has an objective function

$$J = \tfrac{1}{2}\sum_{t=1}^{N} (1+\rho)^{-t}(y_t - y_t^d)^2 + \tfrac{1}{2}\sum_{t=1}^{N} k(x_t - x_t^d)^2$$

subject to

$$y_t = ay_{t-1} + bx_t$$

where y_t is a target variable x_t a policy instrument and the superscript d denotes desired values. We are assuming the policymaker discounts future departures from his desired path for his target. The path for x which minimises the objective function from the vantage point of time period t can easily be calculated. Ex ante, it is optimal but ex post, it is not. Policy will be time inconsistent. This can be seen if we imagine a policymaker who is very interested in the outcome for the economy over the next two years (perhaps the run up to an election) but who attaches little importance to what comes after. When the two years is up (and the election won) he will not wish to pursue the policies in subsequent periods which were 'optimal' from the vantage point of time period t. It does not require much ingenuity to come up with other examples of time inconsistency (the choice of horizons over which policy is designed may be another source of inconsistency). I would hazard a guess that time inconsistency is a more widespread problem for dynamic decision-making than is commonly supposed. Indeed in a recent paper Buiter (1980) draws attention to the prospect of time-inconsistency emerging in games among private agents.

The general nature of time-inconsistency in economic systems makes it unlikely that left to their own devices policymakers would pursue time consistent policies. While if they are constrained (perhaps by constitutional means) to be consistent, policy may no longer be optimal. This, however, may not be so serious a loss. In practical applications in the real world 'optimality' would be a very elusive concept. Stochastic control theory is only optimal for a very narrowly defined class of problems. Most of the problems, however, facing economic policymakers do not fall into this class and we are forced to rely upon approximations. Moreover, although modern control theory derived from the work of Kalman has largely swept the board in economices many control theorists have been unwilling to abandon classical control methods (used for example by Phillips (I954)) and there has been a steady flow of literature on generalising feedback theory to the multivariate case. Its relevance to economics has been examined by Livesey (I979) and Salmon and Young (I979). In a system which is poorly understood an 'optimal' policy may have very undesirable characteristics. To use the analogy of David Livesey, optimal control theory breeds as a very highly strung racehorse which in the right conditions will be a winner but which is prone to catch cold or break its legs on a rough course. A horse with more of the features of a carthorse will not necessarily be first but it will be more reliable and better able to survive the rough and tumble. *Robustness* may be a more preferable feature of economic policy than strict optimality.

References

Buiter, W.H., "The Macroeconomics of Dr. Pangloss : A Critical Survey of the New Classical Macroeconomics", *Economic Journal*, March I980

Holly, S. and Zarrop, M.B., "Calculating Optimal Economic Policies when Expectations are Rational", *E.F.U.* Discussion Paper No. 58. September I979a, London Business School

Holly, S. and Zarrop, M.B., "On Optimality and Time Consistency when Expectations are Rational", *E.F.U.* Discussion Paper No. 68, October I979b, London Business School

Kydland, F.E. and Prescott, E.C., "Rules Rather than Discretion : The Inconsistency of Optimal Plans",

Journal of Political Economy, June 1977

Livesey, D.A., "The Role of Feedback in Economic Policy", *in Optimal Control for Econometric Models*, S. Holly, B. Rustem and M.B. Zarrop (eds), 1979, Macmillans

Phillips, A., "Stabilisation Policy in a Closed Economy", *Economic Journal*, June, 1954

Salmon, M., and Young, P., "Control Methods and Quantitive Economic Policy", in S. Holly et al (op. cit.)

Strotz, R.H., "Myopia and Inconsistency in Dynamic Utility Maximisation" *Review of Economic Studies*, 23, 1955-56

Taylor, J.B., "Estimation and Control of a Macroeconomic Model with Rational Expectations", *Econometrica*, 1979

10. INVESTMENT GRANTS

Michael T. Sumner

INTRODUCTION[1]

The frequency of both innovation and more routine change in the U.K. fiscal stance towards investment has often been noted in the literature. Whatever its other defects, one of which is the creation of uncertainty that diminishes the impact of policy changes if the complaints of the business community are to be believed, the variability of the tax and incentive systems and of their respective rates provides a unique, though little used, source of information on the effects of fiscal policy. The particular episode to be investigated in this paper is the substitution of cash grants for tax allowances in respect of manufacturing investment in plant and equipment between 1966 and 1970.[2]

Two specific questions will be addressed. The grants policy included two years, 1967-8, when the rate of grant was raised from 20 to 25 per cent for a pre-announced period of explicitly limited duration, and the government adhered to its schedule. The announcement of the policy changed intertemporal prices, an instrument of stabilisation policy which has been widely recommended in the literature as a means of utilising substitution effects constructively, but whose efficacy has not previously been examined empirically. While similar devices have been used at other times and in other places, the duration of the temporary reduction in the net price of capital goods, and the government's observance of the rules of the game, make this episode unique. In contrast, the temporary liberalisation of depreciation rules in July 1971, scheduled to last only until July 1973, was made redundant when still more liberal depreciation rules, in the form of immediate write-off, were introduced in the 1972 budget, before the explicitly temporary character of the 1971 measures could have changed investment decisions substantially. The suspension of the U.S. investment credit in October 1966, due to expire in December 1967, met a similarly premature end when the credit was restored after only five months. Future researchers will be able to draw on Canadian experience with the temporary investment tax credit, introduced in 1975 to last until the end of June 1977; but at present the 1967-8 experiment is the only documented instance of an explicitly temporary change in the intertemporal price of investment in which the expectations generated by the announcement have not been falsified by the government's subsequent actions. It should be added that the Canadian government's extension, in the 1977 budget, of the investment tax credit for a further three years, while too late to dampen any impact the credit may have had, will presumably affect the credibility of any future announcements. Unless investment decisions are based on remarkably short memories, the implications of past experience for future policy decisions will be attenuated by the refusal of governments in all three countries to accept the constraint which is imposed on discretionary action when future fiscal changes are announced in advance.

In addition to deliberate attempts to utilise intertemporal substitution effects for countercyclical purposes, announcements of planned tax changes have occasionally been made under rather different circumstances. During the period studied in this paper, there were two occasions when changes in the corporate tax rate could have been anticipated with high probability. The Labour government elected in October 1964 was committed to restoring fiscal discrimination in favour of retentions; and the Conservative government elected in June 1970 entered office with an equally firm commitment to eliminating discrimination, at least for some class of shareholder.[3] In neither case was the future tax rate announced in advance, but the presumption that the total tax levied on corporate profits would be unaffected by the respective reforms, implied that the rate on corporate retentions, which is the rate of primary relevance to investment decisions (King, 1972), would be reduced in the first case and raised in the second. The cost-minimising response to an expected reduction in the corporate tax rate would be to accelerate planned investment, since the cash value of depreciation allowances is reduced with the tax rate; and conversely when a tax rate increase is anticipated. While the 1967-8 episode is the principal concern in this paper, these other instances are worth examining for any information they might provide about the response of investment to expected or announced fiscal changes.

The second, but logically prior, question to be examined

here concerns the equivalence of alternative forms of investment 'incentives'. During the period of the investigation, the instruments adopted included initial allowances, a form of accelerated depreciation, investment allowances, which were a net addition to the depreciation permitted for tax purposes, and cash grants, in addition to the annual writing-down allowances.[4] Given an estimate of 'the' discount rate, it is a trivial matter to compute the present value of tax allowances and grants, but there are obvious reasons for doubting whether such computations accurately reflect the influence of fiscal changes. The calculation of present values is sensitive to the discount rate adopted, and hence to the degree of capital market imperfections assumed. Despite generous provisions for carrying unused allowances forward and, more recently, backwards, tax allowances are not marketable,[5] and so are worth less in some cases than grants of apparently equal present value. The cash value of any allowance depends on the tax rate, which is known with certainty only *ex post*. The frequency of changes in the structure and rates of incentive systems, combined with the long lead time of major investment decisions, has often been cited as a reason for including a substantial discount for uncertainty in evaluations of fiscal inducements. In addition, questionnaire and interview studies conducted in the early 1960's and surveyed by Lund (1976) suggested that tax allowances had made little difference to investment behaviour, and raised the question of whether a more transparent, as well as more certain, form of incentive might be correspondingly more effective. It was these considerations which led to the introduction of cash grants (HMSO (1966)).

Neither of these questions has been subjected to close scrutiny. The only available estimate of the effects of the temporary increase in investment grants was obtained by the Central Statistical Office; the estimate was made 'by averaging the seasonally adjusted quarterly figures of expenditure in the last quarter of 1968 and the first quarter of 1969' and currently stands at 3.9 per cent of manufacturing investment in plant and machinery in 1968.[6] The CSO notes 'the smallness of the effect', but provides no standard of comparison. Moreover, the implicit judgement of what would have happened otherwise begs two questions, *viz.* the time period over which intertemporal substitution was the cost-minimising response and the allocation of the total effect to individual quarters. The rule-of-thumb estimate may be confirmed by a fuller investigation, but regardless of the outcome a firmer methodological foundation appears desirable. The only published econometric study to include the period in question, by Boatwright and Eaton (1972), avoids the issue by adopting as the dependent variable the CSO's smoothed investment series. More seriously, their model implies that the effect of the higher rate grants continued for (at least) fourteen quarters after they had reverted to their previous level, despite the fact that the date of the reversion was known two years in advance with the closest approximation to perfect certainty that can be expected in fiscal matters.

Information on the second question is equally scarce. The CBI, perhaps motivated by the Chancellor's expression of doubt as to the efficacy of investment allowances in his budget statement, conducted a survey of its members in 1965 on the relative merits of alternative incentive schemes: cash grants were regarded with little enthusiasm. A further survey carried out after grants had been introduced suggested that the vast majority of respondents would be completely unaffected by the policy change, a response which was entirely consistent with a standard appraisal of the old and new packages at market interest rates.[7] However, relatively few members of the CBI would be unable to claim tax allowances immediately, because of insufficient taxable incomes, at that juncture, or to perform present value calculations; a larger sample might have yielded a different response.

MODEL SPECIFICATIONS

Studies of investment behaviour concerned with the effects of fiscal policy usually stress the possibilities of substituting capital for labour at a point of time, and are normally classified according to the constraints imposed on the substitution process. Despite some attempted generalisations, the basic distinction is between models which permit equal possibilities for substitution *ex post* and *ex ante*, and those which allow *ex ante* but not *ex post* substitution, or between putty-putty and putty-clay models in current jargon.[8]

When fiscal changes are announced in advance an additional distinction is required between these models on the one hand and clay-clay models on the other. To impose the assumption of a clay-clay technology in the analysis of 'ordinary', unanticipated fiscal changes would be bizarre: the only channel for fiscal influence would then be through induced changes in economic lives; and it would in any case be possible to infer zero substitution possibilities from the more general putty-putty or putty-clay specifications, provided arbitrary restrictions on the form of the production function were not imposed prior to estimation. The clay-clay assumption does not, however, exclude the possibility of intertemporal substitution in response to anticipated fiscal or other changes in factor prices. Moreover, it has an important practical advantage over other specifications.

The implication, noted above, of Boatwright and Eaton's results, that investment was still being affected by the temporary 1967-8 increase in grants as late as mid-1972, illustrates the problem which arises when the possibility of conventional factor substitution is admitted. The higher rate of grant may have induced the adoption of higher than otherwise capital-labour ratios during the two-year period of operation; but investment in 1969 and subsequent years would have been affected only by errors in predicting the construction times of equipment ordered during 1967-8, or by the confident expectation that the government would change its declared policy and maintain the higher rate of grant on a permanent basis. In the absence of such errors and expectations, investment expenditures during 1967-8 and thereafter were based on two different sets of factor prices: the distributed lag of past prices which 'explains' investment in the period after the temporary increase would not contain the higher rate of grant.

The computational advantage afforded by a clay-clay specification should by now be clear. It is the only formulation which permits an assessment of the effects of the temporarily higher grants to be based on all the available information, for the period after as well as before the fiscal experiment. Since the only influence of fiscal policy would be through expectational channels, the effects of the single announcement can be captured by inserting a suitable dummy variable without biasing the other estimated parameters of the investment function.

In contrast, putty-putty and putty-clay formulations can be accommodated only by splitting the sample, a procedure which may, however, permit some inferences to be drawn about the existence of a learning process in decision-makers' evaluation of fiscal policy, and about the intertemporal stability of the investment process itself. Since there is only a single unambiguous instance of the generation of an anticipated price change by fiscal measures, this episode cannot be modelled directly. Instead the significance of anticipatory purchasing of capital goods is inferred from the prediction errors of equations fitted up to the period when the intertemporal transfer of expenditure become profitable. These equations are based on generalisations of Jorgenson's and Bischoff's models.

The model introduced by Jorgenson (1963) contains four essential components. Gross investment is the sum of net investment and replacement. The latter is proportional to the net capital stock; the former is a distributed lag function, for which no adequate justification is provided, of past changes in the static optimal capital stock. Finally, the optimal capital stock is determined from the assumed Cobb-Douglas production function as proportional to physical output divided by the implicit price of capital services relative to the price of output.

Several modifications have been introduced in the subsequent literature. The most immediately obvious generalisation is to substitute a CES for the Cobb-Douglas production function. In view of the results reported by Boatwright and Eaton, who estimated substitution elasticities in the range 0.47 to 0.65, the inconvenience of nonlinear estimation, which is entailed by adoption of the CES assumption, cannot be avoided.

The assumption that replacement investment is proportional to the net capital stock has been criticised by many writers. Radio-active depreciation is not an intrinsic feature of the putty-putty model, and indeed Coen (1975) has explored the relative fits obtained under alternative assumptions about asset lives and time-profiles of deterioration. Partly because the fit criterion did not appear to provide a sufficiently powerful basis for discrimination, Coen's experiments have not been replicated; but a more pedestrian question about replacement investment could not be avoided. The net capital stock series reported by the Central Statistical Office are based on a sectoral rather than an industrial classification, and data for manufacturing are not published; in any case, the construction of the series is inconsistent with the assumption of radio-active depreciation. In the absence of net stock data, all the reported British tests of Jorgenson's model except that conducted by Boatwright and Eaton adopt the gross capital stock as the variable to which replacement is proportional. This substitution is inconsistent with the theory under test,[9] and will yield a biased estimate of the replacement rate. In the solitary exception several net stock series are constructed, but no details are reported. In the present paper a simpler and more direct procedure is adopted by utilising the indentity

$$K_n = (1 - \delta)K_{n-1} + I_n = (1 - \delta)^n K_0 + \sum_{i=0}^{n-1} (1 - \delta)^i I_{n-i} \qquad (1)$$

where I is gross investment, K is the net stock, and δ is the replacement rate. The unobservable variable is proxied by entering two terms, a geometrically declining weighted average of gross investment and a geometric series in the assumed replacement rate; the search over the range of values of δ is terminated when the estimated coefficient on the gross investment term is insignificantly different from the assumed replacement rate, or on the basis of fit. The ratio of the two estimated coefficients is the implied initial value of the net capital stock, K_0.

The remaining modifications of the putty-putty model concern the construction of the implicit rental price of capital services, and apply also to the putty-clay model. In the latter, as formulated by Bischoff (1971), investment again depends on output and the implicit rental; but whereas in the putty-putty model a *ceteris paribus* reduction in the rental will generate positive investment in an amount which is independent of the time-path of output, in the putty-clay model the response to a relative price change is conditional on the behaviour of output. If output is stationary no additions to capacity will be made and relative prices, which influence investment through the *ex ante* choice of capital intensity of new plant, will be of no importance. Bischoff treats the replacement of existing capacity as physically determined by radio-active depreciation. As he points out (n. 22, p. 75), if replacement decisions respond to relative prices then a change in (say) a fiscal parameter will affect investment, even if output is stationary.

As might be inferred from his assumption about replacement, Bischoff follows Jorgenson in defining the implicit real rental (*mutatis mutandis*) as

$$R = \frac{Q}{P} \frac{(r + \delta - q)\ (1 - G)\ (1 - tz)}{(1 - t)} \qquad (2)$$

where the additional symbols are

- Q - price of capital goods
- P - price of output
- r - nominal discount rate
- q - proportionate rate of change of Q
- G - rate of cash grant (which is assumed to reduce the depreciation base of the asset)
- t - corporate tax rate
- Z - present value, computed at r, of tax-allowable depreciation on an investment costing £1.

Apart from the replacement model which underlies this definition, and which is discussed further below, several other characteristics are modified here. First, the assumption that both output, the other principal regressor, and the price of output are exogenous is manifestly inconsistent with any branch of the theory of the firm (e.g. Brechling, 1975). The simplest way of resolving this problem is to postulate cost minimisation for exogenously given output, and hence to replace the output price by the wage rate, W. It is not clear, however, that the specification error in omitting any ratio of money prices is more serious than the measurement error that is likely to be introduced by including it. The relative price of concern in both Jorgenson's and Bischoff's models is the price expected to prevail when the machine under consideration is installed; while static expectations of fiscal parameters, in the absence of definite indications to the contrary, appears a reasonable assumption, it appears much less reasonable when applied to the ratio of machine prices to the wage rate. Furthermore, the use of observed nominal prices implies the assumption of a zero differential in the rates of technical change embodied in men and machines. While it would be desirable to resolve these difficulties by incorporating and testing explicit assumptions about the formation of price expectations and rates of technical change, the simpler alternative adopted here is to experiment with the inclusion and exclusion of the relative factor price ratio.

An important criticism of Bischoff's model is indeed that he treats relative prices in the same way as Jorgenson but under very different conditions. On a strict interpretation, price changes which are expected to occur after a machine is installed are irrelevant in a putty-putty world, since existing equipment can always be transmogrified into a form more suited to the changed conditions. In the putty-clay model, the implicit assumption that expectations beyond the installation date are ignored is not merely implausible but inconsistent with rational behaviour in such an environment. The crucial comparison in selecting the capital intensity of new plant is that between the purchase price of the equipment and the present value of labour costs over the expected life of the machine, so if a relative price term is included in the implicit rental it should be of the form

$Q/[W \sum_{i=1}^{L} ((1 + w)/(1 + r))^{i}]$ where L is the expected life of the asset and w is the expected rate of change of nominal wages. A crude approximation is introduced in the putty-clay formulation to be tested below.

Normal practice in testing the putty-putty model has been to include the term $(r + \delta - q)$ explicitly in the measurement of the rental, but it is not difficult to justify its exclusion. The replacement rate is constant *ex hypothesi*, and it is at least as plausible to assume that the target real rate of return on new investment $(r - q)$ is constant as to suppose that it responds immediately to every disturbance in the *ex post* real rate of return. In the tests reported below the assumption of constancy is imposed and the term $(r + \delta - q)$ is omitted, so that its magnitude is reflected in the estimated coefficients.

The interpretation of the putty-putty model is not affected by the exclusion of $(r + \delta - q)$ from the rental, since the assumption of radio-active depreciation is incorporated through the inclusion of the net capital stock proxies among the regressors. The interpretation of the putty-clay model, however, becomes more flexible: specifically, it is possible to treat replacement as determined, like net investment, by output and relative prices rather than by purely physical considerations. There is, of course, a corresponding increase in the freedom of the firm to postpone or accelerate replacement, and the enhanced potential for intertemporal substitution among different vintages of equipment means that the response of investment to a given exogenous disturbance depends in principle on the history of investment,[10] and hence is unlikely to display constancy.

In a limited sense the influence of expected changes in fiscal policy or in other determinants of the implicit rental can be modelled directly within the putty-putty framework. Using a discrete-time formulation (Sumner, 1973) it can be shown by straightforward but tedious algebra that when a change in (say) the rate of grant is anticipated the rental of capital becomes

$$R = \frac{Q}{P}\,\frac{[(r+\delta-q)(1-G)(1-tZ) + (1-r-\delta+q)\Delta G^{e}(1-tZ)]}{(1-t)} \tag{3}$$

A similar result has been stated by Hall (1977). To make use of this extension it is necessary to know the gestation period of capital goods in order to endow the distinction between the 'current' and 'future' periods with substantive content, so that the expanded definition of the rental cannot be used in the first round of estimation. Moreover, it is clearly necessary to incorporate the terms $(r + \delta - q)$ and $(1 - r - \delta + q)$ explicitly in order to weight the expected change in the grant appropriately. Consideration of these relative weights reveals the significance of the symmetry assumption in the putty-putty model rather dramatically. As the interval before the expected change in the grant rate is reduced, the weight on the first term within the parentheses diminishes and that on the second increases: if the expected change is downwards the rental eventually becomes zero, so that the optimal stock is undefined, as is the problem of disposing of the infinite and now unwanted capital when conditions have reverted to normal. If investment is recognised as an asymmetrical process (Nickell, 1974), the optimal capital stock anticipated for the period after the reduction in grants sets an upper, but still implausibly high, limit on investment while the rate of grant remains at its higher level. The most that can be derived from this extension, therefore, is a standard against which to judge the predictions derived when the extension is ignored, rather than an alternative and more informative method of deriving the predictions themselves.

To summarise the discussion, the basic putty-putty and

putty-clay models to be fitted are respectively

$$I_n = a + \sum_{j=k}^{1} b_j \Delta(Y_{n-j} M^{\sigma}_{n-j}) + d\hat{K}_0 (1 - \delta)^{n-1}$$

$$+ d \sum_{i=0}^{n-2} (1 - \delta)^i I_{n-i-1} \qquad (4)$$

and

$$I_n = a + \sum_{j=u}^{v} b_j Y_{n-j+1} M^{\sigma}_{n-j} + \sum_{j=u}^{v} c_j Y_{n-j} M^{\sigma}_{n-j} \qquad (5)$$

where the additional symbols are

- Y - output
- σ - elasticity of substitution
- M - net-of-tax ratio of unit labour cost to machine price, or reciprocal of the implicit rental.

The time subscript, n, is to be interpreted as beginning at zero. The length and form of the distributed lags are matters that cannot be specified *a priori*. The parameters σ and δ, the depreciation rate, are the best-fitting values from grids ranging from 0 to 1 (in steps of 0.2) and from 0.01 to 0.04 (in steps of 0.01) respectively. The range of values for σ is conventional though for reasons which will become clear the grid is unconventionally coarse. The upper bound on δ was set by doubling Boatwright and Eaton's preferred estimate, and is the quarterly equivalent of Hall and Jorgenson's (1971) annual estimate for the corresponding U.S. aggregate.

Fiscal policy and relative prices operate through the variable M, defined as

$$M = \frac{\alpha(1-t)}{(1-\beta G)(1-\gamma t Z(\lambda))} \left[\frac{W}{Q}\right]^{\theta} \left[\sum_{i=1}^{L} ((1+w)/(1+r))^i\right]^{\mu} \qquad (6)$$

where Greek letters represent weights. Equation (4) was estimated with μ set at zero and θ at both zero and unity; in the estimation of equation (5) θ and μ were set at zero or unity together. *L* was arbitrarily set at ten quarters, on the grounds that any allowance is better than none, and *w* was proxied by the most recently observed rate of change of wage rates. The remaining weights are included to allow for the possibility that cash grants and tax allowances are not aggregated by a conventional present value calculation. Four alternative methods of capturing such a phenomenon were explored: the inverse of the rental is simply scaled up in periods when cash grants are provided ($\alpha > 1$); grants are valued at more than their nominal rate ($\beta > 1$); conversely, tax allowances are undervalued, either directly ($\gamma < 1$), or indirectly by reducing the life (λ) over which allowances are reckoned. In the analysis of the last possibility, attention was confined to the extreme case where only first-year allowances are considered ($\lambda = 1$) in combination with $\beta > 1$. One motive for investigating several mechanisms was as a consistency check; but additionally the precise form of any difference in the valuation of allowances and grants would be relevant in the formation of future fiscal policy, as will be shown below.

Equations (4) and (5) reduce to the clay-clay model, with alternative assumptions about replacement expenditure, when σ is constrained to zero. This model can be estimated for the entire sample period, 1960 (2) to 1976 (3) on the dependent variable, once the period in which intertemporal substitution would have minimised costs has been determined. The same information is needed to define the two sub-periods for estimation of the putty-putty and putty-clay models. Discounting at observed market rates, it would have become worthwhile to anticipate the capital requirements of the period after grants had been reduced to their normal level during 1968 (3); though it would obviously have been more worthwhile to have delayed the anticipation for a further quarter. Accordingly, the clay-clay specialisations of equations (4) and (5) were estimated with a dummy variable which took the value of unity in 1968 (4), minus unity in 1969 (1), and zero at other times. As an additional precaution, this formulation was estimated over the same sub-periods as the other two models, ending in 1968 (2) and beginning in 1969 (3), so as to isolate any effects which spilled over from the two quarters of primary interest.

All the equations were estimated using the Almon interpolation method. The polynomials were restricted to third, or exceptionally second, order; an end-point constraint was imposed, although the results did not appear to be sensitive to this restriction. The precise definitions and sources of data, which relate to U.K. investment by manufacturing industry in plant and machinery at constant 1979 prices, are detailed in the appendix.

RESULTS

In this section the results of estimating the clay-clay and putty-putty models are first summarised. Both of these models were rejected in favour of the putty-clay formulation, which is accordingly presented in greater detail. Finally, the latter estimates are used to draw inferences about some of the other policy questions posed in the introduction.

Clay-Clay

The only advantage of imposing a zero substitution elasticity is that the full sample period can be used for estimation, provided a dummy variable is entered to capture any shift of expenditure in anticipation of the reduction in grants. This formulation, however, can be summarily rejected. The results obtained using the restricted form of equation (5), with the dummy appended, exhibited extreme autocorrelation of the residuals. The dummy picked up a coefficient of 38.2 when allowance for the autocorrelation was made,[11] but the necessity of so doing is clear evidence of misspecification.

The sub-period results summarised in Table 1 indicate that the specification error does not consist merely of imposing an inappropriate pattern on the intertemporal transfer of expenditure. Inferring the effects of the announced grant change from the prediction errors of equation (7), there is no evidence that the impact of the announcement spilled over into the surrounding quarters; though constraining the net effect to zero does appear incorrect. That observation and the persistence of severe autocorrelation in both sub-periods, constitute evidence against the clay-clay hypothesis.

The addition of a proportional replacement mechanism and the substitution of changes for levels of output, in equations (9) and (10), weakens but does not eliminate the

TABLE 1: CLAY-CLAY MODELS

Estimation Period		1960(2)-1968(2)	1969(3)-1976(3)	1960(2)-1968(2)	1969(3)-1976(3)
Equation		(7)	(8)	(9)	(10)
R^2		0.852	0.742	0.897	0.760
DW		0.803	0.810	1.524	0.893
Lag structure		1,11	1,11	1,13	1,13
Cumulative total response of gross investment		28.4	47.5	76.3	30.4
Replacement		3.6	< 0	5.8	< 0
$\sum_{i=0}^{n-2} (1-\delta)^i I_{n-i-1} (\delta = 0.04)$				0.125 (0.019)	-0.017 (0.039)
Grant effect:	1968(3)	4.4		-2.0	
	1968(4)	55.1		38.3	
	1969(1)	-20.3		-47.7	
	1969(2)	7.6		-18.2	

Notes to Table 1: (1) ( ) - standard error

(2) Lag structure refers to the values of u and v in equations (4) and (5).

evidence of serial correlation in the earlier sub-period,[12] while leaving the presumption of specification error in the second unaffected. In neither case does the proportional replacement hypothesis appear plausible: the coefficient on cumulated lagged investment is incorrectly signed and insignificant in (10), and significantly larger than the assumed value (at its upper bound) in (9). The latter result appeared consistently and is discussed further below. In these equations as in the preceding two, the fits are quite poor by the normal standards of time-series analysis.

For completeness, the cumulative total increase in gross investment during the transitional period after a unit step change in output and the long-run response of replacement expenditure are also tabulated. The choice of estimation period and the inclusion of the proportional replacement assumption have pronounced effects on the estimated total change in investment induced by an output change. These variations, and the ridiculous result that in the second period the long run effect of a rise in output was to depress gross investment according to both variants of the model, provide further evidence against the clay-clay hypothesis.

Putty-Putty

The results of estimating Jorgenson's model, which in variously modified forms has been the most popular framework for recent studies of U.K. investment behaviour, are reported next. Despite its frequent use, there are strong grounds for its rejection.

The original form of the model did not provide a satisfactory explanation of investment in either sub-period. For the second of these, the results were not worth reporting; the most obvious defects were a Durbin-Watson statistic below unity and the insignificance of almost all the estimated coefficients. The summary characteristics of the equation (11) fitted to the earlier data set are recorded in Table 2; the evidence of misspecification in this instance takes the less obvious form of a major inconsistency between the assumed and estimated values of the replacement parameter, even when the former was set at its upper bound.

The results improved somewhat when the inverse of the rental was permitted a higher weight in periods when cash grants were available. The best-fitting equation for the first period, (12) in Table 2, was obtained when the grant quarters were weighted 30 per cent more than the remainder. The difference between the estimated and assumed replacement rate was reduced substantially, though it remained significant. In the second sample, the Durbin-Watson statistic rose towards more conventionally acceptable levels, though remaining in the indeterminate range, and the precision of the estimated coefficients improved. The best-fitting equation (14) weighted the grant period 130 per cent more than the remainder; though as comparison with (13) indicates, the difference in the fit of the equation as α was varied over a wide range, was marginal.

TABLE 2: PUTTY-PUTTY MODELS

Estimation period	1960(2)-1968(2)	1960(2)-1968(2)	1969(3)-1976(3)	1969(3)-1976(3)
Equation	(11)	(12)	(13)	(14)
σ	0.2	0.2	0.2	0.2
α	1.0	1.3	1.3	2.3
R^2	0.909	0.944	0.806	0.824
DW	1.739	2.339	1.054	1.263
Sum of lag coefficients	58.6	62.1	28.1	18.4
$\sum_{i=0}^{n-2} (1-\delta)^i I_{n-i-1} (\delta = 0.04)$	0.153 (0.018)	0.073 (0.012)	0.052 (0.038)	0.133 (0.044)

Interpreting the effects of fiscal policy is by no means the only problem posed by these results. The sum of the lag coefficients, which shows the total increase in the net capital stock that would be generated by a unit step change in (YM^{σ}), differs substantially in the two periods,[13] though the form of the lag distribution is quite similar. The coefficients, all of which are well determined except those for the initial response, suggest a longer average lag in the first period of relatively high economic activity. More surprising is the comparison with the results of Boatwright and Eaton, who, using the same estimation method for the intermediate period 1963-70, estimated a noticeably longer average lag. The only common feature of the three sets of estimates is that, unless accurate forecasts with lead times of considerably more than 1.5 years can be made, they fall short of satisfying the rule-of-thumb for successful stabilisation suggested by Phillips (1962).[14]

One other obvious discrepancy between this and the earlier study concerns the replacement rate. Boatwright and Eaton's results indicate the same tendency for the parameter estimate to exceed the assumed value, but by a less clearly significant margin; and their preferred value is half that used here. Their quarterly depreciation rate implies a life for equipment of just over 31 years: the corresponding figure of 15.5 years suggested by the present results is much more difficult to reconcile with the CSO estimates, based on straight-line rather than reducing-balance depreciation, which are the basis of the national accounts. The problem is not merely one of inconsistency with earlier results, but also with the stylised facts. The absolute level of the net capital stock implied by the estimates was about £8B. at end-1970, at 1970 prices; the CSO's estimates of the gross stock of plant and machinery in manufacturing of £27.1B. and the net stock of equipment of industrial and commercial companies of £19.9B. are rather difficult to reconcile with this figure. Still more disturbing is the steady decline in the derived net stock series throughout the sample period.

Some sensitivity tests were conducted, but are not worth reporting in detail. Introducing the price ratio by dropping the zero restriction on θ resolved none of the problems discussed above; rather, the fit deteriorated, consistently with the earlier suggestion of measurement error. Imposing a lower value of the replacement rate caused an imperceptible deterioration in the reported fit, and a larger and more significant difference between the estimated and assumed replacement rates. Finally, because they generated both internal inconsistencies and an implausible series for the net stock, the capital proxies were dropped. The resulting model collapsed to the clay-clay case when all values of M were weighted equally, since for all values of σ above zero the estimated coefficients failed to satisfy the non-negativity requirement. The statistically unacceptable results were improved only marginally when values of α in excess of unity were introduced. Thus, the trend-like capital stock proxies are indispensable, despite the difficulties of interpretation which they themselves create.[15]

The remaining issue to be examined is the effect of the temporary increase in cash grants. The prediction errors from equation (12) for the four quarters beginning in 1968 (3) are respectively *-3.0*, *46.9*, *-14.7* and *28.0*. The predictions for 1969 (1,2) are derived using a 20 per cent grant throughout the preceding period, rather than the figure of 25 per cent which actually obtained in 1967-8 but which was known to be terminating. There is no obvious explanation for the small magnitude of the overprediction in 1969 (1) or for the underprediction in the following quarter; indeed, prediction errors closer to expectation, of *-23.2* and *-20.1*, were obtained when a 25 per cent grant was used in the lagged values of M. The magnitude of the error in 1968 (4) is of more immediate interest. To put this in its putty-putty perspective, suppose that after the temporarily increased grant was announced in December 1966, investment plans which were expected to be completed in 1968 (4) were based on the duly modified form of the rental stated in equation (3). Given the lag distribution it is then a matter of routine calculation to infer the weight that must be imposed on the announced reduction in the grant for the prediction error to be eliminated by increasing M in the period 1967 (1) to 1968 (2). Since this weight depends in principle only on $(r + \delta - q)$ and its complement, a convenient way of summarising the exercise is to state the real discount rate implied by the weight and the value of δ. The net result is a real discount rate in excess of 18,000 per cent per quarter! Thus, this implication of the model amounts to a *reductio ad absurdum*.

The descriptive content of the putty-putty hypothesis has never been at issue, but it has remained a popular 'as if' model for the analysis of investment behaviour. The burden of the preceding argument is that its present status is excessively difficult to justify. The estimated coefficients on the determinants of net investment are highly unstable, and moreover make a very small contribution to the total 'explanation' of investment.[16] The major contribution is provided by the capital stock proxies, which are dominated by trend components. Their share of the explanation cannot be reconciled with the conventional meaning of replacement investment, and their subsidiary implications are unacceptable. Finally, the apparent capacity of the model to analyse explicitly the effects of anticipated fiscal (or other) changes is illusory, because the analysis is incomplete; and its positive element is firmly rejected by the prediction test. There is little reason to prefer a strongly specified model over weaker alternatives when it turns out to be inconsistent with the data.

Putty-Clay

In the putty-putty case the distributed lag in $\Delta(YM^{\sigma})$ makes such a minor contribution to the calculated level of gross investment that the improvement in the performance of the equation when the M series was weighted was perceptible but scarcely dramatic, and in consequence experiments with alternative weighting schemes were not pursued. The putty-clay specification lacks the crutch of proportional replacement, and hence is much more sensitive to the introduction of weighting. Indeed the first two columns of Table 3 indicate that the results of not attaching greater weight to M when cash grants were available are disastrous. Whether or not the factor-price adjustment is incorporated, the fit in the first sub-period is poor and the Durbin-Watson statistic strongly rejects the null hypothesis of random residuals. Both the fit and the error structure improve radically when weights are introduced. The method of introduction is relatively unimportant as judged by these statistical criteria; though methods which reduce the value of tax allowances below their conventional levels, by direct adjustment ($\gamma < 1$) in equation (19) or by arbitrarily considering only first-year allowances ($\lambda = 1$) in equation (20), yield a marginally higher fit than the alternative of raising the values of M in the period of cash grants. The similarity of the statistical results is unfortunate for, as the last two rows of the Table indicate, the economic implications of these alternatives are very different: the total increase in investment in the transition to a level of output which is permanently higher than otherwise by one unit is more than 50 per cent greater when the valuation of grants is raised than when that of allowances is reduced; and there are even larger relative differences in the long-run effects of higher output on replacement investment.

The second part of Table 3 exhibits similar features in the later estimation period. Any method of attributing more weight to cash grants is better than none, though the improvement in statistical results is a little less striking than in the earlier period. The relative performance of the alternative methods, as gauged by fit, is however reversed. There is also some indication of a learning process in the implied evaluation of tax allowances by decision-makers: in particular, the best-fitting weight on the present value of allowances (γ) is 0.6, with an exponent (σ) on M of 0.8 in the first period (equation 19); in the second (equation 23) these are raised to 0.7 and 1 respectively. Thus this admittedly slender evidence suggests that businessmen may have been moving towards a more conventional evaluation of tax allowances, an impression which is strengthened when equations of the same

TABLE 3: PUTTY-CLAY MODELS

Estimation Period	[1960(2)					1968(2)]	[1969(3)			1976(3)]
Equation	(15)	(16)	(17)	(18)	(19)	(20)	(21)	(22)	(23)	(24)
α	1	1	1.8	1	1	1	1	(1.3)	1	1
β	1	1	1	2.0	1	1.2	1	(2.0)	1	1.2
γ	1	1	1	1	0.6	1	1	1	0.7	1
λ	∞	∞	∞	∞	∞	1	∞	∞	∞	1
θ, μ	0	1	0	0	0	0	1	0	0	0
σ	0.4	0.2	0.2	0.4	0.8	1	0.6	0.4	1	1
R^2	0.798	0.797	0.933	0.936	0.956	0.951	0.737	0.890	0.865	0.855
DW	0.630	0.668	1.990	1.949	2.398	2.154	0.846	1.878	1.762	1.714
Cumulative total response of gross investment	21.4	33.0	76.0	79.6	50.2	49.3	23.6	81.6	78.4	24.4
Replacement	1.97	2.08	1.43	1.15	0.56	0.35	< 0	6.16	12.16	< 0

Notes to Table 3:

(1) As there is only a single value of G for the later estimation period, the formulation with ($\alpha > 1$, $\beta = 1$) and ($\alpha = 1$, $\beta > 1$) are indistinguishable.

(2) Balancing allowances are ignored, so declining-balance depreciation in perpetuity is assumed in the construction of Z ($\lambda = \infty$), except where only first-year allowances are incorporated.

(3) The cumulative total response of gross investment and replacement investment to a unit step change in output depends upon the level of M. The fiscal parameters used in Table 3 (and 6) are those prevailing in 1966(1); the relative price component of M (in equations where $\theta = \mu = 1$) is the mean of the values affecting investment (through the distributed lag) in 1966(1).

(4) Third degree polynomials were used throughout except in the estimation of equation (24), for which second-degree functions proved adequate. The lag structure was (in the notation of equation (5)) $u = 2$, $v = 12$.

form are fitted to other data samples. To illustrate, when the first sub-sample is terminated in 1966(4) the best-fitting value of γ is 0.5 with no change in the value σ.

The economic significance of the differences among the alternative weighting schemes is examined more closely in Tables 4 and 5. The former shows the effect of selected fiscal changes on the values of M^{σ}, given the weights of Table 3. The relative magnitudes differ considerably in many instances, and even the direction of change differs on occasion. A tax rate reduction increases the relative price of capital when the present value of tax allowances exceeds unity, as was the case on a conventional calculation at market interest rates when corporation tax was introduced: hence the first variant of M fell in 1965, whereas the other two versions, which undervalue allowances in comparison with the conventional calculation, registered an increase. Similarly the introduction of the imputation system left the first and third versions unaffected, but reduced the second substantially. One aspect of these variations is illustrated in detail in Table 5, which records the simulated results of introducing cash grants. Output is assumed to follow its actual time-path. The only fiscal change recognised in the simulation is the replacement of initial and investment allowances, which are retained in the base run, by grants in 1966 (1). The tax and interest rates are assumed constant throughout the experiment, at levels which would have made the firm using a conventional evaluation indifferent between the two systems of incentives. The simulated results of equations (17-20) showed the same grouping as was noted above, so only one example of each is presented. The base run is the mean of the separate controls for equations (18) and (19); these differ in detail but by amounts which were insignificant when compared with the differences between the grant and allowance runs. The counterfactual estimates of the effect of grants are noticeably different: downward adjustment of tax allowances, in equation (19), implies an effect which develops more slowly, declines more rapidly, and responds to the resumption of output growth more sluggishly, than the estimate produced by a higher valuation of grants. The time profiles are, however, qualitatively similar; and while there remains considerable uncertainty as to the precise effects of grants, there is no doubt that the effect was considerable, despite the equivalence of the two fiscal systems in terms of present value.

TABLE 4: FISCAL POLICY EFFECT

Announcement Date	Policy Change	Percentage Change in M^{σ} $\beta=2,\sigma=0.2$	$\gamma=0.6,\sigma=0.8$	$\beta=1.2,\lambda=1,\sigma=1$
1958(2)	t raised from 0.455 to 0.525	-0.8	-6.6	-9.6
1958(3)	B raised from 0.25 to 0.3	0.4	0.4	6.1
1959(2)	A re-introduced at 0.2, B reduced to 0.1, t reduced to 0.4875	5.2	9.2	5.6
1960(2)	t raised to 0.5125	-0.5	-2.3	-3.5
1961(2)	t raised to 0.5375	-0.4	-2.9	-3.8
1962(4)	A raised to 0.3, C raised from 0.153 to 0.2	2.7	6.8	11.8
1965(2)	t reduced to 0.4	-2.0	10.3	15.5
1966(1)	A and B abolished, G introduced at 0.2	12.6	10.1	8.7
1966(4)	G raised to 0.25	6.5	5.3	15.9
1969(2)	t raised to 0.45	-0.5	-2.4	-3.9
1970(4)	B re-introduced at 0.35, C raised to 0.25, G abolished	-3.7	-10.9	-2.9
1971(3)	B raised to 0.55	0.5	1.4	14.2
1972(2)	B raised to 1 ('free depreciation')	1.1	1.3	11.3
1974(2)	t raised to 0.52	0	-9.4	0

Notes to Table 4:

(1) For notation see Appendix.

(2) The date of the last tax change listed is that of the budget in which the rate was fixed. The new rate applied to profits attributed to the fiscal year 1973/4; and, as discussed in the text, the direction of change could have been anticipated from 1972 (2) at latest.

TABLE 5: SIMULATED EFFECTS OF GRANTS ON INVESTMENT

Date	Base Run A=0.3, B=0.1 C=0.2 Throughout	G introduced in 1966(1) at 0.2			
		Equation (18)		Equation (19)	
		Absolute Change	% Base	Absolute Change	% Base
1966(1)	330.0	(0)		(0)	
(2)	327.6	(0)		(0)	
(3)	314.1	15.0	4.8	0.8	0.3
(4)	303.8	26.3	8.6	7.5	2.5
1967(1)	292.9	35.2	12.0	14.6	5.0
(2)	286.6	38.2	13.3	25.1	8.8
(3)	283.4	40.1	14.2	31.4	11.1
(4)	276.6	39.0	14.1	35.0	12.7
1968(1)	271.4	34.6	12.8	36.6	13.5
(2)	274.2	30.0	10.9	34.0	12.4
(3)	275.3	25.9	9.4	27.3	9.9
(4)	279.1	21.0	7.5	20.1	7.2
1969(1)	283.3	16.4	5.8	14.4	5.1
(2)	292.7	14.5	5.0	10.6	3.6
(3)	307.0	18.2	5.9	10.0	3.3
(4)	317.9	22.1	7.0	8.5	2.7
1970(1)	329.4	25.1	7.6	8.1	2.5
(2)	327.5	23.9	7.3	11.4	2.8
(3)	324.7	21.9	6.7	10.3	3.2
Cumulative Increase		447.4		305.7	

Note to Table 5: $r = 0.1$, $t = 0.4167$ throughout.

The final variation on the putty-clay model was to introduce relative factor prices by relaxing the previous assumption $\theta = \mu = 0$. The results, summarised in Table 6, exhibit similar characteristics to those discussed already. The same distinction between alternative methods of weighting grants and allowances is clearly apparent. Compared with the corresponding formulations of Table 3, incorporating factor prices in M worsens the fit and general plausibility of equations (27) and (29) with $\lambda = 1$; the deterioration is slight in the first sub-period but marked in the second. With the alternative adjustment the fit improves slightly in the first period and substantially in

TABLE 6: RELATIVE PRICE EFFECTS IN PUTTY-CLAY MODELS

Estimation Period	1960(2) - 1968(2)			1969(3) - 1976(3)	
Equation	(25)	(26)	(27)	(28)	(29)
α	1.3	1	1	(1.3)	1
β	1	2.0	1.2	(2.0)	1.2
λ	∞	∞	1	∞	1
σ	0.2	0.2	0.8	0.4	0.6
R^2	0.952	0.941	0.944	0.922	0.786
DW	2.224	2.054	1.920	2.284	1.171
Cumulative total response of gross investment	87.3	79.2	38.4	119.0	25.1
Replacement	1.28	1.30	0.23	14.9	< 0

Note to Table 6: $\gamma = \theta = \mu = 1$ throughout.

the second. There is also a suggestion, implicit in the increase in σ, that more importance was attached to variations in M, whether induced by fiscal policy or relative factor price movements, in the second period than in the first. The relative contribution of the factor price ratio in the two periods is itself consistent with the development of a fuller appraisal of investment opportunities, though also, of course, with numerous other possible explanations. There is clearly scope for a more exhaustive investigation of expectational effects than is possible in this paper.

The Temporary Increase in Grants

In an attempt to isolate the effect of the explicitly temporary character of higher grants, predictions were made for the four quarters between the two data sets. As in the corresponding application of the putty-putty model, the predictions for the second half of 1968 assumed a 25 per cent grant and those for the first half of 1969 a 20 per cent rate. The resulting forecast errors for four of the alternative versions of the putty-clay model are shown in Table 7. The formulations in which allowances are adjusted downwards begin to under-predict immediately, although their performance at the end of the fit period gives no prior warning. All formulations under-predict substantially in the last quarter of higher grants, by amounts which are considerably higher than the CSO's estimate of £51M. The really surprising feature of the results is that the under-predictions continue after the rate of grant had reverted to its former level: the clay-clay and putty-putty models suggest that the extra investment of 1968 was at least partially offset subsequently, whereas the only trace of offset indicated by these better-fitting and generally more plausible equations is a smaller under-prediction in 1969(1) than in the following quarter.

TABLE 7: PREDICTION ERRORS IN THE TRANSITION PERIOD

Period/Source	Equation (18)	(19)	(20)	(26)
1968(3)	12.7	36.9	27.4	0.2
1968(4)	66.4	93.9	84.5	65.4
1969(1)	35.4	46.2	47.6	31.1
1969(2)	66.9	81.8	83.8	63.2

A possible explanation for these unexpected results invokes the distinction between investment demand and the response of the supplying industries. To meet delivery commitments or to complete as much as possible of larger projects, financed by progress payments, before the higher rate of grant terminated, the capital goods industries increased the rate at which orders were executed, but did not revert to previous levels of operation immediately in 1969. This line of argument raises the possibility that part of the prediction errors for 1968 are spurious: it would have been in the interests of both suppliers and customers to have adopted a system of progress payments for projects which would normally have been paid for on completion, and to have accelerated progress payments which would normally have been made early in 1969. If the increased investment was entirely spurious, however, there would have been a corresponding shortfall when payment habits reverted to normal.

Some confirmation that the apparent increase in manufacturing investment was genuine, rather than an economically insignificant departure from established payment practices, may be derived from inspection of the series for investment in equipment by the non-manufacturing sector; but the comparison of these two series also suggests that the macroeconomic significance of explicitly temporary changes in the cost of capital goods is even more difficult to isolate than might have been supposed. The marked increase in manufacturing investment was accompanied by an almost equally pronounced dip in the residual component, with the result that a local peak in total equipment spending did not occur until the first quarter of 1969; after a short pause the growth in total spending then resumed, before reaching a plateau. To conclude that the extra investment in manufacturing was offset by sectoral rather than intertemporal substitution, from the supply rather than the demand side, would however be premature. A crude comparison of the domestic orders on hand and net new orders of the engineering industry indicates some supply response: order books remained short in relation to the inflow of new orders during 1968, and this increased activity does not appear to have been at the expense of the export sector, where orders on hand rose quite slowly in relation to a sharp increase in new orders. While it seems clear that the total impact of the temporarily higher grant was smaller than the evidence of the manufacturing sector alone would suggest, it also seems to have been more prolonged.

If later research confirms the conjecture that the supply-side response to a temporary sectoral stimulus extends and smooths out its macroeconomic impact, an important objection to fiscal changes in intertemporal relative prices would be at least partially answered. The objection, which arises from an exclusive focus on the demand side, is simply the doubt whether an instrument which transfers any amount of investment, however large, between successive quarters with a lead time of two years could be used to advantage. However, unless the supply response is shown to anticipate the effect on demand, the answer would only be partial: to base major policy decisions on the expected state of the economy two years hence requires more confidence in forecasting than can readily be justified; but to depart from announced commitments would ensure that future announcements were heavily discounted; and attempts to apply the same technique over a shorter horizon would reduce the potential magnitude of the effect on investment.

Other Policy Issues

The results throw some light on the subsidiary questions mentioned in the introduction, as well as on the major issues discussed above. First there remains the problem of accounting for the greater weight of cash grants than of tax allowances: the arguments outlined in the introduction stress the simplicity and certainty of grants, but an alternative explanation would point to the simultaneous enlargement of the area within which investment qualified for additional support under the regional programme. If the mere size of the assisted areas was important, however, grants would not have attracted a higher weight in the second sub-period, for the regional boundaries were not redrawn when grants were abolished. On that occasion the magnitude of the regional differential was reduced drastically; but as it had been increased only slightly, on a conventional calculation, when grants were introduced, it would be difficult to argue that the phenomenon identified above as a grant effect was really a consequence of regional discrimination. Finally, if regional discrimination had a significant impact on national investment, this effect would have emerged after the policy was first introduced in the 1963 budget; but inspection of the residuals from equations for the first sub-period does not reveal any such effect.

As is well known, if the present value of depreciation deductions per pound of investment expenditure exceeds unity, a tax cut will unequivocally raise the relative price of capital services. On a conventional calculation this condition was fulfilled after the increase in investment allowances at the end of 1962; but the weight attached to tax allowances in the best-fitting regressions rules out the possibility of this apparently perverse effect.

The short-run consequences of an anticipated change in the tax rate are, to a first approximation, independent of the value of depreciation allowances. Whether the investment takes place before or after the tax change will have little impact on the value of sales proceeds (or of labour cost savings), the bulk of which will in either case be taxed at the new rate; but it will have a major impact on the net price of the investment, since the declining-balance system of annual allowances, the availability of initial or investment allowances, and discounting together ensure that first-year write-offs exceed revenue on any realistic assumptions. Hence an expected fall in the tax rate should induce the acceleration of planned investment; the converse prediction is subject to the qualification that delay will *ipso facto* reduce the value of an investment.

As indicated in the introduction, there were two occasions when changes in the rate of company taxation were predictable: on the introduction of corporation tax with effect from 1965, and on the introduction of the imputation system in 1973. A remarkably consistent feature of all the regressions estimated in the first sub-period was a large overprediction in 1965(2), the quarter in which corporation tax became operative. In all the regressions which weighted allowances and grants differentially, whether for the putty-putty or putty-clay specifications, this residual was invariably the largest, contributing around 20-25 per cent of the residual sum of squares. While there can be no doubt that investment behaved abnormally at this point the episode does not fit into the category of accelerated investment in response to an anticipated tax cut, for the simple reason that there were no equally conspicuous underpredictions in the preceding one or two quarters. Indeed, the short interval between the first definite announcement of corporation tax and its effective introduction would have left little time for any significant advancement of planned investment; but there certainly appears to have been time for cancellation or delay, which are more difficult to explain.

The interval between the announcement of the imputation system and its implementation was considerably longer, but the pattern of residuals accords no more closely with prior expectations. Again the regressions for the second sample consistently exhibit a major error in 1973(1), which accounts for around 15 per cent of the residual sum of squares of the best-fitting equations. At the time when the incentive to delay investment was at its peak, however, the unexplained disturbance took the form of an underprediction. Moreover, there was an almost equal overprediction in the following quarter, when it would have been most profitable to have carried out the projects postponed in anticipation of a lower net price of capital services.

That tax rate changes have an effect on investment was evidenced by the generally inferior results, not worth reporting in detail, when a constant rate was imposed. The two episodes discussed in the preceding paragraphs suggest that anticipated changes also have an effect, but one which is not consistent with a single-equation model of investment behaviour. It may be possible to rationalise the disturbances which accompanied the introduction of corporation tax in a larger model designed to explain dividend and investment decisions simultaneously; though it is not clear that this extension would help in accounting for the errors of 1973. Alternatively, changes in tax rates may be viewed in a more direct fashion than that suggested by a formal model of cost minimisation: the reforms in question were executed by governments with very different public attitudes to the private sector, and their proposals may have been interpreted accordingly.

It is worth adding that Eisner and Lawler (1975) uncovered a similar puzzle in their analysis of the McGraw-Hill capital expenditure surveys. The 1968 survey asked how much investment would be reduced if the 10 per cent surcharge on (US) corporate income tax were enacted. The answer predicted by existing models would be a negative number, since a temporary tax increase is analogous to an expected tax reduction once it has been enacted; but the respondents thought otherwise, indicating an average reduction in investment equal to about 20 per cent of any change in total tax liabilities. Surveys are perhaps not the ideal tool for probing business sensitivity to variations in incentives at the margin, but the parallel with the UK results is striking.

The consistency between the declared and estimated reactions to expected changes in the tax rate and their inconsistency with standard *a priori* reasoning provide an interesting research agenda. In view of these preliminary results it would clearly be imprudent to rely on announced changes in the tax rate as an instrument of macroeconomic control. The response to expected changes in grants or allowances may be 'small', but it is at least in the predicted direction.

CONCLUSIONS

The most robust result of this enquiry is that cash grants were a relatively efficient method of stimulating investment, and provided a bargain in the form of greater investment at negligible cost in terms of foregone revenue. The additional investment induced by the temporary increase in the rate of grant was noticeably larger than the official estimate, and was not immediately offset; but it was nevertheless highly concentrated in time, and occurred after a substantial delay. While the estimated lag structure is probably the most uncertain feature of this or any other study, and clearly does not exhibit stability over time periods in which economic conditions differed considerably, there is no reason to question the truism that investment cannot be altered rapidly, despite numerous attempts by former governments to do so.

The reasons why allowances are less efficient than grants cannot be isolated with any degree of precision. Capital market imperfections and the consequence irrelevance of market interest rates do not provide a satisfactory explanation, at any rate in the extreme form which ignores allowances after the first year of an asset's life. It was still necessary to raise the weight on grants above unity, and this formulation performed badly in the later period, when write-offs were accelerated substantially. The increase in the weight on allowances is difficult to reconcile with an explanation which hinges on the inability of firms with insufficient taxable income to absorb all allowances immediately; casual observation suggests that the non-marketability of allowances was a much more significant limitation in the second subperiod than in the first. It is tempting, in the absence of a more convincing explanation, to regard the perceived difference between grants and allowances as a manifestation of fiscal illusion, further evidence of which is suggested by the transition to both corporation tax and the imputation system.

The results indicate that caution is needed in drawing conclusions of a more conventional kind. An unremarked but obvious feature of the tabulations is that the point estimates of the exponent σ depend not only on the choice between putty-putty and putty-clay technology but also on the way in which the distinction between grants and allowances is made. If relative factor prices perceived by the businessman differ from those observed from the academic arm-chair, econometric estimates of the elasticity of substitution will be a very unreliable guide to technological possibilities. For the purposes of this paper the most important feature of the alternative weighting schemes is their comparative ranking of the various combinations of fiscal instruments, not their absolute measurement of the relative cost of capital goods and labour. As regards the latter, it obviously makes more sense to regard grants as the fixed point of the scale and to reduce the value of allowances than to increase the weight on grants. It is therefore tempting to infer from Table 3 that the elasticity of substitution lies towards the upper end of the range of values estimated for σ. The temptation should, however, be resisted until a much more exhaustive search has been conducted to determine the relative performance of alternative assumptions about the formation of wage-change expectations and about the time-horizon in the putty-clay model.

Finally, the multi-dimensional character of the search procedures required even for the present, relatively modest enquiry should be emphasised, because the detailed conclusions reached may not be independent of the route taken. The degree of polynomial, length of the initial delay, the number of terms included, the exponent on M, and the form and weights used in the construction of M itself, are all questions which could be answered only by resort to search. Even with relatively coarse grids it was obviously necessary to answer some of these questions sequentially rather than simultaneously. Moreover, in many instances the only criterion available was goodness-of-fit, which did not permit sharp discrimination. To illustrate with an extreme case, in the first-year allowances only ($\lambda = 1$) version of the putty-clay model, the coefficient of determination with the best-fitting value of σ fell only from 0.949 to 0.936 as the weight on cash grants (β) was varied from 1.1 to 2.3. Therefore, although only point-estimates can be presented for the parameters estimated by iteration, there is a substantial degree of uncertainty attached to them. Nevertheless, the qualitative results were so insensitive to specification as to justify considerable confidence in the conclusions summarised in this section.

APPENDIX: DEFINITIONS AND DATA SOURCES

I - Gross fixed investment in plant and machinery in manufacturing industry, £M at 1970 prices, seasonally adjusted.

Y - Index of manufacturing production, seasonally adjusted, average 1970 = 100.

Q - Implicit deflator of I.

W - Basic weekly wage rates of manual workers in manufacturing industry, 31 July 1972 = 100, re-based on average 1970 = 100.

r - Average redemption yield on long-dated UK government stocks.

A - Investment allowance (at national rate).

B - Initial allowance (at national rate).

C - Writing-down allowance.

t - Announced tax rate on profits of a company which distributes nothing.

G - Cash grant (at national rate).

$$Z = A + B + C + C\,\frac{(1 - B - C)}{r + C}$$

Data period: 1956(1) - 1976(3).

Sources: for fiscal variables, Melliss and Richardson (1976); for other series, *Economic Trends*, Annual Supplement, No. 2, 1976, and *Economic Trends*, April 1977.

REFERENCES

Bischoff, C.W. (1971). The effect of alternative lag distributions; in G. Fromm (ed.) *Tax Incentives and Capital Spending*. Washington, D.C.: Brookings Institution.

Boatwright, B.D. and J.R. Eaton (1972). The estimation of investment functions for manufacturing industry in the UK. *Economica* N.S. 39, 403-18.

Brechling, F. (1975). *Investment and Employment Decisions*. Manchester University Press.

Eisner, R. and P.J. Lawler (1975). Tax policy and investment:

an analysis of survey responses. *American Economic Review* 65, 206-12.

Griliches, Z. (1963). Capital stock in investment functions: some problems of concept and measurement; in C.F. Christ (ed.) *Measurement in Economics*. Stanford University Press.

Hall, R.E. (1977). Investment interest rates and the effects of stabilization policies. *Brookings Papers on Economic Activity* 1977:1, 61-121.

Hall, R.E. and D.W. Jorgenson (1971). Application of the theory of optimal capital accumulation; in G. Fromm (ed.) *Tax Incentives and Capital Spending*. Washington D.C.: Brookings Institution.

H.M.S.O. (1966). White Paper on *Investment Incentives*. Cmnd. 2874. London.

Jorgenson, D.W. (1963). Capital theory and investment behaviour. *American Economic Review: Papers and Proceedings* 53, 247-59.

Kay, J.A. and M.A. King (1978). *The British Tax System*. Oxford University Press.

King, M.A. (1972). Taxation and investment incentives in a vintage model. *Journal of Public Economics* 1, 121-47.

King, M.A. (1977). *Public Policy and the Corporation*. Cambridge Studies in Applied Econometrics: 3. London: Chapman and Hall.

Lund, P.J. (1976). The econometric assessment of the impact of investment incentives; in A. Whiting (ed.) *The Economics of Industrial Subsidies*. London: HMSO.

Melliss, C.L. and P.W. Richardson (1976). Value of investment incentives for manufacturing industry 1946 to 1974; in A. Whiting (ed.) *The Economics of Industrial Subsidies*. London: HMSO.

Nickell, S. (1974). On expectations, government policy and the rate of investment. *Economica* N.S. 41, 241-55.

Phillips, A.W. (1962). Employment, inflation and growth. *Economica* N.S. 29, 1-16.

Robertson, D.H. (1931). Wage-grumbles; in *Economic Fragments*. London: King.

Sumner, M.T. (1973). Announcement effects of profits taxation; in M. Parkin (ed.) *Essays in Modern Economics: Proceedings of the Association of University Teachers of Economics, 1972*. London: Longmans.

FOOTNOTES

1. The initial stages of this study were conducted at the University of Manchester, with the financial support of the SSRC. The research assistance of C.J. Laing is gratefully acknowledged.

2. The details of the policy will be found in HMSO (1966).

3. On the impossibility of achieving fiscal neutrality between distribution and retentions under the imputation system, see King (1977).

4. For a fuller description and detailed chronology, see Melliss and Richardson (1976).

5. More precisely, allowances are not separately marketable: but as Kay and King (1978) point out, unrelieved tax losses constitute a potential motive for mergers, an activity which peaked in 1968. More recently, the rapid growth of equipment leasing may be partially attributable to the restoration of allowances.

6. This estimate has been revised in successive editions of *National Income and Expenditure*.

7. The reasons for this inertia were explored in a supplementary question. Faced with the alternatives of equivalence of the two incentive systems, delays in assessing the implications of grants, or the irrelevance of either system, two-thirds of the sub-sample selected the third explanation, a choice which is *prima facie* inconsistent with the CBI's inference from its earlier survey that the use of 'sophisticated' methods of investment

appraisal was becoming more widespread.

8. This terminology would perhaps amuse older writers (e.g. Robertson, 1931), by its implication that the distinction is a recent discovery, as much as it would irritate the frustrated amateur glazier, by its inaccuracy.

9. See Griliches (1963) for a lucid discussion of the respective roles of the net and gross capital stocks in the investment function.

10. Cf. King (1972).

11. All absolute figures are in units of £M at constant 1970 prices. For purposes of comparison, the average quarterly rate of manufacturing investment in 1968-9 was 359.7.

12. Some caution should be exercised in interpreting the Durbin-Watson statistic, as the lagged dependent variable appears on the right-hand side of the equation in the capital stock proxy.

13. In Table 1, where a zero value of σ was imposed, the cumulative response of gross investment was recorded to facilitate comparisons between the equations including and excluding proportional replacement. For comparison between equations (9) and (10) of Table 1 and those reported in Table 2, the sum of the lag coefficients for equation (9) was 46.5.

14. In particular at least half of the full effects of a policy initiative should occur within six months of the disturbance it was designed to offset.

15. Bischoff has argued that the capital stock term of the putty-putty model should make no contribution to the explanatory power of the equation, but he also notes that in practice it is an essential component of Jorgenson's model.

16. For example, the distributed lag in $\Delta(YM^{\sigma})$ accounts for only about 10 per cent of the predictions for 1968(3) - 1969(2).

11. THE ROOTS OF THE BRITISH SICKNESS

Samuel Brittan[1]

There are at least two separate problems about the British economy, which are not sufficiently distinguished. First there is the long-standing gap between the growth rate of the United Kingdom and that of other industrial market economies. This goes back over a hundred years. Alfred Marshall remarked that by the 1860s and 1870s "many of the sons of manufacturers" were "content to follow mechanically the lead given by their fathers. They worked shorter hours; and they exerted themselves less to obtain new practical ideas."[2]

Secondly, there is the simultaneous occurrence of high unemployment, high inflation, and incipient protectionism that has affected most Western countries in the 1970s, which is known by the ugly word "stagflation" and which has put a check to many hopes after a generation of postwar prosperity.

The inflationary disorders of the business cycle of the early 1970s, the depth of the subsequent recession, and the troubled and unsatisfactory nature of the latest recovery have been problems common to most countries. But, partly because they were superimposed on an economy which in any case had a low growth rate, they affected Britain with particular severity and gave rise to an orgy of pessimism and self-doubt among British leaders. It was this phenomenon, so surprising in a country of such long-established political culture, which impressed many foreign visitors and which made the diagnosis of the "condition of England" such a growth industry in the United States.

The so-called British disease is thus a mixture of different maladies - slow growth, a severe recent attack of stagflation, and accompanying political strains. Although I hope to find common elements in the explanation of these phenomena, it is first necessary to distinguish them from each other.

LONG-RUN PROBLEMS

The lag in British growth rates goes back at least a century. One estimate made by Angus Maddison[3] suggests that the average level of output per head in sixteen industrial countries rose sixfold between 1870 and 1976, but only fourfold in the United Kingdom. Estimates going back that far have, of course, a heroic dimension. But neither the study of alternative estimates, nor that of subperiods, nor attempted corrections for working hours, upsets the relative orders of magnitude. The estimates are of course of output, not of happiness or welfare.

In 1870, the United Kingdom was the second richest country in terms of output per head among the sixteen, surpassed only by Australia which had a uniquely favourable ratio of labour to land and natural resources. Later the United States overtook Britain. But during the nineteenth century and the first three-fifths of the twentieth century the United Kingdom remained ahead of nearly all the main European countries;[4] and the low growth rate was a matter for concern only to sophists, calculators, and economists.

Since 1960, however, an absolute gap has emerged - whether measured by output, or real wages, or whether the comparisons are made at market or purchasing parity exchange rates, or by the fallible impressions of personal travel. One comparison of gross domestic product (GDP) per head at purchasing power exchange rates suggests that by 1973 most European Economic Community countries were 30 to 40 per cent ahead of Britain.[5]

International corporations are in a good position, compared to merely national concerns, to minimise productivity differentials between plants in different countries. Yet a recent study of such international corporations showed net output per head to be over 50 per cent higher in German and French plants than in corresponding plants in the United Kingdom. Only about half the Anglo-German difference could be attributed to product mix, scale, or capital equipment. The remainder was due to "differences in efficiency".[6] Much more lurid comparisons could be given by selective evidence from particular industries, or anecdotally.

TABLE 1

LONG-TERM GROWTH RATES
REAL GROSS DOMESTIC PRODUCT PER HEAD OF POPULATION (UNITED KINGDOM)
(1970 U.S. Dollars)

	Average of 16 Advanced Countries*	United Kingdom
Growth % per annum		
1870-1976	1.8	1.3
1870-1913	1.5	1.0
1913-1950	1.1	1.0
1950-1970	3.8	2.3
1970-1976	2.4	2.0
GDP per head in U.S. 1970 dollars		
1870	$ 666	$ 956
1976	$4258	$3583
Ratio of U.K. to average GDP per head		
1870	-	1.44
1976	-	.84

*Arithmetical average of United States, Canada, Australia, Japan, United Kingdom, Germany, France, Italy, Switzerland, Netherlands, Belgium, Sweden, Denmark, Norway, Austria, Finland.

Note: The only country with a slower growth rate than the United Kingdom over the century was Australia, where GDP per head in 1976 was 1.19 times that of the United Kingdom. U.S. growth over the century, 1870-1976, was 1.9 per cent per annum, the Japanese 2.5 per cent, the German 2.0 per cent, and the French 1.9 per cent.

Source: Angus Maddison: Phases of Capitalist Development, 1977 Banca Nazionale del Lavoro Q. Rev. 103.

TABLE 2

NET OUTPUT PER PERSON, MANUFACTURING, 1971-1972
(United Kingdom = 100)

	Entire Manufacturing Sector	International Corporations
United Kingdom	100	100
France	155	128
Germany	159	135
United States	216	156*

*North America

Source: Clifford F. Pratten: Labour Productivity Differentials Within International Companies 80 (1976).

TABLE 3

THE INFLATIONARY RECORD
CONSUMER PRICES' AVERAGE PERCENTAGE INCREASE PER ANNUM

	1958 to 1969	1969 to 1977
OECD*	3.3	8.3
United Kingdom	3.8	12.6
United States	2.1	6.4

*Weighted average

Source: OECD Economic Outlook, July 1972, at 16.

RECENT PROBLEMS

Although the lag in the British growth rate is historically deep-seated, the country's special troubles on the inflation and unemployment fronts are, by contrast, recent. The 1949 devaluation of sterling was part of a common adjustment of the parities of most war-devastated countries relative to the United States dollar. Between then and 1967 there was little out of the ordinary in the U.K. macroeconomic experience. The British inflation rate was only very slightly above the average of the twenty-four nations of the Organization for Economic Co-operation and Development (OECD). Registered U.K. unemployment averaged scarcely 2 per cent; and even in the worst recessions, seasonally adjusted adult unemployment rarely touched 3 per cent. (These figures would be very roughly 3 and 4 per cent respectively on U.S. definitions.)[7]

British inflation rates began to rise substantially above the average of industrial countries only in the decade after the 1967 devaluation of sterling. It was in the second half of that decade, from 1972 to 1977, that the British inflation rate really soared. This was a highly inflationary period for the world economy. But while the OECD price level rose by 60 per cent in five years, the British level rose by 120 per cent or twice as much.[8]

The 1970s also saw a reversal of comparative unemployment experience. The British unemployment rate, put onto common definitions, climbed by late 1977 to about 7 per cent, or 2 percentage points above the OECD average.[9] Thus there was no longer either price stability or low unemployment to set off against a low-growth performance. It was not a coincidence that political and social stability seemed threatened in the mid-1970s. I am using the past tense because I believe that on the inflation front, at least, the United Kingdom will no longer diverge so dramatically from the world average.

SUGGESTED EXPLANATIONS

Why has British performance fallen so far behind other countries? A great deal of fun could be had from the many and often contradictory suggestions offered. Both the inequities of British society and excessive egalitarian zeal

TABLE 4

PERCENTAGE OF UNEMPLOYMENT IN OECD AND UNITED KINGDOM*

	Main OECD Countries	United Kingdom
1962-1973 average	2.8	2.4
1973	3.0	2.8
1974	3.3	2.9
1975	5.4	5.1
1976	5.4	7.0
1977	5.4	6.9

*Weighted average on common definition

Source: OECD Economic Outlook, July 1976, at 32; and *id.*, December, 1977, at 28.

have been blamed; so too have inadequate competition and insufficient government intervention. Some people cite the enormous institutional obstacles to change and others the excessive ease with which policies are reversed under a two-party winner-takes-all system; and one could go on indefinitely.

Some of the suggested explanations of British economic performance may shed light on recent years, but cannot conceivably explain the long-term lag in growth rates. Some dwell on transitory phenomena already disappearing or unlikely to last. Some are factually dubious on any basis whatsoever.

For instance, a once popular diagnosis was that British growth was held back by cyclical fluctuations in output, caused by stop-go financial policies. Numerous studies have, however, shown that deviations in U.K. output, measured in relation to trend, were less than in most other countries.[10]

A related explanation was low investment, especially in manufacturing, in the post-World War II period. Close examination reveals, however, that gross investment in manufacturing, as a percentage of value added, was no higher in Germany than in the United Kingdom. Where the United Kingdom did come clearly at the bottom of the league was in the effectiveness of investment in terms of output generated. It is therefore not surprising that profitability and the return on investment were low by international standards.

A contemporary vogue diagnosis is "deindustrialization", which has been used to describe a pathological fall in the ratio of industrial to total employment. But comparative international figures make it clear that this is either not a disease at all, or one from which many other countries suffer as well. The United States, Sweden, the Netherlands and Belgium all had falls in the ratio of industrial to total employment in 1965-1975 of comparable size to Britain's. Germany and France just about maintained the same manufacturing ratio, while Japan and Italy were exceptional in increasing theirs.[11]

One aspect of a relatively slow growth rate has been the fall in the British share of world trade or world exports of

TABLE 5

INVESTMENT IN MANUFACTURING 1958–1972[a]

	Investment Ratio[b] %	Increase in Net Output[c] Per Unit of Investment Index Nos. U.K. = 100
U.K.	13.0	100
U.S.A.	12.2	145
Germany	13.0	190
Sweden	14.4	145
France	16.3	163
Japan	24.6	157

Notes: [a]Or nearest comparable period to eliminate cyclical distortions.

[b]Manufacturing Gross Investment as % of Value Added.

[c]Incremental Output to Capital Ratio

Source: Confederation of British Industry, Britain Means Business 1977, 38 (1977).

manufactures. Repeated investigations have shown that this decline cannot be explained by any special features of either the commodity composition or market outlets for British exports. It is simply that if the United Kingdom has a lower growth rate than competitor countries, one would expect, other things being equal, a declining share of world exports relative to those countries' share. It is thus a consequence rather than a cause.

There is a more specific doctrine relating Britain's slow growth to trading performance. This is that the country has a special difficulty in earning enough overseas to support a full employment level of activity. The doctrine is the theme song of the annual reviews of the Cambridge Economic Policy Group. The essential argument is that even if exchange rates move so as to keep British money costs competitive with other countries', imports will be too high and exports too low to maintain full employment. This would imply that British products are not merely inferior in design, performance, or delivery, but are continually deteriorating in these respects. The Cambridge group's case rests on the very strong assumption that the annual fall in terms of trade required to stay in equilibrium would be so steep and meet such strong union resistance that it could not be brought about without an inflationary explosion.

The whole diagnosis of output limited by a demand or balance-of-payments constraint is open to serious question. The rise in import penetration in the 1960s and 1970s took place in a series of jumps during periods of boom and supply bottlenecks. The increase in British exports, relative to any given increase in world real incomes, has been substantially less than that of exports of other countries. But it is disputable whether such ratios are a true measure of the income elasticity of demand for British exports. Bottlenecks on the supply side - even when the unemployment statistics have been high - have limited the response of British industry to increases in overseas demand.

GOVERNMENT SPENDING

The level of government spending is also often blamed for recent poor performance. We should, however, be very careful in citing figures of the ratio of public spending to the national product, as different definitions produce widely different figures. The Treasury was able to reduce the public-spending ratio by nearly 10 per cent by netting out government interest payments against receipts from nationalized industries, and by excluding capital investment by the latter financed by retained profits or market borrowing. A case could be made for both changes, which brought Britain roughly into line with the common definitions of the OECD.

On the present definition, public expenditure is running at just over 40 per cent of the GDP. This places the United Kingdom in the middle rather than at the top of the international league. There is, however, rarely smoke without fire. A closer look shows that a sudden bulge in spending ratios took place between 1973 and 1975. This came just after the oil price explosion. During these years output fell by 3 per cent, and real national disposable income, taking into account terms of trade changes, fell by 5 per cent.[12] But public-spending plans, which have a momentum of their own, were slow to adjust to changed circumstances; and the period 1973-1975 covered of course two elections. But it was never plausible to extrapolate on the basis of these few years. A political reaction, quite predictably, developed, and the public-spending ratio has since fallen back. The main public argument now is between those who want to freeze the *level* of expenditure and those who want to freeze its ratio to the national product. We had incidentally a similar bulge in the public-spending ratio in the late 1960s which was also followed by a political reaction - in both cases under Labour chancellors.

Was there a dangerous switch of workers from private manufacturing to public service? Up to 1971 the shifts closely paralleled trends in other countries. The shift into public-service employment after 1971 up to 1975 was more worrying. But before ringing the alarm bells too loudly we should, however, note that of the 850,000 workers who entered public-service employment between 1971 and 1975, nearly 650,000 were females, over half part-time.[13] It is stretching credulity to suppose that these women and girls would otherwise have been employed in factories at a conventionally acceptable wage.

TABLE 6

DEFINITIONS OF PUBLIC SPENDING
PUBLIC EXPENDITURE AS A PERCENTAGE OF GDP

	1956-66 %	1975-76 %	1978-79 (official forecast Jan. 1977) %
On goods and services at market prices	21*	26.5	23-24
Goods and services at factor cost	24*	30	27
Total public spending at market prices	35.5	46	42-43
Total public spending at factor cost	40.5	51.5	48
Total public spending at factor cost, pre-1977 definition	45.5	58.5*	not available
Total including tax allowances	not available	70.5	not available

*Estimated

Sources: The Government's Expenditure Plans, Cmnd 6721 (1977); Great Britain, Dep't of Treasury estimates; and General Subcomm. of the Expenditure Comm., Memoranda (Feb. 1977).

Note: A breakdown of the approximate value of tax allowances for 1975-76 as a percentage of gross domestic product is:

Personal	9
Mortgage and Life Insurance	1
Capital Allowances	2
	12

TABLE 7

CHANGES IN EMPLOYMENT, UNITED KINGDOM
(in thousands)

	Total 1959	1959-1971	1971-1976	1959-1976
Private Manufacturing Sector	9,814	-123	-773	-896
Other Private Sector	8,235	- 17	+425	+408
Public Sector (nonmanufacturing)	5,111	+737	+802	+1,539
Total Employed Labour Force*	23,756	+643	+362	+1,005
Unemployment	512	+280	+568	+848

* Minor discrepancies due to public-sector manufacturing, self-employed, and H.M. Forces.

Source: Great Britain, Dep't of Employment.

Let me not be misunderstood. Large parts of public expenditure are not devoted to genuinely public goods and do little to transfer resources to the poor. These expenditures take place only because of the imperfections of the political market. But there is no need to claim that public spending is (a) out of control, (b) higher than in other countries, or (c) in itself a likely cause of economic breakdown or political collapse.

TAX PERVERSITIES

Not surprisingly, international tax comparisons lead to a similar picture. On comparable definitions, the United Kingdom has a tax burden of just over 40 per cent of GNP, half-way down the list, about the same as France and Germany, higher than that of the United States, but a good deal less than the Scandinavian countries.[14] In these comparisons, social security levies are included with taxation where they properly belong.

We come nearer to the source of complaint if we notice that the United Kingdom raises a relatively high proportion of revenue from taxes on households; and the *personal* tax burden did rise sharply in the middle 1970s. Thus people were conscious of a sudden fiscal squeeze which occurred at a time when even gross earnings were under pressure on account of the terms of trade loss. Most of the increase in the personal tax *burden* was due not to any increase in tax *rates*, but to the failure to index the tax starting points and higher rate brackets against inflation. (Looking back over the whole decade from 1965 to 1975, tax thresholds kept up with inflation; and it was the failure to index against rising *real* income which drew so many more people into the income-tax net.)

For most of the postwar period the real trouble has been, however, not average tax rates but the very high marginal rates of tax, both at the top and at the bottom of the income scale. The top marginal rates have been not only higher than in other industrial countries, but were until the 1979 Budget reached at a much lower level of income. These were entirely political taxes. The revenue collected at the top was trivial in statistical terms; and the real effect was certainly to lower revenue, thus reducing what was available for redistribution. As important, from the point of view of the British growth rate, was the diversion of scarce energy and talent into trying to convert income into capital, or into benefits in kind not taxable at these rates.

What proportion of the lag in Britain's growth rate do these tax rates explain? We can only guess. But two facts are worth pondering. One is that these confiscatory rates cannot explain any of the lag before World War II. Secondly, the Western country which most nearly approaches the United Kingdom in the severity of its tax progression, Sweden, has been much higher in the growth league for most of the postwar period. Despite its recent setback, Sweden has a level of GNP per head which is comparable to that of the United States.

Nor can we really ascribe the U.K. growth lag to any generalized fault known as state intervention. For the greater part of the postwar period, there is no evidence that there was more state intervention in the marketplace in the United Kingdom than other Western countries. During the 1950s and most of the 1960s - even during the Labour Governments of 1964-70 - most industrial decisions were made in the marketplace. Moreover, among industrial economies there is little connection between growth rates and the degree of state involvement in the economy. Germany has prospered under free-market doctrines, while Japan and France have prospered under a sort of right-wing *dirigisme* - a common front between government and industrial organizations designed to bypass the market wherever possible. At the level of specific industries, agriculture has been subject to more government intervention than almost any other industry in most Western countries. Yet it has been characterized by a high rate of productivity growth.

A generalization worth venturing is that a country can get away either with a great deal of state intervention or with a great deal of egalitarian social policy, but not with the two together. Sweden, for instance, had a high level of social services and fiscal redistribution but, until recently at least, was a model market economy. Industrial policy was geared to encouraging workers to shift as quickly as possible to the most profitable industries, and investment was guided by world markets rather than by government planning. In France and Japan, on the other hand, "planning" is combined with a highly unequal distribution of income and the bulk of taxation tends to come from sales and turnover levies.

One further tentative generalization may be suggested. The more democratic a country's institutions, the more likely is government economic intervention to hold back rather than encourage growth. Growth depends on change; and change can be disturbing. The general citizen has a dispersed interest in change and efficiency spread over thousands of different decisions. Particular industries and interest groups have a much more concentrated interest in stopping change or in securing inefficient decisions for their own narrow benefit. In a highly democratic society, geographically or professionally concentrated groups have much more influence than do general citizen interests. A concrete example of what I have in mind was the decision of Conservative Premier Harold Macmillan in a conflict over the location of a steel mill between Scotland and Wales at the beginning of the 1960s. The resolution was to have two smaller, suboptimal mills, one in each area.

In its time the steel-mill decision was untypical. Most such decisions would then have been taken in the marketplace. But since 1972 there has been a notable increase in the quantity of government intervention in the United Kingdom and deterioration in quality. We have had a multiplication of discretionary subsidies to individual concerns with no realistic prospects of paying their own way and with no genuine spillover benefits to justify subsidy. The standard of living of U.K. consumers has been reduced and the development of poorer countries impeded by putting barriers on low-cost imports. There have been laws which seem deliberately designed to price out of work the less skilled, the less able, the victims of prejudice, the young, the old, women, and coloured immigrants - all in the name of high-sounding principles such as "the rate for the job".

After 1972, the effects of inflation on a marginal tax structure, which was steeply progressive at the top, were combined with wage-control policies deliberately designed to reduce differentials. According to one set of estimates, adult manual workers had only a very slight increase in earnings in the whole period 1970-1977, while supervisory staff suffered, in typical instances, real falls of 15 to 20 per cent and managers falls of over 30 per cent.[15]

INCOMES POLICY

Perverse regulation, especially in the labour market, has increased in most European countries. If it has been worse in the United Kingdom, it has been from a desire to keep the unions sweet for pay controls. Indeed many of the particular perversities of British economic policy stem from the belief that inflation must be fought by regulation of specific pay settlements. To create a climate in which the unions will tolerate such intervention has been the object of much government activity. This has involved price control, high marginal tax rates, and a special sensitivity to union leaders' views on many aspects of policy. The post-1972 period of especially perverse intervention began, not with a change of government, but with the conversion of the Heath Conservative government to pay and price controls.

This conversion, and the emphasis of subsequent governments on pay restraint, can itself be explained by the fact that the United Kingdom had a much larger jump in inflation rates in the great inflation which hit the Western world in the 1970s than most other countries. Sudden and severe inflation nearly always increases the pressure for direct pay or price controls, however questionable their economic logic.

The severe inflation of the middle 1970s brought with it, moreover, severe unemployment. Whatever the short-term trade-offs between jobs and prices over some normal and moderate range, violent and unpredictable fluctuations in the inflation rate are nearly always bad for employment.[16] British inflation - which reached a high of 20 to 30 per cent in 1975 and declined to single figure rates for a temporary period in 1977/78 was certainly violent and unpredictable; and the business, political and legal systems had certainly not adjusted to these Latin American-type conditions.

When severe inflation is also combined with severe recession, pressures for make-work policies will rise. The vogue of ideas such as the National Enterprise Board and Planning Agreements, or the ability of politicians to dress up make-work policies as industrial regeneration, together with the recurrent bouts of pessimism about the future of capitalism, are all characteristic of severe inflation or slump, and still more of the combination of both.

In my view, however, the exceptionally severe and explosive British inflation has been both a superficial and an ephemeral aspect of the British disease. It has lasted, as already mentioned, for only a decade, and it may be already in the process of passing away.

There is no mystery about the proximate forces behind the recent British inflation. There was an uncannily close relation between the changes in prices and the change in the money supply over the 1970s as a whole. (There was, however, no close fit between year-to-year changes, nor any obvious regular lag. If one had only knowledge of the monetary totals and of the trend growth of output, one would be pretty successful at guessing where the price level would end up over a number of years, but very unsuccessful at predicting short-term changes in either output or inflation.)

STERLING, MONEY, AND EMPLOYMENT

The interesting question is why the money supply was given such a boost. The Heath government of 1970-1974 and its advisers were convinced that the then-prevailing unemployment was a sign of deficient demand and did not want a restrictive monetary policy (or its concomitant of higher nominal interest rates) to stand in the way of an increase in real demand to full employment levels. They were sure that inflation was due to union pushfulness and that there was no danger in boosting demand so long as unemployment was above the then-target level of 2½ per cent (on British definitions).

Until very recently, the orthodox belief of nearly all British policy makers - government, opposition, ministers, civil servants, economic advisers, and independent experts alike - was that fiscal and monetary policy mainly determined real output and activity, except under conditions of extreme excess demand which have not prevailed since the early 1960s. Inflation on this view was almost entirely determined by different forces - namely union pushfulness and import prices - and had to be tackled by completely different means. In the case of wages this meant direct controls or political agreements with union leaders.

Why was this ultra-Keynesian view held for so long?

TABLE 8

MANUFACTURING OUTPUT, EMPLOYMENT, AND OUTPUT PER EMPLOYEE

AVERAGE GROWTH PER ANNUM (%)

	1955-60	1960-64	1964-69	1969-73
Manufacturing Output:				
EEC Five	6.9	6.6	6.5	5.4
United Kingdom	2.8	3.3	3.2	2.8
Manufacturing Employment:				
EEC Five	2.7	1.0	0.2	0.7
United Kingdom	0.6	0.1	-0.2	-1.5
Manufacturing Output per Employee:				
EEC Five	4.1	5.5	6.3	4.7
United Kingdom	2.2	3.2	3.4	4.4

Source: Daniel Jones, Output, Employment, and Labour Productivity in Europe since 1955, Nat'l Instit. Econ. Rev., Aug. 1976, at 72.

Mere intellectual error is apt to be corrected by uncomfortable events. We can understand the attitudes of British policy makers better if we remember that their thinking was based on a long period of a fixed exchange rate. This lasted until the 1967 devaluation, after which a further attempt was made to re-establish a fixed exchange rate regime at a new parity which lasted until the pound finally floated in 1972. With a fixed sterling parity, the prices of internationally traded goods could not diverge far from that of other countries. During this long period the main effects of excessive monetary expansion were on the balance of payments.[17]

There was a further complication. Because of the international role of sterling, the United Kingdom was able to finance current trade deficits for periods of up to two or three years by attracting short-term funds to London at the cost of a modest, uncovered favourable interest-rate differential. But, in contrast to the U.S. position, there was no sizable long-term buildup of funds in London. The temporary inflows invariably reversed themselves in crisis conditions, often after the domestic economy had already come off the boil.

Thus periods of boom, which were mainly due to demand stimulation, came to look like the beginnings of real growth that had been cut off by mysterious external crises. This gave rise to the mistaken belief that only the international functions of sterling prevented a U.K. growth miracle.

The international role of sterling was also made a pretext for imposing a taboo on discussions of the case for floating or devaluing the pound. But like many taboos, this led to an overvaluation of the forbidden activity. When in the end the United Kingdom did float the pound in 1972, the change was seen not just as a sensible way of balancing the demand and supply for foreign exchange,[18] but it was also seen as a patent medicine which would enable the authorities to indulge with impunity in expansionary fiscal and monetary policies - or "take the brakes off", in the metaphor so often used at the time.

The lesson has been learned from the early and middle-1970s. By this I do not mean that inflation has been conquered or that some ideal monetary rule will be followed, but simply that the British authorities have now had irrefutable evidence that budget deficits financed by excess monetary creation lead to an inflationary crisis rather than the much-desired real growth.

Indeed I would argue that the temptation to inflate the money supply in the name of full employment policies is an aspect of the British sickness now more likely to be experienced in the United States than in Britain itself. The great temptation to monetary overexpansion comes from the temporarily benign effect of such expansion on output and employment, and the delayed effect on prices. But the temporary gain to output is very much smaller than it used to be in the United Kingdom, if indeed it exists at all. This is partly because the foreign exchange and other financial markets are now fully alert to monetary indicators. An expansion of the money stock, or mere *fear* of a future budget deficit likely to be financed in this way, has a much more immediate effect than it used to have on the exchange rate and inflationary expectations, and little if any of the stimulus affects output. A temporary trade-off between inflation and employment is nowadays much more likely to exist in a continental economy with little experience of rapid inflation than in an open economy with such experience.

THE ARGUMENT SO FAR

Let me summarize so far. The lag in the British growth rate goes back at least a century, although it took on a new dimension in about 1960 when the level as well as the growth rate of British real income began to fall behind similarly placed European states. In addition the United Kingdom has shared in the poor output and employment performance of the post-1973 economic cycle. But I have suggested that British inflationary excesses (compared to other countries) are recent, unlikely to persist and therefore not the most fundamental aspects of the British disease. Many other much-criticised British policies are also followed to a comparable degree by other governments, working under similar political pressures. Moreover, these errors are too recent to explain the longer-term weaknesses. The tax rates of the 1970s hardly shed light on weaknesses of British management which worried Lord Haldane before World War I.

Can then anything be said of the deep-seated lag in British growth rates? And does British experience throw any light on the stagflation problem, which still remains serious, even if it is likely henceforth to show itself more in Britain in stagnant output and employment, rather than in runaway inflation?

These broader questions bring us to two subjects which are always raised in any discussion of long-run British economic performance. These are the class system and the trade unions.

THE CLASS SYSTEM

Contrary to travellers' tales, the United Kingdom is *not* more stratified than other societies in any obvious statistical sense. Income disparities, even before tax, are less in the United Kingdom than in the United States, Japan, France, or Germany. Rates of occupational mobility between father's and son's occupation are substantial - over 60 per cent of men in the top occupational classes have parents two or more classes below them. Indeed 40 per cent are the sons of manual workers or lower-grade technicians. There is at least as much upward mobility in the United Kingdom as in the United States; and a greater proportion of British university students have working class backgrounds than is the case on the Continent of Europe. Nor are these overnight developments. Economic divisions in the society have been lessening since the turn of the century if not earlier.[19]

Yet, there is a sense in which Britain is more class-ridden than other capitalist or mixed economies. But it is to be found in the features of British society furthest removed from pecuniary matters. They lie in such things as emphasis on the social pecking order, concern with subtle differences of speech and manner, and the educational segregation from an early age of a so-called elite in fee-paying and often unpleasant residential institutions, strangely known as public schools. These features have given us the British novel; and they are a boon to the travel industry. If anyone doubts that they add to the bitterness as well as the gaiety of British life, he should take the first opportunity to see - or at least read - John Osborne's play of the 1950s, *Look Back in Anger*.

One important feature of this type of class division is that it cuts right across the higher echelons of society. Most British managers have not had the traditional upper-class education; and a captain of industry can feel socially inferior over a glass of sherry with a country parson or a retired army major. The old school conservative and the socialist reformer come together in a common dislike of merely commercial values. In all societies people care about their status in the eyes of their fellowmen. In Britain, however, social status has less to do with merely making money than in almost any other Western society.

UNION POWER

The other old-established British institution, which needs to be mentioned, is the trade-union movement. But here again, we must be careful of misdiagnosis. The number of days lost in British industry through strikes, even in the troublesome period of the early 1970s, was less than in the United States or Canada (although more than in Germany or France). The quantities involved are insignificant - just over one day per man year on average. Strikes are overwhelmingly in large concerns. Well over 90 per cent of workers in establishments employing less than 500 do not have any experience of strikes from one year to the next.[20]

Monopolistic union practices are a different matter. Their effect on productivity is difficult to quantify, although the international productivity comparisons cited earlier may give a clue. Let me quote from a profound analysis of the logic of contemporary unionism. The writer shows that unions derive their influence over wages from the power to exclude and that the main losers are other workers. He cites severe restrictions on entry such as:

> ....high initiation fees, excessive periods of apprenticeship and restrictions upon numbers of apprentices, barriers to movements between related trades, and, of course, make-work restrictions, cost-increasing working rules, and prohibition of cost-reducing innovations, not to mention racial and sex discrimination....
>
> There is every prospect that opportunities for

> collective,collusive, monopolistic action in particular labor markets will increase indefinitely whereever organization is possible. This prospect alone suffices to explain the ominous decline of private investment and the virtual disappearance of venturesome new enterprise....
>
> Investors now face nearly all the disagreeable uncertainties of investors in a free-market world plus the prospect that labor organization will appropriate most or all of the earnings which would otherwise accrue if favorable contingencies materialized.[21]

But even this is not the worst of it. Partial unionism is "a device by which the strong may raise themselves higher by pressing down the weak". It makes "high wages higher and low wages lower". This works when "everybody does not try it or when few have effective power". Attempts to apply it universally are incompatible with order." He goes on:

> In an economy of intricate division of labor, every large organized group is in a position at any time to disrupt or to stop the whole flow of social income, and the system must soon break down if groups persist in exercising that power or if they must continuously be bribed to forgo its disastrous exercise....The dilemma here is not peculiar to our present economic order; it must appear in any kind of system. This minority-monopoly problem would be quite as serious for a democratic socialism as it is for the mixed individualist-collectivist system of the present. It is the rock on which our present system is most likely to crack up; and it is the rock on which democratic socialism would be destroyed if it could ever come into being at all.[22]

The author I am quoting does not pretend to have a remedy but talks about the possibility of "an awful dilemma: democracy cannot live with tight occupational monopolies; and it cannot destroy them, once they attain great power, without destroying itself in the process".

This sounds like a despairing British economist writing in the aftermath of the 1974 miners' strike, when union power broke one government and demoralised the whole governing order. In fact the author was an American writing of U.S. trade unions, and passages cited were composed in 1946 by none other than that great libertarian and radical Henry Simons himself.[23] His remarks can be regarded as an elaboration of Dicey's contrast[24] at the beginning of the twentieth century between the effects of individual pursuit of self-interest and its collective pursuit.[25]

DEMOCRACY AND INTEREST GROUPS

Simons's forebodings were followed in the United States by over three decades of unparalleled prosperity in which the membership and influence of U.S. trade unionism, if anything, declined. Unfortunately, a premature prediction is not necessarily a wrong one. We still do not know whether the gloomy forebodings of Dicey and Simon were averted or merely postponed.

The underlying question concerns the impact, not merely of unions, but of all producer and special interest groups on the functioning of the economic system. The problem is not one of inflation, as so often wrongly supposed, but of unemployment. If the total effect of the monopolistic activities of producer groups is to price so many people out of work that the resulting unemployment rate is higher than the electorate will tolerate, then our system of political economy is doomed.[26] If the government in such a situation tries to spend its way into full employment, the result will be not just inflation, but accelerating inflation. So there is no escape that way - as I believe British policy makers are at last learning. We do not know if the sustainable unemployment rate is too high for democratic stability or, if it is, what the role of union-type monopoly is in making it so. The fact that we cannot rule out the pessimistic hypothesis is itself important.

The Simons quotation also raises the question of the effects of uncertain property rights on investment. Investment can take place under state ownership, under workers' cooperatives, or untrammelled private ownership. The private enterprise system can probably adapt to the capture by unions of a large proportion of the return on new investment - provided that proportion is predictable and stable. The main eventual effect might then be higher profit margins and higher gross returns. But a system of confused and unpredictable property rights under a nominally private enterprise system is highly discouraging to investment - and thereby also depressing to employment in the longer run.

It is difficult to pronounce on the breakdown hypothesis in general terms.[27] A great deal depends on things such as the proportion of the population unionized - which is much greater in the United Kingdom[28] than in the United States - as well as on the degree of toleration of under-cutting of union suppliers by others. One need only compare the 1978 U.S. coal strike with the British miners' strikes of 1972 and 1974. Much also hangs on the electorate's toleration of higher unemployment in today's circumstances. This is clearly higher than it was, given the social cushions now available; but we have yet to test its limits on either side of the Atlantic. Nor have we any real idea how high is the sustainable rate of unemployment consistent with avoiding merely an acceleration of the existing inflation rate. A lot hangs on whether it is in the 6 per cent area of the late 1970s or something much higher, such as 10 to 15 per cent.

Moreover, we should not conceive the producer-group threat too narrowly. Collective action to secure real wages incompatible with full employment may come not just through the strike threat alone, but also through political action - import price ceilings, minimum wage laws, and farm support are only some of the more obvious areas. The uncertainty and insecurity of property rights which Simons feared can be the result of regulatory agencies or of political hyperactivity as well as of unions. The real danger is that the end result of action taken by people through collective activity will be unacceptable to the same people in their capacity of consumers and voters - a perverse invisible hand. The fact that Simons was premature in his forebodings in the case of the United States does not mean that they can be dismissed.

THE COSTS OF STABLE INSTITUTIONS

Why have restrictive policies, not only by unions, but by all producer groups, had more impact in the United Kingdom than in many other countries? An interesting hypothesis has been suggested by Professor Mancur Olson.[29] This derives from the old problem of the free rider, which Professor Olson has recently applied specifically to the United Kingdom.[30] The point is that there is very little personal incentive for an individual to participate, whether financially, or by direct action such as striking, or by political lobbying, in group activity, since the gains spill over to others while he bears the costs himself. Long periods of peace and established institutions are necessary for producer groups to overcome this constraint. The passage of time enables such groups to build up selective benefits for their members which will persuade them to participate in collective action. As the years proceed, political linkages become established, voting lobbies become organized; and the biggest allies of all - instinctive habit and group loyalties - have time to become established.

The central conclusion that Olson draws is that "the longer the period in which a country has had a modern industrial pattern of common interest and at the same time democratic freedom of economic organization without upheaval and disorganization, the greater the extent to which its growth rate will be retarded by organized interests".[31] Thus it is not surprising that the British disease should have come first to the country which both pioneered the industrial revolution and has the longest record of civic freedom and settled institutions. On the other hand, countries "where common interest organizations have been emasculated or abolished by foreign occupation, totalitarian governments or political instability", experience rapid rates of growth "after a free and stable legal order is established".[32] The Olson explanation has the great advantage of not having to suggest that Germany gained in a physical sense from having had her industrial plant destroyed in the war. Among Continental countries, it was Italy, where the traditional culture was most deep-rooted, and the wartime destruction was most superficial, that saw the earliest end to the period of "miracle" growth, and the earliest infection by the British disease.

On this interpretation there is nothing peculiarly British about the British sickness; but it is something which will come in time to any country with a settled record of free institutions. It came to New England before California, and it is coming to California before Alaska.

As World War II and its aftermath recede, and settled democratic institutions move into their second generation, producer-interest groups might be expected to gain ground in Western Europe as well. The countries now experiencing the most rapid growth in the Pacific basin are those where industrial development is still a novelty and untrammelled by collective or political pressures.

SELF-CORRECTING FORCES

But there is no need to end on a fatalistic note. As the output gap widens between a slowly growing country held back by restrictive interest groups and other countries employing best-practice techniques, the incentive to catch up also becomes larger. The more atrophied become a country's techniques and habits, the greater becomes the return to innovation. The gains can become so great that it may be possible to make agreements to share them with the restrictive interest groups. Moreover, restrictive practices are never of the same severity across the economy; and if innovation is blocked in traditional or well-organized sectors, talent and capital will drift to newer areas, where group loyalties have not yet "solved" the free-rider problem. In the last resort the returns to political entrepreneurship from trying to change the institutional or political rules in favour of better economic performance may become so great that the changes are made.

LATEST U.K. TRENDS

Unfortunately, there are no useful rules for telling us exactly when self-correcting forces will overcome those for making for relative decline. This is one reason why political economy is still so remote from genuine science. Are we talking about years, decades or centuries?

There was in fact some evidence that corrective forces were beginning a few years ago to develop in the U.K. at grass roots level. Value added per man hour in U.K. manufacturing did rise at faster rates during successive trade cycles of the 1960s, and by 1969-73 it was rising at about the same rate as in other European countries (Table 8).

TABLE 9

THE LATEST CYCLE

	UNEMPLOYMENT %[o]			PRODUCTIVITY[+]		
	1973	1978	Change 1973 to 1978	Average annual growth 1963 to 1973	Average annual growth 1973 to 1978	Average annual decline in growth rate
U.K.	2.8	6.8	+4.0	3.2[x]	0.8[x]	-2.4[x]
U.S.	4.7	5.9	+1.2	1.8	0.1	-1.7
Germany	0.9	3.7	+2.8	4.7	3.2	-1.5
France	2.6	5.8	+3.2	4.5	3.0	-1.5
Japan	1.3	2.5	+1.2	8.9	3.4	-5.5
Canada	5.6	8.4	+2.8	2.4	0.6	-1.8
Italy	3.7	7.4	+3.7	5.4	1.1	-4.3
Sweden	2.5	2.6	+0.1	n.a.	n.a.	n.a.

o = On common OECD definition

+ = GNP divided by employment

x = Excluding North Sea oil

n.a.= Not available

Source: OECD Economic Outlook, December 1978 and July 1976

Even in 1969-73, however, there was one important difference between the United Kingdom and other European countries. The growth in manufacturing productivity in other countries was mainly the result of rising output, with little change in manpower. In the United Kingdom on the other hand, it was due mainly to a fall in the manufacturing labour force with very little change in output itself. The fall reflected the shakeout in the industrial labour force following first the "Wilson" recession of 1966-67 and then the "Heath" recession of 1971-72.

These qualified signs of improvement turned out premature. For in the world economic cycle, following the oil price explosion of 1973-4, the U.K. lost ground heavily. It did much worse than nearly all other OECD countries both in terms of indicators such as prices and employment and in terms of productivity. Yet another phase of relative decline had begun.

The causes of this relapse have a great deal to do with a turn for the worse in British economic policy in 1972. For about that time macro-economic management took a highly inflationary turn, the consequence of which successive governments tried to suppress by pay and price controls. These errors reflected an intellectual climate, which in turn I believe to be susceptible of economic explanation.

But the very fact that this latest relapse is (unlike the long earlier decline) partly attributable to specific policy errors gives us a ray of hope. For if these policy errors are avoided, the tendency for British productivity growth to approach the European average, evident in the early 1970s, could reassert itself. But this has not yet happened. And even if it did, the U.K. would simply be maintaining a constant proportionate GDP gap compared with more fortunate countries. The closing of that gap will be a bigger and more difficult undertaking.

FOOTNOTES

1. I am grateful to The Journal of Law and Economics, Chicago, for permission to use and extend the text of the seventh Henry Simons Lecture, "How British is the British Sickness?", Vol. XXI, October 1978.

2. Alfred Marshall, Memorandum on Fiscal Policy of International Trade (1903), reprinted in Official Papers 404-06 (1926).

3. Angus Madison, Phases of Capitalist Development, 1977 Banca Nazionale Del Lavoro Q. Rev. 103.

4. *Id.*

5. Daniel T. Jones, Output, Employment and Labour Productivity in Europe Since 1955, 1976 Nat'l Inst. Econ. Rev. 72.

6. Clifford F. Pratten, Labor Productivity Differentials Within International Companies (1976).

7. OECD Economic Outlook, July 1976, at 31, 147; *id.*, Dec. 1977, tabs. 7 & 8, at 28.

8. *Id.*, Dec. 1977, 125 tab. 24, at 54.

9. *Id.*, tabs. 7 & 8, at 28; *id.*, July 1976, at 106.

10. For instance, National Economic Development Office, Cyclical Fluctuations in the UK (1976).

11. C.J.F. Brown & T.D. Sheriff, Deindustrialization in the UK (Nat'l Inst. Econ. & Soc. Res. 1978).

12. Central Statistical Office, National Income and Expenditure 1966-76 (H.M.S.O. 1977); The Government's Expenditure Plans, Cmnd. 6721 (H.M.S.O. 1977); and Dep't of Treasury estimates.

13. Great Britain, Dep't of Employment statistics.

14. 1977, UK Economic Trends, Table 10 at 10.

15. Confederation of British Industry, Britain Means

Business 1977, tab. 3.2, at 19 (1977).

16. The general argument is set out in Milton Friedman, Nobel Lecture: Inflation and Unemployment, 85 J. Pol. Econ. 451 (1977). The great discrepancy between traditional accounting rates of return and inflation-adjusted ones suggests that, even without government intervention, business may be slow to adjust pricing policy to rapid changes in inflation and that the profit share might be squeezed.

17. The devaluation of sterling was not opposed because it was inflationary, but inflation - which was not yet seen as a serious domestic threat - was opposed mainly because it threatened to bring about devaluation. It is almost impossible to overemphasize how much damage was infliected by this process of miseducation.

18. The long struggle to maintain a fixed exchange rate and preserve the international role of sterling was frequently criticised by radicals, but for the wrong reasons. The real harm inflicted by these prestige goals was that they misled people into supposing that low British growth was a demand problem, when it was really a supply problem.

19. For substantiation of these assertions see Royal Commission on Distribution, Rept. Nos. 3 & 5, 1976 and 1977. See also Henry Phelps Brown, What is the British Predicament? Three Banks Rev., Dec. 1977, at 3.

20. See Henry Phelps Brown, *supra* note 17; and Concentration of Industrial Stoppages in Great Britain: 1971-75, 86 Dep't of Employment Gazette 9 (1978).

21. Henry C. Simons; Some Reflections on Syndicalism, in Economic Policy for a Free Society 121, 130-31, 146-48 (1948).

22. *Id.* at 122-23.

23. See also his introduction to the volume, *id.* at 5.

24. A.V. Dicey, Law and Public Opinion in England (1963).

25. This is the distinction glossed over by British trade

union leaders when they say with monotonous regularity: "If there is to be a free-for-all, we are part of this all."

26. This proposition is known as the Jay Hypothesis, Peter Jay, Employment, Inflation, and Politics (Inst. Econ. Affairs, 1976).

27. The impact of union power on unemployment, inflation and democratic stability is discussed further in Samuel Brittan, The Economic Consequences of Democracy pt. III, at 185-222 (1977).

28. According to Department of Employment figures, 62% of all male employees belong to a union.

29. Mancur Olson, Jr., The Logic of Collective Action (2nd ed. 1971).

30. Mancur Olson, Jr., The Political Economy of Comparative Growth Rates (1978) (mimeo, Univ. of Maryland).

31. *Id.* at 41.

32. *Id.* at 38.

12. PUBLIC SECTOR BEHAVIOUR: THE STATUS OF THE POLITICAL BUSINESS CYCLE

James E. Alt and K. Alec Chrystal

The hypothesis of an electoral-economic cycle is nearly integrated into the folklore of capitalist democracies.
Tufte

One of the most widely accepted patterns of behaviour on the part of the macroeconomic policy makers in Western democracies is the political business cycle. The idea is that, since macroeconomic policy is guided by incumbent politicians, and since political popularity is influenced by the state of the economy, politicians manipulate the economy to ensure that favourable 'boom' times exist prior to elections, thereby maximising their chances or re-election. This notion has long been popular with the media. A recent example of the acceptance of this view is provided by Brittan (1978) who concludes that: "The first part of a Parliamentary or Presidential term is, therefore, one of stagnation, while the last part of one of prosperity." Formal analyses supporting the political business cycle have started appearing in relatively 'serious' academic economics journals within the last few years, as well as within the political science literature. Good examples are Nordhaus (1975), Macrae (1977), Frey and Schneider (1978), Frey (1978b), as well as books by Frey (1978a) and Tufte (1978).

It should be readily accepted that, if the election cycle does lead to *systematic* cycles of economic policy, then this should be investigated by macroeconomists and incorporated into operational macro models. In what follows, however, we shall argue that in reality the political business cycle has neither a strong theoretical basis nor strong empirical support. In general, we are of the view that such 'political' influences can successfully be subsumed within a random disturbance term which is unlikely to provide a payoff to further econometric investigation.

We proceed by providing in the next section a brief survey of the analytical literature. Then we report an application of Macrae's method to the U.K., which provides no support for the existence of a political business cycle. Finally, we investigate the main components of public sector expenditure and revenue to see if they evidence electoral cyclical behavior. We do not bother to address the issue of whether manipulating the economy wins elections, since there can be no strong presumption that it does [see Chrystal and Alt (1979)], rather the concern is to investigate, first, the targets of policy, and, secondly, the instruments of policy to see if they show cycles which are consistent with an electoral cyclical explanation.

THEORY OF POLITICAL BUSINESS CYCLES

One of the most influential recent papers is that by Nordhaus. His paper really falls into two distinct parts. The first part puts forward a justification for the view that 'democracy' causes inflation, while the second part presents a model of the political cycle in which it is deduced that unemployment falls continuously throughout electoral terms and inflation rises continuously. The first proposition is derived from a model which contains an expectations-augmented Phillips curve and a voting function.

$$\pi_t = f(u_t) + \lambda v_t \qquad (1)$$

$$\dot{v}_t = \gamma(\pi_t - v_t) \qquad (2)$$

$$V_t = g(u_t, \pi_t) \qquad (3)$$

where π is the rate of inflation, u unemployment, v expected inflation, and V the percentage of votes for the incumbent party. If the V function is regarded as a proxy for a social welfare function it can be shown that the vote maximising decision within each period will lead to a socially suboptimal outcome. This is illustrated in Figure 1. LP is the long run Phillips curve. The V_i are the equivote curves with votes increasing towards the origin. The P_i are the short run Phillips curves. The social optimum is at A where LP is tangent to the highest possible V line. However, short run vote maximising behaviour by governments will take the economy to the tangency of a P line and a V line. The locus of democratic outcomes will therefore be the set of

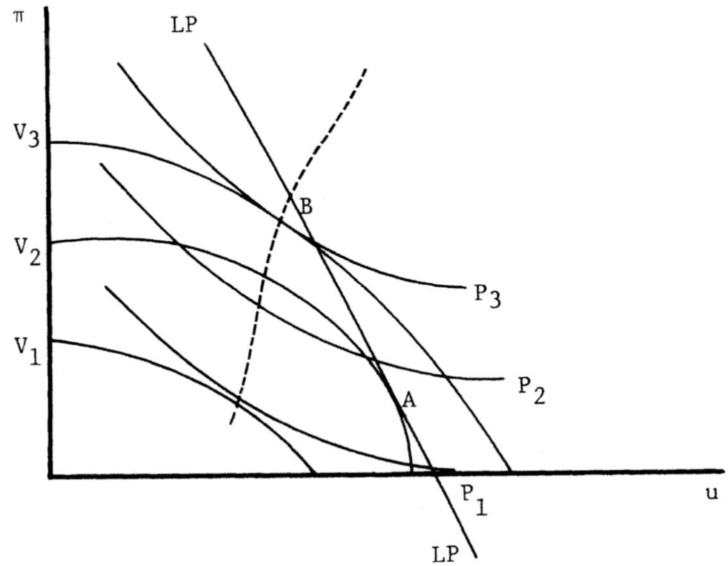

Fig. 1. Equivote and expectations-augmented Phillips curves.

tangencies of the P_i and V_i with the long run outcome at B. At B inflation is unambigously higher than at A but unemployment will only be lower if LP is not vertical.

There are a number of problems with this argument. The most serious is the presumption that governments only get one shot at the economy in each election period. If they are only concerned with the outcome in an election year and get more than one shot per incumbency, they should keep the economy to the left of LP in all but the last year, thereby getting onto the lowest possible P line. This will enable them to get to the highest possible V line in time for the election. In this case democracy could easily produce a *lower* average inflation rate than at A but with a higher average unemployment rate.

Nordhaus generates a cyclical outcome in the second part of his paper by assuming that voters have a decaying memory within election periods, so the voting function becomes

$$V_\Theta = \int_0^\theta g(u_t, \pi_t) e^{\mu t} dt \qquad (4)$$

where θ is the length of the electoral period and μ is the

rate of decay of memories. A specific g function and Phillips curve are assumed so 1 and 3 become

$$\pi_t = \alpha_0 - \alpha_1 u_t + \lambda v_t \tag{5}$$

$$g(u_t, \pi_t) = -u_t^2 - \beta\pi_t \tag{6}$$

So the formal problem is now to maximise

$$V_\theta = \int_0^\theta [-\beta\alpha_0 - u^2 + \beta\alpha_1 u - \beta\lambda v]e^{\mu t}dt$$

subject to $\dot{v} = \gamma[\alpha_0 - \alpha_1 u - (1-\lambda)v]$.

Nordhaus shows that the solution to this problem must be characterized by a continuous decline in unemployment throughout each electoral period accompanied by a steady rise in inflation. It is presumed by Nordhaus that, "Immediately after an election the victor will raise unemployment to some relatively high level in order to combat inflation. As elections approach, the unemployment rate will be lowered until, on election eve, the unemployment rate will be lowered to the purely myopic point." However, there are two critical assumptions which generate these results. The first is that votes depend upon unemployment *squared* whereas only the *level* of inflation enters. Secondly, while actors form inflation expectations for their wage bargain, they do not let these expectations influence their voting behaviour. In other words, voters at election time are pleased by low unemployment, but they completely ignore the inflationary consequences. The result depends entirely upon voters ignoring information which is presumed for other purposes to be available to them. Another major problem with this model is that the jumps which occur immediately after elections are an assumption which would not in reality be feasible. In other words, the model does not deduce a cyclical outcome, rather Nordhaus assumes it. Within incumbencies unemployment falls and inflation rises. What happens at the boundaries is undefined.

A simple test of his result is provided by Nordhaus. He looks at nine countries to see if unemployment is typically lower in the second half of electoral terms than in the first. For six of the nine he concludes that it is not. The three countries that do have this pattern are the U.S., Germany and New Zealand. For the U.S. and Germany much of this is explained by a trend decline in unemployment through the 1960s rather than by a cycle. Even more telling perhaps is the fact that the U.S. and Germany are two Western democracies among those with the lowest long run average inflation rates. So it is hard to accept either the conclusion that democracy causes inflation or that there exists a clear electoral cycle.

A rather more satisfactory piece of empirical work is presented by Macrae. He works in a dynamic programming framework under the assumption that once a voter has been lost he cannot be recovered. Vote loss depends upon current inflation and unemployment, the weights on which are determined empirically. Governments can either assume a myopic electorate, in which case they ignore vote loss beyond the next election, or they can assume strategic behaviour by which governments think about staying in power indefinitely. This framework will be fully evaluated in the next section when we apply it to the U.K. Of the four presidential terms studied by Macrae in the U.S., he concludes that two (1961-4, 1965-8) are consistent with the myopic hypothesis and two (1957-60, 1969-72) with the strategic hypothesis. So even here the political business cycle (which requires myopic behaviour) is far from well established, especially as even in the periods when it is acceptable the myopic hypothesis only marginally outperforms the strategic hypothesis.

It is worth emphasizing that while Macrae makes a distinction between long run optimisation (strategic voting) and short run optimisation (myopic voting) this distinction enters in a highly specific way. All it amounts to is that in the former the optimisation process is conducted continuously over the entire data period whereas in the latter it is conducted within electoral terms only. The framework can still be criticized on the grounds that while actors hold inflation expectations they do not use them when voting. Vote loss is determined solely by current unemployment and inflation. Voters are 'irrational' in the sense that they do not make full use of the information available to them.

The implication of allowing actors to use available information has been pointed out by McCallum [1978]. If the actor/voters understand the model and form expectations 'rationally' this leads to the hypothesis that:

> "...Incumbent governments *cannot*, even if they so dedesire, regularly manufacture booms during the latter portion of their elected terms. Prices may be bid up and inventories drawn down, but output and employment will be unaffected. The argument assumes (i) that

departures of the unemployment rate from its 'natural' level are *initiated* by expectational errors and (ii) that expectations are formed rationally, in the sense of Muth. Under these conditions, Phillips-type relations may exist but will not be exploitable by monetary and fiscal authorities: regular attempts by the authorities to manufacture election-time prosperity will be anticipated by private consumers and firms, and the real effects negated." [p. 504]

McCallum is here pointing to the fact that expansionary policies which are fully anticipated will be offset by the resultant expectations of private actors influencing their market decisions. A fully anticipated expansionary policy will lead to prices being bid up immediately and no change in unemployment. It should also be pointed out that these same expectations should also affect voting behaviour so that there will be no electoral gain to be made from the alleged fact that inflation responds to demand pressures with a lag. Without this lag the political business cycle literature loses its primary raison d'etre.

To support his point McCallum conducts a thorough investigation of unemployment in the U.S. from 1948-1974. He demonstrates that the unemployment time series is well explained as a third order autoregressive process. The addition of a wide variety of dummy variables designed to represent electoral cyclical factors is shown to provide no significant extra explanatory power. Thus it is concluded that the economy which some others allege to show periodic election cycles evidences an unemployment time series which is consistent with the tenets of the rational expectations hypothesis. These tenets are entirely inconsistent with the existence of a political business cycle. However, the McCallum test does not preclude the existence of a regular cycle with peaks in election years.

It is readily admitted by Frey (1978a, Ch. 10) that merely looking at the raw data (be it unemployment, inflation or income) does not provide much support for the notion of a political business cycle. He nonetheless believes in the political cycle but attempts to demonstrate its existence in a completely different way. Rather than looking at the *targets* of economic policy, Frey and Frey and Schneider purport to demonstrate that the *instruments* of policy, notably elements of government expenditure, respond to the proximity of elections and the popularity of the government. It is also claimed that there are significant differences between the behaviour of incumbent parties. For example, in Frey (1978a, p. 151) it is shown that 'expected time to election', 'lead deficit' and party dummies all have a significant part to play in the explanation of government consumption expenditure and transfers in the U.K.

We have elsewhere (Chrystal and Alt, 1979) provided a very detailed critique of Frey and Schneider. In short we found that their theoretical framework left a great deal to be desired and we were unable to replicate their empirical results. Indeed we were so impressed by the very smooth character of the time series for government expenditure and transfers (see Figure 2) that we have been stimulated to explain these from an entirely different point of view. As far as we can see these grow broadly in line with clearly defined macroeconomic aggregates. We will later set out these relationships and show that there is little or no part to be played by electoral cyclical factors, though there is an effect of party differences on transfers.

MACRAE'S MODEL APPLIED TO THE U.K.

There are two main structural relationships in Macrae's model.

$$I_t = aI_{t-1} - bU_t + c \qquad (7)$$

$$V = \frac{1}{2} qI_t^2 + \frac{1}{2} rU_t^2 \qquad (8)$$

Equation 7 is an expectations augmented Phillips Curve. I_t, I_{t-1} are current and lagged inflation respectively (I_{t-1} is a proxy for 'expected' inflation), U is unemployment, c a constant. V is the vote loss by the incumbent party in the current period. q and r are the penalty weights attached to inflation and unemployment (either q or r can be set at 1 so that it is their ratio that is considered); these are presumed fixed for each incumbency.

Macrae proceeds to analyze the optimization problem of the incumbent party in a dynamic programming framework. First he solves for the optimal unemployment level in the terminal year (i.e. election year) by minimizing V subject to equation 7. This gives a decision rule for the election year:

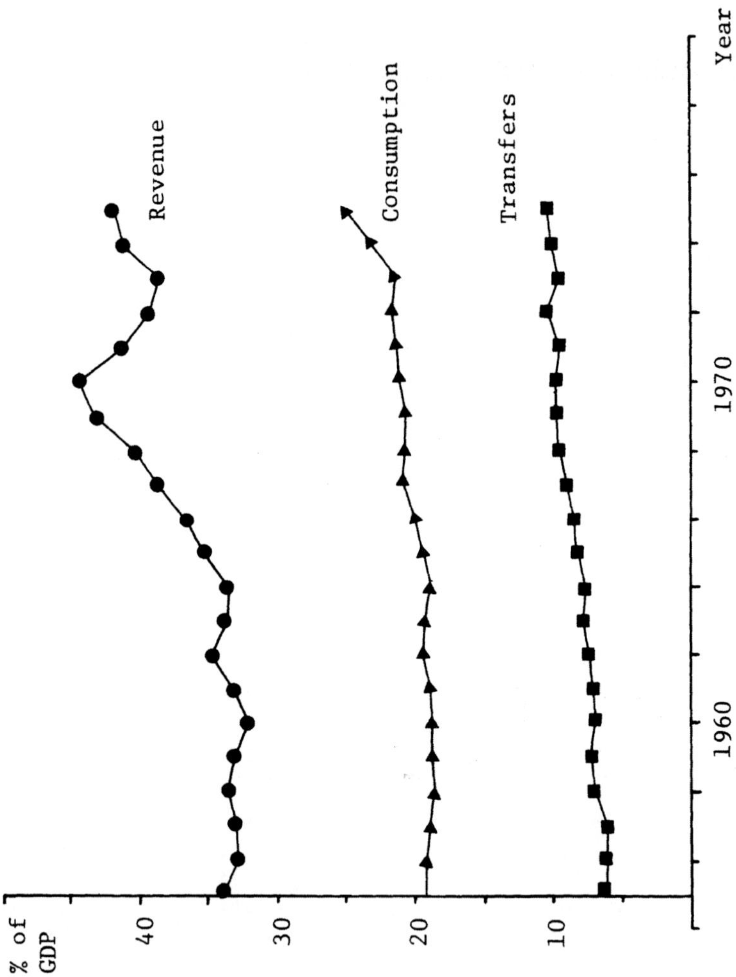

Fig. 2. Shares of GDP in government revenue and expenditure.

$$U_T = \left(\frac{abq}{b^2q+r}\right) I_{T-1} + \frac{bcq}{b^2q+r} \qquad (9)$$

This is the vote loss minimizing decision *given* the inflation in the previous period. Rules are then derived for each successive prior period, working backwards in time so as to both minimize the vote loss in the current period and the vote loss in subsequent periods resulting from current inflation: or in other words to minimize the cumulative vote loss within the decision period.

Political business cycles arise in this model if the government is only concerned to win the next election and ignores the inflationary consequences beyond that point. Thus a test of the hypothesis is provided by comparing long run optimization over an indefinitely long future period with short run optimization for each election period. The former we call strategic behaviour, the latter myopic. Of the four electoral terms examined by Macrae, two were better explained by the strategic hypothesis and two by the myopic -- though it is not at all clear that they were 'significantly' different.

We follow Macrae's methodology for the five major electoral periods in the U.K. between 1951 and 1974. The only deviation from his method is that we allow the Phillips curve to change over time by basing its parameters upon estimates for the current and previous election period. The steps are as follows:

1. Estimate the parameters of the Phillips curve.

2. Using the estimated values of a, b, c for each period and the actual values of U, obtain the best fitting q/r ratios for each election period under the two hypotheses (myopic and strategic) by an iterative simulation procedure.

3. Using the estimated values of a, b, and c and the best fitting q/r ratios under both hypotheses, compare the fitted level of unemployment with that obtained by a 'naive' first order autoregressive process. The comparison is given by the ratio of the error sum of squares under each hypothesis to that obtained under the naive hypothesis.

4. Finally an indirect test of the q/r ratio is provided from opinion polls by regressing popularity loss on squared inflation and unemployment.

Table 1

Political Business Cycles 1951-74

Government	Coefficient of: I_{t-1} a	Coefficient of: U_t b	Constant c	Best-fitting q/r ratio under: Myopic Hypothesis	Best-fitting q/r ratio under: Strategic Hypothesis	Poll-estimated q/r vote loss weights
1951-55	.88 (9.5)	-1.48 (1.5)	3.02 (1.9)	.06 (1.05)	.02 (.11)	-.01
1955-59	.86 (13.4)	- .86 (2.1)	1.65 (2.4)	.20 (5.22)	.15 (1.94)	.11
1959-64	.78 (8.6)	- .69 (2.3)	1.87 (2.8)	.50 (.48)**	.25 (.08)	.20
1966-70	.86 (11.9)	- .41 (1.5)	1.70* (2.1)	.42 (7.59)	.16 (1.14)	.09
1970-74	1.00** (12.7)	- .31 (1.0)	.59 (0.8)	.54 (.64)	.05 (.62)	.73

* Includes a post-1966 dummy variable.

** Actual coefficient 1.08, insignificantly different from theoretical maximum of 1.0.

Note - Bracketed figures in columns 1-3 are t-statistics, equations estimated by OLS over the period of the current and previous government. Bracketed figures in columns 4-5 are goodness-of-fit statistics representing the ratio of the error sums of squares of the hypothesis in the column to the naive hypothesis. Column 6 shows the ratios of the coefficients of the squared values of I and U when quarterly estimates of vote loss were regressed on them, with the constant constrained to zero.

The results are presented in Table 1. The first three columns are estimates of the Phillips curve parameters for each period. Columns 4 and 5 provide the best fitting q/r ratios under each of the two hypotheses. The indicators of accuracy are the bracketed inequality coefficients--the smaller is to be preferred. In all the periods studied the strategic hypothesis does considerably better than the myopic hypothesis with the only exception of 1970-74 (where they are close). In two periods, however, (1955-9 and 1966-70) the naive hypothesis outperforms the strategic hypothesis. The poll estimated q/r ratio in column 6 confirms the ratios fitted for the strategic hypothesis in all but the last period. Thus we are unable to accept that economic policy was determined on the basis of myopic, election influenced, decisions. Rather, we have discovered that policy is consistent with long term optimisation on the part of governments. The only doubt concerns the 1970-4 period where we are unable to distinguish between the possibility of a high inflation penalty weight but myopic optimisation as opposed to a low inflation penalty weight with strategic optimisation.

There may be many objections to the framework used here. Not the least might be the specification of the Phillips curve. We are fully aware of these inadequacies. The important point to notice, however, is that we have tested the hypothesis of myopic electoral horizons *in a framework which is favourable to the hypothesis* and have nonetheless rejected it. An a priori or empirical rejection of the underlying structural relations themselves would not be so convincing. This does, of course, leave open the possibility that political business cycles exist but must be justified in a completely different analytical framework. We cannot counter this possibility until such time as this alternative framework is provided.

AN APPROACH TO PUBLIC SECTOR BEHAVIOR

We have seen above that the time series of inflation and unemployment, two of the most commonly accepted targets of economic policy, do not exhibit electoral cyclical characteristics. We cannot rule out the possibility that other aggregate indicators (such as income) may exhibit electoral cyclical characteristics, but we are of the view that it is fruitless to look at the raw data without some model of what would have been happening anyway. Another approach, however, which will enable us to check our results is to look at the source of policy changes rather than at the targets. If governments are changing their behaviour prior to elections, this should be apparent in the behaviour of their revenues and expenditures. Accordingly, we now investigate the possibility that governments change their shortrun expenditure or tax gathering activity prior to elections in a way designed to increase their popularity. If these are just announcement effects, they are beyond the scope of this paper, but if they are real changes in behaviour then we can examine the data for their existence, even though they may be reversed before affecting unemployment or output. Indeed, Frey, Tufte and Frey and Schneider have done just this and arrived at the unambiguous conclusion that such electoral patterns do clearly exist. We have elsewhere (Chrystal and Alt, 1979) provided a detailed criticism and antithesis of Frey and Schneider which need not be further pursued here. It is sufficient for our present purposes to demonstrate that there exist simple relationships which explain the two major categories of government expenditure -- consumption and transfers -- as well as overall tax revenue. There is no extra explanatory power to be achieved in these relationships by the addition of political cyclical factors. In fact, the only major cycle evident in the residuals for any equation is electorally *counter-cyclical* in the revenue function.

Government Consumption

The approach we adopt is to estimate an equation which relates expenditure to the level of aggregate income. We then investigate the residuals from this equation both by inspection and by adding a variety of political dummies. The basic equation for government consumption relates the level of real expenditure to the level of real GDP. The functional form chosen can be justified in the same way as a 'permanent income' function which includes current GDP and lagged expenditure. We have also discovered by trial and error that post-1974 data necessitates the inclusion of an inflation term to pick up the effects of inflation supplementation prior to the introduction of cash limits (this term is not significant on pre-1974 data). The equation is:

$$G.\ Cons_t = -2.8 + .53G.Cons_{t-1} + .12GDP + .09INFL_{t-1}$$
$$\quad\quad (5.9)\ (9.3) \quad\quad\quad (8.6) \quad (4.6)$$

$\bar{R}^2 = .99$ D.W. = 1.9 Data: Quarterly 1955-1976.2

Estimator: Two stage least squares

This equation fits extremely well by normal criteria. Neither inspection of the residuals nor addition of election dummies provides any support for the existence of electoral shifts in this component of expenditure. Figure 3 plots these residuals. The only remotely possible cycle is one which peaks in 1967. This is exactly the opposite of what we are looking for, since this is early in an incumbency. The other curiosity in the residuals is the large underprediction for 1975.1. The explanation for this seems to be that real GDP was abnormally low at the same time as inflation supplements were paid out for the financial year 1974-5. Thus nominal expenditure rose by something like 15% in one quarter, subsequently to return to trend.

Table 2 shows the results of adding a variety of dummy variables. 2) The Frey-Schneider popularity deficit (FSPD). This is significant but it has the wrong sign according to the Frey and Schneider hypothesis. b) A dummy through the last four quarters of each incumbency. This is marginally significant but again has the wrong sign. c) A two-quarter pre-election dummy. This is insignificant. d) An acceleration dummy (1234) for the four pre-election quarters. Again this is insignificant with the wrong sign. e) A Labour Party dummy shows no significant shift between Labour and Conservative.

In short, we would strongly argue that there is no obvious effect upon aggregate government consumption expenditure of election cycles, political popularity or even the ideology of the incumbent party. In this respect our results are strongly at variance with those of Frey and Schneider and Frey (1978a).

Government Transfers

The form for the transfers equation is the same as for consumption:

TABLE 2

Political Dummies in Government Consumption Equation

		$\bar{R}^2$	D.W.
1.	Other variables plus − .02FSPD* (2.2)	.99	1.9
2.	Other variables plus − .25FOURQD* (1.76)	.99	1.85
3.	Other variables plus − .18 TWOQD* (.99)	.99	1.85
4.	Other variables plus − .077AccD* (1.5)	.99	1.83
5.	Other variables plus + .04LABOUR (.26)	.99	1.9

FSPD = Frey-Schneider Popularity Deficit

FOURQD = Four pre-election quarters

TWOQD = Two pre-election quarters

AccD = 1,2,3,4, for four pre-election quarters

LABOUR - Labour incumbency

*Wrong sign

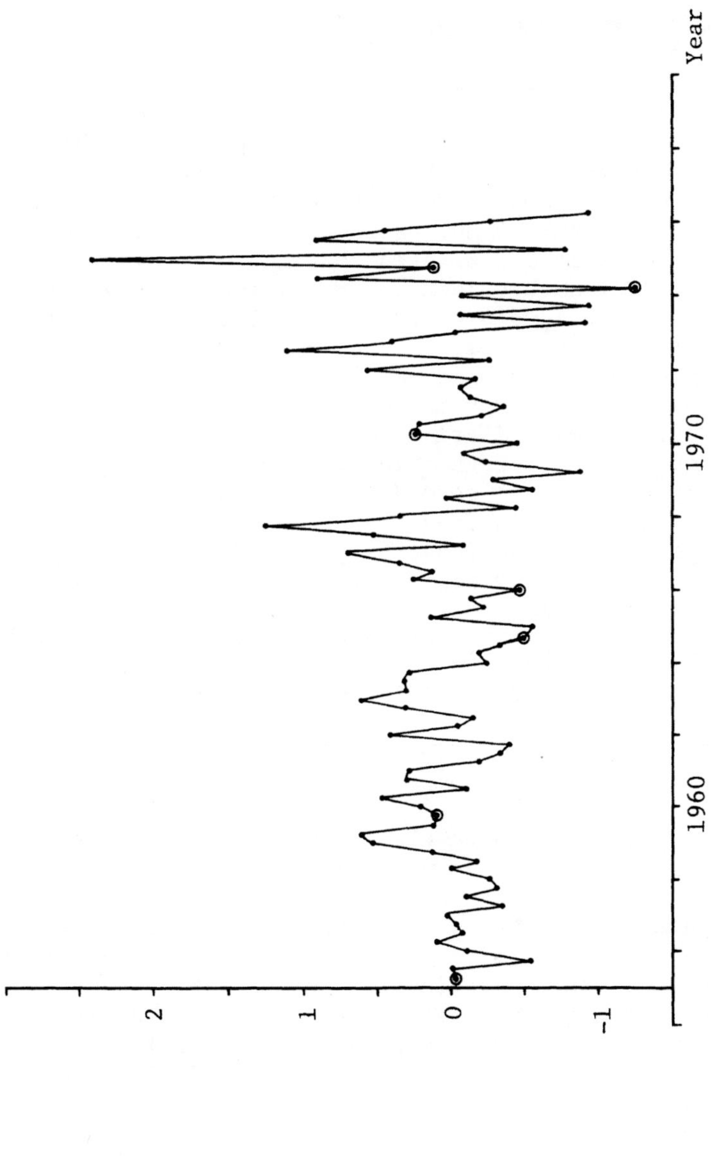

Fig. 3. Government consumption function residuals (election quarters circled).

$$GTrans_t = \underset{(7.7)}{-4.3} + \underset{(8.2)}{.09GDP_t} + \underset{(2.2)}{.2GTrans_{t-1}} + \underset{(6.9)}{.75UNEMP} + \underset{(4.8)}{.52LABOUR}$$

$\bar{R}^2 = .98$ D.W. = 2.2 Data: Quarterly 1955–1976.2

Estimator: Two stage least squares

Unemployment is included because a major automatic component of transfers is associated with unemployment benefit. It was obvious from the residuals that there was a shift in the function during Labour governments, and this is reflected in the LABOUR dummy. Further inspection of the residuals in Figure 4 and estimation of election dummies as shown in Table 3 indicates that there is little else of a political nature left to be discovered. In particular, there are no obvious pre-election cycles. In all election periods the residuals are either negative or within one standard error of the fitted value. The biggest errors come again in the first two quarters of 1975. It appears that in transfers inflation supplementation comes in the second quarter, after the budget, so the first quarter is unusually low and the second quarter unusually high. Similarly other deviations from trend will no doubt have institutional explanations, but these deviations do not seem to be in any way related to electoral cyclical factors. It is not surprising to find an ideological preference in Labour periods for transfers but this is nothing to do with a political business cycle. Indeed it would be worrying if we could find *no* difference between governments.

Government Revenue

It only takes a quick glance at the revenue series to see that this behaves very differently from either category of expenditure. In the first place there is a strong seasonal pattern, yet it is one that changes over time. Secondly, as we shall see, there are major cycles in the series even after adjusting for seasonality and detrending. Our basic equation has revenue growing both in relation to total government current expenditure (GCons + GTrans) and GDP. There is a first quarter dummy (split in three over the period to pick up the change in seasonality) and a fourth quarter dummy:

TABLE 3

Political Dummies in Transfers Equation

		$\bar{R}^2$	D.W.
1.	Other variables plus − .004FSPD* (.74)	.987	1.95
2.	Other variables plus + .014FOURQD (.15)	.984	2.2
3.	Other variables plus + .08TWOQD (.67)	.984	2.2
4.	Other variables plus + .007AccD (.19)	.984	2.2

FSPD = Frey-Schneider Popularity Deficit

FOURQD = Four pre-election quarters

TWOQD = Two pre-election quarters

AccD = 1,2,3,4 for four pre-election quarters

*Wrong sign

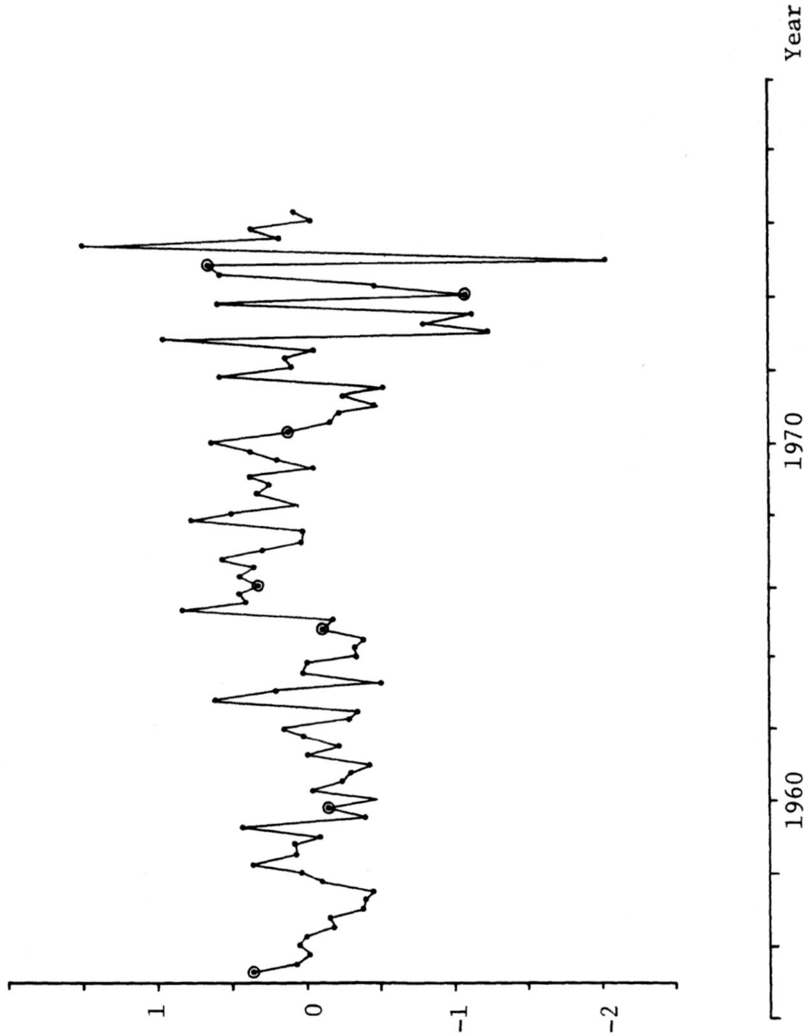

Fig. 4. Government transfers function residuals (election quarters circled).

$$REV_t = -17.9 + \underset{(6.6)}{} 16.7QIA + \underset{}{} 13QIB + 3.4QIC - 1.6Q4 + .57TOTG$$

$$\begin{array}{l} REV_t = -17.9 + 16.7QIA + 13QIB + 3.4QIC - 1.6Q4 + .57TOTG \\ \quad (6.6) \quad (19.9) \quad (18.2) \quad (3.0) \quad (3.0) \quad (4.2) \\ \quad + .36GDP \\ \quad (5.6) \end{array}$$

$\bar{R}^2 = .97$ D.W. = 0.73 Data: Quarterly 1955-1976.2

Estimator: Two stage least squares

What is absolutely clear from the residuals (Figure 5) of that equation is that there is a clear cycle left in the errors. The D.W. statistic is ample testament to that. But this is not an election cycle, as Table 4 shows. Indeed, for present purposes the cycle in the residuals looks rather troublesome for political business cyclists. Tax revenue is very close to its predicted value in all election periods since 1955 except one. That is 1970 where the all-time *peak* of revenue relative to trend is reached exactly in the *election quarter*. It then declines towards 1972 and starts to rise again in time for the 1974 elections.

The message that we receive from these residuals and from their comparison with those for expenditures is twofold. First, none of the series exhibits a political business cycle. Secondly, Keynesian fiscal policy is overwhelmingly concentrated in the revenue side of public sector accounts. Accordingly, we added to the Revenue equation unemployment and the balance of payments as 'targets' which may pick up the remaining revenue cycle. We include the balance of payments in three different ways: (a) the base figures (BOP (in real terms)), (b) BOP squared when in deficit only (BOPSD), and (c) BOP squared when in surplus only (BOPSS). This is to pick up asymmetry between deficits and surpluses. The result with dummies not reported is:

$$\begin{array}{l} REV_t = DUMMIES + .82TOTG + .34GDP + 1.4BOP + .114BOPSD \\ \qquad\qquad\qquad (5.2) \quad (5.2) \quad (5.0) \quad (3.3) \\ \qquad\qquad - .47\ BOPSS - 1.17\ UNEMP \\ \qquad\qquad\quad (2.1) \qquad (2.4) \end{array}$$

$\bar{R}^2 = .98$ D.W. = 1.5 Data: Quarterly 1955-1976.2

Estimator: Two stage least squares

It is clear that adding these targets does contribute to the explanation of revenue and reduces considerably the cycle in the residuals. We do not intend to pursue this

TABLE 4

Political Dummies in Revenue Equation

		$\bar{R}^2$	D.W.
1.	Other variables plus + .07FSPD* (2.3)	.98	1.4
2.	Other variables plus − .04FOURQD (.07)	.98	1.5
3.	Other variables plus + .26TWOQD* (.43)	.98	1.5
4.	Other variabls plus + .05AccD* (.29)	.98	1.5
5.	Other variables plus + 1.2LABOUR (2.2)	.98	1.5

FSPD = Frey-Schneider Popularity Deficit

FOURQD = Four pre-election quarters

TWOQD = Two pre-election quarters

AccD = 1,2,3,4 for four pre-election quarters

LABOUR = Labour incumbency

*Wrong sign

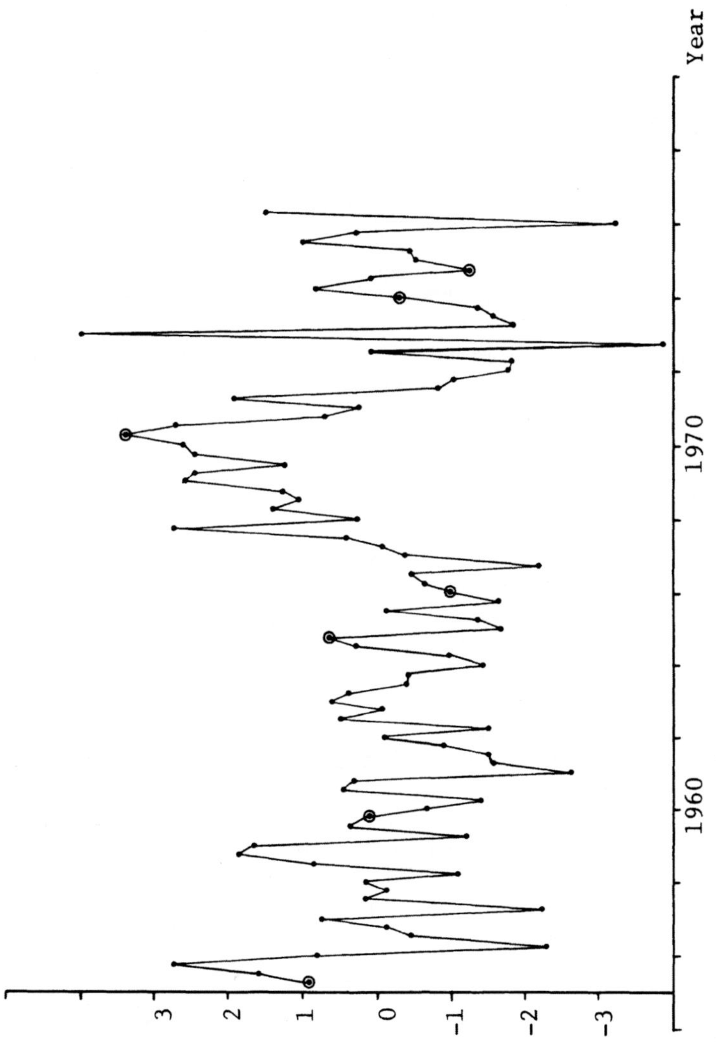

Fig. 5. Government revenue function reisudals (election quarters circled).

line of investigation further in this paper since our intended point should by now be established. Revenue does show a clear cycle about trend, but it is to be explained by Keynesian stabilization policies and not by governments pursuing electoral advantage by manufacturing booms prior to elections. The only political dummy which has any influence on revenue is the LABOUR dummy. This might be thought to reflect the fact that the higher transfers have to be financed, however, this cannot be entirely true as total government expenditure is already in the equation.

SUMMARY AND CONCLUSIONS

1. We have discussed the theoretical underpinnings of political business cycles and argued that they are deficient in that it is assumed that actors behave not only in a myopic fasion but also inconsistently. Even if actors do behave in this way, the optimal path for governments to follow is far from clear cut.

2. We have applied to the U.K. the dynamic programming technique previously applied to the U.S. by Macrae. We reject the hypothesis that the course of inflation and unemployment is explained by the recurrence of short run election targets, in favour of long run optimising behaviour.

3. We investigate the time series of government consumption, transfers and revenue. No 'political' factors are found to affect consumption. Transfers are significantly higher under Labour Governments. Revenue is clearly used to correct for deviations of targets from desired levels and is also higher under Labour. However, there is not a shred of evidence in these variables of cyclical variation due to the proximity of elections. Indeed the peak of revenue relative to trend arises exactly in an election quarter.

4. If there is a political business cycle in the U.K. it must be associated with one of three possibilities:

(i) Monetary policy changes are linked to elections. This seems highly unlikely in view of the lags involved.

(ii) The cycle is based on 'policy illusion', i.e. the policy makers lead us to believe that things are different from the underlying reality. This is plausible but not the province of a macroeconomist.

(iii) Governments time elections at the most favourable time within a short run horizon. This seems trivially obvious but again should not trouble economists.

In short we conclude that the political business cycle is something that the economics profession in the U.K. need not take too seriously. The major error in the previous literature has been a failure to distinguish the question of whether politicians *ever try* to manipulate the economy for electoral advantage from the more important question (from the standpoint of economics) of whether they *systematically succeed.* A clear answer to the latter question for the U.K. is that they do not.

ACKNOWLEDGEMENT

This research was supported in part by the National Science Foundation under grant SES-8006488.

REFERENCES

Brittan, S., The Election and the Economy, *Financial Times,* 26 June 1978.

Chrystal, K.A. and Alt, J., Some problems in formulating and testing a Politico-Economic model of the U.K., University of Essex Discussion Paper, 1979.

Frey, B. (1978a), *Modern Political Economy,* Martin Robertson.

Frey, B. (1978b) The Political Business Cycle: Theory and Evidence, in J.M. Buchanan et al., *The Economics of Politics,* IEA, 1978.

Frey, B. and Schneider, F., A Politico-Economic Model of the U.K., *Economic Journal,* June 1978, pp. 243-253.

McCallum, B. J., The Political Business Cycle: An Empirical Test, *Southern Economic Journal*, 1978, pp. 504-515.

Macrae, D., A Political Model of the Business Cycle, *Journal of Political Economy*, 1977, pp. 239-263.

Nordhaus, W., The Political Business Cycle, *Review of Economic Studies*, 1975, pp. 167-190.

Tufte, E., *Political Control of the Economy*, Princeton, U.P., 1978.

DISCUSSION: KERRY SCHOTT

It is very important that Alec Chrystal and James Alt have done this research on the apparent existence of the political business cycle since the political business cycle is fast becoming accepted as factual in economic ideology. The available evidence now, more than ever before, suggests that there is virtually no support for the existence of a political business cycle. It may be useful to summarize the story so far before I add a few comments.

Following the work of Downs (1957) it was hypothesised that a political business cycle exists. Governments aim to win elections and they manipulate the economy to do so. This causes a political business cycle. If this hypothesis is true we would expect to observe cycles in economic activity caused by changes in government controlled economic instruments. Booms would be appropriately timed to coincide with election campaigning and voting day.

Studies relating economic activity to the relevant election dates have, however, shown only scant support for the political business cycle. See for example Nordhaus (1975), Tufte (1978) and Frey (1978). Undeterred by these results, these proponents of the existence of a political business cycle have argued that the apparent lack of support in the aggregate data simply means that the political business cycle is invisible. This invisibility occurs because of the swamping effect of international trade and capital movements, the swings in the pure business cycles and the lack of regular intervals between elections in many countries. This argument may be correct but it also suggests that the effect of political manipulation on the economy is at least not quantitatively larger than effects from other sources. Politicians wanting to win elections may affect the economy but only in a small way.

Arguing on similar lines it is also worth noting that if more sophisticated spectral analysis was to be applied to the aggregate economic activity data the most likely outcome would still provide no evidence for a political business cycle. The political business cycle is not likely to be sufficiently regular to separate it out from other economic cycles which in any case may themselves be irregular.

The evidence that economic instruments have been used to cause a political business cycle is also shaky. The main supporting argument for the existence of a political business cycle along these lines is Frey and Schreider's (1978) work. Chrystal and Alt (1979) have attacked this argument in an earlier paper and as we have just heard (in Part III of the present paper) there is no evidence of any change in economic instruments to generate a political business cycle. It is also worth noting that some econometric models of national economies have attempted to endogenise the public sector and while this work is not directly aimed at examining the existence of a political business cycle it does tend to support the conclusions from Section III of Chrystal and Alt's paper. Some of this econometric work (reviewed by Davis (1976)) treats government revenues and expenditures in a more satisfactorily disaggregated way than have Chrystal and Alt and the empirical evidence is still not there to support the political business cycle. So to conclude the story, it does look as if we should not accept the existence of a political business cycle as part of economic theory. At the very least we should be terribly cautious of such a concept.

I would now like to say that this conclusion is not at all surprising. The research work in this area has been developing along lines of inquiry which certainly should be questioned and which is far from satisfactory in any methodological sense. The three assumptions implicit behind the political business cycle hypothesis display a misleading notion of politico-economic behaviour and should have initially been thought about more carefully. The three assumptions used are:

(i) governments aim to win elections and hence act to maximise their votes,

(ii) citizens vote and reveal stable preferences defined over specified objectives, and

(iii) governments have complete (or sufficient) control over the economy so they can manipulate the economy to achieve their aim of winning elections, given voting preferences.

Let's examine each of these assumptions in more detail.

Assumption (i). Governments aim to win elections

Few people would quibble with this assumption as a description of the behaviour of central government politicians in our parliamentary democracy. However, setting up a model of government behaviour in this way does overlook the structure of government in important ways. Politicians may aim to win elections but they are serviced by a bureaucracy which need not share their goal; bureaucratic behaviour can be governed by quite different motives. It has been suggested by Niskanen (1971) that bureaucrats aim to maximise the size of their bureau's budget since this increases their power and their ability to pursue satisfactory behaviour. This obviously can conflict with the governing politician's aim, and if the diaries of Richard Crossman (1976) are to be believed, along with reports like those of Jo Haines (1977), there is no evidence of conflict between politicians and their civil service. The main point to be made is that central government is not a monolithic single minded institution guided solely by the desires of governing politicians. There are other influences from other tiers of government and outside sources, which sometimes may override or at least constrain the political behaviour of vote maximising politicians.

Assumption (ii). Citizens vote and reveal stable preferences

It is fundamental to the political business cycle hypothesis that the stated intention and current behaviour of government causes citizens to vote. Yet as Brian Barry (1978) has pointed out, there is no rational economic explanation for why an individual should vote at all. The probability that any individual's vote will alter the outcome in a general election is infinitesimally small and the cost of voting, in terms of time and effort, is not insignificant. So a rational economic person is not likely to vote! Riker (1968) suggests that people get satisfaction from voting because it affirms their allegiance to the political system. This may be true, but this argument still leaves aside the problem of why people vote for different parties when their individual vote is most unlikely to make any difference to the election outcome.

The perceived behaviour of mass voting is not yet explained rationally.

A more well known theoretical problem related to voting behaviour concerns preferences. From the public choice literature we know that a single vote cast over a multitude of alternative policies does not reveal either policy priorities or the intensity of voter's preferences. Simple majority voting need not reveal the optimal collective decision as the work of Arrow (1951) and Buchanan and Tullock (1962) has amply demonstrated. Furthermore, individuals can and are likely to alter their preferences over time.

Now what all this seems to imply is that the theoretical foundations of voting behaviour, implicit in the political business cycle are very shaky. We do not have any well understood rational notions about why people vote in the first place. Given that they do vote, it is clear that their single vote does not contain much information about which of the party policies are most desired. Hence when politicians pursue policies on the basis of signals from single majority voting preferences, their information is terribly imperfect. And in addition, if voters change their preferences over time, previously revealed policy preferences cannot be used as a guide to present policy actions. (This incidentally denies the existence of Nordhaus' (1975) iso-vote curves.)

Assumption (iii). Governments have sufficient control over the economy to manipulate it to win votes

This basic assumption is familiar to economists and needs little comment here. It is well known that the objectives of economic policy frequently conflict with each other and that trade-offs between targets are necessary. The timing of the impact of economic policy instruments is uncertain as is the quantitative effect of such measures. In this uncertain and imperfect world, the degree of control that the government can exert over the economy is far from complete and our own imperfect understanding of the economy adds to the problem.

So this consideration of the assumptions behind the

political business cycle hypothesis suggests it is not surprising that there is so little evidence for the hypothesis. I hope these comments and the more substantial work of Alec Chrystal and James Alt have indeed convinced you that the political business cycle should not be treated too seriously. On a more constructive note, it seems that an improved understanding of the economic behaviour of the public sector would best be approached by disaggregating the public sector in terms of its different institutions as well as in terms of its different functions. The increased size of this part of the economy certainly warrants more careful and thoughtful attention than it has so far received from economists.

REFERENCES

Arrow, K. (1951). *Social Choice and Individual Values*. New York: John Wiley.

Barry, Brian (1978). *Sociologists, Economists and Democracy*. Chicago: University of Chicago Press.

Buchanan, J.M. and Tullock, G. (1962). *The Calculus of Consent*. Ann Arbor: University of Michigan.

Chrystal, K. Alec and Alt, James (1979). Some Problems in Formulating and Testing a Politico-economic Model of the UK. *University of Essex Discussion Paper*.

Crossman, Richard (1976). *The Diaries of a Cabinet Minister*. London: Hamish Hamilton and Jonathan Cape.

Davies, Jeffrey M. (1976). The Determination of Government Expenditure for Short Term Forecasting and Policy Simulation Models. *Journal of Public Economics*.

Downs, A. (1957). *An Economic Theory of Democracy*. New York: Harper and Bros.

Frey, B. (1978). *Modern Political Economy*. London: Martin Robertson.

Frey, B. and Schneider, F. (1978). A Politico-economic Model of the U.K. *Economic Journal*.

Haines, Joe (1977). *The Politics of Power.* London: Hodder and Stoughton.

Niskanen, W. (1971). *Bureaucracy and Representative Government.* New York: Aldine-Atherton.

Nordhaus, W. (1975). The Political Business Cycle. *Review of Economic Studies.*

Riker, W.H. and Ordeshook, P.C. (1968). A Theory of the Calculus of Voting. *American Political Science Review.*

Tufte, E. (1978). *Political Control of the Economy.* Princeton, N.J.: Princeton University Press.

13. PORTFOLIO SELECTION IN PRACTICE

W.B. Reddaway

I must apologise for having given this talk a somewhat grandiose title: it will in fact consist in various reflections on my experience in helping to manage my College's investment portfolio for some 26 years, together with a rather feeble attempt to consider, on an *ex-post* basis, how these can be related to the theory of portfolio selection, which I must confess that I had never studied until I agreed to give the talk, and have only skimmed in part even now.

What seems to me to make the experience of my College portfolio of some interest to people other than members of the College is the combination of two facts. First, we have pursued a very simple policy, which many commentators have described as "simple-minded", but which I might describe in this conference as a "satisficing" policy rather than a maximising one; and secondly, that the results have been consistently rather better than many people would have expected in the light of the principles adopted - as is explained below.

COLLEGE OBJECTIVES AND PRINCIPLES ADOPTED

The principles adopted by the investment committee basically reflected the College's objectives and outlook. Up to 1953 the College had held no equities, but had had its endowment invested partly in real property and partly in government securities. With the real property the policy had been a "buy and hold" policy, under which there were few if any attempts to buy a property with a view to re-sale in a few years, and little or nothing in the way of active development beyond such minor improvements as building a new barn for a farmer-tenant. The main objective of the members of the Finance Committee who wanted to shift from gilt-edged securities to equities was to avoid the effects of the terrible inflation which was prevailing in those years (perhaps 3% or 4% a year - but that was a major matter when the return on gilt-edged was of a similar size): consequently, they were happy to propose that the principles governing investment in equities should be rather similar to those used for properties - i.e. "buy and hold", with a wide spread of investments, and no attempts to be clever by trying to spot the moments when it would be wise to go liquid and hope to re-purchase later at lower prices. In this way I personally felt confident that the outcome would be markedly better than by continuing to hold gilt-edged - apart from anything else, those were the days in which the "yield gap" meant that one started with a considerably higher return from equities, and the prospects were that this return would increase, whereas on gilt-edged it would remain stable in money terms. The general strategy seemed likely to give the College a satisfactory income in real terms for the next century or two.

The main principles were

a) to be continuously invested in equities (the typist showed unwitting insight when she recorded the decision to hold no more "guilt-edged" securities);

b) to give these a wide spread over different industries and to select them as if we were buying "for keeps";

c) not to attempt elaborate investment analysis, either ourselves or through advisers, in choosing the holdings, and to invest about the same amount in each;

d) to make the most of our tax-exempt status by giving a slight preference (ceteris paribus) to shares which gave a high immediate return and for which double tax relief (which was useless to us) was not important.

The starting of the system illustrated the working of the principles. The investments committee of four met with what was then the back page of the Financial Times, which gave simple information about a thousand or so companies, divided into so-called "industry" sections. It was agreed that we would choose at least one from each section, unless we decided unanimously to miss one out (we in fact omitted greyhound racing and - somewhat illogically - insurance). As each section was called, anybody could make a suggestion (usually on the basis of some prior knowledge), and we applied the principle of "one white ball and you are in", unless the number of suggestions seemed excessive. In this way we chose 48 holdings in an hour.

At the time when we did this there was no provision for having an annual valuation and review: we had no such thing for properties, and the philosophy had been that we were buying "for keeps". We soon decided however that there should be an annual valuation (if only to see how we were doing, on income as well as capital) and that this would provide a good occasion for an annual review.

This annual review has very limited objectives. Its main object is to ensure that the portfolio still broadly conforms to the basic principles, when valued at the latest prices. Thus any share which has risen greatly in price may be sold completely, on the ground that its yield now seems too low (we tend to brand these as "glamour stocks" or "suitable only for surtax-payers"); or we may sell part, to bring it down to our normal size-range - this is the usual outcome; or, occasionally, we may decide to let it run as an out-size holding - usually because it is an investment trust, which automatically provides "spread", or because "oil is a very big industry, with few suitable companies, so Shell can count as two".

The review does make possible proposals for changes on other grounds, either to get rid of some holding which no longer seems suitable, or to introduce something which a member has come to favour; it also enables any new funds to be introduced, or sales to be made to pay for College buildings etc. But the atmosphere is usually very hostile to changes of a general kind, largely for expense reasons, and the normal length of the meeting is about two or three hours. After that the portfolio is fixed for the year, apart from any actions needed to deal with rights issues, take-over bids and the like.

This sketch of the committee's guiding principles would be seriously incomplete if I did not add that they leave room for considerable flexibility of interpretation, and even so we do not always stick rigidly to what are basically self-imposed restrictions on our freedom of choice: I would be happy to enlarge on that in the discussion. Nevertheless, for today's purpose they serve to give an adequate picture of a Fund which is the antithesis of a Go-Go Fund (we call it a Come-Come Fund - we make our selection, sit by passively, and take what comes). The principles exclude the two main ways in which an economist might hope to apply his professional ideas:-

a) By spotting the right moments at which to shift temporarily from equities into bonds or cash.

b) By spotting the industries in which to have a large investment or nothing at all.

Indeed, the principles might be said to go a long way towards ensuring that our portfolio would be so like that used for a good index of share prices that differences in the results would be expected to be of little interest.

Despite all this, however, the results are different, to an extent which seems to me important (I hesitate to use the word "significant", since I can think of no formal statistical test). I have myself no satisfactory explanation of the reason, and I throw the puzzle open to the audience. I can however offer some very varied pieces of information which may seem relevant, at least negatively.

MAIN RESULTS

We do not keep any elaborate statistical records, but since 1961 I have published in the Investors' Chronicle a commentary on the results shown at each annual review, over the pseudonym of Academic Investor. For this purpose the portfolio has been treated as a unit trust, which pays out all its income each year: if additional funds come in (e.g. from legacies), or if funds are withdrawn (e.g. for new College buildings) the number of units is increased or decreased by notional transactions at the mid-market price shown at the valuation, with allowance for expenses. The annual article (usually published in August or September) gives the full run of the results from investing £100 in such units in 1953 in terms of both income and capital valuation, together with "control" figures based on investing £100 in the Financial Times index.

An abbreviated table is given below[1]:-

Table 1

Capital Value and Income from £100 Invested in 1953

Valuation date (end-July)	Value at Mid-market Prices*		Annual Income† (gross††)	
	College	Based on FT Index	College	Based on FT Index
1953	(96.5	(96.5)	-	-
1961	310	222	16.48	10.98
1967	431	253	26.3	13.4
1973	703	306	39.5	13.4
1974	432	169	43.4	14.1
1975	517	202	42.4	14.7
1976	633	262	48.8	15.7
1977(8 Jun)	750	326	53.8	16.7
1978	912	352	64.2	19.0
	Total for 25 years		706.3	291.1

* All purchases made in 1953 were lumped together to start the series, which begins at 96.5 because of buying expenses, etc.

† "Annual income" represents broadly one year's cash income on the securities held at the time of valuation, taken at the rate for the last full year and omitting special payments; exceptionally, the "indicated" payments for the present year may be used instead.

†† For the College portfolio the income excludes any irrecoverable tax; for the FT column, 4 per cent was deducted to make a rough allowance for this factor, up to 1965.

It will be seen that by 1978 the capital valuation had reached a level 2.6 times that of the F.T. Control, and the income was 3.4 times as great. In part this reflects the imperfection of the F.T. index for comparisons of this sort, in so far as it is a geometrically weighted index and confined to blue chips: nothing else was available when we started, and we have simply continued to use it. This point is discussed further below.

In order to combine the effects of higher income and greater appreciation into one figure, notional "accumulating" units were calculated from the above table, for which it was assumed that each year's income was reinvested in the basic index at the end of the year, at the mid-market-valuation price. The results of these calculations are given in table 2, which shows that the £100 notionally invested in our unit in 1953 would have been worth £4,310 in 1978, against a control figure of £1,242 - a superiority of about 3½ times.

Table 2 also serves to bring out two important points:-

a) In all 25 of the completed years, the College portfolio showed a higher income than the FT as a percentage of the valuation at the start of the year. In view of our selection policy, it is not surprising that this superiority should apply initially, but it might easily have disappeared as our shares rose in market value, in view of our tendency to make few changes.

The difference averages 1½%, which is clearly important for the College; it has been rather larger in the last three years, when we have been making special efforts to raise the yield to offset inflation.

b) On income and capital appreciation taken together, the College has done better than the FT in 21 years, and worse in 4, but the difference has seldom been spectacular: we liken ourselves to a plodding tortoise, who can be relied on to keep on steadily progressing, rather than an erratic hare. The fact that our average gain compared with the FT is over 5 percentage points shows that our superiority is more in capital appreciation than in income - which might seem to suggest that one is more likely to achieve a good cap-

Table 2

Results of Investing £100 in 1953, on an Accumulation Basis

Valuation date*	Accumulation Value		Income in next Year†		Income Plus Capital Appreciation	
	College	FT Control	College	FT Control	College	FT Control
1953	96.5	96.5	7.82	5.44	43.6	22.5
1954	138.6	118.2	7.39	5.80	49.4	44.7
1955	207.0	171.1	5.84	4.58	-12.5	-12.6
1956	181.2	149.5	7.61	5.72	24.7	18.0
1957	225.9	176.4	6.78	5.24	- 1.6	- 7.8
1958	222.3	162.7	7.52	6.56	47.4	39.7
1959	327.6	227.2	6.55	5.61	39.1	36.4
1960	455.7	309.9	5.46	4.97	8.1	5.5
1961	492.7	327.0	5.70	4.82	- 1.7	-11.4
1962	484.3	289.7	6.79	5.81	30.5	26.2
1963	632.0	365.6	6.24	5.44	21.7	18.8
1964	769.1	434.3	6.04	5.28	- 2.3	- 6.5
1965	751.5	406.1	6.97	5.96	10.7	7.3
1966	831.9	435.8	6.74	5.90	17.2	17.4
1967	974.9	511.6	6.17	5.30	44.9	38.5
1968	1413	708.5	6.04	3.92	- 7.0	-19.2
1969	1314	572.5	7.56	4.79	7.6	0.9
1970	1414	577.6	7.79	4.34	29.7	19.6
1971	1833	690.9	6.26	3.83	29.5	29.9
1972	2374	897.4	5.06	3.70	- 5.0	-11.8
1973	2256	791.5	6.18	4.61	-32.3	-40.2
1974	1527	473.3	9.81	8.70	29.5	28.2
1975	1978	606.8	9.44	7.77	31.8	37.5
1976	2606	834.4	8.50	6.37	27.0	30.8
1977	3310	1091	8.60	5.80	30.2	13.8
1978	4310	1242				
Average	-	-	7.00	5.46	19.4	13.0

* End-July, except for 1977 (8 June)

† As % of valuation

ital appreciation in the coming year by rigorously making no attempt to consider future share prices at all.

At the risk of a slight digression, it is useful to apply the retail price index to the accumulating figures in table 2, and give the picture in real terms for some selected years and the real growth rate for various periods.

Table 3

The Accumulating Unit at 1953 Prices

Valuation date*	Accumulation Value (£, at 1953 prices)		Compound Growth Rate† (% p.a.)	
	College	FT Control	College	FT Control
1953	96.5	96.5	-	-
1961	424.7	281.9	20.4	14.3
1967	633.1	332.2	6.9	2.8
1973	980.9	344.1	7.6	0.7
1974	569.8	176.6		
1975	594.0	182.2		
1976	671.6	215.1	-2.1	-6.2
1977	678.3	242.4		
1978	881.4	254.0		
	Whole period 1953-1978		9.3	4.0

* End-July, except for 1977 (8 June)
† Since previous date

As Table 3 shows, 1953 to 1961 was the period of equities' glory. Since then the FT index, even on an accumulating basis, has not kept up with inflation: the same is true for the College since 1973, despite a substantial recovery in the last four years.

Finally, it is useful to conclude this section by

making a rough attempt to assess how far these results reflect the deficiencies of the FT index as a pace-setter, even though it is widely used for that purpose by fund managers. So far as the capital valuation is concerned, one can get a rough check on the extent of the bias for the period since 1962, when the All-share index was started. The comparative figures are:-

	July 1978 as % of July 1962
FT Index	189
All-Share	257
College	318

These figures imply that the All-Share index gained relatively to the F.T. by an average of almost 2% a year (compound) during this period. Without making a systematic analysis, I know from preparing the annual articles that this average is very far from applying to each and every year, and I have no idea whether it would apply to the years up to 1962, if an All-Share index were calculated for that period: but it is interesting to see what happens if we simply assume that the "true" capital appreciation to take as yardstick in each year is 2 percentage points higher than that shown by the F.T.

My impression is that the dividend yield on the two index-numbers is usually much the same, so I tried the effect of raising the final "control" column in table 2 by 2 units in each year; the result was to reduce the number of years in which the College did better from 21 to 19, and of course to reduce the average superiority for the whole 25 years from 5.4% to 3.4%. The "control" figure for the 1978 value of 100 accumulating units was raised by a factor of 1.64 from £1,242 to £2,038, which reduces the College "superiority ratio" from 3½ to rather over 2.1.

These are probably the most important results, and they are given "with all reservations" solely as orders of magnitude. Anyone who wishes can apply the factor 1.64 to the 1978 values in Table 1 (both capital and income, on the assumption that the dividend yield is the same), or deflate the College superiority ratios to 1.6 for capital and 2.1 for income.

INDIVIDUAL SECURITIES AND THE ANNUAL REVIEWS

All the above results relate to the portfolio as a whole, and it is painfully obvious to us that we made innumerable mistakes on individual holdings. Each of the annual articles by Academic Investor emphasises our failure in detail to choose an optimum portfolio, by contrasting the percentage movements over the year in the prices of the most successful shares and the least successful - and the range is commonly more than 100% of the opening price. Our candid critic, Mr. H. Ind-sight, never wearies in his caustic comments on our shortcomings, and he is not impressed by our statement that we do not even attempt to make prospective assessments of price movements.

This point was also brought out on a more long-term basis by a special article published in the Investors' Chronicle for 11 July 1975, which also threw light on the cumulative effects of our annual reviews. Thanks to the good offices of a friendly stockbroker[2], this article showed what would have happened if we had simply sat tight on our original 48 securities from 1953 to June 1975, apart from dealing with rights issues, bids etc.

The short answer, so far as the aggregate outcome went, was that we would have done slightly better on capital valuation (an index of 768, against the actual figure of 648), but somewhat worse on income, so that in one important sense our annual reviews had made little difference. The comment made by "Stockbroker" on the high quality of our original selection makes a strange bedfellow with my knowledge of how that selection was made.

On individual holdings the picture was dramatic: two of the original holdings would have fallen in (money) value by half, whilst the two champions had valuations 46 and 37 times their original cost. The result would have been, if we had really let the original portfolio ride, that these two holdings would have come to represent over 20% of the total valuation - a position which would hardly have been acceptable on risk-spreading grounds.

Finally, although it seems that the annual reviews contribute very little to the results, nevertheless it seems relevant to throw some light on the personal equation of one of the people who has played a leading part in them: after all, the portfolio has had to endure the annual ordeal of being reviewed and altered - we now hold only eight of the original 48 holdings, even counting companies which took them over - so the reviews are definitely part of the story.

The main point which I can offer is not exactly a flattering one. Although I played a large part in drawing up the deliberately restrictive principles under which we have operated, I have frequently felt that it ought to be possible to do better by allowing just a little more scope for economic judgement. So I tried the limited experiment, after various annual reviews, of dividing the next year's portfolio into two halves, according as my (very feeble) intuition suggested that the price-movement over the coming year would be above or below the median. The idea was that if there were a preponderance of successes, I might propose that we somewhat increased the size of the holdings in my "upper" half, and reduced that for those in the "lower" half.

The results of several experiments were consistent: at dividing the portfolio in this way, "Academic Investor's intuition" is neither better nor worse than spinning a coin.

It would be nice, of course, to believe that the outcome of this contest between Academic Investor's intuition and the spinning coin would be different, if one could test something a bit more directly relevant to our problems. "Picking the 50 members of the team" from a universe of many thousand companies is not the same thing as dividing the team into two parts; similarly a long-term assessment of future performance is much more relevant to what we do than a guess at the price-movement over the coming year. Possibly also doing things "for real" produces a better judgement than the hypothetical exercise. But I can offer no evidence of any kind to support a belief that I (or any other member of the Committee) have any skill at these things - unless it be the persistent way in which the College portfolio beats the index.

In brief, my main impression from 26 years of portfolio management is the need for humility. Our principles reflected a basic recognition of our colossal ignorance about what the future will bring forth. Our performance has, by the simple test we use, been relatively satisfactory (though by the more fundamental test of "beating inflation", rather than the index, the last six years have been disquieting, to say the least). But if I dig beneath the surface I know full well that the good results came through good fortune, or at least for reasons that were quite unforeseen. Doubtless that was inevitable when one was running a Come-Come Fund, and perhaps we deserve some credit for adopting that system and not becoming more ambitious with the passage of time. I class myself with the humble cobbler, who has the good sense to stick to his last.

RELATION TO THE THEORY OF PORTFOLIO SELECTION

So much, then, for what we have done - and done by the light of nature, without any reference to the theory of portfolio selection. What light does that theory throw on our activities, or our activities throw on the theory?

With some guidance from colleagues at Cambridge who work in that field I have made a quick dip into the literature, in the hope of providing some answers to these questions. Broadly speaking, I found two types of book, which seemed to me to be almost unrelated. At the risk of grossly over-simplifying the matter, I see these two branches of the literature (and my reactions to them) as follows.

First, there is what I had vaguely pictured as the classic literature, dealing with the theory of how an investor should select a portfolio to maximise his expected rate of return for any given willingness to face risks. I must confess that I have not spent much time on this analysis, which doubtless casts an unfavourable light on me, rather than on the literature. It seemed to me to be concerned with the refinements of how to handle mathematically a whole lot of data which simply are not available - about prospective returns from all the securities, their variances and co-variances. Nor did I see how one could produce proxies for them, except by showing a degree of faith in history repeating itself in detail which I certainly do not possess. Moreover it often seemed to reduce "the future return" to a single-period result, which I could only interpret as being the coming year's dividend plus the rise in share price over the year - and this seemed to put all the emphasis on the share price a year hence, which is so hard to predict, and which is liable to be here today and gone tomorrow. This did not seem to me of much help to a continuing Institution like a College, which needs a continuing real income, even though in principle one could repeat the exercise by redistributing the portfolio in the light of next year's revised "data": the importance of switching expenses seemed somehow to be overlooked.

All this is doubtless very unfair. One can perfectly well argue that an investor's behaviour will not be fully logical unless he makes assessments of all these prospective returns, variances and covariances, however crude these may be, and that therefore it is helpful to know what one should assess and how one should use the assessments. Maybe a more conscientious study of the literature would have given me some useful insights, which I could apply. But to carry on one's economic life - and particularly portfolio management - with full logic would require one to work a 48-hour day, and at present I feel that this literature is directing my attention to the less rewarding parts of the problem: it does not seem to allow enough for the sheer ignorance about the future which affects us all.

As against this, I found a second branch of the literature which seemed to be dealing with many of the problems with which experience had confronted me, and even claiming to give answers to a good number of them - though in a manner which still leaves my basic problem unsolved.

I take as archetype of this literature the book by

B.G. Malkiel, called "A Random Walk down Wall Street;" I have also found "The Money Game", published over the pseudonym of Adam Smith, both entertaining and instructive. The characteristic of both books is that they are firmly founded on real-life experience and make use of much empirical testing: both make considerable use of the ideas set out by Keynes in chapter 12 of the General Theory.

The essence of Malkiel's approach, so far as it seems relevant to this talk, is that he starts from two possible ways of selecting a portfolio of equities:-

a) The "chartist" approach, which claims that everything which is relevant to assessing whether a share price is likely to rise or fall is reflected in past share prices and various Stock Exchange statistics - e.g. the volume of dealing, the purchases or sales in "odd lots", etc. Hence one can decide what to buy or sell by studying these, without even knowing what the company does, let alone looking at its accounts.

b) The "fundamentalist" approach, whereby one studies all sorts of data about each company and the industry in which it works the quality of its management, etc: one thus forms a view above all about its prospective, future earnings. This and other data (e.g. the balance sheet) enable one to assess the fundamental value of its shares, which can be compared with the market price.

Malkiel first examines the work done by a number of academic researchers to test whether any of the numerous chartist approaches (or "technical trading rules") will yield sufficiently successful predictions to cover the brokerage and other expenses involved in making the necessary switches. His conclusion is that none of them survive the ordeal of proper testing - including especially the need to apply the rules to different periods from the ones used to inspire them.

This conclusion seems to me inherently plausible, at least so long as the rules are truly mechanical. The proviso is important - rival chartists often proclaim different conclusions from the same basic data - but it makes me a bit dubious about the reason which Malkiel gives (page 133) for believing that if any system really did work, it would be bound to destroy itself, because everyone would try to apply it: acceptance of the "fact" that the system worked would not necessarily be widespread, especially since it would only do so "on average", and varying interpretations of how to apply it to to-day's "facts" would also prevent a universal stampede of people trying to beat the gun.

This onslaught on the claims of the chartists is, so far as it goes, a welcome result for our committee: we certainly never attempt anything like these systems, and apparently we lost nothing by ignoring them.

Malkiel's analysis of the results of the fundamentalists' approach is a bit more relevant: our self-imposed principles reduce the scope for applying fundamental analysis, but the vague intuitions which we use to make decisions within the area which remains open might euphemistically be regarded as primitive attempts to follow the fundamentalists' principles.

Be that as it may, the empirical results which Malkiel reports are also of a strikingly negative character. I may mention two of his tests.

First, he discusses in chapter 4 the "Firm - Foundation theory of Share Prices," according to which the most important reason why a company should show a high price-earnings ratio is that its earnings are expected to show a high growth-rate over a long period: this is "tested" on page 86, using the growth-predictions supplied by 18 leading investment firms, and the test looks very convincing. We are warned however that neither the growth-rate nor its duration can be predicted very accurately, so that a good analyst who made unusually accurate predictions should be able to pick out the winners. The crucial questions are, then, how accurate are these predictions on average, and can some analysts systematically beat the average?

The answer to these two questions is given on pages 140-142. Past predictions of one-year and five-year growth-rates for profits were collected from 19 of the best investment firms, and compared with actual results. The five-year estimates were, on average, worse than the predictions from several naive forecasting models, even for "predictable" industries like utilities; the one-year estimates were wrose than the five-year estimates; and there was no consistency of performance by particular analysts from year to year.

Malkiel's second test is to consider the performance of professionally managed Funds of various kinds. (I almost said that this "comes nearer home", but the management of the College Fund is certainly not professional!) Typical of his conclusions is the following from page 151: "Over long periods of time mutual fund portfolios have not outperformed randomly selected groups of stocks." Moreover "there seems to be no relationship between good performance by a Fund in one period and superior returns in the next" (page 152). The only concession which he makes is that on average, "riskier" funds do better than the rest - but he adds that "randomly selected portfolios of riskier stocks also tended to outdistance the market".

THE EFFICIENT MARKETS THEORY

The main conclusions which might seem to follow from these results appear to be as follows:-

a) It is extraordinarily hard to know what prices "ought" to prevail in the market, because in logic they "ought" to depend on future events (whether "fundamentals", like future earnings, or "future prices for the share in question" - if one equates the Stock Exchange to a casino), and these things are highly uncertain.

b) Nevertheless, in the words of Professor Samuelson, (quoted on p. 167) "If intelligent people are constantly shopping around for good value, selling those stocks they think will turn out to be overvalued and buying those they expect are now undervalued, the result of this action by intelligent investors will be to have existing stock prices already have discounted in them an allowance for their future prospects. Hence, to the passive investor, who does not himself search out for under- and over-valued situations, there will be presented a pattern of stock prices that makes one stock about as good or bad a buy as another. To that passive investor, chance alone would be as good a method of selection as anything else."

This second point is, I understand, referred to as "the efficient markets theory". Personally I find this a bit of a deceptive title when the future prospects are so hard to assess. The pattern of share prices seems to me to change far more violently between one day and another than can be rationally accounted for by changes in the known facts - I am thinking of our annual "winners and losers" table.

It is nevertheless a comforting thought for portfolio managers - and one on which our Committee implicitly acts - that the prices in the market have some element of fundamental rationality, and above all that it is very difficult in practice to do very much better than follow a semi-random principle of selection within the various investment strata. This provides a semi-rational justification for not living laborious days trying to make impossible forecasts; but it still leaves us with the hope that a little systematic (if not particularly intelligent) guess-work may keep our results above the index in most years.

Perhaps one should note that Samuelson confines his statement to a "passive" investor "who does not himself search out for undervalued and overvalued situations". It is not really clear to me how this description should be interpreted, since if the passive investor is not prepared to do any work, there is no way for him to make his selection except by some sort of chance process: the statement then seems close to being a tautology, but perhaps one should take it as a condemnation of simple rules like buying only shares which have risen (or fallen!) in price over the last year, or which have a high (or low) dividend yield.

In one sense our Committee is certainly passive: it only considers action once a year. Its "searching out" is also of a rudimentary and largely intuitive kind. But it does go through the whole portfolio at the annual review, and apply a consistent and persistent strategy of a kind - if only not to attempt a forecast of future share prices. Since Malkiel's analysis implicitly or explicitly is much concerned about predicting future prices - whether on a short or medium run (he is not interested in our time-horizon of a century of two) - this refusal to consider future prices at all is a real point of difference.

Malkiel himself states the random-walk theory which follows from belief in the efficiency of markets, following the quotation from Samuelson with this definition

> "Fundamental analysis of publicly available information cannot produce investment recommendations that will enable an investor consistently to outperform a buy-and-hold strategy in managing a portfolio." (p. 168).

Nevertheless he does not wholly believe in it, at least in this strong form (page 172) and he provides (on pp. 201-209) seven principles to be used for managing a portfolio of common stocks. None of these is really in conflict with what our Committee does, except possibly no. 5: "If possible, keep a small reserve to take advantage of market declines..."; the nearest that we get to this is doing only a very small amount of borrowing to gear our portfolio,[3] so that the amount could be increased at any annual review if we so desired. On the other hand the following might almost have been taken from Academic Investor's 1961 articles:-

2 "Maintain a diversified portfolio suited to the risk level you are prepared to assume."

3 "Your tax status and income needs should also influence the type of portfolio chosen."

6 "Adopt a buy-and-hold strategy. Trade as little as possible. Above all do not let your broker churn your account."

7 "Avoid short-term switch-hitting to outguess the market."

I feel almost like Le Bourgeois Gentilhomme, who learned that he had been talking prose all his life: I am not sure that I am equally pleased to find after 26 years that we have been broadly following a recognised theory of portfolio selection - even though we adopted our policy long before Malkiel's book was published.

Nevertheless, these are only principles, and Malkiel adds (pages 240-243) four "rules" for successful stock selection. These, with my comments, are as follows:-

Rule 1: "Confine purchases to companies that appear able to sustain above-average earnings growth for at least five years." - This seems to be crying for the moon, since Malkiel has shown that successful earnings-projections are beyond human power. But perhaps the key word is "appear": if so, our procedure is somewhat different and our time-horizon longer, as we do not attempt any projections for individual holdings, but pretend that our intuitions are aimed at getting a portfolio which will give a good income in real terms over the next century or two.

Rule 2: "Never pay more for a stock than can reasonably be justified by a firm foundation of value." - In a crude way we try to follow this by choosing "as if it were for keeps", and not in the hope of a quick re-sale at a profit.

Rule 3: "It helps to buy stocks whose stories of anticipated growth are ones on which investors can build castles in the air." - On principle, we do not seek for "help" of this kind, which is relevant to attempting to predict future share-prices.

Rule 4: "Trade as little as possible: in general, hold on to the winners and sell the ones that don't work out." - We do not really observe this, though we believe in keeping down the trading. We normally do some trading each year to "balance" the portfolio after the annual review - or rather, we remove the major imbalances, since we allow a fair tolerance in both directions from our norm. We are probably less ruthless in selling the ones that have fallen in price than the rule would suggest: since the future is uncertain we are never sure whether or not "they haven't worked out" - Malkiel seems again to be implying that the investor can make effective projections, after "showing" that he cannot - and retaining them keeps down the amount of trading! We do sometimes cut our losses, but there is a bit of a presumption in favour of buying more to bring the value of the holding within the normal range for that year. Our weak compromises of simply keeping the existing holding ("sending it to hospital") provide Mr. H. Indsight with an assured flow of caustic comments: my impression is that they are fairly evenly divided between "you should have cut your loss" and "you should have built up the holding".

CONCLUDING REMARKS

After this brief visit to one part of portfolio selection theory, I would like to end my talk with a few remarks about the problem with which I started: What, if anything, can we learn from the fact that, even if we take the modified results which allow for the deficiencies of the FT index, the College's portfolio has beaten the adjusted index in 19 years out of 25 and established a cumulative superiority of more than 2 to 1?

In reporting the results of various Funds, or various analysts, Malkiel was at pains to explain that pure chance would ensure that some did much better than the average: on page 164 he gives the analogy that if 1,000 contestants flipped coins, eight could expect to perform the apparently skillful feat of flipping seven heads in a row. Is the outcome simply explained by saying that our slap-happy methods really gave us an even chance of beating the modified index each year, and that our fund simply happens to be one of the few which Chance would decree to win 19 times out of 25?

One can obviously assess the chance of doing this (or better) - I made it about 1 in 137, so it is not negligible. I am bound to say however that I find the whole logic of the "one in a hundred chance" a bit dubious. Granted that some Fund had to be the "one", we should clearly be very grateful if Lady Luck had simply decreed that it should be ours, and that might be considered the end of the matter: we were the lucky one. But this ex-post result does not really dispose of the fact that ex-ante we were very concerned about this particular Fund from 1953 onwards. A true believer in the strong version of the random walk would (or should) have been prepared, in 1953, to give us odds of at least 100 to 1 against our achieving as good results as we did in fact achieve. When a Fund is named in advance it seems a bit more puzzling that it wins against such odds, even though the random walk theory tells us that one Fund out of every 137 will do so. Some other factor seems to be needed.

Basically, I do not myself see anything very surprising in our results: if I had been offered that 100 to 1 bet in 1953 I think that I would have accepted it, and certainly I would have accepted an even-money bet that we would beat the FT index, even with its handicap of 2% a year. But then I do not, in my heart of hearts, believe in the theory of efficient markets, if this asserts that it is impossible (or even particularly difficult) for an investor with no inside information to beat a reliable index over a period of 5 years or more. I did not believe it in 1953, and I certainly do not believe it now.

My problem is rather the opposite. The information cited by Malkiel - and other less systematic information about the UK which has come my way - seems to show that on average professional management seems to give results similar to the random walk prediction. Given all the expertise and effort devoted to these Funds, one might reasonably expect that on average they would show a clear superiority.

This all makes it rather difficult for me to say what it is in our procedures which has made them produce better results than random selection. Obviously it cannot all be attributed to our initial selection, despite the "Stockbroker" exercise: given the need for something akin to our annual reviews, to avoid the risks inherent in excessive concentration of the portfolio, the explanation has to cover that too. The best that I can offer is common sense in applying simple principles and a refusal to try for short-term gains.

I end up, therefore, where I began. I feel that there must be <u>something</u> in what we do that gives us an advantage over random selection. I would not find this at all surprising if it did not also seem to imply that we do better than the average result achieved by professional managers. My problem is really concerned, therefore, with the performance of the latter: perhaps the solution is that all investors taken together must do worse than a good index, because of switching expenses, but the professionals' average equals it.

On one point I am completely clear. I have no faith whatever in the theory that "if anyone found a method of beating the index it would only continue to work if he kept absolutely quiet about it". Our results have been published regularly since 1961, the portfolio has been published annually since 1970, and I have yet to hear of anyone copying either our methods (which are regarded as naively eccentric) or our portfolio, or even our century-long objectives: perhaps that is not surprising - other operators are more interested in swiftly moving hares than in plodding tortoises with eyes concentrated firmly on the long view.

REFERENCES

Academic Investor (1978). Academic Investor looks back on a good year. *Investors' Chronicle*, 25 August 1978.

Malkiel, B.G. (1973). *A Random Walk down Wall Street*. New York: W.W. Norton and Co.

Smith, Adam (1969). *The Money Game*. London: M. Joseph.

FOOTNOTES

1. The full run of years is shown in the Investors' Chronicle for 25th August, 1978.

2. Contact with this gentleman was established when he wrote a letter to the I.C. which said that our portfolio contained some excellent holdings, but also some obvious duds. On being challenged he named six: over the next year two were amongst our worst performers but two were amongst the best, and on average they were close to our over-all movement.

3. The published results of our portfolio treat all assets and income alike, whatever the source of finance, and are therefore not affected by this gearing.

14. VERDOORN'S LAW - THE EXTERNALITIES HYPOTHESIS AND ECONOMIC GROWTH IN THE U.K.

M. Chatterji and M. Wickens

Introduction

In a pioneering paper Kaldor (1966) put forward the view that in order for an economy to achieve a higher rate of economic growth it is necessary to raise the rate of growth of manufacturing output and this could be achieved by transfers of labour from the non-manufacturing to the manufacturing sector. Kaldor argued that the main engine of this growth is the presence of Verdoorn's Law in manufacturing. Using cross-section data from twelve countries, Kaldor tested Verdoorn's Law and found it to be broadly supported.

Our purpose in this paper is to re-assess Kaldor's views using quarterly time series data for the U.K. for the period 1961-1977. First, we wish to test Verdoorn's Law with these data. Secondly, we wish to analyse the effects on economic growth of factors other than Verdoorn's Law and in particular we wish to analyse the effect of the Externalities Hypothesis. Finally, we wish to reconsider Kaldor's proposition about the effects of a labour transfer on the growth of output in the U.K.

In Section 1 we discuss Verdoorn's Law, the Externalities Hypothesis and Kaldor's Proposition regarding the transfer of labour. A simple two sector growth model is constructed to analyse the relationship between these hypotheses. In Section 2 we briefly review the literature on Verdoorn's Law and discuss some of the issues raised by the debate. In Section 3, we report estimates of some simple models suggested by Kaldor in order to test Verdoorn's Law, the Externalities Hypothesis and Kaldor's Proposition. These simple static specifications are found to be inadequate. Accordingly in Section 4, we generalise these simple models by the addition of further explanatory variables and a dynamic structure. In Section 5 we report estimates of these more general models which are shown to be much more satisfactory than the simple models of Section 3. Section 6 contains an evaluation of the quantitative importance of Kaldor's Proposition and Section 7 contains our conclusions.

Section 1 : Verdoorn's Law, the Externalities Hypothesis, and Kaldor's Proposition

In his Inaugural Lecture, Kaldor (1966) put forward the proposition that a transfer of labour from agriculture and services to manufacturing thereby increasing the rate of employment growth in manufacturing and reducing the rate of employment growth in agriculture and services, will permit faster growth of the economy as a whole. This proposition we shall refer to throughout as Kaldor's Proposition. Kaldor viewed his proposition as being a direct consequence of the presence of Verdoorn's Law in manufacturing.[1] Verdoorn's Law states quite simply that there is a positive relationship between the rate of productivity growth and employment growth, viz:

$$p_m = \alpha + \beta e_m \ , \ \beta > 0 \tag{1}$$

where p_m is the proportional rate of productivity growth in manufacturing and e_m is the proportional rate of employment growth in manufacturing. Thus the greater is employment growth in manufacturing industries the larger will be output growth in manufacturing and, as a result, in the whole economy.

In addition to this direct effect on total output of employment growth in manufacturing, Kaldor also suggested that there would be a secondary effect operating through induced productivity growth in non-manufacturing. Thus Kaldor says "...the rate of growth of manufacturing production...will tend, indirectly, to raise the rate of productivity growth in other sectors". Kaldor (1966 p.18). We shall call this proposition the Externalities Hypothesis, as it suggests that the manufacturing sector generates external economies in which the growth of manufacturing output is positively related to productivity growth in non-manufacturing industries. Presumably part of these external economies is technical progress which is embodied in new machines.

According to our interpretation, therefore, Kaldor's Proposition is about the effect of employment growth in manufacturing on the total growth of output and rests on two hypotheses. The first, and the most important, is the presence of Verdoorn's Law in manufacturing, and the second is the Externalities Hypothesis.

Cripps and Tarling have put forward an even stronger proposition: "The suggestion is that even in the absence of increases in the labour force, transfers of labour from agriculture and services to manufacturing employment will permit faster growth of the economy as a whole, and *this transfer does not impede the growth of output in the sectors which give up labour*". (Cripps and Tarling (1973) italics added). The main difference between the Cripps-Tarling Proposition and Kaldor's Proposition is that Kaldor does not require the labour transfer to increase the rates of output growth in both sectors, but only that the overall growth rate should increase. On the other hand, Cripps and Tarling require in addition that the labour transfer be a Paretian improvement in the sense that both sectors' output growth rates should increase.[2] Clearly Kaldor's Proposition is subsumed in the Cripps-Tarling Proposition. In other words, the Cripps-Tarling Proposition is sufficient but not necessary for Kaldor's Proposition to be valid.

In order to examine these propositions in greater detail, we construct the following simple model. The economy is conceived of as consisting of two sectors: a manufacturing sector denoted by "m" and a non-manufacturing sector denoted by "n". The following notation is used:

(i) Q_m, Q_n denote output in manufacturing and non-manufacturing respectively.

(ii) E_m, E_n denote employment in the two sectors.

(iii) P_m, P_n denote productivity (output per man) in the two sectors, i.e. $P_m = Q_m/E_m$ and $P_n = Q_n/E_n$.

(iv) Y denotes aggregate output measured in non-manufacturing output units.

(v) p denotes the price of manufacturing output in terms of non-manufacturing output and is assumed constant.

(vi) lower case letters denote proportional rates of growth; for example

$$q_m \equiv \frac{1}{Q_m} \quad \frac{dQ_m}{d_t}$$

The main variable which the model seeks to explain is y, the growth rate of total output. By definition

$$Y = Q_n + pQ_m \tag{2}$$

and hence by differentiation,

$$y = \theta q_n + (1-\theta)q_m \tag{3}$$

where θ is the share of non-manufacturing in total output.

Kaldor's view that Verdoorn's Law applied to manufacturing yields the "productivity function" for manufacturing:[3]

$$p_m = \beta e_m, \ \beta > 0 \tag{4}$$

The "productivity function" for non-manufacturing is obtained by combining two elements. The first of these is the assumption (accepted by Kaldor) that non-manufacturing is characterised by decreasing returns to employment so that productivity growth and employment growth are inversely related. The second is the assumption (discussed earlier) that the growth of the manufacturing sector yields externalities which increase productivity growth in non-manufacturing. These two assumptions together imply that:

$$p_n = \lambda e_n + \mu q_m, \quad \lambda \leqslant 0, \ \mu \geqslant 0 \tag{5}$$

where μ measures the strength of the external effect.[4,5] Since for both sectors $q \equiv p + e$, it follows from (4) that

$$q_m = (\beta + 1)e_m \tag{6}$$

and from (5) that

$$q_n = (\lambda + 1)e_n + \mu(\beta + 1)e_m \tag{7}$$

Hence,

$$y = \theta(\lambda + 1)e_n + (\beta + 1)\left(\theta\mu + (1 - \theta)\right)e_m \tag{8}$$

Assuming an overall labour constraint and an initial static position, the transfer of labour from non-manufacturing to manufacturing implies an increase in e_m and a simultaneous decrease in e_n i.e. $de_m > 0$ and $de_n < 0$. Kaldor's Proposition may be interpreted as implying that the consequence of a transfer of labour such that $de_m > 0$ and $de_n < 0$ is an increase in y, i.e. $dy > 0$. The Cripps-Tarling Proposition may be interpreted as implying that the consequence of $de_m > 0$ and $de_n < 0$ is that dq_m is positive whilst dq_n is non-negative. We shall examine the Cripps-Tarling Proposition first.

From (6) and (7) it is clear that

$$dq_m = (\beta + 1)de_m \tag{9}$$

and

$$dq_n = (\lambda + 1)de_n + \mu(\beta + 1)de_m \tag{10}$$

Since $(\beta + 1) > 0$ and $de_m > 0$, it follows that $dq_m > 0$. The sign of dq_n depends crucially on the value of λ. If $\lambda + 1 = 0$, then this is sufficient to guarantee $dq_n \geq 0$, if however $\lambda + 1 > 0$, then $\mu > 0$ is a necessary but not sufficient condition for $dq_n \geq 0$. In either event, Verdoorn's Law ($\beta > 0$) is obviously not critical. Thus, so long as the marginal productivity of labour in non-manufacturing is positive ($\lambda + 1 > 0$), the Externalities Hypothesis and not Verdoorn's Law is the critical element for the validity of the Cripps-Tarling Proposition.

Turning to Kaldor's Proposition, we obtain from (8) that

$$dy = \theta(\lambda + 1)de_n + (\beta + 1)\left(\theta\mu + (1 - \theta)\right)de_m \tag{11}$$

It should be clear from (11) that neither Verdoorn's Law nor the Externalities Hypothesis is critical for this proposition. The restrictions $\beta > 0$ and $\mu > 0$ are not (either separately or jointly) necessary or sufficient.

This simple model has shown therefore that if the marginal productivity of labour in non-manufacturing is zero so that $\lambda + 1 = 0$, then the Cripps-Tarling Proposition is valid independently of the Externalities Hypothesis or Verdoorn's Law. *A fortiori*, the same is true of Kaldor's Proposition. However, in the possibly more plausible case when the marginal product of labour in non-manufacturing is positive, so that $\lambda + 1 > 0$, the Externalities Hypothesis is critical for the Cripps-Tarling Proposition though not for Kaldor's Proposition.[6] More importantly the model suggests that Verdoorn's Law is not critical for either proposition.[7] Hence it would appear that the emphasis placed on Verdoorn's Law by Kaldor and subsequent authors, and their relative neglect of the Externalities Hypothesis has not been warranted.[8] Accordingly in Section 8 we attempt to empirically investigate the Externalities Hypothesis as well as Verdoorn's Law using time series data for the U.K. Before presenting our own estimates in Section 3, we briefly review the issues raised by the empirical work of Kaldor and other authors in Section 2.

Section 2 : Empirical Tests of Verdoorn's Law

In order to test his theory Kaldor did not estimate (1) but rather the equivalent relationship

$$p_m = a + bq_m \qquad (12)$$

where q_m is the rate of output growth in manufacturing. Using data for the rates of growth of twelve countries over the period 1953-54 to 1963-64, Kaldor estimated (12) on a cross-section basis and obtained a well determined estimate of b in the neighbourhood of $\frac{1}{2}$. As $p_m \equiv q_m - e_m$, it follows that $\beta = \frac{b}{1-b}$ and hence $\beta > 0$ is equivalent to $0 < b < 1$. Given the precision of his estimate of b, Kaldor had no difficulty in accepting the hypothesis $0 < b < 1$. Hence he inferred that the equivalent hypothesis $\beta > 0$ was also acceptable. In other words, Kaldor verified his hypothesis of interest by an indirect method.

In a critique of Kaldor's methodology, Rowthorn (1975), argued that the appropriate method would be to estimate (1) directly and then test the hypothesis $\beta > 0$. This was indeed the method employed in a detailed study by Cripps and Tarling which basically confirmed Kaldor's findings.[9] However, Rowthorn demonstrated fairly convincingly that the Cripps-Tarling results are crucially affected by the removal of Japan from their sample. The omission of Japan makes it impossible to reject the hypothesis $\beta = 0$. This led Rowthorn to reject Kaldor's assertion that manufacturing is characterised by Verdoorn's Law, and hence also to reject Kaldor's Proposition.

In reply to Rowthorn, Kaldor (1975) argued that the

choice of estimating (1) or (12) really depends on whether one regards e_m or q_m as being exogenous (i.e. independent of the error term); and he asserted that q_m being demand determined is exogenous.[10] He further shows that dropping Japan from the sample does not seriously affect the robustness of his results providing that (12) is the equation estimated.

Parikh (1978) tested Verdoorn's Law with the Cripps-Tarling data in a simultaneous equation framework using Two Stage Least Squares (2SLS). He concluded that there was no evidence in support of Verdoorn's Law. Stoneman adopted a procedure similar to Parikh but used a long historical annual time series for the U.K. alone. His conclusion was similar to Parikh's that"Verdoorn's Law does not apply to manufacturing".

All of the above studies define growth rates over a long period, usually peak to peak. Hence, they can be thought of as testing the long-run validity of Verdoorn's Law and Kaldor's Proposition. One of our points of departure from this framework is to use quarterly growth rates for the U.K. and hence to analyse the dynamics of Verdoorn's Law, the Externalities Hypothesis, and Kaldor's Proposition. This is surely relevant to any study of growth. However, we begin by estimating the simplest static formulations largely with a view to throwing further light on whether employment growth or output growth is the appropriate exogenous variable. The results are reported in the next section.

Section 3 : Verdoorn's Law and the Externalities Hypothesis - Preliminary Estimates

In this section we report estimates of the simple models discussed in sections 1 and 2 paying equal attention to Verdoorn's Law and to the Externalities Hypothesis. The data used is for U.K. manufacturing and non-manufacturing including agriculture and services for the period 1961(2) to 1977(2) and is seasonally adjusted. We would prefer to use unadjusted data but this is not available for all the series.[11] We begin by examining Verdoorn's Law for manufacturing industries.

Verdoorn's Law

The basic estimating equations are obtained by adding disturbance terms to equations (1) and (12). It will be recalled that Rowthorn favoured using (1) as the estimating equation and Kaldor preferred (12). The OLS estimates obtained are

$$\hat{p}_m = \underset{(3.27)}{0.008} + \underset{(0.50)}{0.187}e_m, \quad \bar{R}^2 = -0.014, \quad \hat{\sigma} = 0.0172,$$

$$T = 64, \quad Q_{20} = 24 \qquad (13)$$

and

$$\hat{p}_m = \underset{(3.35)}{0.003} + \underset{(20.94)}{0.869}q_m, \quad \bar{R}^2 = 0.897, \quad \hat{\sigma} = 0.00059,$$

$$T = 64, \quad Q_{20} = 302 \qquad (14)$$

where the numbers in parentheses are t statistics, T is the sample size, and Q_{20} the Box-Pierce residual correlogram statistic which will be assumed to have a limiting χ^2 distribution with 20 degrees of freedom under the null hypothesis of serially uncorrelated errors.[12] The critical value of a χ^2_{20} variable with a significance level of 5% is 32 indicating that Q_{20} is insignificant in equation (13) but highly significant in equation (14). Seasonal dummies are not included in these equations as they are insignificant, no doubt due to the fact that seasonally adjusted data has been used.

According to Verdoorn's Law, β, the coefficient of e_m, is positive. The estimate of β obtained from equation (13) is 0.187 and is not significantly different from zero whilst the estimate from (14) is 0.869/(1-0.869) = 6.63 with an asymptotic t value of 2.74[13] which strongly supports Verdoorn's Law. However, given the massive residual serial correlation in (14), estimates obtained from (14) are not reliable. Furthermore, it is possible that both sets of estimates suffer from asymptotic bias due to the endogeneity of the regressors. As indicated earlier, this can be removed by using an appropriate instrumental variable estimator.[14]

Using the first four lags of e_m as instrumental variables for e_m and q_m, the following results were obtained:

$$\hat{p}_m = \underset{(2.75)}{0.007} - \underset{(0.27)}{0.115}e_m,\ \bar{R}^2 = -0.026,\ \hat{\sigma} = 0.017,$$

$$T = 60,\ Q_{20} = 23,\ K_3 = 9.4 \qquad (15)$$

and

$$\hat{p}_m = \underset{(3.48)}{0.004} + \underset{(6.53)}{0.673}q_m,\ \bar{R}^2 = 0.842,\ \hat{\sigma} = 0.0070,$$

$$T = 60,\ Q_{20} = 95,\ K_3 = 25.2 \qquad (16)$$

Once again the estimate of β obtained from the employment equation (15) is not significantly different from zero and the estimate of β obtained from the output equation (16) which is 2.06 supports Verdoorn's Law but is implausibly large. Furthermore, the Box-Pierce statistic indicates serially correlated disturbances in equation (16) but not in equation (15). The statistic K_3 provides a test for the validity of the instruments. If the instruments are valid, then K_3 is distributed as a χ^2_3 variable.[15] Since $\chi^2_3(.05) = 7.8$ and $\chi^2_3(.025) = 9.4$, the instruments are clearly unacceptable for equation (16) and barely adequate for equation (15). However, the instrument test is only valid when the model is not misspecified. A significant test statistic could also occur when the model is misspecified due, say to omitted variables if these latter are correlated with the instruments. Thus equations (13) to (16) may well be misspecified. Further investigation into this possibility will be made in Section 4.

In the meantime, these results suggest that Rowthorn's version of Verdoorn's Law is to be preferred to Kaldor's which (i) produced implausibly large estimates of β, and (ii) given the massive residual serial correlation in equations (14) and (16) and the significance of the instruments, seems to indicate some misspecification. The main problem with Rowthorn's model is that the estimates of β are not significantly different from zero; in fact the estimate from equation (15) is negative. This,taken together with the fairly high value of the instrument test statistic in equation (15), cannot be regarded as providing any serious evidence in support of Verdoorn's Law in manufacturing.

The Externalities Hypothesis and the Cripps-Tarling Proposition

Both of these hypotheses can be tested by adding a constant and a disturbance term to the "productivity function" for non-manufacturing (equation (5)) to yield

$$p_n = \mu + \lambda e_n + \mu q_m + u \tag{17}$$

The Externalities Hypothesis requires $\mu > 0$ whilst a sufficient condition for the Cripps-Tarling Proposition is $\lambda = -1$. OLS estimation of (17) yields:

$$\begin{aligned} p_n &= \underset{(3.23)}{0.003} - \underset{(3.84)}{0.887}e_n + \underset{(5.42)}{0.301}q_m, \quad \bar{R}^2 = 0.388 \\ \hat{\sigma} &= 0.0077, \ T = 64, \ Q_{20} = 111 \end{aligned} \tag{18}$$

These results appear to offer strong support for the Externalities Hypothesis and the Cripps-Tarling Proposition as the hypothesis $\mu = 0$ can be rejected in favour of $\mu > 0$ and the hypothesis $\lambda = -1$ cannot be rejected. However equation (18) is not satisfactory as it possesses highly serially correlated residuals which may reflect misspecification. It may also exhibit simultaneous equation bias. In an attempt to remove this bias, equation (17) was re-estimated using instrumental variables. Using the first four lags of e_m and e_n as instruments for e_n and q_m, the following results were obtained:

$$\begin{aligned} \hat{p}_n &= \underset{(3.06)}{0.004} - \underset{(1.98)}{1.322}e_n + \underset{(2.50)}{0.284}q_m, \quad \bar{R}^2 = .334, \\ \hat{\sigma} &= 0.0080, \ T = 60, \ Q_{20} = 95, \ K_6 = 6.1 \end{aligned} \tag{19}$$

Once again these results suggest that $\mu > 0$ and that $\lambda = -1$ cannot be rejected, thus corroborating the Externalities Hypothesis and the Cripps-Tarling Proposition. The statistic K_6 is not significant and hence indicates that that the instruments appear to be valid. However, the statistic Q_{20} is highly significant and reflects the presence of serially correlated residuals. These results suggest that both the Externalities Hypothesis and the Cripps-Tarling Proposition may well be correct, but like the results on the productivity function for manufacturing, there is a strong possibility that the productivity function for non-manufacturing is misspecified. Further investigation into this possibility is carried out in Section 4.

Section 4 : A General Model

The models estimated in the previous section were very much basic models and, as we showed, need considerable re-specification in order to fit the data more closely. The re-specification could take the form of adding further explanatory variables and/or adding dynamic structure to the models. In re-specifying the "productivity functions" of manufacturing and of non-manufacturing industries we shall focus attention on both possibilities. In particular, we shall concentrate on (i) the effect on productivity of operating at less than full capacity, (ii) the role of capital accumulation, and (iii) dynamic specification.

(i) Capacity Utilisation

Productivity changes can be thought of as resulting from short-run movement to capacity output with more or less fixed factor inputs (i.e. movements *to* the production frontier) and long-run movements due to changes in factor inputs (i.e. movements *along* and *of* the frontier). A possible explanation for the results of equations (13) to (16) which indicate that variations in productivity growth in manufacturing are largely due to variations in output growth and not employment growth, is that most short-run variation in productivity is caused by changes in capacity utilisation which, not surprisingly, is being picked up by output changes. A comparison of the standard deviation of productivity, output, and employment over the sample, which are 0.018, 0.019 and 0.006 respectively support this view. In the light of this, the residual correlograms of equations (14) and (16) and the very high implied returns to scale of these equations, it is probable that in effect these equations are using q_m to explain itself. Much of the short run variation in output and therefore of movements to the production frontier is due to variations in the utilisation rate of factor inputs. This suggests that the growth rate in average hours worked in manufacturing (h_m) may capture movements in capacity utilisation and should be included as an additional explanatory variable.

(ii) Capital Accumulation

Verdoorn's Law focuses attention on the relationship between productivity growth and employment growth, ignoring the role of capital growth.[16] It would seem more sensible, however, to allow capital growth to have an independent influence on productivity growth since capital accumulation often embodies technical progress and may be expected to raise output per man. In contrast to the growth of hours whose effect on productivity has been interpreted as measuring movements to the production frontier, capital growth reflects movements of the frontier. In order to capture the effects of capital accumulation, the rate of growth of capital stock in manufacturing and non-manufacturing industries should be included in the productivity functions.

At this point it is necessary to consider whether it is sensible to include the growth of average hours and capital stock into both the employment and output versions of the manufacturing productivity function. Kaldor's argument for favouring the output version of Verdoorn's Law in manufacturing is that q_m is an exogenous variable. But the results of Section 3 have raised severe doubts about the validity of this assumption. A further consideration is that output growth will almost certainly be correlated with hours growth and capital stock growth. Indeed a possible reason why the coefficient of q_m is so large in equations (14) and (16) is that it contains omitted variable bias due to the correlation between q_m and the omitted variables (hours and capital growth). On the other hand, employment growth is much less likely to be dependent on growth of capital or hours. In view of these arguments it was decided not to use the output version of Verdoorn's Law (equation12) any further but to generalise the employment version of Verdoorn's Law by including capital and hours growth as additional variables.

Accordingly, we may write the productivity functions for manufacturing and non-manufacturing as:

$$p_n = \alpha + \beta e_m + \gamma h_m + \delta k_m \qquad (20)$$

and

$$p_n = \pi + \lambda e_n + \mu q_m + \eta h_n + \phi k_n \qquad (21)$$

where k_m, k_n are the rates of growth of the capital stock in manufacturing and non-manufacturing respectively whilst h_m and h_n are the respective growth rates of average hours.[17]

(iii) Dynamic Specification

Equations (20) and (21) though considerably more general than their earlier counterparts (equations (1) and (5) respectively) are still completely static. They imply that any adjustment takes place instantaneously. In the empirical work of Kaldor, Cripps and Tarling, Rowthorn and Parikh, the data used were cross-section and the interpretation of their results and those of Stoneman who used growth rates measured peak to peak from 1800, concerned the long-run. One advantage of our use of quarterly time series data is that it is possible to examine the dynamic response of productivity growth to changes in the growth of employment, hours and capital and thus distinguish between short-run and long-run effects. Fairly general formulations which incorporate the idea that the response of productivity growth to changes in the growth of employment, hours and capital is distributed through time are:

$$p_m(t) = \alpha + \sum_{s=0}^{5} \beta_s e_m(t-s) + \sum_{s=0}^{5} \gamma_s h_m(t-s) + \sum_{s=0}^{5} \delta_s k_m(t-s) + \sum_{s=1}^{5} \varepsilon_s p_m(t-s) + u(t) \qquad (22)$$

and

$$p_n(t) = \pi + \sum_{s=0}^{5} \lambda_s e_n(t-s) + \sum_{s=0}^{5} \mu_s q_m(t-s)$$

$$+ \sum_{s=0}^{5} \eta_s h_n(t-s) + \sum_{s=0}^{5} \phi_s k_n(t-s)$$

$$+ \sum_{s=1}^{5} \psi_s p_n(t-s) + v(t) \qquad (23)$$

where u(t) and v(t) are assumed to be random disturbance terms each with zero mean and constant variance.

Equations (22) and (23) can be related to the literature. First, they can be regarded as transformed production functions in which the lagged variables can be interpreted as capturing the short-run behaviour of the frontier, of factor efficiency or, in the case of the externality terms, embodied technical progress. Second, they are similar in some respects to Hazledine's (1974) productivity function in which output per man hour is thought to be a quadratic function of employment; productivity falls as employment either exceeds or drops below a certain optimal level. Finally, they can be related to Okun's Law which postulates that *short-run* deviations in output from its capacity level are related to short-run deviations of the unemployment rate from the natural rate. Since changes in the unemployment rate are inversely related to changes in the employment rate, a fall in the unemployment rate will cause a short-run increase in employment and hence in productivity. Thus Okun's Law can be viewed as a short-run version of Verdoorn's Law. For further details of these various interpretations see Chatterji and Wickens.

Section 5 : Estimates of the Dynamic Model

Before reporting the estimates of our general dynamic models, we note a number of difficulties associated with the estimation. The first of these concerns the construction of a capital stock series for both manufacturing and non-manufacturing from which k_m and k_n can be derived. The capital stock series is calculated from total investment using a constant depreciation rate which was chosen on the basis of a rough grid search to be 0.02 per quarter.[18] Another difficulty was the absence of a quarterly series for average hours worked in non-manufacturing. Hence we were forced to use average hours in manufacturing as a proxy for average hours in non-manufacturing on the presumption that the two are closely correlated. Accordingly we used h_m instead of h_n in equation (23). Having obtained unrestricted estimates of (22) and (23), we attempted to find a more parsimonious dynamic specification which would capture the essential short and long run features of the unrestricted estimates of (22) and (23). Besides the appeal of simplicity such formulations may well provide more efficient estimates. It is these restricted estimates which are reported here.

Our preferred estimates were obtained using OLS and are:

manufacturing:

$$\begin{aligned} p_m(t) = &- \underset{(2.25)}{0.011} + \underset{(6.57)}{0.742}\, h_m(t) + \underset{(3.26)}{0.705}\, \Delta_3\, e_m(t-1) \\ &- \underset{(2.00)}{0.241} \sum_{s=1}^{4} e_m(t-s) - \underset{(2.40)}{2.043}\, \Delta_3\, k_m(t-1) \\ &+ \underset{(9.39)}{0.249} \sum_{s=1}^{4} k_m(t-s) - \underset{(13.15)}{0.19}\, \Delta_4\, p_m(t-1) \end{aligned} \qquad (24)$$

$\bar{R}^2 = 0.649$, $T = 56$, $\hat{\sigma} = .0105$, $Q_8 = 4.93$,

where $\Delta_s\, x_t \equiv x_t - x_{t-s}$.

non-manufacturing:

$$\hat{p}_n(t) = \underset{(2.33)}{0.0055} + \underset{(5.18)}{0.325}\, h_m(t) - \underset{(2.36)}{0.500}\, e_n(t)$$

$$- \underset{(3.31)}{0.231} \sum_{s=0}^{5} e_n(t-s) + \underset{(3.04)}{0.064} \sum_{s=0}^{4} q_m(t-s)$$

$$+ \underset{(4.08)}{3.099}\, k_n(t) - \underset{(3.75)}{2.886}\, k_n(t-1) - \underset{(4.65)}{0.352} \sum_{s=1}^{2} p_n(t-s) \qquad (25)$$

$\bar{R}^2 = 0.654$, $T = 56$, $\hat{\sigma} = 0.0058$, $Q_8 = 6.0$.

The corresponding long-run steady growth solutions are:

$$p_m = - 0.011 + 0.742\, h_m - 0.96\, e_m + 1.00\, k_m \qquad (26)$$

$$p_n = 0.0032 + 0.191\, h_m - 1.107\, e_n + 0.188\, q_m + 0.125\, k_n \qquad (27)$$

From equations (24) and (26) it can be seen that productivity growth in manufacturing has a significant and quite large transitory response to employment growth in manufacturing but that in the long-run, the cumulative effect of employment growth on productivity growth is significantly negative. This implies that manufacturing is characterised by a strong but short-lived Verdoorn's Law and that this effect is more than offset in later periods leaving no Verdoorn's Law effect in the long-run. This phenomenon, which is in contrast to some of the earlier results can best be explained by means of the simple diagram on the next page. The diagram shows a production function relating output to employment. The function is drawn for a given level of capital stock and for a given socio-legally determined maximum level of hours. The slope of any ray through the origin measures productivity. In the short-run, the economy is assumed to be operating inside the frontier at some point A with employment of E_A and hours less than the maximum. The increases in demand lead to simultaneous increases in employment (to E_B) and hours to their maximum level, i.e. to point B where productivity is higher. The move from A to B is a manifestation of Verdoorn's Law. In the longer run, however, increased output demand can only be met by increased employment and the economy moves from B to C accompanied by a fall in productivity. This is a manifestation of the inverse relationship between employment growth and productivity growth.

Diagram 1. Output, Employment and Productivity

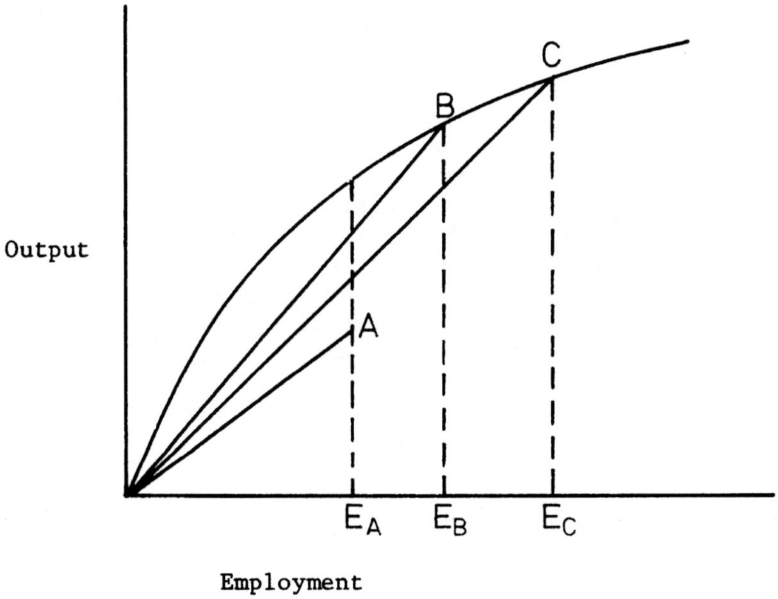

Turning to other variables, equations (24) and (26) show that the growth of average hours and capital have significant positive effects on productivity growth in the long-run, thus confirming once more our earlier conjectures. In addition, however, there is a large negative transitory response to new investment and a negative transitory feedback. The constant term implies a significant negative rate of disembodied technical progress but,since capital will embody technical progress, the total effect of technical progress would not be expected to be negative.

Turning to non-manufacturing productivity, equation (25) indicates that employment growth has a fairly strong and negative instantaneous effect on productivity growth and a much larger long-run effect.

As with manufacturing industry, these results show that changes in capacity utilisation, as proxied by the growth rate of hours in manufacturing, as well as changes in the growth rate of capital have a significant influence. Capital growth has a strong instantaneous effect which is largely but not entirely offset in the following period. The distributed lag function on the lagged dependent variable shows that there is marked negative feed-back for about six months which attenuates the sum of the distributed lag coefficients to produce reduced long-run multipliers.

The estimates of the distributed lag function for employment growth in non-manufacturing indicates a fairly strong and negative instantaneous effect of employment growth on productivity growth and a much stronger total effect with a long-run multiplier of 1.107 which is not significantly different from - 1, and suggests that the Cripps-Tarling Proposition receives support in the long-run.[19] The estimates of the distributed lag function for output growth of manufacturing industries indicate a weak short-run impact but a significant and moderately strong long-run influence. This confirms the Externalities Hypothesis but suggests that it is primarily a long-run phenomenon.

Section 6 : Kaldor's Proposition Reconsidered

The central issue of concern to Kaldor and to Cripps and Tarling is whether or not a transfer of labour from non-manufacturing to manufacturing industries will raise the rate of growth of total output. We have argued that Kaldor's Proposition rests on two hypotheses, Verdoorn's Law and the Externalities Hypothesis, but we have found evidence to support the existence of only the latter. Nevertheless, we have shown that this is a sufficient condition for Kaldor's Proposition to hold. It remains to estimate from our results the quantitative importance of this transfer. We shall consider below only the long-run implications.

From equations (26) and (27) we obtain the long-run output growth equations for manufacturing and non-manufacturing:

$$q_m = -0.01 + 0.74\,h_m + 0.04\,e_m + 1.00\,k_m \tag{28}$$

$$q_n = 0.19\,h_m - 0.11\,e_n + 0.19\,q_m + 0.13\,k_n \tag{29}$$

Using the CSO estimate of the share of non-manufacturing in total output computed for the index of industrial production we have $\theta = 0.745$ when equation (3) becomes:

$$y = 0.745\,q_n + 0.255\,q_m$$

and hence the long-run reduced form equation for total output growth is:

$$y = 0.00 + 0.48\,h_m + 0.02\,e_m - 0.08\,e_n + 0.40\,k_m + 0.10\,k_n \tag{31}$$

Since the purpose of the exercise is to analyse the effects of *reallocating* labour, we shall assume that total employment is unchanged.[20] Hence a transfer of one per cent of non-manufacturing employment raises manufacturing employment by 2.112 per cent. This transfer implies a one percentage point fall in the growth rate of non-manufacturing employment (e_n) and an increase of 2.112 percentage points in the growth rate of manufacturing employment (e_m).[21] Substituting into (31) that a *sustained* transfer of $e_n = -1$ implies $e_m = 2.112$ we find that $y = 0.12$, implying that the growth rate of total output increases by only 0.12 percentage point.

As sustained transfers are not feasible in the long-run due to the existence of constraints on labour, it is perhaps of more interest to examine the effect of a *once-for-all* transfer of labour. These calculations are made in Chatterji and Wickens using a dynamic simulation of the original model, equations (24) and (25) together with (30). It is found that there are no significant gains in output growth beyond the first two quarters and these are completely offset in later periods reaching the long-run value of zero in about two years.

Although this is true if one considers the *growth rate* of output (as Kaldor and Cripps and Tarling did), it may be the case that even a once-for-all transfer could have permanent effects on the *level* of output. These calculations suggest that the gains in cumulative output from the once-for-all transfer increase during the first year and then decline steadily. But after five years output is only approximately 0.28 percent higher than it would have been without the transfer.

Section 7 : Conclusions

The main conclusions to be drawn from our results are as follows. First, Verdoorn's Law does not hold for the U.K. manufacturing industry in the long-run. This result is consistent with the results obtained by Rowthorn, Parikh and Stoneman. Secondly, U.K. manufacturing industry is characterised by a short-run Verdoorn's Law which is analagous to Okun's Law. This result cannot be compared with previous empirical work because the earlier literature cited concentrated exclusively on long-run tests. Thirdly, the Cripps-Tarling Proposition and, *a fortiori*, Kaldor's Proposition regarding the possibility of increased output growth by a transfer of labour do hold but are due almost entirely to the Externalities Hypothesis rather than Verdoorn's Law. Again this result is not easily comparable with the previous literature as earlier researchers did not attempt to test these propositions directly. Fourthly, the impact of the labour transfer on economic growth, though positive, is of little quantitative significance. The long-term pay-off of the labour transfer in terms of an increased growth rate of output is only 0.12 percentage points and if the labour transfer is applied only once, then the pay-off in terms of an increased growth rate of output is highly transitory but very small in the long-run. Finally, it is possible to conduct a similar analysis considering an investment transfer instead of a labour transfer. The results of this exercise, which are reported in Chatterji and Wickens, are found to be much larger.

APPENDIX

A Test for the validity of the Instruments

The test statistic is obtained by multiplying the sample size by the R^2 obtained from an OLS regression of the residuals obtained from the instrumental variables estimation against the instrumental variables. The asymptotic distribution of this test statistic is obtained as follows:

Consider the linear model

$$(A.1) \quad y = X\beta + u$$

where y is a $T\times 1$ vector of observations on the dependent variable, X is a $T\times k$ matrix of observations on k explanatory variables, u is a $T\times 1$ vector of disturbances which are assumed to be distributed $N(0,\sigma^2 I_T)$ and β is a $k\times 1$ vector of coefficients. It is assumed that X is stochastic such that $\text{plim}\,(X'u/T) \neq 0$ and $\text{plim}\,(X'X/T) = M_{xx}$ is finite non-singular.

Let Z be a $T\times p$ matrix of observations of $p > k$ linearly independent instrumental variables for which $\lim\,(Z'Z/T) = M_{zz}$ is finite non-singular and $\text{plim}\,(Z'X/T) = M_{zx}$ has full column rank. On the null hypothesis that the instruments are valid for X it is assumed that the limiting distribution of $Z'u/\sqrt{T}$ is $N(0,\sigma^2 M_{zz})$ and, on the alternative hypothesis that the instruments are not valid, $\text{plim}(Z'u/T) \neq 0$.

In order to derive a test statistic suitable for H_0 we shall consider the distribution of the explained sum of squares of a regression of the instrumental variables residuals of (A.1), namely $\hat{u}$, on the instruments Z, i.e. we consider the distribution of $\hat{u}'Z(Z'Z)^{-1}Z'\hat{u}$. Now

$$\begin{aligned}\hat{u} &= y - Xb = -X(b-\beta) + u \\ &= \left[I_T - X(X'P_zX)^{-1}X'P_z\right] u\end{aligned}$$

where $b = (X'P_zX)^{-1}X'P_zy$ is the IV estimator of β and $P_z = Z(Z'Z)^{-1}Z'$. It follows that

$$\hat{u}'P_z\hat{u} = u'\left(P_z - P_zX(X'P_zX)^{-1}X'P_z\right) u$$

$$= u'\ A\ u$$

where $A = P_z - P_zX(X'P_zX)^{-1}X'P_z$ is an idempotent matrix with rank $p - k$. On H_0, the limiting distribution of $u'P_zu/\sigma^2$ is the same as that of $u'Au/\sigma^2$ which converges to that of

$$u'Z\left(M_{zz}^{-1} - M_{zz}^{-1}M_{zx}(M_{xz}M_{zz}^{-1}M_{zx})^{-1}M_{xz}M_{zz}^{-1}\right) Z'u/\sigma^2$$

which is a χ^2_{p-k}. If σ^2 is consistently estimated by $\hat{u}'\hat{u}/T$, the required test statistic is given by

$$K = T\ \frac{\hat{u}'P_z\hat{u}}{\hat{u}'\hat{u}} = T.R^2_{\hat{u}.z}$$

where $R^2_{\hat{u}.z}$ is the squared multiple correlation coefficient from the regression of $\hat{u}$ on Z. In view of the above results, the distribution of K on H_0 can be approximated by a χ^2_{p-k} with large values leading to a rejection of H_0. Note that unless $p > k$ the test cannot be used.

ACKNOWLEDGEMENTS

This paper is part of a larger project on dynamic macro-econometric model building. We wish to acknowledge, with sincere thanks, the SSRC for providing financial support for the project. We also wish to thank Hassan Molana for his invaluable assistance and Pravin Trivedi for his comments on an earlier draft.

REFERENCES

Chatterji, M. and M.R. Wickens (1980). Productivity, Factor Transfers and Economic Growth in the U.K. *Economica.* (forthcoming).

Cripps, T.F. and R.J. Tarling (1973). *Growth in Advanced Capitalist Economies, 1950-1970.* Cambridge University Press.

Hazledine, T. (1974). Employment and Output Functions for New Zealand Manufacturing Industries. *Journal of Industrial Economics,* 22, 161-198.

Kaldor, N., (1966). *Causes of the Slow Rate of Economic Growth of the United Kingdom.* Cambridge University Press.

Kaldor, N., (1975). Economic Growth and the Verdoorn Law - A Comment on Mr. Rowthorn's Article. *Economic Journal,* 85.

Parikh, A., (1978). Differences in Growth Rates and Kaldor's Laws, *Economica,* 45, 83-91.

Rowthorn, R. (1975). What Remains of Kaldor's Law? *Economic Journal,* 85, 10-19.

Stoneman, P., (1979). Kaldor's Law and British Economic Growth: 1800-1970. *Applied Economics,* 11, 309-319.

FOOTNOTES

1. Certainly this interpretation is also imputed by Stoneman (1979).
2. It may be the case that the Cripps-Tarling Proposition can be implicitly inferred from Kaldor's Inaugural Lecture. However, Kaldor has not explicitly stated the Cripps-Tarling Proposition.
3. Throughout this paper we are interpreting Verdoorn's Law as a *partial* effect in a structural equation. It is possible to interpret Verdoorn's Law as the *total* effect of e_m (or q_m) in a reduced form equation for p_m. This however implies that other factors which may have an influence on productivity growth, for example, capital accumulation, can be represented as functions of e_m and possibly p_m(or q_m) alone which is surely unreasonable. Furthermore, if one takes this view that the effects of capital accumulation etc. are included in the formulation of Verdoorn's Law, it is difficult

to argue that the validity of Verdoorn's Law implies a reallocation of labour. Accordingly, we interpret Verdoorn's Law as the partial effect of employment growth and allow explicitly for the separate influence of other variables such as capital accumulation etc. in Section 4.

4. As with Verdoorn's Law, we are interpreting the Externalities Hypothesis as a partial effect in a structural equation. This approach is also implicitly adopted by Stoneman who has also tested a version of the Externalities Hypothesis. However, it is possible to view the Externalities Hypothesis as the *total* effect of q_m in a reduced form equation for p_n. In this case the Externalities Hypothesis is trivially true and not of much interest.

5. The "productivity functions" (4) and (5) can be integrated to yield the production functions:

$$Q_m = A_m E_m^{\beta+1}, \quad \beta + 1 \geq 1 \text{ and}$$

$$Q_n = A_n E_n^{\lambda+1}, \; E_m^{\mu(\beta+1)}, \quad \theta \leq \lambda + 1 \leq 1, \; \mu > 0,$$

where A_m, A_n are constants. Thus $\beta = -1$ and $\lambda = -1$ represent the limiting case of zero marginal productivity of labour in the two sectors.

6. Kaldor has hinted that the marginal productivity of labour in agriculture may well be zero. Whilst this may be plausible for *agriculture*, it is improbable for *non-manufacturing* as a whole.

7. Of course, if Verdoorn's Law is true so that $(\beta + 1) > 1$, then the *likelihood* of $dq_n \geq 0$ and $dy > 0$ is increased. This is also true of the Externalities Hypothesis.

8. Exceptions are Stoneman and Cripps and Tarling. But the latters' main emphasis is still on Verdoorn's Law whilst Stoneman's specification of the Externality Hypothesis is somewhat strange.

9. There are, however, some qualifications for the later periods of study.

10. In fact the choice between using (1) or (2) as the estimating equation is important if OLS is to be used but if a suitable consistent estimator is used, either (1) or (2) can be chosen.

11. For a detailed account of the data sources see Chatterji and Wickens (1980).

12. Strictly the Box-Pierce statistic applies to the original disturbances and not to the residuals.
13. See Phillips and Wickens (1979), Chapter 2, for details of this calculation.
14. This is similar to the approach adopted by Parikh and Stoneman.
15. For details of this test, see the Appendix.
16. See footnote number 3.
17. We have deliberately not worked in a production function framework, but if we assume a simple Cobb-Douglas production function, then we can write:

    $$q_m = (\beta + 1)\, e_m + \gamma h_m + \delta k_m$$

    The dependence of q_m on h_m and k_m is now clear and the corresponding productivity function is $p_m = \beta e_m + \gamma h_m + \delta k_m$ which is of the preferred form.

18. Unrestricted estimates of (22) and (23) as well as the methodology underlying our choice of preferred restricted specifications is fully described in Chatterji and Wickens.
19. For details of this test and other statistical calculations in this section, see Chatterji and Wickens.
20. We do not discuss the method whereby this transfer of labour is to be achieved. Kaldor's suggestion was S.E.T.
21. For details of these calculations see Chatterji and Wickens.

DISCUSSION: N. KALDOR

Messrs. Chatterji and Wickens' paper is a further addition to the increasing literature on the 'Verdoorn Law' which seems to be in vogue at present. I am not sure that I succeeded in understanding just what they are after, but I think there are a number of statements which I regard as false or misleading and which need to be pointed out.

(1) I never intended to put forward the view that 'the main engine of economic growth was the presence of Verdoorn's Law in manufacturing', though I can see that superficial readers of my inaugural lecture may have formed that impression.

I did suggest that the main engine of economic growth for industrially developed countries was the manufacturing sector, and that this is due to (a) the importance of exports from the point of view of growth; (b) the manufacturing sector has the peculiarity that it accumulates its own resources, i.e. it manufactures the capital goods which it uses and provides the savings for it through the profits which its own investment activities generate; (c) in its expansion, it absorbs labour from the agricultural and/or the services sector of the economy, where labour, in the relevant sense of the word, is in surplus. As a result of that, the growth of output of the manufacturing sector does not cause a diminution of output of these other sectors, but on the contrary, it stimulates their growth.

(2) I also disagree with their exposition of the Verdoorn Law. They use Rowthorn's formulation which can be put as

$$P_m = f(e_m), \quad f' > 0$$

This is not a *necessary* condition of the law (though it may be a *sufficient* one) for the simple reason that if output, and not employment, is regarded as the exogenous variable, any statistical error which occurs in the endogenous variable e_m sets up a change of the opposite sign in P_m and thus generates a spurious negative correlation which has the effect of making the relationship appear a great deal weaker than it is if set in the form which I prefer:-

$$e_m = f(q_m), \quad f' > 0 < 1 \qquad \text{(ii)}$$

The usual formulation

$$P_m = f(q_m), \quad f' > 0 \qquad \text{(iii)}$$

I regard as unsatisfactory since, in view of t identity $P_m \equiv q_m - e_m$, it may be no more than a tautology unless equation (ii) holds; whereas if (ii) holds, (iii) is automatically satisfied.

(3) I disagree with their statement that manufacturing output cannot be regarded as "exogenous" for any number of countries. Of course the export demand for any one country depends on the growth of output of all other countries, but this no more invalidates the exogeneity condition than the fact that the demand for, say, matches in a particular country or region depends on the total output of that country or region from which its consumers are drawn. I cannot, therefore, accept their criticism of the use of cross-section data which I still feel avoids some of the pitfalls of time-series data. Assuming, however, that these pitfalls do not matter, the time series data should serve to confirm the findings of cross-section data.

(4) So, far from saying that I regard the exogeneity of the growth of q_m as being grounded on the Verdoorn Law, I repeatedly expressed the opposite view. I did so explicitly both in my paper in *Economica*, August 1958, and in my reply to Rowthorn in the *Economic Journal*, December 1975, where I said that:

> 'The important thing to note is - and herein lies Rowthorn's misunderstanding - that the existence of increasing returns to scale in industry (the Verdoorn Law) is not a necessary or indispensable element in the interpretation of these equations. Even if industrial output obeyed the law of constant returns, it could still be true that the growth of industrial output was the governing factor in the overall rate of economic growth (both in terms of total output and output per head) so long as the growth of industrial output represented a *net*

> *addition* to the effective use of resources, and not just a transfer of resources from one use to another.'
>
> (p. 894)

(5) My assumption that labour is not a constraint on output as a whole or on the output of any particular sector such as manufacturing is basic to my whole approach in economics. It is, of course, a denial of the basic neo-classical hypothesis according to which in a market economy there is both full employment and a "pareto-optimal" allocation of the labour force. As against that I assert that in agriculture and services the marginal social product is normally zero (or could even be negative for all kinds of reasons, such as that too much labour prevents the optimum organisation of the individual production unit, such as the optimum sized farm in agriculture) or else leads to excess capacity (as in the case of distribution) and the division of sales among too many selling units. The reason why a 'pareto-optimal' full employment equilibrium does not exist in these cases is partly because the land constraint may be binding, and the fact that there are limits to the range within which labour and land are effective substitutes for one another at the margin; partly because of imperfect competition and the absence of homogeneous and linear production function in services, which means that there is always a minimum scale of production (higher than zero) below which unit costs are rising with a further fall in sales. Given these facts, the marginal (social) product of labour is normally in excess of the average product of labour in manufacturing industry and is very much below it in both agriculture and services. This is the basic reason for my rejection of neo-classical economics. As far as I understand, all these points are subsumed by Messrs. Chatterji and Wickens under the notion of the "externalities hypothesis", but calling it by that name is not just a matter of semantics - it concedes the general validity of the neo-classical approach to economics (which I deny).

(6) The Verdoorn Law is however essential for the existence of "circular and cumulative causation" which I regard as critical for understanding the nature of the process of economic development, but the assumption of which is incompatible with neo-classical economic theory (i.e. the theory of general equilibrium). The latter regards the essence of the economic problem as the allocation of scarce resources

between different uses; but it is the *rate of creation* of resources (and the factors that promote it or inhibit it) rather than their allocation which are the really important issues to be considered.

I agree that the main difference between economists like myself and those who believe in neo-classical theory, is essentially a difference in empirical assumptions. It is not always easy to isolate an aspect of reality the observation of which is capable of rejecting the one hypothesis and not the other. For example, if we were to find that the rate of growth of agricultural production is fairly close to two per cent per annum among a large number of countries differing in other respects, whereas the rate of growth of labour productivity in agriculture can be either much higher or much lower than this, depending on both fertility and the growth in numbers engaged outside agriculture (which in turn is a reflection of the growth of demand in the other sectors of the economy which draw their additional labour requirements from agriculture), this would be sufficient, in my view, to reject the neo-classical hypothesis and to support the opposite hypothesis, that of surplus labour. Such examples could be multiplied.

15. THE WAGE EQUATION AND RATIONAL EXPECTATIONS

Patrick Minford and Michael Brech[1]

In much of the discussion of wage equations, the role of the trade union in setting the nominal wage level in a highly unionised economy like the UK has generally either been disregarded or treated as a source of exogenous 'militancy'. There are, however, distinguished exceptions in the literature and the number is steadily increasing; the earliest contribution was Sargan (1964), and recently Johnston (1972), and Johnston and Timbrell (1973).

In addition to these the hypothesis of dual labour markets has been extensively explored - see Laidler and Parkin (1975) - and not just in developed countries; the literature of developing countries is rich in such models, as pioneered by Lewis (1954) and exemplified in Harris and Todaro (1970) and Minford and Ohs (1976). This seems a most fertile approach and we have built on it here. The links between unionised and the competitive or 'residual' sector are two-fold: the real wage paid in the competitive sector shifts the supply curve of labour to the union intermediary in the unionised sector and employment in the unionised sector shifts the supply curve in the competitive sector.

The theoretical basis of our approach is fully described in Minford (1980) and only the briefest account can be given here. The union maximises the discounted value of its potential members'[2] utility; this leads naturally to the inclusion of measures of uncertainty about price and quantity developments, as well as the expected level of competitive sector real wages and a lagged adjustment term, within the equation for the planned union real wage. The union then sets the nominal wage for an assumed one-year contract period by adding to the planned real wage its estimate of expected inflation.

The competitive labour market is supposed to be continuously cleared by non-contract real wages. The competitive real wage is therefore determined by the level of activity and supply factors such as the real social security benefit rates, the tax rates, and labour force trends; also by the determinants of the unionised real wage, since the union employment feeds back on this market by withdrawing labour from it.

Largely for convenience, we assume that our aggregate wage rate statistics record only unionised rates; the one country in which this does violence to the known facts is the USA, and in this case the interpretation of our equation differs, but the specification if we were to allow the proper weight to the competitive sector would not differ much.

Expectations are taken to be rational. We have been confined, by the unavailability of a full model for each country, to single equation estimation methods. We have used a variant of the approach of Sargent (1973), whose expectations proxies are least square predictions from available information. We have however imposed more structure than this in order to increase estimation efficiency. We project expected activity levels from the reduced form of a simple macroeconomic model; the exogenous variables used are world trade and the ratio of the public sector deficit to GNP, with freely determined lags.

For expected inflation, we used a two-stage procedure. We follow the monetary approach to the balance of payments in which (Laidler and Parkin) under fixed rates domestic prices (CPI) are determined by world prices and so by world money supply (MI) but under floating rates by domestic money supply. Domestic money supply is in turn related under both regimes to the public sector deficit in each country; this medium term relationship is subject to a short run error process. So under fixed rates we aggregated public sector deficits in order to project the world money supply from this aggregate, and projected each country's prices from their relationship with the world money supply. Under floating rates we projected each country's prices from its own money supply projection which we derived from its own public sector deficit. Full details are given in Brech, Ioannidis and Minford, (1978)

In the case of the UK adjustment was made to the PEXP series for the years 1974 and 1975. The MI series on which they were based plunged in 1972 and 1973 (even though M3 was rising extraordinarily rapidly). This was a period of monetary turbulence caused by a combination of a sharply rising deficit, a booming economy, with rising interest rates, and Competition and Credit Control legislation. The PEXP series drops from 9.4% in 73(4) to 0 in 75(2) before rising back to 10% in 75(4). We took the step of keeping PEXP at 10% throughout this period in the light of the conflicting monetary data. This at least prevents extreme low observations from affecting the sample results.

The issue arises that in the usual model variances are assumed constant, whereas here they change over time. We assume specifically that:

a) the error processes in our inflation and output reduced forms (but *not* in the wage equation itself) are heteroscedastic.

b) their variances are related to current and lagged values of variables known to economic agents, who form their expectations of these variances according to their expectations of these variables.

For example the variance of inflation errors seems to be related to the square of inflation itself (Minford and Hilliard, 1978), while the variance of output errors may be related to the square of output deviations from trend.

Assumption a) implies that our estimation procedure of the inflation and output reduced forms suffers from inefficiency; this is in addition, however, to whatever inefficiency arises from our single equation techniques. Further research may make it possible to reduce this as the other sources of inefficiency.

In implementing b), our approach has been, in the absence of much work to determine the relevant explanatory variables, to use the current squared actual forecasting errors as one proxy, in addition to the suggested squared inflation rate and squared output deviation from trend. The squared error will clearly be a noisy proxy of the true variance but will be related to it. It may therefore give an indication of any effect.

The Wage Equation

The wage equation is written as:

$$\Delta logW = \alpha_0 + \alpha_1 PEXP + \alpha_2 b_{-1} + \alpha_3 TX_{-1} + \alpha_4 t +$$
$$\alpha_5 Q + \alpha_6 VARP_{-1} + \alpha_7 VARE_{-1} + \alpha_8 log\frac{(W)}{(P)}_{-1} + \alpha_9 PRES_{-1}$$

where the variable definitions and expected signs are as follows:

$\Delta logW$ The change in the national wage rate index expressed at an annual rate.

PEXP The expected change in prices over the coming year, assuming an annual wage round; constructed as described above. $\alpha_1 = 1$ (no money illusion).

b Benefits-to-earnings ratio; available for several countries (source: Holden & Peel, 1979). $\alpha_2 > 0$.

TX The marginal tax rate. $\alpha_3 > 0$

Q Expected demand pressure corresponding to

$(\underset{-1}{E}\ log^{y}/y^*_{+1} - (I-\gamma)\ \underset{-1}{E}\ log^{y}/y^*)$, where $y(y^*)$ = actual

(equilibrium) output. Two series were used:

a) *QL*: lagged real GNP to represent the demand conditions during which the wage claim is formulated, on the assumption that $y/_{y^*}$ is serially correlated,

so that $(^{y}/y^*)_{-1}$ will be a good proxy for expected

demand pressure in the next four quarters.

b) *QEXP*: the prediction from the reduced form of a macro-model (arguments: world trade and PSBR/GNP with various lags), see above .
$\alpha_5 > 0$.

VARP Variance of unanticipated inflation.

a) *VARP1:* the square of unanticipated inflation over the year prior to the claim.

b) *VARP2:* the square of average inflation over the year prior to the claim. The justification is a strong relationship found by Minford and Hilliard (1978) between the size of errors in forecasting inflation and the square of inflation itself.

VARE Variance of unanticipated employment.

a) *VARE1:* the square of unanticipated output over the year prior to the claim.

b) *VARE2:* the square of output deviations, from a loglinear trend, over the year prior to the claim.

α_6, α_7 depend on the relative seriousness with which 'job risk' and 'real income risk' are regarded. Possibilities are (for further discussion see Minford, 1980):

(1) $\alpha_6 > 0, \alpha_7 > 0$, where job risk is regarded as being of little importance (presumably because society provides high social insurance benefits). Higher variance requires higher real wages to compensate higher real income risk.

(2) $\alpha_6 < 0, \alpha_7 < 0$, where job risk is of prime importance (social insurance is low). Higher variances require lower real wages to increase the probability of retaining jobs.

(3) $\underset{(>)}{\alpha_6 < 0}, \underset{(<)}{\alpha_7 > 0}$, represent intermediate environments.

$\left(\frac{W}{P}\right)_{-1}$ Real wages over the previous year. $0 < -\alpha_8 < 1$.

$PRES_{-1}$ Unanticipated inflation during the previous year. This splits the lagged adjustment term into a component representing the intended (real) discrepancy and that due to unanticipated inflation. $0<\alpha_9=1+\alpha_8$.

Results

We estimated the wage equation over quarterly data from 1960.1 to 1975.4. We imposed the constraint that $\alpha_1 = 1$, using a standard F-test on the constraint. The Cochrane-Orcutt iterative method of OLS was used, to allow for serial correlation of up to second order. The results are summarised in Table 1 and reported fully for each country in the Tables at the end.

In general, they were consistent with a unit coefficient on expected inflation, though in some countries the constraint was rejected in certain combinations of variables. Expected demand pressure usually entered with a positive sign though in several cases not significant; the exceptions were Cananda, France and the UK. The lagged real wage almost invariably entered with a significant negative sign, the only exception being Belgium. Unemployment benefit was only significant and of the right sign in the case of Canada.

The variance terms had some effect in almost all countries: they were positive in Canada, Japan, France and Belgium, negative in the US, Germany and mixed in Italy and the UK (*VARP*+, *VARE*-). This suggests, plausibly, that job security is greatest in the first four countries so that concern is predominantly about real income, while in the US and Germany job security is the major concern of unions: while in Italy, where there is a combination of high unemployment in the South and a virulent inflation, both job security and real income are of concern. The UK and Italy have obvious similarities.

The power of the preferred equation (as indicated in the country Tables for Table 1) to explain *nominal* wage changes is high. Col. 1 of Table 1 shows the $\bar{R}^2$ for the equation in the form $\Delta \log W = 1.0\ PEXP + \ldots$. It also parenthesises the percentage of the $\bar{R}^2$, other than that due to seasonal factors, contributed by expected inflation (*PEXP*) alone, with a unit coefficient. It is striking how large this is in general; the exception is Germany where the *PEXP* series seems to be at fault.

TABLE 1

SUMMARY OF RESULTS FOR WAGE EQUATION

	$\bar{R}^2$ (of which *PEXP*,%)	Unit coefficient on *PEXP*?	Real wage coefficient significant?	Demand pressure significant?	Variance effects significant?	Other significant effects?
U.S.A.	.65 (74)	Yes	Yes	Yes?	Yes. Both −.	No
CANADA	.77 (73)	Yes	Yes	No	Yes. Both +.	b?
JAPAN	.81 (21)	?	Yes	Yes	Yes. Both +.	No
GERMANY	.40 (−12)	?	Yes	Yes	Yes? Both −?	No
FRANCE	.39 (77)	Yes	Yes	No	Yes. Both +.	No
ITALY	.59 (54)	Yes	Yes	Yes(QL only)	Yes. VARP + VARE −.	$PRES_{-1}$
BELGIUM	.73 (55)	Yes	Yes?	Yes	Yes. Both +.	$PRES_{-1}$
N'LANDS	.57 (28)	?	Yes	Yes?	No	No
U.K.	.81 (49)	Yes	Yes?	No	Yes. VARP + VARE −.	No

(For fuller details see tables at the end)

Price expectations

A key point in this approach is the unit coefficient on *PEXP*; a non-unit coefficient would imply money illusion, a proposition that is unacceptable theoretically. Rejection of a unit coefficient therefore implies some form of misspecification. We carried out the F-test for all countries. The US, Canada, Italy, France and the UK gave insignificant F-values. For Belgium, the F-values are with only 2 exceptions insignificant; however, these were only marginally significant and can probably be disregarded. For Japan, the F-values varied between 2 and 9; for Germany from 2 to 12; for the Netherlands from 3 to 6 casting doubt on the specification of some of these equations.

The results for Italy, Belgium and the Netherlands must be seen in the context of indexation arrangements for the bulk of the post war period. Indexation has varied in detail and in the proportion of price inflation compensated; it has never been total. Bargaining in these countries therefore still involves forming price expectations, in order to calculate the element not covered by indexation. Our *PEXP* term, while a misspecification in these cases,is clearly not unduly serious judging by the results; *PEXP* must be seen as crudely proxying the joint effect of both the indexed and the expected inflation terms.

Pressure of Demand

Whether the pressure of demand affects real wages has significance in principle for the long run equilibrium of output; if it does not affect them, then equilibrium output will vary according to world demand conditions, whereas if it does affect them equilibrium is the level at which demand pressure is zero. However we must distinguish dynamic questions from equilibrium ones. It is presumably absurd to argue that real wages could in the long run not adjust in response to continued excess supply or demand; the question is whether there is evidence of short run response (the alternative being that unions decide to stabilise real wages in the face of quantity shocks).

In fact for only four countries, Belgium, Germany, Japan and Italy, is there very strong evidence of short run response, with elasticities around 0.75 for the first three and as high as 2 for Italy. For the US and the

Netherlands the evidence is there but weak that there is some response, of the order of 0.1 - 0.4. For France and the UK there is no evidence of any response at all. It is possible that the UK (in which the sign was often negative) could be affected by the use of a wage rate rather than earnings series.

Of the two proxies for demand pressure, *QL* generally performs better than *QEXP*, perhaps because of the inadequacy of our reduced form.

Lagged real wages and adjustment

Only in Italy (and perhaps Belgium) was there any evidence of a distinction between the inflation catch-up term $PRES_{-1}$, and the real wage adjustment effect. This could partially reflect the effects of indexation of wages in Italy and Belgium.

The rate of adjustment indicated by the lagged real wage varied considerably. The fast adjusters (with some 80% occurring in the first year) are the USA, Canada, and Germany. Japan, France, Italy and the Netherlands are a middle group (with some 50%). The UK and Belgium are slow adjusters (only 10-20%).

Variance terms:

It is perhaps not surprising that the upheavals of the recent decade should affect real wage behaviour. Both unemployment and inflation have risen strongly and become less predictable. To measure the variances (i.e. of the errors in prediction) for these, we have used both the squared deviations from our predictors, *QEXP* and *PEXP*, these being VARP1 and VARE1, and more direct measures, VARP2 being the squared rate of inflation itself and VARE2 the squared deviation of output from trend.

The evidence suggests that these measures are picking up significant effects. Only the Netherlands shows no impact at all. It appears that there are strong institutional differences in response to variance, as noted above. The more 'competitive' societies, Germany and the US, have a negative response. The more stuctured societies, Canada, Japan, France, Belgium, have a positive response while the UK and Italy are in a special position. We have not been able to test how closely these results mirror differences in the social security system as our theory suggests they should. They do however seem to follow an intelligible pattern.

Other effects:

It is unfortunate that we have lacked good quarterly data on marginal tax rates, since Johnston and Timbrell reported interesting findings on this for UK annual data. We have also found in our annual work on the UK that a tax rate variable may enter, though usually not at a high level of significance. It is perhaps to be expected that in quarterly data it will be harder to disentangle this effect. Only for Canada could any evidence of the benefit ratio effect be found (though on annual data we also found evidence for Belgium). However, subsequent work suggests that it is the benefit level, not the ratio, that should enter the wage equation (as opposed to the labour supply equation); we did not test this here.

Incomes Policy experiments:

Among the nine countries studied, the UK is the only one that has carried out prices and incomes policies regularly over the postwar period. In our rational expectations models, incomes policies, unless permanent, can have no permanent effect on inflation. However, they may have temporary effects, before, during or after their implementation. Furthermore, one who believed that expectations were adaptive might expect to find permanent effects within our equations, reflecting a misspecification of expectations formation. So an examination of the UK evidence on this is a further indirect test of our model.

Incomes policies have been variously claimed to have the following effects:

(1) They reduce inflation, temporarily or permanently, by
a) reducing the ('politically possible') growth of money supply

b) reducing *expected* inflation, for any *given* monetary growth

c) for given expected inflation, reducing the rate of

wage increase and so actual inflation.

(2) They reduce unemployment, temporarily or permanently, by lowering real wages (so making it possible to employ more people along a given marginal product curve).

Our model suggests the following way in which these effects may enter, corresponding to:

1) a) In an ARIMA process for money supply growth a set of incomes policy dummies, D_i, for different stages of the policy (eg. 'before', 'after', 'during tough phase', 'during lax phase') may enter. So we may have $\beta(L)\Delta logM = \gamma(L)\varepsilon + \alpha_i D_i + \gamma_0$, where M = money supply ($M1$), L is the lag operator, and ε a random error term. This tests jointly for effects on the budget deficit and the money supply process that is centered around the normal deficit. Notice that incomes policy cannot change γ_0 which is set by the long run equilibrium of the model.

b) The dummies may enter the inflation/money supply relationship as $\phi_2(L)\Delta logP = \phi_0 + \phi_1(L)\Delta logM_{-1} + \beta_i D_i$ where P = consumer prices.

Notice again that they cannot alter the long run relationship between inflation and monetary growth,

ie. $\frac{\phi_0}{\phi_2}$ or $\frac{\phi_1}{\phi_2}$, which is set by the model.

1) c) In the wage equation we may have

$$\Delta logW - PEXP = (b_{-1}, TX_{-1}, \ldots) + \gamma_i D_i$$

The dummies - which have in some previous work been entered on the slopes of the function (see Parkin and Sumner, 1972) - should enter additively because the hypothesis here is that the union reacts rationally to the components of the function (the partials of the arguments are unchanged) but is shifted off its rational choice by the policy. Again, long run expected real wage growth will be unchanged.

2) To test for effects on real wages, we have;

$$\Delta logW - \Delta logP = \Delta logW - PEXP + \eta = (b_{-1}, TX_{-1}, \ldots) + \gamma_i D_i + \eta$$

where $\eta = (PEXP - \Delta logP)$ is independent of $(b_{-1}, TX_{-1} \ldots)$ but may be negatively related to D_i; eg. any effect on log wages may have had an equal effect on log prices so leaving real (actual) wages the same. So we must regress

$$\eta = \delta_i D_i + \varepsilon$$

Then $(\gamma_i + \delta_i)D_i$ will represent incomes policy effects on the rate of change of real wages. If they do not cancel out, there will be a continuing effect on the level of real wages. This effect will be gradually eliminated by the negative lagged real wage term in the wage equation. If γ_i are insignificant, then we do not need to carry out this test.

The D_i were constructed from data on policy periods set out by Tarling and Wilkinson (I978). We identified the year before (D_1), the year after (D_4), years of pay freeze or zero norms (D_2), and other years of policy (D_3). Experiments with dummies constructed in other ways (eg. a single dummy for all periods; separate dummies for each year of the policy, Ist, 2nd etc) made no difference. The results are shown in Table 2.

Table 2: Tests of Incomes Policy Effects for U.K.

1.(a) *Money Supply:* (*t - ratio parenthesised*)

$$\underset{}{\Delta logM} = \underset{(2.41)}{0.044} + \underset{(0.38)}{0.01D1} - \underset{(-0.42)}{0.01D2} - \underset{(-0.43)}{0.01D3}$$

$$+ \underset{(1.08)}{0.02D4} - \underset{(-1.813)}{0.27\Delta logM_{-1}} + \underset{(1.887)}{0.24\Delta logM_{-2}}$$

$$+ \underset{(2.13)}{0.28\Delta logM_{-3}} + \underset{(0.46)}{0.06\Delta logM_{-4}}$$

$\bar{R}^2 = 0.44$ SE = 0.0253 DW = 2.02 Q = 2.76

1.(b) *Inflation on money supply:*

$$\Delta logP = \underset{(-0.71)}{-0.01} - \underset{(0.01)}{0.0005D1} - \underset{(-.255)}{0.0016D2} + \underset{(.086)}{0.0006D3}$$

$$+ \underset{(0.3109)}{0.0016D4} + \underset{(1.305)}{0.2258\Delta logP_{-1}} + D\sum_{i=1}^{16} \alpha_i logM_{-i} + (1-D)\sum_{i=1}^{16} \beta_i logM^*_{-1}$$

$$\sum_{i=1}^{16} \alpha_i = \underset{(2.82)}{1.738} \qquad \sum_{i=1}^{16} \beta_i = \underset{(1.77)}{1.23}$$

[Almon 3rd order polynomial, no endpoint restrictions]

$\bar{R}^2 = 0.784$ SE = 0.0078 DW = 1.861

1.(c) *Wage equation*

$$\Delta logW - PEXP = \underset{(.472)}{0.4154} - \underset{(.54)}{0.1114log\left(\frac{W}{P}\right)_{-1}} - \underset{(.349)}{0.07626QL} + \underset{(1.705)}{0.0317D1}$$

$$+ \underset{(1.318)}{0.0303D2} + \underset{(1.621)}{0.0345D3} + \underset{(2.6)}{0.05D4} + \underset{(3.176)}{5.2371VARP2}$$

$\bar{R}^2 = .6983$ SE = .0322 DW = 1.9521

2. *Inflation errors:*

$$\eta = \underset{(2.352)}{0.034} - \underset{(-2.585)}{0.0341D1} - \underset{(-2.084)}{0.0327D2} - \underset{(-2.793)}{0.0436D3} - \underset{(4.684)}{0.0577D4}$$

$\bar{R}^2 = .3052$ SE = 0.260 DW = 0.4024

1(a) We failed to find any impact on the money supply growth rate itself of the dummies. For the full period we found that the impacts were of the right sign but insignificant.

1(b) For the UK foreign money supply was found to dominate the fixed period, domestic the floating. We therefore set up an equation:

$$\Delta logP = A(L)(D)\Delta logM^{*} + B(L)(I-D)\Delta logM + \lambda\Delta logP_{-1} + \beta_i D_i + \varepsilon$$

where M^{*} = world money supply ($M1$), D = I for the fixed period, 0 otherwise, and $A(L)$, $B(L)$ were Almon polynomials stretching over sixteen quarters. Neither the β_i nor λ were significant, picking up respectively the temporary effects and any carry over to subsequent periods.

1(c) Finally when the dummies were inserted into the wage equation we found that there was some slight *positive* effect, especially in the periods before and after the policy. While this is of course not the intention of these policies, it could happen, since the politicisation of the wage process could lead groups to get more (as well as less) than the economics alone would dictate.

2 We decided in view of our various results in I(c) to investigate whether the policies also raised (rather than lowered) real wages. We found here that the inflation prediction errors, were *negatively* correlated with the dummies implying that these episodes caused an unanticipated rise in inflation especially before and after the policies. The two effects roughly cancel out on real wages. We therefore concluded that these policies seem to have had no effect on real wages.

However, we do not emphasise the positive effect on nominal wages which seems peculiar. It could simply reflect some misspecification. We prefer to say that there is certainly no evidence whatsoever that these policies have, as claimed, *either* lowered inflation *or* lowered real wages (and so raised employment).

Conclusions

The role of unions in the wage-setting process has often been represented as a source of exogenous wage-push or 'militancy'; some have argued further that this makes incomes policy necessary to restrain such forces. We have attempted in this paper to show that a theory of wages based on unions in no way supports such views. Unions are assumed to be maximizing agents, inter temporally, within a stochastic environment. They form their expectations rationally on the basis of the information available. There are adjustment costs in real wage change and there is a contract period (whose optimum length partly depends on these costs). Unions compete with a secondary, competitive labour market.

Such a framework has yielded on the whole plausible estimates when confronted by the data. A unit coefficient on expected inflation is not generally rejected. Lagged adjustment is supported almost uniformly. Expected demand pressure is found to have strong effects in several countries, and of the rest only three show no signs of any positive effects. Variances of output and inflation have significant effects, not previously found in empirical work on wages. Finally, when we looked in detail at the UK's experience with incomes policy we found, in line with our theory, no evidence whatever of the virtuous effects alleged in some quarters; this is consistent with previous findings (especially Parkin and Sumner, 1972) taken as a whole and Henry and Ormerod (1978) even though this work proceeded within different frameworks.

Our general conclusion is therefore that, just as industrial structure has no bearing on inflation, neither does the structure of the labour market. Inflation originates and is perpetuated elsewhere in the system; the labour market merely reflects and passes it through, as one element in the transmission process.

REFERENCES

Brech, M., C. Ioannidis and A. P. L. Minford (1978). Prices, money supply and budget deficits under fixed and floating exchange rates; and the projection of rational expectations, Working Paper No. 7806, University of Liverpool.

Harris, J. R. and M. R. Todaro (1970). Migration, Unemployment and Development: A Two Sector Analysis, *American Economic Review*.

Henry, S. G. B. and P. A. Ormerod (1978). Incomes Policy and Wage Inflation: Empirical Evidence for the UK 1961-1977. *N.I.E.S.R. Review*, August.

Holden, K. and D. A. Peel (1979). The benefit-income ratio for the UK, *International Labour Review*, Vol.118, No.5.

Johnston, J. (1972). A Model of Wage Determination Under Bilateral Monopoly, *Economic Journal*, Vol. 82.

Johnston, J. and M. C. Timbrell (1973). Empirical Tests of a Bargaining Model of Wage Rate Determination, *Manchester School*, June.

Laidler, D. W. and J. M. Parkin (1975). Inflation: A Survey, *Economic Journal*, December.

Lewis, W. A. (1954). Economic Development with Unlimited Supplies of Labour, *Manchester School*.

Minford, A. P. L. (1980). A Rational Expectations Model of the UK under fixed and floating exchange rates, (Working Paper No. 7902, University of Liverpool) *Carnegie-Rochester Conference Series on Public Policy*, Vol. 12 (On the State of Macroeconomics eds. K. Brunner and A. Meltzer).

Minford, A. P. L. and G. W. Hilliard (1978). The Costs of Inflation, in *Contemporary Economic Analysis* (M. J. Artis and A. R. Nobay, eds), Croom-Helm.

Minford, A. P. L. and P. R. Ohs (1976). The Supply Responses of Malawi Labour, *East African Economic Review*, June.

Parkin, M. and M. T. Sumner (eds) (1972). *Incomes Policy and Inflation*, Manchester University Press.

Sargan, J. D. (1964). Wages and Prices in the United Kingdom: A Study in Econometric Methodology, in Hart, P. E., G. Mills and J. K. Whitaker, eds., *Econometric Analysis for National Economic Planning*, London, Butterworths.

Sargent, T.J. (1973) Rational Expectations, the Real Rate of Interest and the Natural Rate of Unemployment, Brookings Papers on Economic Activity, No. 2 1973, 429-472

Tarling, R., and F. Wilkinson (1977). The Social Contract: Post-war Incomes Policies and their Inflationary Impact, *Cambridge Journal of Economics*, I, 395-414.

FOOTNOTES

1. We are grateful to John Hunter and Christos Ioannidis for carrying out some of the regressions and for helpful suggestions. We have also benefited from discussions with Ken Holden, Dave Peel, Ken Wallis and Mike Wickens and from the comments of Nicholas Kiefer and two referees. This paper reports some results from our SSRC research project into the international transmission mechanism.

2. Defined as all those who would be employed in the industry with a competitive labour market.

RESULTS FOR U.S.A. ($\Delta logW-PEXP$ = dependent variable)(1) t ratios 1961.1-1975.2

QEXP	QL	$\log(W/P)_{-1}$	VARP1	VARP2	VARE1	VARE2	b_{-1}	$PRES_{-1}$	ρ_1/ρ_2(3)	F(2)	$\bar{R}^2$	S.E.
0.20 (3.27)		-0.65 (3.61)							-0.39 / 0.31	2.13	0.35	0.018
	0.62 (2.38)	-0.15 (1.11)							-0.33 / 0.38	5.14	0.29	0.019
0.12 (1.76)		-0.96 (4.80)	-9.02 (2.33)		-6.78 (0.77)				-0.52 / -0.43	0.00	0.41	0.017
	0.18 (0.65)	-0.79 (3.31)	-0.19 (3.16)		-10.46 (1.17)				-0.48 / -0.42	0.00	0.38	0.018
0.09 (1.31)		-1.01 (5.30)		-3.00 (2.83)	-9.77 (1.13)				-0.55 / -0.45	1.34	0.43	0.017
	0.11 (0.40)	-0.91 (3.92)		-3.67 (3.83)	-13.15 (1.55)				-0.52 / -0.44	0.00	0.42	0.018
0.12 (1.67)		-0.96 (5.11)	-7.96 (2.26)			-8.97 (1.12)			-0.50 / -0.42	1.34	0.42	0.018
	0.20 (0.74)	-0.78 (3.59)	-9.91 (2.83)			12.47 (1.56)			-0.46 / -0.43	2.35	0.39	0.018
0.10 (-1.51)		-0.96 (5.24)		-2.39 (2.52)		-7.47 (0.95)			-0.52 / -0.43	0.00	0.43	0.017(4)
	0.19 (0.72)	-0.80 (3.81)		-2.89 (3.15)		-10.15 (1.29)			-0.48 / -0.44	0.00	0.41	0.017

(1) Each equation contains a constant, a time trend and seasonal dummies, not reported.
(2) F-test on constraint that $\alpha_1 = 1$.
(3) Coefficients of 2nd order AR error process estimated by Cochrane-Orçutt iterative technique
(4) Preferred equation. $\bar{R}^2$ in the form $\Delta logW = 1.0\ PEXP + \ldots$ is .65. Excluding the effect of seasonal dummies, $\bar{R}^2$ is .62; the share of this contributed by 1.0 *PEXP* is 74%.

RESULTS FOR CANADA ($\Delta logW-PEXP$ = dependent variable)[1] t ratios 1961.1-1975.2

QEXP	QL	$\log(W/P)_{-1}$	VARP1	VARP2	VARE1	VARE2	b_{-1}	$PRES_{-1}$	ρ_1/ρ_2[3]	F[2]	$\bar{R}^2$	S.E.
		-0.48 (-2.89)							-0.12 / 0.00	0.28	0.55	0.036
-0.51 (-2.29)		-0.55 (13.19)					0.00 (0.46)		-0.22 / -0.05	0.90	0.57	0.033
-0.66 (5.81)		-0.78 (-5.81)		4.33 (2.79)	15.80 (1.93)		0.00 (1.13)	-0.65 (-1.73)	-0.48 / -0.26	0.78	0.67	0.023
	-0.46 (2.80)	-0.85 (-4.86)		5.19 (2.74)	17.21 (1.77)		0.00 (0.78)	-0.66 (-1.56)	-0.38 / -0.19	0.92	0.63	0.027
-0.46 (-2.20)		-0.82 (-4.92)	3.46 (0.40)			4.54 (2.99)	0.00 (1.56)	-0.14 (0.40)	-0.47 / -0.22	2.57	0.66	0.025
	-0.25 (-1.35)	-0.84 (-4.08)	19.98 (0.26)			5.85 (4.14)	0.00 (1.16)	-0.07 (-0.18)	-0.43 / -0.19	3.36	0.64	0.026
-0.52 (2.86)		-0.79 (-5.82)		2.86 (1.36)		3.15 (1.76)	0.00 (1.83)	-0.40 (-1.04)	-0.50 / -0.24	2.64	0.67	0.023 (4)
	-0.33 (2.04)	-0.88 (-5.42)		2.44 (1.07)		4.55 (2.59)	0.00 (1.52)	-0.35 (-0.86)	-0.45 / -0.20	4.29	0.65	0.024
		-0.69 (-5.25)		0.12 (0.06)		5.63 (3.13)		-0.28 (-0.66)	-0.36 / -0.16	8.09	0.63	0.027
	-0.11 (-0.57)	-0.48 (-2.38)					-0.00 (-0.24)		-0.13 / -0.02	0.00	0.53	0.036

(1) Each equation contains a constant, a time trend and seasonal dummies, not reported.
(2) F-test on constraint that $\alpha_1 = 1$.
(3) Coefficients of 2nd order AR error process estimated by Cochrane-Orcutt iterative technique.
(4) Preferred equation. $\bar{R}^2$ in the form $\Delta logW = 1.0\ PEXP + \ldots$ is .77. Excluding the effect of seasonal dummies, $\bar{R}^2$ is .70; the share of this contributed by 1.0 *PEXP* is 73%.

RESULTS FOR JAPAN ($\Delta logW - PEXP$ = dependent variable)[1] t ratios 1961.1-1975.2

QEXP	QL	$\log(W/P)_{-1}$	VARP1	VARP2	VARE1	VARE2	b_{-1}	$PRES_{-1}$	ρ_1/ρ_2 (3)	$F^{(2)}$	$\bar{R}^2$	
0.66 (3.83)		-0.29 (-1.88)		4.93 (4.22)	7.39 (0.81)				-0.18 / -0.43	0.00	0.76	0.054
0.53 (3.58)		-0.27 (-2.07)		5.42 (5.71)		0.70 (1.05)			-0.17 / 0.43	1.72	0.77	0.054
	0.73 (4.06)	-0.40 (-3.19)		5.17 (6.24)		0.09 (0.12)			-0.10 / -0.47	3.89	0.77	0.052
0.78 (4.50)		-0.35 (-2.42)		6.94 (4.55)	5.08 (0.58)			-0.52 (-1.95)	-0.23 / -0.47	5.15	0.77	0.053
	0.74 (4.85)	-0.53 (-3.70)		5.77 (4.50)	7.04 (0.84)			-0.35 (-1.40)	-0.17 / 0.51	5.42	0.78	0.052
	0.20 (1.31)	-0.41 (-1.93)	-0.96 (-0.26)		26.05 (2.62)			0.33 (0.81)	-0.15 / -0.33	10.31	0.70	0.061
0.70 (4.67)		-0.48 (-3.86)		8.24 (6.93)		1.51 (2.51)		-0.82 (-3.21)	-0.30 / -0.51	2.36	0.80	0.05 (4)
	0.69 (4.00)	-0.53 (-3.82)		6.58 (5.78)		0.77 (1.00)		-0.51 (-1.78)	-0.16 / -0.49	4.24	0.79	0.051
-0.06 (-0.46)		-0.15 (-0.85)							-0.04 / -0.20	5.86	0.65	0.063
	0.01 (0.09)	-0.14 (-0.74)							0.05 / -0.20	6.64	0.65	0.066

(1) Each equation contains a constant, a time trend and seasonal dummies, not reported.
(2) F-test on constraint that $\alpha_1 = 1$.
(3) Coefficients of 2nd order AR error process estimated by Cochrane-Orcutt iterative technique.
(4) Preferred equation. $\bar{R}^2$ in the form $\Delta logW = 1.0\ PEXP + \ldots$ is .81. Excluding the effect of seasonal dummies, $\bar{R}^2$ is .52; the share of this contributed by 1.0 *PEXP* is 21%.

RESULTS FOR GERMANY ($\Delta logW-PEXP$ = dependent variable)[1] t ratios 1961.1-1975.2

QEXP	QL	$\log(W/P)_{-1}$	VARP1	VARP2	VARE1	VARE2	b_{-1}	$PRES_{-1}$	ρ_1/ρ_2 (3)	F (2)	$\bar{R}^2$	S.E.
	0.80 (5.29)	-0.88 (-4.56)							-0.16 / -0.14	5.72	0.36	0.041
0.58 (4.01)		-0.56 (-2.74)							-0.07 / -0.08	1.27	0.30	0.044 (4)
	0.73 (4.29)	-0.91 (-4.84)	-10.02 (-1.29)		-30.56 (-0.70)				-0.18 / -0.18	7.25	0.36	0.042
	0.84 (4.90)	-0.83 (-3.88)	-9.43 (-1.21)			-0.78 (-0.50)			-0.20 / -0.19	8.93	0.36	0.042
0.49 (3.28)		-0.69 (-2.46)	-5.07 (-0.53)		-0.81 (-1.81)			-0.00 (-0.01)	-0.11 / -0.15	7.44	0.30	0.044
	0.78 (4.24)	-0.78 (-3.12)	-12.04 (-1.45)		-24.00 (-0.54)			-0.61 (-0.77)	-0.17 / -0.19	6.70	0.36	0.042
0.52 (3.04)		-0.58 (-3.12)	-5.24 (-0.47)			1.69 (-1.45)		-0.65 (-0.77)	-0.051 / -0.08	7.60	0.26	0.045
	0.83 (4.73)	-0.75 (-3.06)	-11.95 (-1.38)			0.18 (0.09)		-0.75 (-0.76)	-0.18 / -0.18	8.47	0.35	0.042

(1) Each equation contains a constant, a time trend and seasonal dummies, not reported.
(2) F-test on constraint that $\alpha_1 = 1$.
(3) Coefficients of 2nd order AR error process estimated by Cochrane-Orcutt iterative technique.

(4) Preferred equation. $\bar{R}^2$ in the form $\Delta logW = 1.0\ PEXP + \ldots$ is .40. Excluding this effect of seasonal dummies, $\bar{R}^2$ is .34; the share of this contributed by 1.0 *PEXP* is -12%.

RESULTS FOR FRANCE ($\Delta logW-PEXP$ = dependent variable)[1] 1961.1-1975.2

t ratios

QEXP	QL	$\log(W/P)_{-1}$	VARP1	VARP2	VARE1	VARE2	b_{-1}	$PRES_{-1}$	ρ_1/ρ_2[3]	F[2]	$\bar{R}^2$	S.E.
0.01 (1.00)		-0.73 (2.27)	13.49 (1.59)		90.78 (1.97)			0.46 (1.07)	-0.25 / -0.19	0.00	0.19	0.044 (4)
0.02 (1.32)		-0.58 (2.15)		5.60 (1.52)	103.91 (2.28)			-0.12 -0.18	-0.24 / -0.18	0.05	0.19	0.044
	-0.29 (-0.81)	-0.49 (1.90)		0.07 (2.52)	112.11 (2.45)			0.38 (0.70)	0.24 / 0.20	0.10	0.17	0.045
0.02 (0.59)		-0.93 (2.46)	22.69 (2.08)			3.11 (0.82)		0.50 (1.08)	-0.21 / -0.13	0.19	0.14	0.046
	0.01 0.03	-0.70 (1.92)	11.34 (1.13)			-0.58 (-0.19)		-0.61 (1.23)	-0.18 / -0.12	0.64	0.19	0.047
	0.02 (1.19)	-0.56 (1.84)		5.95 (1.46)		-0.60 (-0.18)		0.07 (0.10)	-0.18 / -0.12	0.44	0.11	0.047
-0.00 (-0.03)		-0.21 (0.71)							-0.08 / -0.07	2.45	0.13	0.048

(1) Each equation contains a constant, a time trend and seasonal dummies, not reported.
(2) F-test on constraint that $\alpha_1 = 1$.
(3) Coefficients of 2nd order AR error process estimated by Cochrane-Orcutt iterative technique.
(4) Preferred equation. R^2 in the form $\Delta logW = 1.0\ PEXP + \ldots$ is .39. Excluding the effect of seasonal dummies, $\bar{R}^2$ is .39; the share of this contributed by 1.0 *PEXP* is 77%.

RESULTS FOR BELGIUM ($\Delta logW-PEXP$ = dependent variable)(1) t ratios 1961.1-1975.2

QEXP	QL	$\log(W/P)_{-1}$	VARP1	VARP2	VARE1	VARE2	b_{-1}	$PRES_{-1}$	ρ_1/ρ_2(3)	F(2)	$\bar{R}^2$	S.E.
0.25 (0.97)									-0.31 / 0.06	1.41	0.38	0.046
	0.68 (2.77)								-0.39 / -0.04	1.71	0.45	0.044
	0.85 (4.88)	-0.25 (-1.56)	17.01 (2.77)		45.70 (2.39)			0.51 (1.97)	-0.71 / -0.32	0.04	0.59	0.038
0.78 (3.96)			14.55 (2.80)		68.41 (3.35)			0.64 (2.14)	-0.66 / -0.28	0.12	0.54	0.04
	0.99 (4.66)	-0.16 (-0.88)		3.49 (1.70)	33.60 (1.50)			0.30 (0.80)	-0.65 / -0.25	0.35	0.55	0.039
0.78 (3.59)		-0.25 (1.22)	1.55 (2.16)			8.30 (3.27)		0.31 (0.95)	-0.59 / -0.19	3.38	0.54	0.04
	0.84 (4.58)	-0.44 (-2.45)	18.14 (2.81)			5.25 (2.25)		0.32 (1.00)	-0.66 / -0.26	2.67	0.58	0.038(4)
1.02 (4.26)		-0.17 (-0.93)		4.60 (2.21)		8.21 (3.24)		0.01 (0.12)	-0.59 / -0.18	8.08	0.54	0.04
	1.00 (4.75)	-0.34 (-1.90)		4.31 (2.21)		4.52 (1.84)		0.03 (0.01)	-0.63 / -0.23	6.49	0.56	0.039
0.49 (1.76)		0.37 (1.75)							-0.36 / 0.01	1.24	0.40	0.045

(1) Each equation contains a constant, a time trend and seasonal dummies, not reported.
(2) F-test on constraint that $\alpha_1 = 1$.
(3) Coefficients of 2nd order AR error process estimated by Cochrane-Orcutt iterative technique.
(4) Preferred equation. $\bar{R}^2$ in the form $\Delta logW = 1.0\ PEXP + \ldots$ is .73. Excluding the effect of seasonal dummies, $\bar{R}^2$ is .65; the share of this contributed by 1.0 *PEXP* is 55%.

RESULTS FOR ITALY ($\Delta logW-PEXP$ = dependent variable)[1] t ratios 1961.1-1975.2

QEXP	QL	$\log(W/P)_{-1}$	VARP1	VARP2	VARE1	VARE2	b_{-1}	$PRES_{-1}$	ρ_1/ρ_2[3]	F[2]	$\bar{R}^2$	S.E.	
	2.43 (4.64)	-0.20 (-1.00)		10.41 (2.21)	-235.92 (2.32)			0.74 (1.06)	-0.04 -0.19	0.21	0.35	0.062	
	2.12 (4.73)	0.31 (-1.46)	16.47 (2.22)		-0.02 (2.28)			1.81 (2.82)	-0.04 -0.14	0.00	0.35	0.062	
	0.28 (0.64)	-0.35 (-1.28)					0.01 (2.00)		0.17 -0.05	0.36	0.20	0.074	
-0.02 (-1.06)		-0.44 (-1.62)					0.01 (1.43)		0.16 0.04	0.02	0.21	0.073	
	2.25 (4.33)	-0.48 (-2.60)	27.79 (4.07)		-274.91 (-3.64)		-0.01 (-0.88)		-0.09 0.17	1.13	0.42	0.063	
-0.004 (-0.18)		-0.49 (-1.61)	5.55 (0.55)		-0.02 (-1.69)		-0.01 (1.29)	1.47 (1.92)	0.14 0.05	0.00	0.25	0.072	
	3.09 (5.12)	-0.20 (-1.12)		15.08 (4.78)	-0.03 (-3.83)		-0.01 (-1.56)	0.61 (0.99)	-0.10 -0.19	0.27	0.47	0.072	(4)
0.00 (0.16)		-0.61 (-2.98)	3.79 (0.43)			8.05 (1.08)	-0.09 (0.03)	0.91 (1.15)	0.07 0.04	0.00	0.22	0.073	
	1.54 (2.70)	-0.56 (-2.59)	15.81 (2.34)			4.18 (1.87)	-0.01 (-1.43)	1.17 (1.74)	-0.02 -0.08	0.72	0.31	0.068	
	2.10 (2.99)	-0.41 (-1.84)		8.96 (2.57)		4.44 (1.0)	-0.014 (-1.55)	0.31 (0.41)	0.03 0.08	0.28	0.33	0.068	

(1) Each equation contains a constant, a time trend and seasonal dummies, not reported.

(2) F-test on constraint that $\alpha_1 = 1$.

(3) Coefficients of 2nd order AR error process estimated by Cochrane-Orcutt iterative technique.

(4) Preferred equation. $\bar{R}^2$ in the form $\Delta logW = 1.0\ PEXP + \ldots$ is .59. Excluding the effect of seasonal dummies, $\bar{R}^2$ is .57; the share of this contributed by 1.0 *PEXP* is 54%.

RESULTS FOR NETHERLANDS ($\Delta logW - PEXP$ = dependent variable)(1) t ratios 1961.1-1975.2

QEXP	QL	$\log(W/P)_{-1}$	VARP1	VARP2	VARE1	VARE2	b_{-1}	$PRES_{-1}$	ρ_1/ρ_2(3)	F(2)	$\bar{R}^2$	S.E.
0.13 (0.41)		-0.53 (-1.63)							0.03 / 0.01	3.12	0.52	0.055
	0.42 (1.24)	-0.63 -(1.86)							0.05 / 0.03	2.91	0.53	0.054(4)
0.08 (0.23)		-0.67 (-1.57)	-4.77 (-0.76)		-15.4 (-0.62)			-0.47 (-0.86)	0.06 / 0.05	3.88	0.5	0.056
	0.43 (1.11)	-0.75 (-1.85)	-3.37 (-0.5)		-6.58 (-0.25)				0.05 / 0.03	6.55	0.51	0.055
0.14 (0.39)		-0.51 (-1.29)		5.6 (0.99)	-10.96 (-0.46)			-0.55 (-0.96)	0.06 / 0.01	3.58	0.51	0.057
	0.49 (1.17)	-0.55 (-1.42)		6.68 (1.2)	-0.78 (-0.03)			-0.45 (-0.79)	0.06 / 0.01	6.42	0.52	0.055
0.12 (0.35)		-0.47 (-1.25)	-4.53 (-0.76)			2.11 (0.58)		-0.49 (-0.92)	0.03 / 0.02	5.72	0.5	0.056
0.17 (0.5)		-0.36 (-0.97)		5.74 (1.04)		1.82 (0.52)		-0.57 (-1.03)	0.04 / -0.02	6.02	0.51	0.056
	0.5 (1.33)	-0.46 (-1.23)		7.02 (1.28)		2.18 (0.62)		-0.45 (-0.8)	0.05 / -0.02	6.23	0.52	0.055

(1) Each equation contains a constant, a time trend and seasonal dummies, not reported.

(2) F-test on constraint that $\alpha_1 = 1$.

(3) Coefficients of 2nd order AR error process estimated by Cochrane-Orcutt iterative technique.

(4) Preferred equation. $\bar{R}^2$ in the form $\Delta logW = 1.0\ PEXP + \ldots$ is .57. Excluding the effect of seasonal dummies, $\bar{R}^2$ is .23; the share of this contributed by 1.0 *PEXP* is 28%.

RESULTS FOR U.K. ($\Delta logW-PEXP$ = dependent variable)[1] t ratios 1961.1-1975.2

QEXP	QL	$\log(W/P)_{-1}$	VARP1	VARP2	VARE1	VARE2	b_{-1}	$PRES_{-1}$	ρ_1/ρ_2[3]	F[2]	$\bar{R}^2$	S.E.
-1.03 (-2.37)		-0.30 (-1.77)		2.63 (1.19)		-1.82 (-7.60)			-0.02 / -0.44	1.22	0.69	0.033[4]
	-0.06 (-0.26)	-0.33 (-1.70)		7.04 (4.42)		-0.84 (-0.31)			0.03 / -0.38	0.84	0.65	0.034
-0.96 (-2.17)		-0.28 (-1.58)		3.40 (1.53)	-3.72 (-0.81)				0.01 / -0.43	1.12	0.69	0.033
	-0.04 (0.17)	-0.24 (-1.23)		7.53 (4.79)	-4.88 (-0.96)				0.05 / -0.37	0.25	0.66	0.034
	-2.37 (-0.95)	1.07 (2.80)	-0.25 (-3.34)		0.37 (0.06)				0.21 / -0.41	0.44	0.61	0.037
		-0.25 (-1.26)		7.72 (7.28)	-4.93 (-0.98)				0.05 / -0.37	0.17	0.66	0.034
		-0.03 (-1.81)		7.34 (6.90)		-0.77 (-0.29)			0.03 / -0.38	0.42	0.66	0.034
	-0.77 (-3.88)	0.06 (0.35)							0.25 / -0.35	1.86	0.54	0.04
-1.55 (-8.03)		-0.32 (-2.46)							-0.03 / -0.42	0.88	0.68	0.033

(1) Each equation contains a constant, a time trend and seasonal dummies, not reported.

(2) F-test on constraint that $\alpha_1 = 1$.

(3) Coefficients of 2nd order AR error process estimated by Cochrane-Orcutt iterative technique.

(4) Preferred equation. $\bar{R}^2$ in the form $\Delta logW = 1.0\ PEXP + \ldots$ is .81. Excluding the effect of seasonal dummies, $\bar{R}^2$ is .80; the share of this contributed by 1.0 *PEXP* is 49%.

16. A MULTIVARIATE APPROACH TO DATA ANALYSIS

John Matatko and David G. Mayes

I. INTRODUCTION[1]

Recent studies of major macro-economic relationships such as the consumption, investment demand, and money demand functions (see Davidson, Hendry *et al.* (1978), Bean (1979), Hendry and Mizon (1978)) have emphasised the use of preliminary data analysis in the modelling of economic relationships. For instance, the authors of the consumption function study mentioned consider such historical properties of the data used as time plots of consumers' expenditure, disposable income, a.p.c. etc., before moving to specify a consumption function. Thus the strategy followed is one of 'soft-modelling' where specification is not independent of perceived properties of the data (for a full account of such specification searches see Leamer (1978)). The studies cited are concerned with single equation problems. When dealing with systems of equations involving many endogenous variables, the empirical properties of the data are less readily observed. Simple time series plots of the variables themselves or of ratios will be less easy to interpret because of the multicollinearity among these variables.

In this paper we discuss one possible approach to discovering and describing the time series properties of data and apply it to data sets made up of the major components of national income and expenditure, as well as monetary series, of both the UK and US. We shall argue that the results do indicate that important and interesting properties of the data are brought out in the analysis and that these will form a useful, preliminary guide to the model-builder in his search for a specification which provides an adequate description of the data.

The major difficulty in drawing out the properties of a set of variables, as opposed to a single variable, is the need to establish them from the co-variation of the set. The more co-linear are the variables, the more difficult does it become to see what additional variation is contained in any subset of the data series. We suggest the use of principal components analysis,[2] since this provides the user with linear combinations of variables which have maximal variance subject to being mutually uncorrelated and which have variances whose sum equals that of the original variables. (They 'exhaust' the original variation.) These components are, however, not invariant to linear transformations of the data. Principal components analysis thus gives a decomposition of the variation of a set of original variables into a variation which is due to a set of orthogonal components. The movement of these components is easier to interpret than the original variables since the former are uncorrelated. If we interpret the variables used as endogenous variables in a dynamic model, then, conditional on values of the exogenous variables, time paths are implied, as the solution of a set of difference equations. These properties will, of course, depend upon such properties of the structural difference equations such as their linearity, order and restrictions on their coefficients (again see Davidson *et al.* (1978) for a single equation example). This solution of the model may be decomposed using principal components, as described above, and comparisons made between the time series properties of the solution and the actual time paths of the endogenous variables. (Indeed, Geweke (1977) has derived a complete decomposition by principal components in the frequency domain - 'Spectral Factor Analysis'. However, the number of observations required for this approach is far in excess of the data available to us.) By considering the time series behaviour of the components, the model-builder may well discover the type of cyclical variation which his model fails to explain. He may also see, by looking at the weights of the variables on a particular component, the source of the variation and, from the amount of variance explained by that component, its importance in the data set. Such an analysis then, although in no way actually forming part of the estimation process of model-building, is valuable either as a preliminary step in 'soft-modelling' a system or as a check on the properties of a system which has already been estimated.

The empirical results in this paper shed light on one further problem in applied econometric work: the extent of multicollinearity in major macro-series. An early, but widely quoted, study (Stone (1947)) showed that the first three principal components of 17 macro-series for the US 1922-39 (in fact a breakdown of national income and expenditure) explained 98% (81%, 11%, 6% respectively) of the variance of the original data. He identified these components, or factors, as, respectively, total income, its first difference, a linear trend. Since these results are extremely pessimistic for econometric estimation[3] using such data, we present results showing the influence of the major components in similar data sets for both US and UK in the post-war period. In view of the fact that PCs are not invariant under linear transformations, we examine the robustness of any results when several, widely used, data transformations are applied to the data. We also discuss their effect on the time series properties of the components.

Since results will be dominated by variables which are largest in absolute magnitude, the identification of subsets of data which exhibit independent variation will be made more difficult. We therefore present results using standardised data (i.e. the correlation rather than the covariance structure is decomposed). This is, of course, a natural approach when data are measured in different units, as with the monetary series.

In the following sections II, III and IV, we give results for various principal component analyses using different transformations. For the reasons given above, we shall stress the time series movements of each of the major components. We shall also draw particular attention not only to the extent of multicollinearity but also to those variables in each data set which either 'group together' as a component or exhibit independent variation. In particular we apply canonical correlation as well as regression analysis in order to 'identify' movements in components. The last section presents a brief summary of results and conclusions.

II. THE UNITED KINGDOM, 1954-1976

In examining the United Kingdom we have endeavoured to make our choice of variables as similar as possible to that already presented for the United States by Stone (1947). However, there are a number of minor differences caused by differences in the methods of national accounting used by the government statisticians in the two countries. Furthermore, we feel it is preferable to deal with the sorts of variates which are normally used in models of the United Kingdom because these themselves are naturally developed from the concepts which are embodied in the official statistics. We have, therefore, taken the expenditure and income breakdowns of the UK economy as summarised in Table 1 (more recently 1.1) of the *National Income and Expenditure* (Blue Books) each year with increased detail where appropriate to approximate to the US categories. These variables are set out in Appendix Tables 1A and 1B. Unlike Stone, we present full separate analyses of income and expenditure. Results of an aggregation experiment are given in Section IV. This distinction between expenditure and income variables is in any case desirable, first because they reflect different sorts of behaviour as is clear when the components from the correlation matrix of the differences of the deflated variables are considered and secondly because putting both sides of a set of accounts into the same matrix in a sense over-identifies the variation we wish to examine.

A Reconsideration of Stone's Results

Stone's (1947) original analysis presented results for variables expressed in nominal terms and components calculated from the covariance matrix. A similar calculation on our UK Income series gave the result that the first component plainly dominated totally, explaining for 99.7% of the variance. The largest weights on this component are Y4, Y2 and Y12, the largest variables in absolute size. Obviously Stone's result identifying the first component with aggregate income arises from the use of unstandardised variables: aggregate income is the sum of the variables used and this sum is dominated by its largest items. Such a result could clearly be obtained here.

Effects of Deflation and Standardisation on the First Principal Components

In this section, for reasons of space, we merely present a brief discussion of results from levels (note: fuller results are available on request from the authors). Even after deflation the first principal component dominates (explanation > 90%) in both income and expenditure data. Standardisation still leaves this component as an approximately equally weighted average of all the variables, except stockbuilding. The latter stands out as a source of independent variation. The importance of this component falls, after the transformation, to approximately 75% explanation.

Effects of First Differencing (Correlation Matrix)

All the discussion thus far has been in terms of levels of variables, but the major feature of the variance even in the constant price series has been the general trend. If we take differences of the data to remove this feature, we can explore the further structure of the fluctuations in income and expenditure rather more closely. The same arguments about the use of deflation and correlation rather than covariance matrices still apply so in Table II.1 and Table II.2 we have only shown the principal components of the correlation matrix of deflated variables. The variance is now much more diverse and the first three components of the income series only explain 60% of the total variation. The first three components of the expenditure series explain nearly 80% of the total variation. The usual rule of thumb adopted in this sort of case (see Lawley & Maxwell (1971) for example) is to consider all components which explain up to 5% of the total variation. This would comprise the first six components in these two cases which is an unusually large number. We have restricted our main analysis to the first three components although there are some remarks which can usefully be made about the second three.

Whether we take expenditure or income we can see from Fig. II.1 that the first component shows the cyclical pattern of the series closely with peaks in 1960, 1964, 1968 and 1973. This similarity is lost with the second component other than the variation in the 1970s. Unlike the data on levels, the difference data show far from uniform weights on the first component. In the case of income (col. (1) Table II.2) the main positive weights are on income from employment in the private sector, income from self-employment, rental income, distributed and undistributed profits, stock appreciation and capital consumption in the personal sector. A similar pattern is observed for expenditure with the main weights on consumers' expenditure on non-durables and services, private investment in other fixed assets, private stock-building, exports, imports and net property income from abroad. These then are the main variables which vary pro-cyclically, public stock-building on the other hand varies counter-cyclically.

To a large extent, the second components reflect the influence of the variables with low weights in the respective first components. In the case of income, the component clearly reflects the behaviour of the public sector with positive weights for income from the public sector, public stock appreciation and capital consumption and a negative weight for income tax paid by corporations. This could, therefore, perhaps be construed as the way in which the cycle of fiscal policy differs from the general cycle. The second expenditure component comprises three main facets: it has negative weights on the major parts of government expenditure, positive weights on the parts of private expenditure with low weights in the component and negative weights on imports and exports.

Statistical "Explanation" of Individual Variables

The main interest and space in Stone's article is devoted to showing and explaining how well the first three principal components "explain" the original macro-economic variates, in the sense of giving the results of the regression of these variables on the components in differenced form. The maximum percentage of variation explained by the first three components is 87.5% (consumers' expenditure on non-durables) but all bar two (X5 and X10) have more than 60% explained.[4] There is a corresponding reduction in the proportion of variation explained by the first component, but the proportion is over 50% for most of the major economic aggregates. Since the first component is now related largely to cyclical rather than trend behaviour, stockbuilding is well explained by it. Also since housing investment has a rather different cycle from the general run of the economy, it is not surprising that it has a large proportion of its variation explained by the second component.

Fig. II.1

Graph of First Principal Components,
UK Income and Expenditure, Real Differences, Correlation Matrix

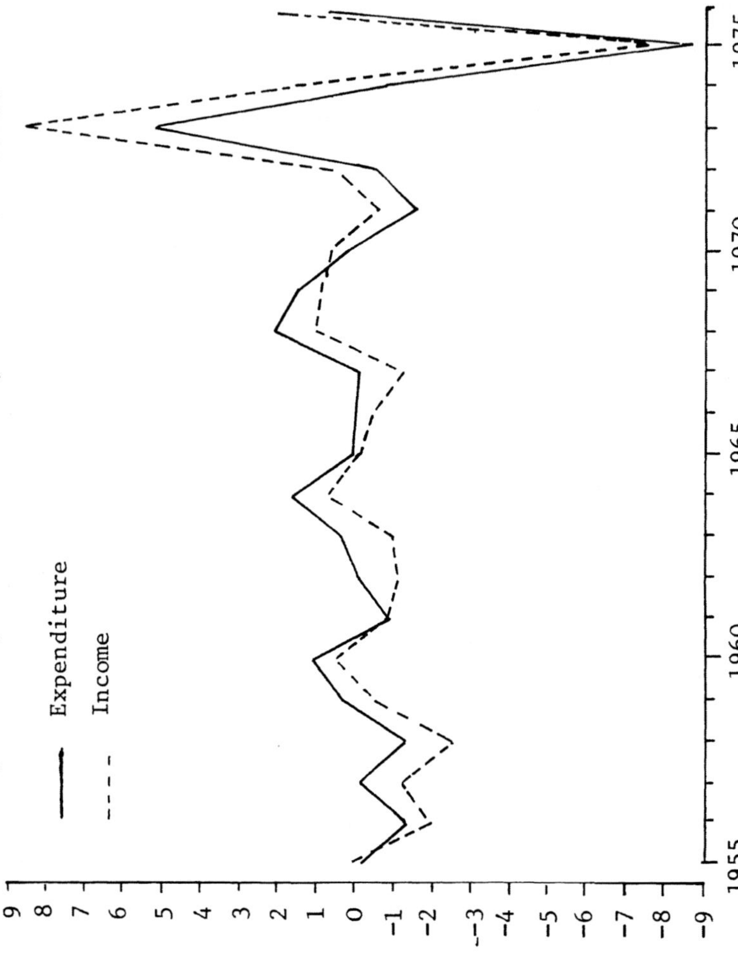

TABLE II.1

Principal Component Analysis of UK National Income 1954-1976, 22 Series

Component			1	2	3
			% of variance explained		
Variable	Mean (£m)	99.6833	36.2815	15.0086	9.0188
			Weights on variables		
Y1	2847.8	-0.1033	-0.0051	0.4444	0.1410
Y2	4264.4	-0.1913	-0.0933	0.3608	0.1591
Y3	733.3	0.0205	0.1237	-0.1864	-0.2754
Y4	27256.6	-0.9411	0.2305	0.1984	0.3264
Y5	585.2	-0.0206	0.2926	-0.1716	-0.0523
Y6	809.6	-0.0274	0.3032	0.0312	0.1750
Y7	2205.2	-0.0797	0.2547	-0.1947	0.0027
Y8	2395.9	-0.1004	0.2419	0.0030	0.0276
Y9	302.7	-0.0124	0.3027	-0.0584	-0.0293
Y10	2799.5	-0.0880	0.2536	-0.1333	0.2098
Y11	1334.4	-0.0236	0.1392	-0.3008	0.3439
Y12	3950.7	-0.1466	0.2932	-0.0479	-0.2146
Y13	405.3	-0.0103	-0.0210	-0.2044	-0.4741
Y14	1239.1	-0.0518	0.1685	-0.0964	-0.0257
Y15	131.7	-0.0001	-0.0054	-0.2491	0.0761
Y16	189.7	-0.0136	0.2705	0.2128	0.0169
Y17	982.5	-0.0790	0.3045	0.1617	-0.1277
Y18	72.5	-0.0064	0.2039	0.2863	-0.0466
Y19	882.5	-0.0324	0.2698	-0.0785	0.0861
Y20	1638.5	-0.0676	0.1915	0.1965	-0.1621
Y21	1550.1	-0.0640	0.1091	0.2909	-0.2963
Y22	182.3	-0.0082	0.0537	0.1410	-0.3971
			Correlation of Real Differences		

TABLE II.2

Principal Component Analysis of UK GDP (Expenditure)

1954-1976, 17 Series

Component		1	2	3
		% of variance explained		
Variable	Mean (£m)	36.8577	23.4901	8.4884
		Weights on variables		
X1	2236.7	0.0751	0.3726	-0.2231
X2	21867.3	0.3729	-0.0248	-0.0308
X3	4194.9	0.3496	0.1056	-0.0331
X4	853.3	0.0972	0.3443	-0.4576
X5	1216.1	-0.0788	0.1954	-0.0402
X6	2736.6	0.3108	0.2080	-0.1130
X7	642.0	0.1071	-0.3689	-0.2267
X8	1349.4	0.3129	0.0260	-0.2864
X9	80.8	-0.0563	-0.3843	-0.3283
X10	1443.4	-0.0673	-0.2946	-0.1944
X11	260.1	0.3526	0.0271	-0.0460
X12	50.1	-0.2874	0.0391	-0.2980
X13	10206.6	0.2757	-0.2415	0.1764
X14	10717.1	0.3111	-0.1806	0.1443
X15	14139.8	0.1464	-0.3357	0.1312
X16	4693.0	-0.0952	-0.2687	-0.5229
X17	495.8	0.3057	-0.0014	-0.1092
		Correlation of Real Differences		

Income Variables (Correlation Matrix)

Similar calculations for the income data series show a similar general structure. Here it is only two aspects of corporate profits (Y11 and Y13) and the residual error which are not well explained by the first component of the data in levels. This picture is substantially changed when we consider the components of the differenced data. Two of the major income variables (Y1 and Y2) are explained by the second component rather than the first. The third component provides the explanation of Y11, Y13 and the residual error which we noted were poorly explained when expressed in levels. Here, in differences, it is the trading surpluses of public corporations and other public enterprises and forces pay which are explained least well.

A Monetary Data Set

So far in this section, we have confined our interests to the real sector, but it is now possible to obtain monetary statistics for the United Kingdom over the period 1954-76. This allows us to develop our analysis a stage further, for not only can one consider the principal components of the monetary variables, but the relation between the monetary and the real sector and the relation between monetary and real variables and the major aggregates of the U.K. economy.

The separation of monetary and real variables is the result of the historical development of the publication of data, and most models of the UK economy (e.g. NIESR (1979)) treat them as a single coherent structure together with price determination. One approach, therefore, would be to form a single large data set of all the variables, but our purposes here is to examine the characteristics of the monetary data and then compare these with those of the real variables.

The choice of the monetary data set is more arbitrary as it cannot be based on some direct equivalent of the summary national accounts data. Rather than pick a definition relating to that in use in one of the current models, we have followed our procedure of taking the earliest available statistics and have, therefore, used the variables from Crouch's (1967) model (see Appendix Table IC). These comprise the main components of the money supply, the major rates of interest and the major monetary actions of the government. Thus between them, the full range of monetary instruments and targets should be included.

Monetary Variables (Correlation Matrix)

In the analysis which follows, no attempt is made to consider the covariance matrix of the monetary variables as the variables are not all in the same units of measurement (some are in £ and others are rates of interest). The striking feature of the results in levels is the similarity between the monetary and the real data. The first component has largely uniform weights on each of the variables and results in a general trend being observed over time. The second component on the other hand has a strong positive weight on Bank Lending, a smaller weight on Domestic Credit Expansion and negative weights on the Public Sector Borrowing Requirement and Sales of Public Sector Debt. This results in a cyclical time path, but not an identical path to the real sector fluctuations. Deflation indicates Bank Rate movements as a source of independent variation.

First Differences of Monetary Variables (Correlation Matrix)

These cyclical patterns are again present if we discard the levels of the variables and consider first differences. The proportion of the variance explained by each component again assumes a less steep profile with the first explaining 37% and the first three 68%. The first component reflects the general movement in the series, while the second contrasts the London Clearing Banks' Account, Sales of Public Debt and Domestic Credit Expansion with Special Deposits, the Consol and Treasury Bill Rates. This latter component reflects the two sides of monetary policy, with a similar relation for the third component among the remaining variables.

TABLE 3

	Differences							
	Nominal				Real			
	Correlation				Correlation			
	% of variance explained							
	1	2	3	Rest	1	2	3	Rest
	33.2386	25.7092	15.8333	25.2189	36.7122	18.0068	13.4787	31.8023
	Weights on variables							
1	0.0463	-0.4470	-0.3177		0.0136	-0.5601	-0.1713	
2	-0.1070	0.0001	0.5823		-0.2522	-0.0143	0.4533	
3	-0.4009	-0.2781	-0.0190		-0.4173	0.0878	-0.1505	
4	-0.3255	-0.0560	-0.0014		-0.2974	0.2797	-0.3516	
5	-0.4501	0.0029	0.0157		-0.3665	0.2016	-0.0067	
6	-0.1678	-0.4444	0.0243		-0.3572	-0.1556	0.1563	
7	-0.1883	0.0413	0.5854		-0.1898	0.3153	0.2302	
8	-0.4437	0.0099	0.0468		-0.3774	0.2359	-0.1324	
9	0.0420	-0.4995	0.1483		0.0584	0.1039	-0.5405	
10	0.1220	-0.4689	-0.0145		0.1972	0.1673	-0.3981	
11	-0.3172	0.2176	-0.3629		-0.2942	-0.4584	-0.0767	
12	-0.3734	0.0614	-0.2451		-0.3232	-0.3623	-0.2596	

Statistical "Explanation" of Individual Variables

All variables in both levels and differences are well explained by the first three components, the lowest being differences in the yield on Consols at 46.9%. In terms of levels, minimum lending rate stands out as the one variable not well explained by the first component, although its first differences are clearly (59.2%) explained. It is interesting the way that the Public Sector Borrowing Requirement is distinguished when expressed in differences. Its path is picked up by the third component alone. It is clear that the borrowing requirement and Domestic Credit Expansion do not move hand in hand. There are thus several important different components in the monetary sector in a way which is not so true of the real sector. This helps to explain why analysis of monetary variables has proved rather more difficult for econometricians and that monetary sectors have frequently been omitted from macro-models.[5]

III. THE UNITED STATES, 1954-1976

Introduction and General Remarks

In looking at the United States for the period after the Second World War, we are able to make a double comparison, one not only with the United Kingdom during the same period, but also with the United States itself in the interwar period. One of the major features of this comparison is that despite the fundamental similarity of the three data sets in that the first component of the correlation matrix of the original variables reflects the overall trend and the second the general economic cycle, the contexts are clearly different. This is not surprising as the time path of national income during the two periods in the United States is strikingly different, with the occurrence of the Slump between the wars in contrast with the continuing growth in the post-war period.

The time periods for these US data and those we have just considered for the United Kingdom are identical and the variables used are as close as definitional changes will permit to those used for the inter-war period.[6] The categories used are set out in Appendix Table II.

The first feature of the US data which stands out in relation to that observed for the UK is the lack of effect from deflation. The first two components of the correlation matrices of nominal and real values of the income series are shown in Figure III.1 and this similarity is also reflected in the components of the first differences of the variables. This presumably reflects the much steadier development of price inflation in the United States compared with the United Kingdom.

The reason why cyclical fluctuations are not initially apparent is because their size is relatively small compared with the general levels of the variables. The first principal component in levels has a range twice as great as that in differences. The second and third components, like their counterparts in the levels of variables show most of their influence for the period 1973-6.

The use of differences has separated out some of the variables influencing the fluctuations by spreading the variance more evenly over a large number of components. Farm incomes, for example, form the major weight in the fourth component (which explains 9% of the total variance) and capital consumption adjustment in proprietors' income (USY4 and USY7) are the main weights in the fifth component (7% of the variance). The third component introduces Rental Income of Persons as the major weight which did not appear in the discussion of levels. We now consider in detail the components of the income and expenditure variables.

Income Variables - Deflated (Correlation Matrix)

Again for reasons of space, we confine our detailed discussion largely to first differences. We note, in passing, that a strong trend remains even in the deflated results.

Turning to differences, Table III.1, we find generally a much lower level of explanation, as is to be expected. In fact, farm income is almost 'missed' altogether, less than 10% of its variance being due to variation in the first three principal components. Now only wages and salaries and the corporate income series of the main income variables correlate highly with the first component. Interest and Non-Farm Income appear relatively strongly with the same sign in the second component, and rent has over 60% of its variation due to the third component. It is interesting that for levels and differences neither of the two adjustments, stocks or capital consumption, appears heavily weighted on any single one of the components. They do not then appear to behave as mutually consistent aggregates. Finally, we note that if the differences transformation is made, then we require six components to obtain a better overall fit than 90%, for levels, the first three give approximately 89%.

The most striking feature of differencing the real data is the elimination of trend. What remains demonstrates the relative amplitude of cyclical variation from 1970 onwards. All variables except two (capital consumption and net interest) show negative weights and thus move opposite to the graph. We see thus an almost steady fall in the size of changes in most main income variables (USY1, USY6, USY11-13) from 1965 to 1970 then a very wide cyclical movement between 1970-75, the 1973 recession being clearly marked. Rent and interest do not, having low weights, follow this pattern closely. Thus, as we might expect, cyclical economic movement is shown clearly in the differences, income which flows from production identifying directly with this but earnings from capital following a different path.

Fig. III.1

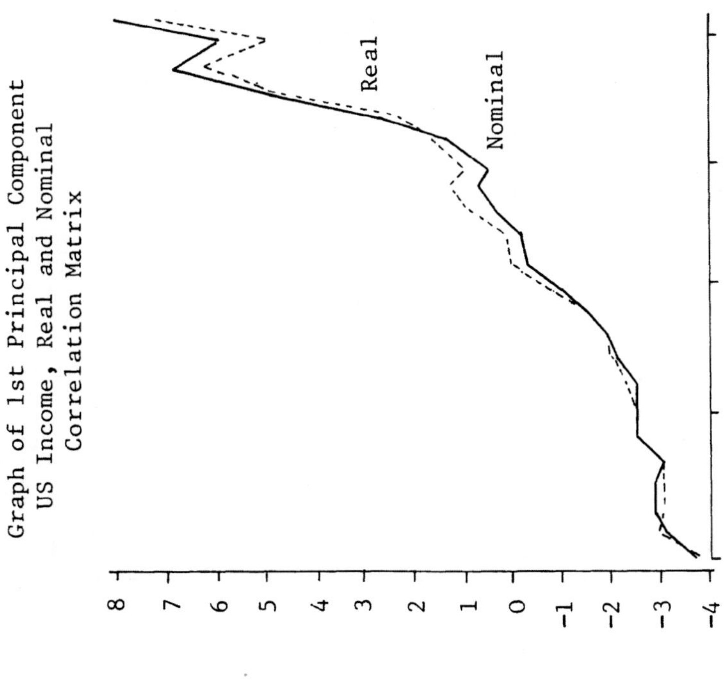
Graph of 1st Principal Component
US Income, Real and Nominal
Correlation Matrix
8
7
6
5
4
3
2
1
0
−1
−2
−3
−4
1955
1960
1965
1970
1975
Real
Nominal

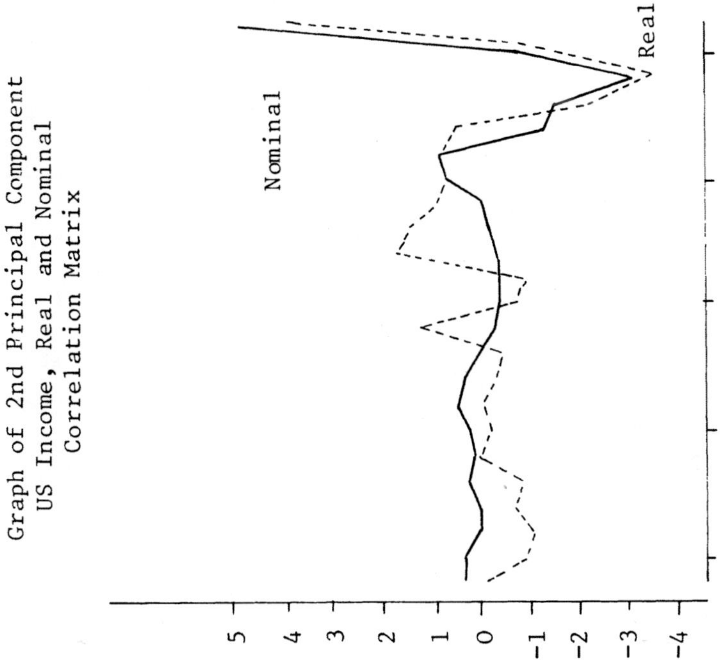
Graph of 2nd Principal Component
US Income, Real and Nominal
Correlation Matrix
5
4
3
2
1
0
−1
−2
−3
−4
1955
1960
1965
1970
1975
Nominal
Real

TABLE III.1

Principal Component Analysis of US National Income 1954-1976, 16 Series

Component		1	2	3
			% variance	explained
Variable	Mean (£m)	36.7915	18.9910	12.4934
			Weights on	variables
USY1	433.4	-0.3454	0.0015	-0.0039
USY2	49.6	-0.2581	0.1228	0.3054
USY3	16.3	-0.1124	0.0102	0.0663
USY4	1.4	0.1811	-0.2223	0.3143
USY5	45.0	-0.3318	-0.2532	-0.0463
USY6	0.5	-0.2480	0.4159	-0.1212
USY7	1.4	-0.0826	-0.2193	-0.3783
USY8	23.0	-0.0842	-0.4551	0.0519
USY9	6.2	-0.0021	0.2334	0.5530
USY10	32.8	-0.3650	-0.0718	0.1410
USY11	41.4	-0.3863	-0.0446	0.0110
USY12	19.1	-0.3161	-0.0133	-0.1803
USY13	22.4	-0.3761	-0.0467	0.0399
USY14	4.2	-0.1381	0.4504	-0.3088
USY15	2.2	0.1947	0.0690	-0.4065
USY16	27.3	0.0493	0.4142	0.1429
		Correlation of Real Differences		

Fig. III.2

Graph of First, Second and Third Principal Components by Time, US Expenditure Real Levels, Correlation Matrix

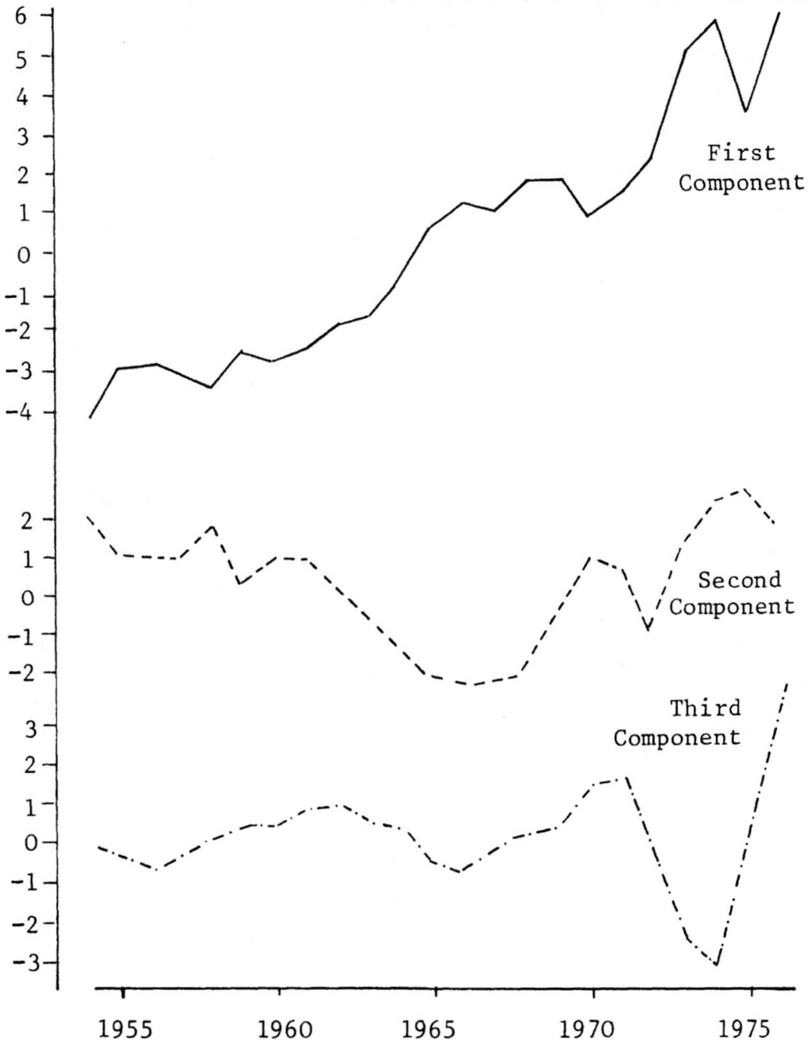

Expenditure Variables Deflated (Correlation Matrix)

In terms of levels the first principal component explains 78% of total variation and is a trend-like variable, with some of the properties of an average.

Dealing now with differences (Table III.2), again the proportion of total variance due to the first three components falls to 67.8: it requires six components before 95% explanation is reached. Fig. III.3 shows the first component with considerable cyclical variation but with some trend remaining. As might be expected, inventories have a large positive weight as do durable and non-durable consumption, producers' investment in durable equipment, and imports. These are the usual main categories of aggregate demand (imports negatively) and it should be noted that these are picked out by a 'standardised' principal component.

Examination of Fig. III.2 shows this component apparently leading the first component in levels in its dating of peaks and troughs. The second and third components are further dominated by the fluctuations after 1970. The second explains variation in series 'missed' by the first, particularly residential investment in farm building, the third, explaining 11% of overall variation, gives heaviest weights (Table III.2) to exports, and government spending - the only truly 'exogenous' categories of demand.

Finally, comparing results with levels and differences, we see that again the explanation of the individual variables by the first three components drops. Only consumer non-durable expenditure has a 90% explanation in terms of these orthogonal variables.

A Monetary Data Set

The US monetary variables are rather different in some ways from those used for the United Kingdom. Both contain measures of money stock and long and short interest rates, but the relatively small size of the US public and overseas sectors makes the breakdown of DCE less important. More important perhaps are Federal Reserve requirements and bank reserves. These latter are reflected in USM8 and USM9 (see Appendix Table II.E).

TABLE III.2

Principal Component Analysis of US Expenditure 1954-1976, 13 Series

Component		1	2	3
		% of variance explained		
Variable	Mean (£m)	43.24	13.38	11.16
		Weights on variables		
USX1	76.5	0.260	-0.296	0.114
USX2	246.0	0.356	-0.257	0.093
USX3	247.7	0.291	-0.080	0.018
USX4	35.2	0.303	0.040	-0.183
USX5	55.0	0.357	0.232	-0.183
USX6	39.3	0.254	-0.397	0.281
USX7	0.8	0.018	0.526	0.230
USX8	0.8	0.257	0.252	0.198
USX9	6.5	0.362	0.010	-0.033
USX10	53.9	0.201	0.374	-0.513
USX11	47.8	0.362	0.196	0.082
USX12	101.0	-0.031	0.277	0.554
USX13	111.9	0.048	0.183	0.397
		Correlation of Real Differences		

Fig. III.3

Graph of Principal Components 1, 2 and 3 by Time,
US Expenditure, Real Differences, Correlation Matrix

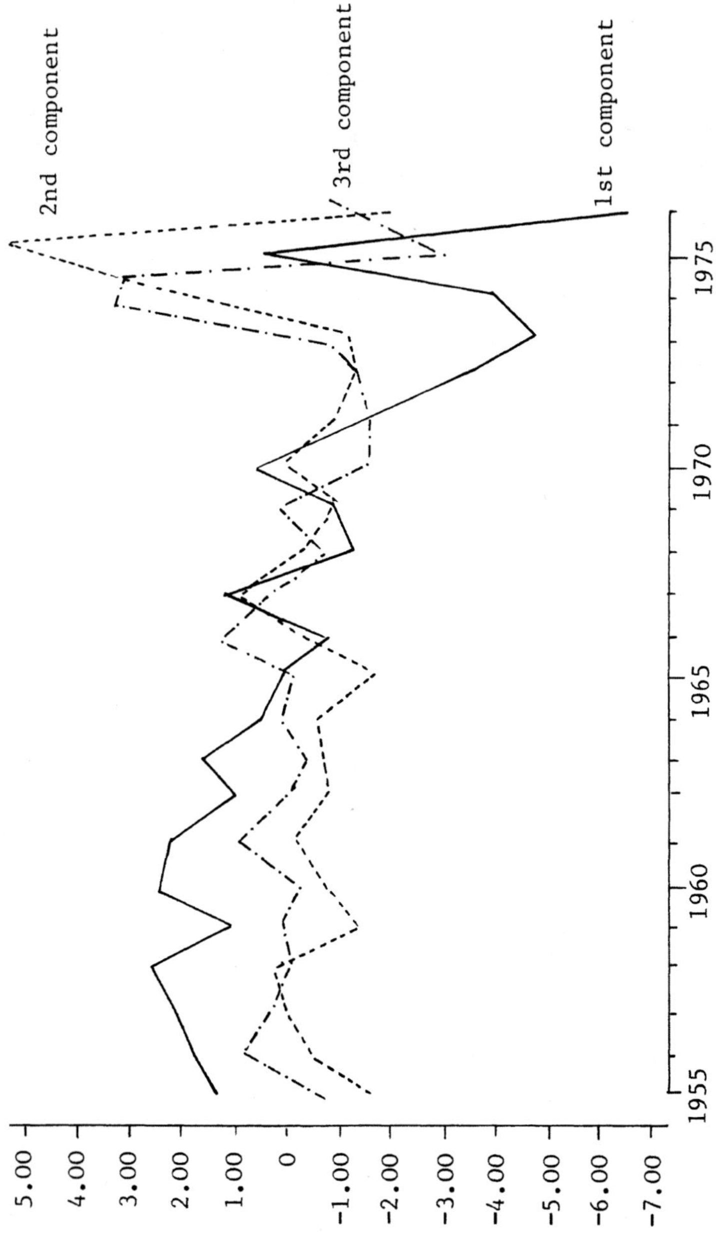

Monetary Variables - Levels (Correlation Matrix)

Considering first the results for variables in level terms, we this time draw attention to the results for nominal levels as the first two components present a particularly clear decomposition of money market variations. The first with stocks, interest rates and reserves having the same sign shows a secular movement. The second, which it should be recalled is orthogonal, gives opposite signs to interest rates on the one hand and to stocks and reserves on the other. This would appear to be movement along a given demand for money schedule. In real terms, the first component, although explaining now only 68.2% of the total, gives a similar weight pattern (Table III.3). The second variable now plainly shows the influence of federal reserve requirements and actual reserves with demand deposits tending to co-vary positively with reserves. The only interest rate to vary strongly indirectly is the bond rate. As the variables are in level terms, all are, as expected, well explained by the first three components (90%+) with only the reserve variables showing low explanation by the first component.

First Differences of Monetary Variables (Correlation Matrix)

Fig. III.4 shows that changes in the monetary sector, as in the real, in the US over the period are dominated by post-1970 years. The wide fluctuation of the first component (explaining 40.1% of the total) between 1972 and 1975 covers twice the total range previously covered. This component shows too a demand for money schedule weight pattern, with stocks and interest rates opposite in sign.

It can also be seen that the second component represents interest rates, treasury bills and bank loan rate (Table III.3), and that this moves in a similar but lagging fashion to the first in the post-1970 era. From Table III.3, the weights of the first component show reserve requirements varying directly with stocks but the second component uses the contra-cyclical aspect of reserve requirements. These reserve variables then have the same sign as interest rates and opposite to stocks on the second component.

The relative stability of the earlier years can clearly

TABLE III.3

Principal Component Analysis of US Monetary Statistics
1954-1976, 9 Series

	Differences							
	Nominal				Real			
	Correlation				Correlation			
	% variance explained							
	1	2	3	Rest	1	2	3	Rest
	38.4503	31.9894	12.4400	17.1203	40.0901	32.3586	9.2662	18.2848
	Weights on variables							
USM1	-0.1264	0.4828	0.3937		-0.3957	0.1223	-0.1120	
USM2	-0.1731	0.4871	-0.0730		-0.4370	0.1146	-0.0107	
USM3	-0.3863	0.0217	0.1152		-0.1942	-0.2825	0.8249	
USM4	-0.0236	0.5556	0.1702		-0.3624	0.3325	0.2125	
USM5	-0.3614	-0.2961	-0.0073		-0.0463	-0.5064	-0.3683	
USM6	-0.1141	-0.2080	0.8034		0.3317	-0.2763	0.3306	
USM7	-0.4213	-0.2761	0.1665		0.0058	-0.5472	-0.0784	
USM8	-0.4942	0.0836	-0.2444		-0.4324	-0.2752	-0.0599	
USM9	-0.4888	0.0796	-0.2538		-0.4293	-0.2713	-0.0839	

Fig. III.4

Graph of First Principal Component by Time
US Monetary Statistics, Real Differences, Correlation Matrix

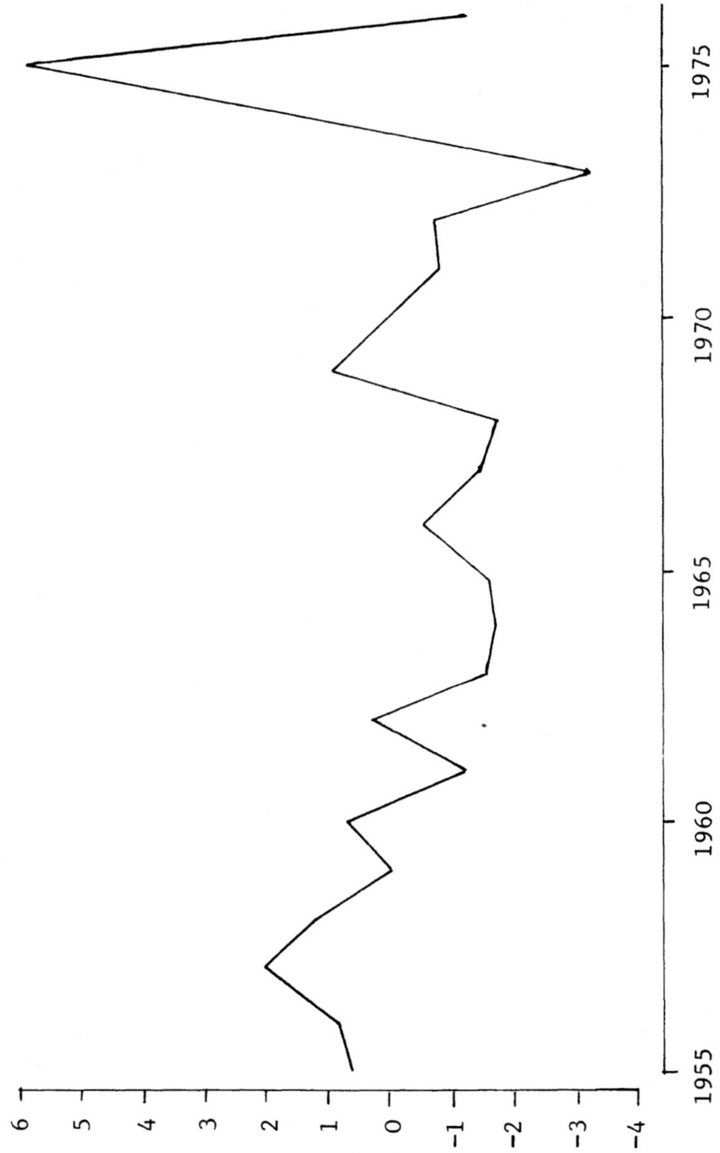

be seen to have given way to a period of strong fluctuation in the changes of the main monetary aggregates.

Identification of Components - Canonical Correlation Analysis

In this much abbreviated section, we report a further attempt to use multivariate analysis to relate variations in the real and monetary sector. To identify movements in the real sector of an economy with those in the monetary sector, the canonical variates of the two sectors are calculated. These are linear combinations of the two sets of variables which have maximal correlation. They are pairwise mutually uncorrelated. As explained in footnote 9, these calculations are here illustrative and are presented only for the US, the two sets of variables being an aggregated expenditure set and the set of monetary variables.

The correlation between the variates is only slightly less than 1. All the investment variables have opposite signs to those for consumption and imports, and move in the opposite direction to all the monetary variables except for the bond rate and reserve requirements. This presumably indicates timing differences and behaviour at the 1975 turning point. The second pair of variates displays cyclical variation showing major turning points in 1960, 1965, 1970, 1973 and 1975. The investment variables again move together opposite to the consumption and imports expenditure categories, but opposite to the bank loan rate and both reserve variables. We note that only on this variate do the reserve variables have the same sign. (In the work cited above, we have used, in places, simply excess reserves.) The 1973 downturn is well 'caught' on this variate. This perhaps indicates the support that real and monetary sector interactions have as an explanation of cyclical behaviour in the 1970s is strong.

Summary of Aggregation and Identification Experiments

In this section we have seen that the result of aggregation is, as may be expected, to offset some of the standardisation effects. The first components turn out to be almost equally weighted averages (except for stockbuilding). We still, however, appear to be able to isolate important sources of cyclical variation, that from stockbuilding being particularly clear. Again we find cyclical variation most clearly marked in results from differencing.

The most positive result from the identification attempts is the designation of exports as a key exogenous variable, both in terms of trend-like variation and in terms of cyclical variation in income/expenditure changes. Tax changes are indicated as a separate source of variation but it would seem that a more complex lag structure is needed. (It should be remembered that this study deals with annual, not quarterly, data and hence the lag structure would not necessarily be either long or complex.) Finally the illustrative result quoted using canonical correlation analysis would suggest that both long-term and cyclical variation in real sector movements may be related convincingly to corresponding movements in the monetary sector.

V. CONCLUSION

In earlier sections of this study we have advocated the use of principal components as a method of preliminary data analysis suitable for gaining an empirical understanding of economic data sets. We have applied this analysis to UK and US data sets for the post-war period. In addition, we used data at different levels of aggregation and for monetary as well as real variables. Our findings have been discussed in detail in each section, particular attention being given to attributing meaning to the weighting and time series behaviour of the components.

In this section, we return to the question raised in the introduction. We have seen that Stone's results on the 'dimensionality' of economic data are weakened by the use of standardisation but broadly hold up if the data are expressed in level terms. Table V.1 shows that in level terms, not more than 4 components are needed to explain more than 90% of the variation in any of the 7 sets of series. This is plainly due to trend domination. The use of differencing eliminates this effect and allows other, previously obscured, factors to play a more important role. Although the number of components necessary for 90% explanation increases with the number of series, it does not do so substantially, with the US data showing a smaller change than that for the United Kingdom. The '90% dimensionality' roughly doubles with differencing, being between 5-6 for the US sets, and 5-8 for the UK. Thus, although the number of necessary components is usually well below half the number of series used, the conclusion of Stone's work is severely weakened in this case.

Additionally, we have examined the time series behaviour of the major components and drawn attention to those variables which have produced each particular type of cyclical behaviour. A simplified attempt was made to identify the components with exogenous sources of variation and to relate movements in the real and monetary sectors. Exports were seen to be associated with a major UK component, and for the US highly associated canonical correlates were found between monetary and real sectors. Aggregation was found not to affect results greatly.

In conclusion, we repeat our claim that such analyses (in particular examination of the time plots of components) can be of great use in modelling a system of relationships, either as a preliminary step in helping to understand data properties in soft-modelling, or as a check on the properties of a fitted model.

TABLE V.1

Number of Components Needed for 90%+ Explanation

	No.of Series	Levels	Differ-ences
U.S.			
Income	16	4	6
Expenditure	13	3	6
Money	9	2	5
U.K.			
Income	22	4	8
Expenditure	17	3	7
Money	12	4	6
Income/ Expenditure	11	3	5

APPENDIX

TABLE 1

United Kingdom: Variables Used

A. Expenditure

Code	Variable
	Consumers' Expenditure *
UKX 1	on durable goods
UKX 2	on non-durable goods
UKX 3	on services
	Private GDFI
UKX 4	on dwellings
UKX 5	on other buildings
UKX 6	on other fixed assets
	General Government GDFI
UKX 7	on dwellings
UKX 8	on other fixed assets
	GDFI by Public Corporation
UKX 9	on dwellings
UKX 10	on other fixed assets
	Change in stocks and work in progress
UKX 11	private
UKX 12	public
UKX 13	Exports of goods and services
UKX 14	Imports of goods and services
	Current Expenditure
UKX 15	by central government
UKX 16	by local authorities
UKX 17	Net property income from abroad

B. Income

Code	Variable
	Income from Employment
UKY 1	from public corporations
UKY 2	from public authorities
UKY 3	Forces pay
UKY 4	other
	Income from Self-employment
UKY 5	professional
UKY 6	farm
UKY 7	other
UKY 8	rents
UKY 9	other income
	Corporate Profits
UKY 10	interest and dividends
UKY 11	UK taxes on income
UKY 12	undistributed profits
UKY 13	other uses
	Public Trading Surpluses
UKY 14	public corporations
UKY 15	other government enterprises
	Stock Appreciation
UKY 16	personal
UKY 17	companies
UKY 18	public corporations
	Capital Consumption
UKY 19	personal
UKY 20	companies
UKY 21	public sector
UKY 22	residual error

C. UK Monetary Variables 1954-1976

Name	Variable
UKM 1	London Clearing Banks Current Accounts
UKM 2	Notes and Coin held by the public
UKM 3	Bank of England Security Portfolio
UKM 4	Special Deposits
UKM 5	Bank Rate (Min.Lending Rate)
UKM 6	Currency in Circulation
UKM 7	2½% Consol Yield
UKM 8	91 day Treasury Bill Rate
UKM 9	Public Sector Borrowing Requirement
UKM 10	Net Sales of Public Sector Debt to Non-Bank Private Sector
UKM 11	Bank Lending to Private and Overseas Sector
UKM 12	Domestic Credit Expansion

*The division of Consumers' Expenditure into its three components was on the basis of the major breakdown shown in *National Income and Expenditure* 'Consumers' Expenditure at current prices' (Table 4.9 in 1976).

TABLE II

United States: Variables Used

D. US Expenditure Variables

	Personal Consumption Expenditure on
USX 1	durables
USX 2	non-durables
USX 3	services
	Non-residential Investment
USX 4	structures
USX 5	producers durable equipment
	Residential Investment
USX 6	non-farm structures
USX 7	farm structures
USX 8	producers durable equipment
USX 9	Change in business inventories
USX 10	Exports
USX 11	Imports
	Public Sector Purchases
USX 12	federal
USX 13	state and local

Source: Report to the President, Council of Economic Advisers, Table B2.

E. US Income Variables

	Income from Employment
USY 1	wages and salaries
USY 2	supplements
	Proprietors' Income
USY 3	farm income
USY 4	farm capital consumption
USY 5	farm inventory valuation adjustment
USY 6	non-farm income
USY 7	non-farm capital consumption
USY 8	non-farm inventory valuation adjustment
USY 9	rental income of persons
USY 10	capital consumption adjustment
	Corporate Income
USY 11	profits tax liability
USY 12	dividends
USY 13	undistributed profits
USY 14	inventory valuation adjustment
USY 15	capital consumption adjustment
USY 16	Net Interest

Source: Report to the President, Council of Economic Advisers, Table B19.

F. US Monetary Variables

USM 1	Currency
USM 2	Demand deposits
USM 3	Large Certificates of Deposit
USM 4	Other Time and Saving Deposits at Commercial Banks
USM 5	3 Month Treasury Bill Rate
USM 6	BAA Corporate Bond Rate
USM 7	Average Bank Loan Rate to Business
USM 8	Federal Reserve Bank Member Reserves
USM 9	Federal Reserve Bank Required Reserves

REFERENCES

Bean, C. (1979). An econometric model of manufacturing investment in the UK. Treasury Working Paper No. 12.

Crouch, R.L. (1967). A model of the UK's Monetary Sector. *Econometrica.*

Davidson, J., Hendry, D., Srba, F., Yeo, S. (1978). Econometric modelling of the aggregate time series relationship between consumers' expenditure and income in the United Kingdom. *Economic Journal.*

Dhrymes, P.J. (1970). *Econometrics.* New York: Harper and Row.

Geweke, J. (1977). The dynamic factor analysis of economic time series models. In *Latent Variables and Socio-Economic Models*, D. Aigner and A. Goldberger (eds.). North Holland.

Hendry, D., Mizon, G. (1978). Serial correlation as a convenient simplification not a nuisance: a comment on a study of the demand for money by the Bank of England. *Economic Journal.*

Kendall, M.G. (1957). *A Course in Multivariate Analysis.* London: Griffin.

King, B.J. (1966). Market and Industry Factors in Stock Price Behaviour. *Journal of Business Supplement.*

Lawley, D.N., Maxwell, A.E. (1971). *Factor Analysis as a Statistical Method.* London: Butterworths.

Leamer, E. (1978). *Specification Searches.* Wiley.

London Graduate School of Business Studies (1976). Relationships in the basic model. Econometric Forecasting Unit, Appendix to Discussion Paper No. 34.

Matatko, J.M., Mayes, D.G. (1979). Real and Monetary Sector Interactions. University of Exeter Working Paper.

National Institute of Economic and Social Research (1979).

Listing of National Institute Interim Model IV.

Renton, G.R. (1975). *Modelling the Economy.* London: Heinemann.

Stone, J.R.N. (1947). On the interdependence of blocks of transactions. *Journal of the Royal Statistical Society, Supplement*, Vol. IX, No. 1, 1-45.

Surrey, M.J.C. (1971). *The Analysis and Forecasting of the British Economy.* Cambridge: Cambridge University Press.

Theil, H. (1971). *Principles of Econometrics.* Amsterdam: North Holland.

FOOTNOTES

1. The initial part of this article has been substantially altered (on the advice of the editors) from that of the original paper delivered at the AUTE, entitled "The description of the UK and US economies: a multivariate approach". The original article with the many tables and figures which had to be omitted because of the page limit on this version, is available from the authors.

2. Since we are concerned with data description, we do not consider estimation problems. The method of principal component analysis is well explained in many text-books, e.g. Lawley and Maxwell (1971), Dhrymes (1970), Theil (1971).

3. I.e. is the 'dimensionality' of economic data really 3?

4. See Theil (1971), pp.53-54. The r-squared between any variable and any component is equal to the square of the weight of the variable on that component times the corresponding latent root. Full tables of the percentages explained of each variable are available on request from the authors.

5. This is not, of course, the only reason why monetary sectors are omitted, the general lack of long-run data has been a considerable hindrance in the past.

6. We do not repeat the arguments made in Section II above for the use of standardised data, i.e. results from the correlation matrix are emphasised.

7. For a discussion of the use of multivariate analysis in simultaneous equation systems, see e.g. Dhrymes (1970), Chap.5.

8. Although we employ total tax yield as the policy variable, this cannot be taken as exogenous. It is the tax rates which are exogenous.

9. This is part of work reported elsewhere (Matatko and Mayes, 1979) and is for present purposes simply illustrative of the multivariate methods used in the work cited.